# FIDEL CASTRO

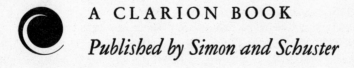

By Herbert L. Matthews

A CLARION BOOK

*Published by Simon and Schuster*

A Clarion Book
Published by Simon and Schuster
Rockefeller Center, 630 Fifth Avenue
New York, New York 10020
Copyright © 1969 by Herbert L. Matthews

FIRST PAPERBACK PRINTING, 1970

SBN 671-20526-9
Library of Congress Catalog Card Number: 69-14284
Manufactured in the United States of America

*To my sister, Rosalie,*
*and my brother, John*

# Contents

INTRODUCTION   *9*

1   FIDEL   *15*
2   CUBA   *39*
3   FROM MONCADA TO THE SIERRA   *63*
4   SIERRA MAESTRA   *93*
5   THE REVOLUTION BEGINS   *131*
6   THE ROAD TO MARXISM   *165*
7   PIGS AND MISSILES   *199*
8   THE ECONOMIC STRUGGLE   *237*
9   THE WORLD OUTSIDE   *275*
10   CASTRO'S COMMUNISM   *314*
11   FIDEL CASTRO'S REVOLUTION   *336*

BIBLIOGRAPHY   *365*
INDEX   *369*

# Introduction

"IT IS unfortunate," wrote Carlyle, "though very natural, that the history of this period [the French Revolution] has so generally been written in hysterics. Exaggeration abounds, execration, wailing; and on the whole, darkness."

Such is the fate of all true revolutions, until generations have died and passion is spent and students pick at the bones in the graveyard with detached curiosity. We who write as the history is being made can claim no such independence of judgment. But we can offer something more precious—a living testimony.

"By their works ye shall know them"—but not only by their works. Castro, after all, has had to live for years in the closest contact with his revolutionary associates, and he has by no means been unapproachable to a foreigner like myself whom he gets to know. It is twelve years since I went up to the Sierra Maestra and interviewed him for *The New York Times* at a moment when the Batista Government and the United Press International had pronounced him dead. One learns something of a man after many visits and long hours of talk with him and his associates over so many years. Since there is no separating the man from his creation, it has been necessary—up to a point—to combine the account of Castro's life with a description of the Cuban Revolution.

This, perforce, is a book without an ending, since Fidel Castro is very much alive in 1969 and the Cuban Revolution is going full blast.

As will be seen, I find myself generally at odds with scholars like Theodore Draper, Boris Goldenberg and Andrés Suárez, who have done such remarkable work in gathering documentation on the Cuban Revolution and drawing conclusions from the masses of material which they patiently and usefully collected.

To me, there is a dimension missing in such works—the third dimension which comes from the solidity and impact of life. A man who deals with living realities may be handicapped by his subjective reactions as a human being, but the material he deals with is true. A man who works only from speeches, articles, documents and decrees is playing a guessing game, however brilliantly he plays it.

What I have in mind was expressed with far more authority than I can offer by Arnold J. Toynbee in the chapter of his book *Acquaintances* on Sydney and Beatrice Webb. He read the galleys of their work on Lenin and was dissatisfied.

"They were including in it circumstantial and detailed accounts of Lenin's public acts" [wrote Professor Toynbee (pages 117–18)]: "his speeches; his manifestoes; his pamphlets; his political and administrative directives. All this was certainly pertinent and, indeed, essential; but it was also the kind of thing that was the stuff of which official documents are made; and by this time I knew enough about official documents to have realized that there are limits to their usefulness as aids to knowledge and understanding. . . .

"They had taken, too much at its probably deceptive face-value, the documentary evidence for Lenin's public acts, and they were refusing to consider Lenin's personal character, though this was the para-documentary evidence that was the indispensable key to the interpretation of the documents themselves."

The leading American authority on the Cuban Revolution and Fidel Castro for the academic world and officialdom has been

Theodore Draper, who is a Senior Research Fellow at the Hoover Institute on War, Revolution and Peace, of Stanford University, California. I have therefore felt it necessary to refer often to his writings on Cuba and, much as I disagree with his conclusions, I hope that my constant references will be taken as a tribute to his indefatigable and punctilious scholarship.

I would like to pay a special tribute to the American photographer and author, Lee Lockwood, on whose book *Castro's Cuba, Cuba's Fidel,* I have drawn freely. I have done so because it is essentially a series of long interviews with Castro, taped and then checked for accuracy by Premier Castro himself. This is authentic, firsthand material for biography, although it has to be used with circumspection.

Anyone writing a book on the Cuban Revolution is also indebted to Professor Robert Freeman Smith of the University of Rhode Island, whose work on the background of the revolution, as author and editor, is invaluable.

I give page and book references in my text, and not as footnotes. There is a bibliography of the principal books cited at the end. In the case of speeches by Fidel Castro, Raúl Castro, Ernesto Che Guevara, President Osvaldo Dorticós and some other leaders, there is no need for references. The texts of all important speeches have been published—generally the day after they were given—in the official Havana newspapers.

I desire to express my thanks to the following individuals and publishers for their kindness in permitting me to quote from their works:

Lee Lockwood, The Macmillan Company, New York.

Theodore Draper, Frederick A. Praeger, Inc., New York.

# FIDEL
# CASTRO

# 1 FIDEL

T̲H̲E̲ ̲C̲U̲B̲A̲N̲ Revolution is Fidel Castro's revolution.

The documentation is mountainous. A whole library of books has already been written. But the key to understanding lies in the extraordinary young man who transformed his country, shook up a hemisphere, and brought the world to the brink of a nuclear war.

It will not be easy to study him—now or ever. Fidel (he must be called that, since all Cubans refer to him by his first name when not addressing him more formally as *Comandante*—Major) is a man who has permitted little of a personal nature to be known about his life. In this respect, he is like the only other towering figure in Cuban history— José Martí, the "Apostle" of the struggle for independence from Spain.

Although so different in character, both men kept their intimate lives to themselves. As Edmundo Desnoes, the young Cuban author who is a director of the Instituto del Libro in Havana, has written: "They are public men who have surrendered themselves to a cause."

Fidel Castro is an expression of the times in which we live. Unconsciously, he was setting a standard with the beard, the asocial and in some ways antisocial behavior, the rebelliousness, the violence. He comes out of the secular and religious unrest of our times, which has spawned amusing and intriguing fashions like long-haired youth and miniskirted girls, parodies like the hippies, and—in a more serious way—Black Power, the guerrillas and the mercenaries.

Pro-Fidelista Cuban intellectuals always make the point that Fidel Castro is the culmination of a whole progression of Cuban history, especially of the past century beginning with the wars of independence in 1868. Naturally, this is a claim that Castro and his followers make even more emphatically, and it is an arguable interpretation.

There is a new Cuba because of Fidel Castro, and in this sense he represents a beginning even more than he does a continuation of the past. The rebelliousness of the new generation everywhere means a change in values; it means a different world; it has meant a different Latin America.

Although he was the first of his generation in the Western Hemisphere to come to power, and although there has been no second Fidel Castro, he was not and is not an "accident." Nothing could be more misleading than to think of him as a freak or as a meteor flashing across the Cuban skies to burn out in nothingness.

Fidel Castro has stamped his seal on Cuba and it can never be erased. His influence on hemispheric affairs is still uncertain, although it is obviously great. He is the first man in the history of Latin America to achieve worldwide stature and fame during his lifetime.

It is not to his credit—very much to the contrary, in fact—that Fidel Castro willingly brought us all to the verge of a nuclear world war in 1962. Whatever his reasons, the incident bespoke a man of extraordinary ruthlessness, daring and determination.

Fidel Castro is the romantic revolutionary who keeps cropping up in history, like Cromwell in England or John Brown in the United States. This type of individual embodies all the suppressed, yearning forces of his age and gives expression to them.

Such men are made, up to a point, by the attacks they draw

upon themselves. Few contemporary figures have been so vilified as Fidel Castro. Both worship and vilification distort the true image. Fidel is one of the most extraordinary men of our times, but he is neither saint nor devil. Take him for what he really is.

He was born on his father's sugar plantation near Birán, on the north coast of Cuba's easternmost Oriente Province. The father, Ángel Castro y Argiz, was an immigrant laborer from Galicia, Spain. The mother, Lina Ruz González, was a Cuban Creole from the same part of Oriente. Her family was also from Galicia, which makes Fidel a pure *Gallego* so far as descent is concerned. This places him, geographically and racially, alongside another dictator, Generalísimo Francisco Franco of Spain.

Ángel had two children—Lidia and Pedro Emilio—by his first wife and seven after his wife died by Lina Ruz, who had been the house servant. They were Angela, Agustina, Ramón, Fidel, Raúl, Ernma and Juana. Fidel was born on August 13, 1926. He was an illegitimate child, but his father married his mother soon after his birth. Of the nine children, all of whom are alive, three were to play a role in Fidel's career—Ramón, his older brother; Juana, the youngest sister, who played a minor part; and Raúl, four years younger than Fidel, who played a most important part.

Raúl linked his fate to that of Fidel at the time of the mad attack on the Moncada Barracks in Santiago de Cuba, July 26, 1953, and he has been with his brother ever since. Raúl needs— and deserves—a book to himself to do him justice. A public image of him has been created outside of Cuba that has little relation to reality. Like Fidel, he has been the subject of many exaggerated reports, with the greatest emphasis on his shortcomings and his relative unattractiveness in the Sierra Maestra years and the early stages of the revolution. His figure will emerge more clearly in this account as his brother's career is traced.

Fidel has a sense of family, an attachment, that is very Latin, but he keeps it for his private, not for his public, life. He has an aunt in Galicia, Spain, with whom he keeps in touch. Carlos Rafael Rodríguez, who is now a Cabinet Minister dealing with agricultural and economic affairs, told me in October 1967 that on his last trip to Spain he took to the aunt a gift from Castro.

The relationship between Fidel and his father, Ángel Castro, is generally considered to have been bad. Certainly it was never affectionate, as was his relationship with his mother, even when she disapproved of what he was doing. Fidel, for his part, disapproved of what his father was doing.

Lee Lockwood, in his book, *Castro's Cuba, Cuba's Fidel* (page 25),* tells about an evening in Oriente Province spent with Castro and some of the Premier's associates.

> In a curiously detached voice [writes Lockwood], he begins to speak about his father. He had owned a large sugar plantation on the other side of the mountains. He had been a *latifundista,* a wealthy landowner who exploited the peasants. He had paid no taxes on his land or income. He had "played politics for money."

Ángel was rough, hardworking, shrewd and thrifty. He worked his way up until he owned about 700 *caballerías* (23,300 acres) of land. He, his wife and the older sons, Pedro Emilio and Ramón, had the typical peasant's emotional attachment to their land. They were instinctively conservative, and it can be taken for granted that Ángel never understood, and could never approve of, the political radicalism of his sons Fidel and Raúl.

Ángel died in 1956 while Fidel was in Mexico preparing for the *Granma* invasion, and so the father never had any heartaches about the land he had worked so hard to acquire. But when Fidel's agrarian reform was put into effect in May 1959, and the Castro plantation was included in the breakup and nationalization of the latifundia, Lina Ruz de Castro, and Fidel's older brother Ramón, who had taken over the management of the family property, were outraged. In fact, Señora Castro had started protesting as early as 1957 when the 26th of July underground went around burning as much sugar cane as they could, not sparing the Castro plantation.

However, during the Sierra Maestra period of 1957 and 1958,

---

* I have listed in the bibliography at the back of the book all the books referred to in my text that have a bearing on the Cuban Revolution, together with their publication details.

Ramón helped his two guerrilla brothers, reputedly using the family farm as a depot and transit point for arms and supplies. Later, he became reconciled to the revolution and won his mother over to a grudging acceptance. For years Ramón has been directing the agrarian reform for his brother in the eastern end of the island.

None of her disapproval, according to close friends, diminished Lina's affection for Fidel or his for her. Someone who was present when news of his mother's death was brought to Fidel in 1965 told me he was deeply moved.

The large Castro family has always remained close with one exception—Juana, or Juanita as everyone calls her. She never reconciled herself, Fidel's friends believe, to the loss of the family property or to the fact that because of her unsympathetic feelings about the leftist trend of the revolution, she could play no role in the regime.

Juanita and, at the time, her mother were helping counter-revolutionaries in the critical years of 1962–63. Fidel knew it, but closed his eyes. When things got too bad and Juanita said she wanted to leave Cuba, her brother not only made no objection but let her go with lots of her possessions in a large collection of luggage. Normally, departing Cubans could take only one valise and the equivalent of five dollars.

Once in exile, Juanita made and wrote bitter and accusatory statements about the Cuban Revolution and even about her brother Fidel. They were eagerly lapped up in the United States by receptive Americans and Cuban exiles, but since Juanita was at all times out of touch with governmental affairs and with the ruling group and was, indeed, emotionally and actively trying to harm her brother, her assertions cannot be accepted as factual. In many respects they were obviously wild exaggerations.

Her only importance thus far in the revolution lies in the fact that she, a sister of Fidel, should have defected. He was distressed and bitter about it but, so far as I know, referred to the affair only once. This was in a speech at the University of Havana on March 13, 1966: "The imperialists have not hesitated with their detestable attempts to bribe, corrupt and even recruit close relatives, as they have done with us, as they have done with my own family, to utilize them later as repugnant instruments for hire."

Normally, Fidel never talks about his family, his personal affairs, or his personal life, even with his closest associates.

Teresa Casuso, who was working in the Cuban Embassy in Mexico City and was closely involved with Castro and the 26th of July group who were then preparing to invade Cuba, unwittingly provides a typical example of Fidel's reticence. She learned from one of the Cuban youths that Fidel's father had died in October 1956.

"Although I was seeing a lot of Fidel at the time, he had never mentioned it," she wrote in her book *Cuba and Castro* (pages 131–32), after her defection and exile. "Then I realized that all the boys had spoken of their fathers except Fidel. Apparently there was some hidden wound relating to his childhood which had never healed. Such disunity within a family is a rare thing in Cuba."

While Fidel's relations with his father were never close, there was no "hidden wound" and no disunity. He simply had kept his private affairs and his feelings to himself, as he always did.

There was one exceptional occasion that clearly moved and delighted his intimate friends. On an evening during the *zafra*, or sugar harvest, in the winter of 1966, while they were all sitting in a house out in the country, Fidel started to reminisce about his childhood. Apparently he talked for hours. "If I had only had a tape recorder!" Celia Sánchez said to me regretfully. (Celia, as she is always called in Cuba, has been one of Fidel's closest associates since the early weeks in the Sierra Maestra.) A year and a half later I heard of that same incident from Rodríguez, who had been present.

Evidently there are a number of personal letters from Fidel dating from before the revolution. Celia Sánchez and Carlos Franqui, the ex-newspaperman who prepared a first, and still unpublished, volume of Fidel's autobiography, have a number of such letters among the documentation of the revolution. Naty Revuelta, who was close to Fidel at the time of the Moncada Barracks attack in 1953, also has some letters.

Several personal letters that Fidel wrote from the Isle of Pines prison after Moncada are reproduced in the book that Luis Conte Agüero published in Havana early in 1959. It is called *Cartas del Presidio* (Letters from Prison) but presumably because of the personal revelations, especially those concerning the background for Fidel's divorce, the book was quickly suppressed.

Anyone working on the Cuban Revolution or on the life of Fidel has to be reconciled to the fact that he does not want to talk about himself. One result is that his enemies have succeeded in putting out a number of wild and damaging stories about his youthful career, especially at Havana University.

He has lived under such a glare of publicity since 1959 that his actions, at least, are public property. His thoughts and feelings are, and always will be, his own. He does not wear his heart on his sleeve.

In the reminiscences of his childhood, Fidel recounted how, as a boy of six or seven, he told his father he wanted to go to school. Ángel saw little need for the schooling that neither he nor his wife had had as children. He refused. Whereupon Fidel said he would burn the house down if they did not send him to school. Evidently his parents suspected that he might do so and complied. The story illustrates how early in life the fierce flame of rebelliousness burned inside his body.

So he was sent off to stay in Santiago with godparents who, it seems, treated him rather badly, not even giving him enough to eat, but he went to school—a Jesuit school called the Colegio Dolores.

On graduation, his father—or perhaps it was his mother, who was devoutly religious—sent him to another Jesuit school, this time to the fashionable Colegio Belén a preparatory school, in Havana. This was in 1942 when Fidel was sixteen years old.

He had inherited his family's attachment to the land, which is more in evidence than ever in 1968, the tenth year of the revolution. At Belén his best subjects were Agriculture, Spanish and History—all of which were to serve him in his later career. In 1944 he was voted "the best school athlete."

The next year he graduated. The school Yearbook for June 1945, which the director of the Colegio proudly showed to me and my wife in 1959 after Fidel's triumph, seemed to the charming old

Jesuit to be strikingly prophetic. The text, as Jules Dubois gave it in his biography of Castro (page 15) reads:

> *1942–1945.* Fidel distinguished himself always in all the subjects related to letters. His record was one of excellence, he was a true athlete, always defending with bravery and pride the flag of the school. He has known how to win the admiration and the affection of all. He will make law his career and we do not doubt that he will fill with brilliant pages the book of his life. He has good timber and the actor in him will not be lacking.

This showed remarkable acumen on the part of Fidel's teachers, even if later they were to have good reason to regret that they ever saw or heard of a youth named Fidel Castro. The Jesuit teachers were almost all Spanish priests. In 1960 and 1961, during a political conflict, Fidel expelled nearly all the Spaniards. Moreover, the Colegio Belén was swallowed up along with all the Church schools when the regime took complete control of education.

Nevertheless, the school record stands. There is no reason to doubt that it was deserved.

The Yearbook had noted that Fidel was to "make law his career." In reality, he was to make revolution his career. Since there were no courses in that profession at the University of Havana, Fidel entered the Faculty of Law in 1945.

The period that Fidel spent at Havana University is a controversial one. His enemies—Cuban and American—have created a "black legend" about his university career, while his brother Raúl and his associates and friends, most of whom were at the university at the same time or just before and after Fidel defend his activities with equal passion.

Castro himself, whether he is fed up with the malicious reports, or disdains to defend himself, or really has something to hide, will not talk about his life at that time. In his still-to-be-published autobiography, the university period is blank. He mentioned a political aspect of his university career in his famous speech of December 1, 1961, when he claimed to have been deeply interested in, and attracted to, Marxism, but it is a well-known fact by now—and his closest associates confirm it—that this was pure political tactics for the end of 1961 and had almost no relation to the facts.

Theodore Draper, in his book *Castroism,* falls into one of those traps that have, at times, ensnared all students of the Cuban Revolution who take literally everything that Fidel Castro says for public consumption. He writes (pages 113–14):

> Like the vast majority of ambitious but aimless young Cubans, who wished to study the least and prepare themselves for nothing or anything, he chose to enter the Law School of the University of Havana. Years later, he recalled guiltily: "I ask myself why I studied law. I still don't know. But I attribute it in part to those who said, 'He talks a lot; he has the makings of a lawyer; he is going to be a lawyer.' Because I used to argue and discuss, they made me believe that I was qualified to be a lawyer. Possibly, that was one of the reasons why I studied law, because they made me believe it." As he himself has admitted, he was not a good student; he belonged to those who "never went to class, never opened a book other than on the eve of examinations." In one of those self-revealing outbursts, Castro cried: "How many times have I deplored the fact that I was not forced to study something else!"

It is certainly arguable, as Draper writes, that for Fidel "the university was less an institution of learning or a professional training school than a nursery of hothouse revolutionaries," and that Fidel "was early tempted to get his more meaningful and exciting experiences in extra-school political adventures."

However, Raúl Castro showed me the final university reports signed by the professors in all the courses his brother had taken. The thirteen or fourteen slips were obviously genuine. Eight or nine of the professors wrote *sobresaliente* (excellent), three gave him *notable,* and only two were *aprovechado* (approved, which is to say passing). In other words, Fidel did brilliantly at the university, in spite of what he said about himself.

Law is an obvious choice for a Latin American youth thinking of going into politics. Fidel's legal training was useful to him when he ran for Congress in 1952. He practiced law briefly from 1950 to 1952. According to some of his biographers he made little

money because he insisted on representing poor people unable to
pay or those with politically hopeless cases.

On one notable occasion, October 16, 1953, when he was tried
for leading the attack on the Moncada Barracks in Santiago de
Cuba, his legal status gave him the right to defend himself. Out of
that defense was later to come his most effective piece of revolutionary propaganda: *"La Historia me absolverá"* (History Will
Absolve Me).

As is so often the case with the Cuban Revolution, a lot depends
on what document you choose to cite. Jules Dubois, in his 1959
biography, *Fidel Castro* (page 107), quotes from an article in the
Havana magazine *Bohemia,* written by Fidel in Mexico on Christmas Day, 1955. It shows a man proud of his university record and
defending it (the full text is published in Gregorio Selser's *La
Revolución Cubana* (pages 102–11).

> Thousands of students who are today professional men [Castro
> wrote] saw my actions in the university for five years. I have always
> counted on their support. . . . These men can be witnesses to my
> conduct. There they saw me, from the beginning, without experi-
> ence but full of youthful rebellion. . . .
>
> In an era of unprecedented corruption, when many youthful
> leaders had access to dozens of government positions and so many
> were corrupted, to have led student protests against that regime for
> several years, without ever having appeared on a government
> payroll, is worthy of some merit.

In any consideration of a particular student at the University of
Havana—and this goes for most of the universities of Latin
America—one must look at the other side of the picture.

It was the normal thing for professors to be absent much of the
time, leaving the teaching to young and inept assistants. The
methods of teaching were antiquated and books were scarce. A
student had himself to put into the university at least as much as
he got out. Student gangs ran black markets in textbooks and
terrorized other students and professors.

The "black legend" aspect of Fidel's university career concerns
two things: the rivalry, amounting to gangsterism, of two student
groups; and the great uprising in Bogotá, Colombia, on April 1,

1948, known as the *Bogotazo*. Castro was there with two Cuban comrades representing Havana University at a student conference.

Fidel always claimed that he carried a revolver during his Havana University days to defend himself. It was, indeed, a dangerous time for students involved in the intrauniversity struggles or in politics. Fidel never kept out of a fight and he was always in the ferment up to his neck, and—as always—in the lead.

In an interview I had with President Batista in June 1957 when we talked about Fidel, the General asked me how I thought he might come to terms "after all the crimes this man Castro has committed, beginning in his student days when he killed two men."

At least four students really were killed in the factional strife. A former student, a close friend of Fidel's named Emilio Tró, who was a founder of the Unión Insurreccional Revolucionaria (UIR), had been killed in 1947. Along with its rival, the Movimiento Socialista Revolucionario (MSR), the UIR could be rated as a terrorist organization.

"It was in this second group [the UIR]," writes Andrés Suárez, a Cuban exile, in his book *Cuba: Castroism and Communism* (page 14), "which initiated the scheme of leaving alongside its victims a note reading 'Justice is slow but sure,' that Fidel Castro began his career in 1945, when he came to the university to study law." Suárez then goes on to suppose that Castro "prepared those macabre notes."

This is typical of the way Castro's enemies overreach themselves so far as the historical record is concerned. There is not the slightest shred of evidence that Fidel took part in any killings at the university or wrote those macabre notes. It is a case of guilt by association and of wishful thinking.

Fidel was a roughneck from all the genuine evidence. In my book *The Cuban Story* (page 140), I wrote of seeing a United States intelligence report which described Fidel as "a typical example of a young Cuban of good background who, because of lack of parental control or real education, may soon become a full-fledged gangster."

He was letting off steam and in the process following a line of violence that had become endemic in Cuba years before. If Fidel Castro had really killed anybody during his university years, convincing evidence would have been found by his Cuban enemies and the United States Central Intelligence Agency.

The only legal case in which Fidel was involved concerned a police sergeant who was fatally wounded during a student demonstration in July 1948. A fellow student accused Fidel of firing the shot but the supposed witness later retracted and the case was dropped.

The other part of the "black legend" concerned the *Bogotazo* where Fidel and one of his companions, Rafael del Pino, were to be accused of killing anywhere from one to a half-dozen priests during the sanguinary rioting in Bogotá on April 9, 1948.

Jules Dubois, who was in Bogotá during the whole *Bogotazo* as a correspondent for the *Chicago Tribune,* wrote in his book on Castro (page 24):

> No priest had been killed in Bogotá. . . . The author had luncheon with the Apostolic Delegate to Colombia at the Italian embassy a week later, and he reported that he had not received any word of casualties in the clergy.

The Colombian Government called in a team from Scotland Yard to investigate the uprising. The report made by the British investigators, who were headed by Sir Norman Smith, referred to Castro and del Pino as "two Cubans" who had certainly made a nuisance of themselves, but there is no indication in the report that they had killed anybody or were charged with having done so.

False reports not only distort a true picture; they backfire. The falsity of the "black legend" of Fidel Castro in his university career has led to a "white legend" which is not an accurate picture either. The truth is that Fidel was a rebellious, rambunctious troublemaker, always looking for and sometimes making mischief —in short, a wild young man.

When an expedition of Dominicans and Cubans was organized in 1947 to invade the Dominican Republic and overthrow the dictator, Generalísimo Rafael Leónidas Trujillo, Fidel Castro was with it, submachine gun and all. This was the incident of Cayo Confites, so named for the place in the Bay of Nipe in Oriente Province from which three ships bearing the adventurers set sail.

The Venezuelan Government was helping financially and morally. Protests from Trujillo and words of caution from the United States Embassy persuaded President Grau San Martín to squelch the undertaking. In order to escape arrest, Fidel jumped from the ship he was on and swam ashore—legend, and possibly truth, having it that he made the long swim hanging on to his submachine gun.

When he entered Colegio Belén at the age of sixteen, Fidel was already tall, heavy and powerfully built. He has never permitted himself to get out of training.

The role that Fidel's physical strength has played in his life and career is so obvious that one is inclined to overlook it. He started out as a ten-pound baby. The manager of the neighboring United Fruit Company's sugar plantation in Oriente in the early thirties remembers the sturdy active boy running around his father's property. In schools and at the university he was an outstanding athlete.

So when the great trials of his life began, he had the physique and stamina to stand them. Twenty-two months of imprisonment after Moncada did not wear him down. He thrived on the grueling hardships of the two years of guerrilla fighting in the Sierra Maestra.

In the early years of the revolution he worked eighteen or twenty hours a day, every day of the week. It was such a fantastic performance that many Cubans believed he kept going on Benzedrine or some such stimulant.

He took nothing, except enormous quantities of food. He rarely drinks liquor and does not enjoy it when he does. Even now, in his early forties, he eats hugely and works hard enough for two men, but he does take time off now and then for rest and sport.

Good health and exceptional strength are not necessities, as history has proved. In Cuban history, José Martí was frail. Che Guevara, with his severe, chronic asthma, was in constant distress, but he went through the great hardships of the Sierra Maestra, survived three wounds, one of them serious, and went on to his destined end in the jungles of Bolivia. Yet one can still insist that Fidel Castro's physical strength played a key role in his career. Aside from anything else, it helped to bolster his image as a charismatic hero.

It was while he was at the university that Fidel fell in love with and married a student in the Faculty of Philosophy—Mirta Díaz-Balart. The Díaz-Balart family did not approve. The father and a son, Rafael, were government officials, which made it a Romeo-and-Juliet affair that was fated to end unhappily for Fidel.

The couple were married on October 12, 1948, in the Roman Catholic Church at Banes, in Oriente Province, where Mirta was born. The honeymoon, ironically, was in Miami, Florida. Their only child, a son—Fidelito—was born on September 1, 1949.

At its best, the marriage could not have been easy, considering Fidel's overpowering personality and, especially, his revolutionary activities. He was a married man during the preparations for the attack on the Moncada Barracks in 1953. The break with Mirta came while he was in prison in the Isle of Pines after Moncada.

On July 17, 1954, he wrote to Conte Agüero (Letter VII in *Cartas del Presidio*) about hearing on the radio that "the Ministry of the Interior has dismissed Mirta Díaz-Balart." For Fidel, this was a vile calumny intended to ruin him. It gave the idea that his wife was working for the Batista Government which he and his comrades had sacrificed so much to destroy.

Nothing more is divulged in the letters about the incident, although the divorce proceedings that Mirta introduced are referred to in Letters XIII and XIV.

The story behind the incident was told to me by a close associate of Fidel's who had innocently become involved. Mirta's brother Rafael, who has then a subsecretary in the Ministry of the Interior, came to this family friend one day and said that Mirta was desperate for money. He, Rafael, would give her 100 pesos (then worth $100) a month, but because of the fact that Mirta's husband was none other than Fidel Castro, it had to be done discreetly. He asked the friend to take the money regularly and pass it on to his sister.

This went along smoothly for months, but as it happened, Rafael was getting the 100 pesos out of Ministry funds by putting

Mirta's name down as an employee. In time, Batista's Minister of the Interior learned about it and happily published the fact that Fidel Castro's wife had been on the payroll of the Ministry.

Fidel was not only horrified; he was saddened and bitter. In one of his letters from prison he refers to the event as "a new, unknown and terrible sadness." Despite his political radicalness, his antisocial disposition and a certain promiscuity when it came to women, he seems to have had a typically Catholic and Latin attitude toward marriage and its sacredness.

Moreover, there was Fidelito. Fidel's affection for his son is very deep. Every one of his friends bears witness to that. The boy at first stayed with his mother and had a few years at school on Long Island in the United States. In fact, he was there when Fidel was in the Sierra Maestra, but came back in time to be able to ride into Havana on a tank with his father on January 8, 1959, the day that Fidel made his triumphant entry.

From then on the father had charge of his son, but the curtain descended so far as the public was concerned. Fidelito went quietly to school like any other Cuban boy. Fidel sought no favors for him and never mentioned him outside the restricted circle of his friends. Fidelito became a *becado,* a scholarship student. For his part, he is so embarrassed by the attention his parentage gives him that he insists on going by another name at school. It is a thin disguise for the tall, good-looking youth of nineteen who is so much his father's son. He is said to be a good student and is now in Havana University.

Mirta remarried. Fidel did not. Teresa Casuso, in her book, writes of a romance and a proposal of marriage by Fidel to a beautiful Cuban girl she calls Lilia, who was living in Mexico City in 1956. "Fidel's plan was to marry Lilia and take her with him on the [*Granma*] expedition," she writes. The engagement lasted only a month, it seems.

Other women came along, but no one else has written about a possible marriage, so far as I know. Two of his friends have said to me that he never really loved any woman except Mirta—which may be a case of romanticizing. He simply was not made for marriage; his life has been so bound up in his work that there is no room for a normal married life.

There is no need to get into the eternally fruitless speculation as to whether men or external factors are chiefly responsible for history. However, this book will reflect the firm conviction, which I stated earlier, that the Cuban Revolution is Fidel Castro's revolution. I would agree with a judgment I ran across in a posthumous, unfinished essay by Professor Marc Bloch of the Sorbonne University: "It is men that history seeks to grasp. Failing that, it will be an exercise in erudition."

Trying to "grasp" all of Fidel Castro would be a hopeless task. Men like him have enormously complicated characters. Yet there is a great deal that can be grasped, some of it obvious, some that one sees and understands only after long acquaintance.

My own first impression of him was that he is certainly one of the most brilliant talkers I have ever met, not in the sense of being clever, witty, cultured, but in his ability to express ideas and thoughts with great clarity and fluency. When the subject is something about which he feels strongly and emotionally there is a passionate, urgent rush in his language that is irresistibly convincing. This is what I felt so intensely in the Sierra Maestra on the morning of February 17, 1957, as he crouched next to me whispering (we were surrounded by Bastista's troops) the hopes, the dreams, the convictions that were, in time, to become realities.

It having been my fortune, as a correspondent for *The New York Times,* to cover the Spanish Civil War, I kept being reminded—and I still am—of the Spanish anarchists whom I got to know in those years. Spain was unique in offering fruitful ground for the anarchist movement that grew out of the early Marxist developments in Western Europe. Fidel, after all, is of pure Spanish blood.

The Spanish anarchist is a rash, antisocial, brave, proud, arrogant type—and he is also undisciplined, disorganized, unpredictable, individualistic. He is moved by an idealism which contains much that is noble, but also much that is impractical and utopian. (The anarcho-syndicalist movement was strong in the Cuban labor unions from the 1890s to well into the 1920s but it lost out to the Communists, and Castro could not have felt its influence.)

In the eager discussions about Fidel, when he first took over in Havana, becoming Premier and then ousting the President whom he himself had chosen—Manuel Urrutia—it was a commonplace to say, "Fidel always wants to win." This is true.

Fidel Castro is a perfect example of Max Weber's charismatic leader. He has the overpowering personality and magnetism to attract devoted followers and to win mass support. He has the force of character to innovate, to bring change. A charismatic leader can be good or evil in Weber's concept, although the general idea is that he is a hero. Fidel is a hero to many and an evil demagogue to others, depending on the point of view. But however you take him, there is no doubt that he has charisma.

In view of Fidel Castro's career, it should not be necessary to point out that he is, and always has been, a man of exceptional personal courage. Some of his enemies will not concede this, but it is a fact that he is brave to the point of rashness. In the Sierra Maestra, his guerrilla followers were constantly trying—in vain—to induce him not to expose himself to unnecessary danger. Che Guevara was once misquoted as saying that Fidel used to hang back, but this was not the case, and Che denied that he ever said any such thing.

There is a true story of Fidel's boyhood (I heard it from his brother Raúl and from others) that illustrates his determination to win. It concerns the period when Fidel was at the Jesuit preparatory school of Belén in Havana.

He quarreled with an older and bigger lad who beat him until he could fight no longer. The next day Fidel went for his enemy and was beaten up again until they were separated. The third time the result was no more favorable, but the other boy had had enough—and presumably conceded a moral victory to Fidel.

"The most important feature of Fidel's character," his brother Raúl said to me when I last saw him in October 1967, "is that he will not accept defeat."

Every phase of his life, from childhood to the present, proves this point. It will be seen as his political career is traced—through Moncada, the Sierra Maestra and the agonizing gestation and growth of the revolution—that Fidel never gave up; he never lost heart; he seems immune to discouragement and dismay.

This is an aspect of his character that his enemies, including the United States State Department, took years to understand. There never was a time when sabotage, subversion or even invasion held any hope of eliminating Fidel Castro. So long as he lives he will never accept defeat for himself or his revolution.

This goes equally for Cuba's economy. Fidel is fighting back against early defeat in this field, and will go on fighting until—presuming it is humanly possible—he achieves a due measure of success.

It has been a vital part of the composition of Fidel's character that he has always had a passion to be his own master. He hates to be restricted or under discipline. His twenty-two months of imprisonment after the Moncada Barracks attack—four of them in solitary confinement—must have been almost unendurable to him. He can exercise self-discipline, but in that case he is still his own master.

From the time he was old enough—let us say his Havana University days—Fidel would never take orders from anybody. In fact, he would rarely take advice.

This "lone wolf" characteristic, which is so profoundly a part of Fidel's nature, should have been noted from the beginning by his Cuban middle-class enemies and by Americans in the State Department. There would have been less naïve zeal in picturing a Fidel Castro "captured" by the Cuban Communists or a Castro Government as a satellite of the Soviet Union.

As Raúl Castro put it to me, "Fidel never wanted to join any party because he didn't want to be restricted or be under any orders or discipline. He never could stand for any kind of formalism. This is a trait he has never abandoned. Even in matters of protocol and diplomacy, Fidel just cannot be bothered about formalities."

One of the first things I noted about him in the chaotic ferment of the year 1959, when I paid three visits to Cuba, was that he does not confide completely in anybody, not even in his brother Raúl. If there is any exception to this rule it would be Celia Sánchez, the young woman who joined the tiny guerrilla band in the first weeks of the Sierra Maestra adventure and has been an inseparable part of Fidel's life ever since. The relations between Celia and Fidel are one of the intriguing mysteries of the Cuban

Revolution. In any event, she is the soul of discretion and never divulges confidences.

There is no use trying to guess what Fidel Castro is going to do at any given time. Felipe Pazos, who was a resistance leader during the insurrection and was president of the National Bank of Cuba for the first ten months of 1959 (he went into exile afterwards) once put the problem to me in clever fashion.

"Your logic and mine," he said, "are not always applicable to Fidel or to the Cuban Revolution, which has a logic all its own. It is something like working in a fourth dimension."

The fact that Fidel always kept his own counsel partly explains why the first few years of the revolution were an endless and bewildered guessing game for Cubans and Americans. Those working with him in the government (I heard this from a number of them, starting in 1959) say that Castro is calculating. He thinks over and maps out an action or program, often for a long time. Many of his apparently abrupt and emotional acts are planned in advance. Curiously, this is a well-known trait of another *Gallego,* who is likewise a dictator—Generalísimo Franco. Both men, so different in other respects, are enigmatic, aloof, baffling even to their closest associates.

All the major figures of history (witness Lyndon B. Johnson and Richard M. Nixon in the United States) are men—and women— of tremendously complicated characters. There is always a variety of opinions about them, and a core of mystery that goes down the years in the pages of historians.

One should approach such figures with an intellectual humility and diffidence that has been blatantly absent in nearly all the writing about Fidel Castro. A whole breed of Cubanologists has flourished since 1959. I believe one can apply to them a wise judgment from an essay by the British historian, C. V. Wedgwood: "Though specialization is essential for learning, it is fatal to understanding." A nation in revolution is a vivid phenomenon. So is a revolutionary leader.

Such men have idiosyncrasies that are unimportant, but also traits of character that influence a nation's life.

One of Fidel's oddities is that he lives, so to speak, outside "the money economy." He never has any money with him and, of course, needs none for his daily life, since he is surrounded by people who take care of all his problems in the way of food, clothing, housing and transportation.

He has kept a number of sleeping places and one "home base" since the early months of the revolution. The base is the upper floor of a small house where Celia Sánchez and a sister live in the Vedado district of Havana. It is simple, ugly, badly but comfortably furnished. Luxury not only has never meant anything to Fidel; it positively irritates him and makes him uncomfortable.

His disdain for money is a lifelong part of his character; although Ángel Castro was moderately wealthy by the time Fidel was growing up, he seems to have kept his sons on small allowances.

When Fidel has needed money, which he has desperately in his career—for the Moncada attack, the *Granma* expedition, the arms and supplies for the Sierra Maestra—it has been for a revolutionary purpose, not for himself.

For those who do not know Cuban history it needs to be pointed out that the Castro regime is the first honest government that Cuba has ever had—honest in the sense that its leaders have not enriched themselves. Cuban history in Spanish colonial times and since independence in 1898 had been an uninterrupted course in political and economic corruption.

Whatever the future brings, Cubans know that Fidel Castro has no money deposited in the United States or Switzerland, and that he will never go off, as his predecessor General Fulgencio Batista and his henchmen did, with hundreds of millions of dollars in foreign banks or Florida real estate. The same dishonesty can be ascribed to Batista's predecessors—Carlos Prío Socarrás, Ramón Grau San Martín, and so on back into history.

There were, of course, exceptions among Cuban officials in this century, but they merely proved the rule. The tradition that Fidel Castro naturally and unconsciously followed was that of José

Martí and other leaders of the rebellious Cuban forces in the wars of independence from 1868 to 1898.

Fidel's contempt for money went so far that when he first came to power in 1959 he even grumbled because banks were charging interest. This was not only a throwback to medieval Catholic doctrine about the evils of "usury"; it was also one of the many ways in which Fidel's ideas resembled some of the pre-Marxist schools of socialism and modern anarchism.

It is this anti-money instinct that inclines him—as it did Che Guevara—to feel that the rewards of labor should be moral rather than materialistic. There is a utopian streak in Fidel's character that he himself has recognized on occasion.

Fidel is neither religious nor antireligious. Not only did I note this from my own experiences but I have heard it from some of the most important churchmen in Cuba—Catholic and Protestant—and also from Castro's closest associates.

He respects the religion of the Roman Catholic Church into which he was born, but it has no appeal to his emotions. His mother was intensely religious. It is also possible that a vestige of his Jesuit education clung to him. The religious atmosphere of the schools that he went to did not irritate him as it did his brother Raúl, who followed the same school path at four years' distance.

The French author, Robert Merle, in his book *Moncada, Premier Combat de Fidel Castro* (pages 117–19), relates an amusing conversation with Raúl on this subject. Raúl simply could not stand the praying that he had to do. "For myself, frankly, I had enough of prayers. I liked sports and devilry," Merle quotes Raúl as saying.

Fidel, in that respect, was more conformist, no doubt because he did not care one way or another. In 1960–61 he expelled a number of Spanish priests from Cuba and there was a period of conflict in those years when he was carrying his revolution into the Communist camp. However, his motives were political, not antireligious nor even anticlerical. It was a campaign against certain individual priests who, he believed, were plotting, or at least agitating, against his regime in collaboration with the Americans.

An ambassador in Havana told me a story in May 1966 which he said he knew to be true. An old Cuban Government official and a friend of Castro's was dying. Castro visited him and it was Fidel who said to him; "But you must have Monsignor Zacchi [the Vatican Chargé d'Affaires] to come in and give you the last sacraments."

A Canadian diplomat in Havana told me that at the time of the conflict with the Catholic priests, Fidel expelled some Canadian priests, along with the Spaniards. Ottawa protested, and since Canada has had uninterrupted diplomatic and trade relations with Cuba, not only did Fidel arrange for the Canadian priests to return, but the Cuban Government paid all their travel expenses.

There was a period of a few months when Fidel wore a religious amulet that had been put around his neck by an old woman during the triumphant procession to Havana in January 1959. The gesture touched him, but obviously the amulet engendered no religious emotions in him.

It is worth noting at this point that the Vatican has never broken diplomatic relations with Cuba. There is an internuncio in Havana, Monsignor Cesare Zacchi (who, interestingly, was ordained a bishop in 1967), and there is a Cuban Ambassador to the Holy See, Luis Amado-Blanco, who has the reputation of being a devout practicing Catholic.

Fidel's indifference toward religion in his own life is a revealing trait in his character because it applies just as much to that secular religion known as Communism. The attraction of Marxism-Leninism to Castro was in political, economic and international fields. It never had an emotional appeal to him. In all such matters, the safest key to unlocking Castro's motives is pragmatism.

The same trait, incidentally, applies to Fidel's attitude toward race. He has no feelings of superiority or antagonism toward Negroes or Orientals, for instance. In himself, he is racially color-blind. Politically, and in his relations toward the United States, it is another matter. He has used the equality of Negroes in revolutionary Cuba and the racial troubles in the United States to great effect in his propaganda.

His personal habits are his own business, of course, and they would not be worth mentioning if so much had not been written about them. His multitudinous enemies have asserted that he is sloppy, unwashed, neglectful of his person, and so on.

The truth is simple. He is one of those men—and there are infinite numbers of them—who like to shed the artificial restraints of society. However, when he has to—which is most of the time in Havana—he is as spotlessly clean and orderly as any official should be. His beard and fatigue uniform give outsiders a falsely stupid impression. But it is still a fact that given the chance, he reverts to nature.

The last letter in *Cartas del Presidio* is written to his sister Lidia. It is about an apartment to be rented for him, Raúl and two of the sisters. In it he writes of himself as being of "a bohemian temperament and naturally disorderly" (*poco ordenado*). Then he adds, "There is nothing more agreeable than having a place where one can throw on the floor as many cigar butts as one pleases without the subconscious fear of a maid who is waiting like a sentinel to place an ashtray where the ashes are going to fall."

It has been his fate, ironically, to be living in a house in Havana that Celia Sánchez sees to it is kept spotlessly clean.

I felt from the beginning in 1959—and I have not changed my mind in 1968—that the press coverage of the Cuban Revolution is the worst failure in the history of American journalism. To be sure, it has been one of the most difficult stories of our times to cover from month to month and year to year in an authoritative and understanding way. The story has been a bewildering one to follow. Fidel had to find his way, gropingly, making mistakes, changing his policies and methods as he went along.

One can see, looking back, that the changes in what he did, as compared to the changes in what he said, were not substantial; they were formal. Fidel made the revolution he always had in mind but made it differently than he expected to—and certainly differently than the Cuban middle classes, the Americans and many foreign sympathizers, including myself, expected him to make it.

He has a strong pragmatic, opportunistic streak in him that defies ideological or dogmatic classification, even though he calls himself a Marxist-Leninist. He must respond to the inexorable pressures of Cuban history and tradition, the Cuban character, the influence of the United States, the politics of the socialist bloc of nations, the working of economic "laws" and the world markets— especially for sugar. He and his revolution have been caught up in the stormy winds of the Cold War, but the revolution can be properly understood only as a Latin American phenomenon.

The scene changes with every visit to Cuba, but one is watching a continuing drama with the same actors and the same leading man. Fidel Castro has never stepped out of character. His role is that of a revolutionary, and he is going to go on playing it until he dies.

His comrade Che Guevara was also a born revolutionary, and he played out the role until he died on a jungle battlefield in Bolivia. In the letter that he wrote to his five children in Cuba, to be opened if he were killed, Che exhorted the children to become "good revolutionaries."

There never has been a more revolutionary period in history than this last half of the twentieth century. What is more natural than that an elemental type—the revolutionary—should be an embodiment of our times?

What is a revolutionary? A rebel, obviously, one who goes against the environment in which he lives, who sets out to destroy, to overturn, and then to create a different, a better, world. The processes of destruction and creation are agonizing—and so the revolutionary is the enemy of society. But he always wins because the act of destruction forces himself, or those who come after, to make a new society.

Revolution, in some form or other, has to take place in our world. It is taking place in the United States and Great Britain, as well as in other countries. Those who seek to hold it back are fighting a lost cause. They are trying to preserve a world that has been doomed.

# 2 CUBA

FIDEL CASTRO came out of Cuban history as naturally as sugarcane grows out of Cuban soil. The revolution that he is making has to be interpreted in Cuban terms.

When Christopher Columbus saw the lush, green Cuban shore on his first voyage he wrote that this was "the fairest island human eyes have yet beheld." The true wealth of the country does, indeed, lie in the rich soil that made Cuba "the sugar bowl of the world" and, for smokers, the source of incomparably the finest cigars to be found anywhere. Its untapped resources of nickel are second in quantity only to those of the United States. Professor Lowry Nelson, in his classic study, *Rural Cuba,* called the island "one of the most favorable spots for human existence on the earth's surface."

Spain held it for four hundred years, until long after all her other colonies in the New World had been lost. They were, on the whole, years of misrule, spoliation and brutality. Most of the native Indians were killed off, so that all Cubans are "immigrants"

—Spanish and Negro or a mixture of both, except for a small percentage.

As the winds of freedom swept over the hemisphere, Cuban patriots began fighting for independence and went on fighting for generations. The struggle was long, costly and heroic. A rebellious spirit was bred into Cubans, which helps a little to explain why Castro's revolution has endured. Fidel, like all other Cubans of this century, had learned the history and heard the stories that were handed down from one generation to another. Something revolutionary was there, deep in Cuban hearts, to be awakened.

For thirty years Cuban patriots fought and died in two Wars of Independence—the Ten Years War from 1868 to 1878, and the revolt that José Martí inspired in 1895, which was to lead to the misnamed "Spanish-American War" of 1898 and to independence —at least from Spain.

Whether the Cuban rebels could alone have won their independence if, as General Máximo Gómez and other patriots desired, the United States had helped with artillery and ammunition can never be known. During the bitterly fought guerrilla war of 1868–78 United States "nonintervention"—not to mention its sale of arms to Spain—helped the Spaniards. The Cuban rebels rose again in 1895 and fought and were still fighting hard in 1898 when an American public, aroused by the wildest sort of yellow journalism, but also responding to a genuine and generous desire to help the Cubans, intervened. The still-mysterious blowing up of the battleship U.S.S. *Maine* in Havana harbor on February 15, 1898, was the spark that set off the American explosion.

It was what Secretary of State John Hay most unfortunately called "a splendid little war," lasting 114 days and costing only 2,500 American lives, mostly from disease.

"You know the history of the Yankee intervention," Fidel Castro said in a speech in Santiago de Cuba on July 26, 1962, "that when the Spaniards were on the verge of defeat, they came to pick up the fallen mangoes [i.e., the ripe fruit on the ground]. They intervened, and would not let [General] Calixto García enter this city of Santiago de Cuba."

No Cubans were present when the treaty of peace was signed in Paris. The name of the conflict in all American history books, and

doubtless for all time, was given as the "Spanish-American War."
Even when such a distinguished historian as Professor Frank
Freidel of Harvard published a book on the war in 1958, which he
called *The Splendid Little War,* there was no mention, no understanding and no explanation of the Cuban version of what was to
them their Second War of Independence. They had fought for
thirty years, not just for 114 days.

In 1960, the noted and then very old Cuban historian, Emilio
Roig de Leuchsenring, whose nationalistic ideas strongly influ-
enced the Cuban thoughts against the United States on which Fidel
Castro's generation was nourished, published a book. It was
called: *Cuba no debe su Independencia a los Estados Unidos*
(Cuba Does Not Owe Her Independence to the United States).

A succinct picture of the price that Cuba and the Cuban people
had paid for their bitter struggle against Spain is given by Boris
Goldenberg in his book *The Cuban Revolution and Latin America*
(page 100):

> The country had been laid waste. Almost 400,000 people had
> died, many in big "concentration" camps into which the Spanish
> General Weyler had collected a large part of the population. The
> 1899 census showed a population of 1.5 million inhabitants—
> 60,000 less than ten years earlier. The number of cattle had fallen
> by 80 per cent and tobacco production by about the same amount.
> The sugar harvest of 1895 had amounted to one million tons: now
> it was hardly more than 300,000. The health of the population was
> causing anxiety for yellow fever claimed many victims. Bridges and
> roads had been destroyed.

Although Che Guevara was a "Cuban" only briefly by a special
process of naturalization, he was able to express Cuban feelings as
well as any of the revolutionaries. In an article for the magazine
*International Affairs* of October 1964 he gave a typical summary
of how generations of Cuban nationalists felt about the beginnings
of the Republic:

> The Paris Peace Treaty of 1898 and the Platt Amendment of
> 1901 were the signs under which our new Republic was born. In the

first, the settlement of accounts after the war between the two Powers led to the withdrawal of Spain and the intervention of the United States. On the island, which had suffered years of cruel struggle, the Cubans were only observers; they had no part in the negotiations. The second, the Platt Amendment, established the right of the United States to intervene in Cuba whenever her interests demanded it.

In May 1902 the political-military oppression of the United States [i.e., the occupation] was formally ended, but her monopolistic power remained. Cuba became an economic colony of the United States and this remained its main characteristic for half a century.

Two features of the peace settlement led to a still-unended bitterness among Cuban nationalists. They were to keep the embers of revolutionary anti-Yankeeism red-hot.

Both were inscribed in the Platt Amendment that Guevara mentioned, which was, by United States insistence, written into the Cuban Constitution and the peace treaty between Cuba and the United States in 1903. The key Article III read as follows:

> That the government of Cuba consents that the United States may exercise the right to intervene for the preservation of Cuban independence, the maintenance of a government adequate for the protection of life, property, and individual liberty, and for discharging the obligations with respect to Cuba imposed by the Treaty of Paris on the United States, now to be assumed and undertaken by the government of Cuba.

Article VII stipulated that "the government of Cuba will sell or lease to the United States land necessary for coaling or naval stations." Out of this clause came the big American naval base at Guantánamo Bay on the southeastern coast of Cuba.

The Platt Amendment was abrogated in 1934, but not before there had been a number of American military interventions in Cuba. Until then, Cuba was only half independent. Guantánamo Bay is still an American base since, legally, the treaty arrangement can be abrogated only with the consent of both parties. Its strategic value as a protector of the Panama Canal has been greatly reduced in these nuclear-bomb days, but it still serves as a base against the threat of leftist revolution in the Caribbean and as a beachhead in Marxist-Leninist Cuba. The Castroites feel about it—although for different reasons—the way the pro-Franco Spaniards feel about Gibraltar.

The practical effect of the Platt Amendment—and this was intentional—was to forestall a social revolution in Cuba and insure order and stability for Cubans and for the American investors who were then acquiring huge tracts of land very cheaply and embarking on a banking and economic control over Cuba.

Before the war, President McKinley could have extended recognition of belligerency to the Cuban rebels against Spain, but he feared to do so because, as he said, that would "subject us to embarrassing conditions of international obligation" to the Cuban rebels. This meant that as early as 1898 the United States was against revolution in Cuba.

There was nothing Machiavellian or sinister in this. It was a natural response to American interests and to the prevailing economic and social philosophy of those times. In fact, most of our contemporaries in Europe marveled that the United States did not annex Cuba, and that so much was done with good will and good intentions—not to mention good results—during the four-year occupation that followed the war.

In the "Joint Resolution of Congress for the Recognition of the Independence of Cuba," April 20, 1898, it was stated:

> That the United States hereby disclaims any disposition or intention to exercise sovereignty, jurisdiction, or control over said island except for the pacification thereof, and asserts its determination, when that is accomplished, to leave the government and control of the island to its people.

This pledge was honored to a considerable degree—but by no means wholly.

In 1938, Herminio Portell Vilá, one of Cuba's most distinguished historians, began publishing his classic four-volume study of the relations of Cuba with Spain and the United States. In his introduction, quoted on page 73 in *Background to Revolution* (edited by Professor Robert F. Smith), he wrote:

> The frustration of the Cuban revolution [1868-98]—of its formidable effort and its awakened national conscience striving to

make a truly new state—was the work of the United States, dictated by those with an appetite for annexation. No nation has been so victimized without [developing] a deep resentment in its resistance to the aggressor, a resentment which permeates the organization of its society and its very life.

(Portell Vilá, incidentally, has chosen since 1960 to live in exile in the United States rather than in a Cuba that has turned authoritarian.)

Therefore, Cuba's long struggle for independence did not end in 1898 so far as nationalists and "revisionists" as they were called, were concerned. Fidel Castro grew up and spent his university years with the conviction that the fight for independence had simply been transferred from Spain to the United States.

José Martí had warned his fellow Cubans that "Cuba must be free of Spain and of the United States," but from the viewpoint of Cuban nationalists, freedom was lost to the United States. Cuba became a colony in the sense that it was dependent on the United States for capital, technical knowledge, trade, ideas of government and economics, and even to a considerable degree for its culture and manners.

Martí, poet, orator, journalist and martyr, the "Apostle" of the 1895–1898 War of Independence, has had roughly the place in Cuban hearts and minds that Abraham Lincoln occupies in the United States. He caught the tide of events in Cuba in the 1880s when slavery was abolished and for the first time it became possible to conjure up a mass following for a revolution against Spain. His eloquence, fervor and all-absorbing dedication to the cause of independence permitted him to achieve at least temporary unity among the Cuban emigrés in the United States and around the Caribbean.

As all Cuban leaders have known, there is nothing more difficult than to bring Cubans together and keep them together. Martí had a pure quality about him that was to make him the ideal inspirer and organizer of Cuban liberty, but one could not imagine him as a political leader after independence. Tomás Estrada Palma, who was also a resistance leader and who became the first President of the Republic, was made of sterner stuff but even he could not hold off the greedy, bribe-taking, cynical officials around him. Estrada Palma died in poverty and ignominy.

José Martí was more fortunate; he died a hero and a martyr in a Spanish ambush on May 19, 1895. The column led by General Máximo Gómez that Martí had joined was betrayed by a Cuban guide.

Cuban history, curiously, has a dark strain of treachery that runs through its pattern. There was a traitor in Castro's group in Mexico when the *Granma* invasion was being prepared—none other than Rafael del Pino who had been with Fidel in Bogotá. There were others in the Sierra Maestra. It was because of treachery, according to Che Guevara, that Castro's force was almost entirely wiped out soon after the landing. One delator, Eutimio Guerra, was naïve or greedy enough to try twice. He was caught and executed a few hours after I left Castro in the Sierra Maestra on February 17, 1957.

Martí's populist ideals broke down quickly in the early scramble for power when the Cuban Republic was formed. His name was honored in a perfunctory way for a quarter of a century.

Then there was a renaissance. By coincidence it came around the time that Fidel Castro was born, when university students agitated for—and got—academic reforms. It was in the mid-1920s that Havana University became a fiery center of rebellion. The works of José Martí were taken down from library shelves, dusted off and read. His figure again symbolized what was best in Cuban history and the Cuban people—a noble fatherland, an economically independent nation, a united, brotherly people. The students who led the revolutionary explosion that overthrew the brutal tyrant, President Gerardo Machado, in 1933, had been fed on Martí's idealism. When Fidel Castro went to Havana University, it was not Marx and Lenin that he read most of all, as he later boasted for political reasons, but José Martí. When he was in the Isle of Pines jail after the Moncada Barracks attack, reading omnivorously, there was a little of Lenin but a lot of Martí.

This does not mean that Fidel Castro is the direct heir of José

Martí or that Cuba today fulfills Martí's dreams. Life and history are not so simple. Yet the spirit is there in Cuba today. Fidel Castro has carried on a Martían tradition; his revolution has fulfilled some of Martí's hopes, although in many other respects today's realities are far from Martí's dreams.

But after all, Martí could only dream. He never lived to deal with the harsh realities—and they are indeed harsh—of ruling Cuba in the face of the "formidable neighbor's" enmity. Martí's task was child's play compared to Castro's.

Fidel Castro was to say—in a speech at the University of Havana on March 13, 1965—that after Spain "a much greater power arose elsewhere, a more fearful power—Yankee imperialism. The struggle against that power became the great historic task of our people in this century, to achieve independence from that power, to resist its aggressions, and to maintain on high the flag of revolution."

This feeling was not a Castroite invention. Professor Smith, in *The United States and Cuba* gives (page 103) an earlier example: "After the cabinet reorganization in June 1922," he writes, "one Havana newspaper came out with double-page headlines declaring, 'HATRED OF NORTH AMERICANS WILL BE THE RELIGION OF CUBANS.' " This was four years before Fidel was born.

It would be totally unrealistic to take into account only Cuban feelings and overlook how Americans on the continent always felt about Cuba. *Look* magazine of April 9, 1963, has a cartoon in which an irate American wife asks her husband: "What I'd like to know is, what *is* Cuba doing only ninety miles from our shores in the *first* place?"

Probably the most famous of many historic pronouncements on what Cuba has meant to the United States appeared in a letter that the then Secretary of State, John Quincy Adams, wrote to Hugh Nelson, United States Minister to Spain, on April 28, 1823:

These islands are natural appendages of the North American continent, and one of them [Cuba] almost within sight of our shores, from a multitude of considerations, has become an object of transcendent importance to the commercial and political interests of our Union. Its commanding position . . . gives it an importance in the sum of our national interests with which that of no other foreign territory can be compared, and little inferior to that which binds the different members of the Union together.

With the nuclear missile crisis of 1962, a new tactical factor was introduced, but strategically speaking the threat from Cuba is one of the recurrent themes of American history.

The island's geographic position is a dominating one. Its western end points into the Gulf of Mexico. The Straits of Florida separate it from the United States by only 90 to 100 miles. On the southwestern side, the peninsula of Yucatán in Mexico is 150 miles away. The Windward Passage at the eastern end, between Cuba and Haiti, which is only 50 miles wide, takes about two-thirds of all Atlantic Ocean traffic entering and leaving the Caribbean or coming from or going to the Panama Canal. Geopoliticians have likened the Windward Passage to the Strait of Gibraltar—and incidentally compared the Caribbean Sea to the Mediterranean Sea as a sort of *Mare Nostrum* for the United States. Oil, iron ore, bauxite, tin and copper from South America and the West Indies (all highly strategic materials) come in ships through the Windward Passage or sail close to Cuba.

When air travel developed, a new strategic element was added. Cuba is more than 700 miles long. It lies across the most direct air routes from the North Atlantic to and from the Panama Canal and northern and western South America.

It has been a basic feature of American strategy since the thirteen colonies won their independence that the island of Cuba must be denied to a strong or hostile power. America did not worry about Spain once Florida was acquired in 1819. She ceased to become a threat after all the Latin American colonies except Cuba had won their independence. The English, the French and the Germans were the nations America worried about most at various times.

The situation had so little changed as this century was beginning that Secretary of State Elihu Root, in a letter written on February 9, 1901, to General Leonard Wood, commander of the United States occupation forces in Cuba, had this to say:

> It would be hard to find a single statement of public policy which has been so often officially declared by so great an array of distinguished Americans authorized to speak for the Government of the United States, as the proposition stated, in varying but always uncompromising and unmistakable terms, that the United States would not under any circumstances permit any foreign power other than Spain to acquire possession of the island of Cuba.

Root mentioned Thomas Jefferson, James Monroe, John Quincy Adams, Ulysses S. Grant, Henry Clay, Daniel Webster, James Buchanan (all but two of them Presidents), and he could have named others. In our era, he also could have added Eisenhower, Kennedy and Johnson.

> The United States [Root's letter goes on to say] has, and will always have, the most vital interest in the preservation of the independence which she has secured for Cuba, and in preserving the people of that island from the domination and control of any foreign power whatever. . . .
>
> We are placed in a position where, for our own protection, we have, by reason of expelling Spain from Cuba, become the guarantors of Cuban independence. . . .
>
> It would be a most lame and impotent conclusion if . . . we should . . . be placed in a worse condition in regard to our own vital interests than we were while Spain was in possession.

It was an irony of history that we were so placed in 1962. Before the Cuban Revolution, it would have taken a wild imagination to conceive of the possibility of a hostile, powerful, nuclear-armed Russia reaching across 4,000 miles of land and sea to turn Cuba into a serious—in fact, a desperate—threat to the security of the United States. Even now, the situation seems to go against any criteria of logic, common sense or strategy—but there it is, and there it will be as long as Fidel Castro lives and Cuba is a Communist country.

American power was used steadily in those six decades before the revolution, but, alas, it was used primarily to maintain enough stability and enough control over, or collaboration from, Cuban Presidents to assure the safety of American investments and American residents and to prevent a revolution.

The second of two bungling American ambassadors to Havana during the Batista dictatorship (both political appointees), Earl E. T. Smith, made a most damaging remark to the U.S. Senate Subcommittee to Investigate the Administration of the International Security Act. This was in August 1960, and the statement has already become historic.

> Senator [Eastland], let me explain to you that the United States, until the advent of Castro, was so overwhelmingly influential in Cuba that, as I said here a little while ago, the American Ambassador was the second most important man in Cuba; sometimes even more important than the [Cuban] President.

This will take its place with a famous and often-quoted statement by the blunt U.S. Marine general, Smedley D. Butler, in 1931. John Gunther, for instance, puts it at the head of Chapter 8 of his recent book, *Inside South America:*

> I helped make Mexico safe for American oil interests in 1914. I helped make Haiti and Cuba a decent place for the National City Bank boys to collect revenues in. I helped purify Nicaragua for the international banking house of Brown Brothers. . . .

The shameful course of Cuban politics was uninterrupted. President Gerardo Machado, having served his first term of office from 1924 to 1928 without being particularly worse than his predecessors, decided to retain power. American business and banking interests approved, according to historians of the day, but Machado could hold his post only by a tyranny and brutality that became intolerable. Even then, the United States tried to save Machado and, failing that, worked successfully to prevent a revolution.

Machado was ousted by Cuban military officers in August 1933. A period of confusion and virtual chaos ensued, out of which came "a sergeant named Batista" who, incidentally, had nothing to do with the overthrow of Machado or with the revolutionary violence that preceded it. Fulgencio Batista became Colonel, Chief of Staff of the Army, and President (1940–44), and Cuba went back to its muddle of graft and corruption.

One of Fidel Castro's major accomplishments—and a reason why his advent brought a definitive revolution—was that he destroyed the political system that had been in effect since the beginning of the century. At that time a Cuban ruling class was formed, composed in part of the men who had achieved prominence in the wars of independence and in part of upper-class Cuban and Spanish landowners, bankers, businessmen, professional elements and high-ranking military officers. These groups dominated politics for six decades. Insofar as a middle class developed, its objective was to join the upper economic and political level. Now and then an upstart like Batista, who had Negro and Chinese as well as white blood, would break into the charmed circle—but only to copy the methods and actions of the ruling group.

Politics, from the beginning of the Republic, was a spoils system, a profession, a means of enriching oneself and one's family, and of gaining a spurious social prestige in the process. There were honorable exceptions, of course, but the rule was that politicians, high army officers, bankers, businessmen and landowners served themselves and their families, not their country and their people.

The United States supported their system because it protected American property; permitted generations of Americans to make money in or from Cuba; provided friendly Cuban governments in a country of the highest strategic value to the United States; and, finally, ensured a crude sort of stability and order.

In theory, Cuba was sovereign, so that internal violence and political corruption were the business of Cubans and required American military intervention to restore order only on occasions in the first few decades of the Republic.

Cuba, to be sure, could not have developed industrially and agriculturally without United States investments and managers. There was a high degree of good intentions and honest idealism in United States relations with Cuba, especially in the earliest years of the Republic, but there were also greed and callousness. Business is business, and it is naïve to expect investors to place anything ahead of the safety and profitability of their investments. It would also have been naïve to expect Cuban businessmen to welcome a revolution that would take over their businesses, or to expect Cuban politicians to go along with young revolutionaries who would sweep away their jobs.

It is not reasonable to believe that the old system could have been changed peacefully. By the time Fidel Castro came along this had to be acknowledged in an official way even in Washington. It was done in a passage of the White Paper put out by the State Department in April 1961, on the eve of the Bay of Pigs invasion. Arthur Schlesinger, Jr., then a White House Assistant to President Kennedy, prepared the Paper:

> The character of the Batista regime in Cuba made a violent popular reaction almost inevitable. The rapacity of the leadership, the corruption of the Government, the brutality of the police, the regime's indifference to the needs of the people for education, medical care, housing, for social justice and economic opportunity —all these, in Cuba as elsewhere, constituted an open invitation to revolution.

Although there were some social and economic reforms during the "liberal" regimes of Grau San Martín and Prío Socarrás, the 1961 White Paper's description could fairly be applied to every Cuban administration during the Republic. The last years of the Machado regime were as brutal as Batista's final years in office. There was no prospect of a democratic evolution. Cuba was ripe for revolution.

It stood to reason that when the revolution came, it was going to destroy the existing system of land tenure and try to break the predominance of sugar in the economic system.

In the scramble after 1898, land ownership became highly concentrated—much of it in American hands. A large part of the rural population was made landless and dependent for work on the great sugar plantations.

Fernando Ortiz, Cuba's most famous twentieth-century historian, wrote a book called *Cuban Counterpoint: Tobacco and Sugar.* Passages from the translation by Harriet de Onís are reproduced in Smith's *Background to Revolution* (pages 171–74). Ortiz listed the "principal characteristics" of the Cuban sugar industry in these only too accurate terms: "mechanization, latifundism, sharecropping, wage-fixing, super-capitalism, absentee landlordism, foreign ownership, corporation control and imperialism." And he added:

> Tobacco has created a middle class, a free bourgeoisie; sugar has created two extremes, slaves and masters, the proletariat and the rich. . . . Tobacco has always been under the control of home government. . . . Sugar, on the contrary, has been under foreign control superimposed on the island's government. The history of Cuba, from the days of the conquest to the present moment, has been essentially dominated by foreign controls over sugar, and the greater the value of our production, the greater the domination.

Sugar was for generations a symbol of Cuban subjection to the United States and of American power over the island. Cuba was not a "monoculture" country, and it is possible to demonstrate statistically, as Draper does in his book *Castroism,* that sugar did not play as great a role in the economy of Cuba as is generally thought.

However, Draper rightly adds that sugar was "largely responsible for Negro slave labor, for the devastation of magnificent forests, for the profit-hungry displacement of other crops, and for the attraction of so much foreign capital. The main United States investment was situated at the sorest and most vulnerable point, not only of the Cuban economy but of the Cuban national psyche, and whatever was or had ever been wrong with the sugar industry was linked in the most direct and intimate way with U.S. capital and trade."

This was not a uniquely Cuban phenomenon. Lord Acton, in one of his essays on the French Revolution, wrote: "Adam Smith says that to prohibit a great people from making all they can of every part of their own produce, or from employing their stock and industry in the way they judge most advantageous for themselves, is a manifest violation of the most sacred rights of mankind."

Referring to the Sugar Act of 1934 and to the reciprocal trade agreement of the same year, which gave United States goods tariff preferences in Cuba, United States Ambassador to the Castro Government, Philip W. Bonsal, pointed out in a generally hostile article in the January 1967 *Foreign Affairs* that "Cuba's share in our market did not rest upon a contractual basis but was dependent on the will of Congress. Cuts were made from time to time in the Cuban quota for the benefit of domestic areas or even of other foreign areas. The need for Cuba to avoid actions or attitudes which might put her in a bad light with Congress at quota time was a fact of life generally understood."

It was not only understood; it was resented. "The natural advantages of sugar in Cuba are obvious," Che Guevara wrote in his *International Affairs* article, "but the predominant fact is that Cuba was developed as a sugar factory of the United States."

As was stated before, the whole system of land tenure in Cuba was badly distributed from the social point of view.

> The 1946 Census [writes Professor Sidney W. Mintz of Yale University, quoted in *Background to Revolution*, page 184,] "indicated that 20 percent of the farmed area was held by less than one tenth of one percent of the farms—that is, one fifth of all Cuban farmland was divided up among slightly more than one hundred farms. Of the total number of farms, 70 percent were 63 acres or less in area, but accounted for only 11 percent of the farmland. In other words, the Cuban land situation was archetypal for Latin America: a bimodal distribution, with a few enormous latifundia at one end and many very small farms at the other."

This census, incidentally, was the last of its kind taken before the revolution. It also showed that 8 percent of all landowners held more than 71 percent of the land. Small holders (up to about 30 acres) owned 39 percent of all the farms but only 3.3 percent of the cultivable land.

Sugar was not the only product or service in which Americans played a major role. One of the most often quoted descriptions of the situation in Cuba before the revolution comes from a United States Department of Commerce publication of 1956:

The only foreign investments of importance are those of the United States. American participation exceeds 90 percent in the telephone and electric services, and about 50 percent in public service railways, and roughly 40 percent in raw sugar production. The Cuban branches of United States banks are entrusted with almost one-fourth of all bank deposits.

Professor Maurice Zeitlin of Wisconsin University, in his book *Revolutionary Politics and the Cuban Working Class* (page 288), adds: "Private U.S. capital also owned the most important cattle ranches, the copper mine, the major tourist facilities and hotels, and together with British capital almost the entire oil business."

The Cuban upper classes were perpetuating a system that in many ways was unjust, selfish and ultimately unwise. There were injustices in more ways than the land tenure. In a textbook on Cuba that I wrote in 1964, I said (page 64):

> Because of constant political instability and lack of trust in the courts, businessmen and investors sought quick high profits, or hoarded their savings when they did not send them abroad. They got the government to protect them by instituting high tariffs, and they protected themselves with monopoly practices. The American system of mass production at the lowest possible prices was not applied in Cuba.
>
> The tax system, inherited from the Spanish colonial practice of indirect taxation, favored the wealthy ruling classes. Since Cubans did not trust their government officials or their financial system, there was widespread tax evasion. Compared to what we pay in the United States, direct taxes on personal income were very light in Cuba. Rich Cubans could and did live in greater luxury than American multimillionaires.

The question of whether Cuba was and is an "underdeveloped" nation is a matter of definition and depends in part on what statistics are used and who uses them. So far as the Cuban Revolution is concerned, the problem is unimportant. Cuba—in national terms —was relatively prosperous at the time of the revolution.

This is usually the case with modern social revolutions. They come out of social and economic imbalances, oppression, frustrated expectations, magnetic leadership, contagious political doctrines, mass misery—all of which can be present in a prosperous or relatively prosperous nation.

It is hard for Americans to understand that they can be disliked and resented for the things that they do or have done in the past when they have meant well or when they do not know what their predecessors did. It never occurred to Americans, in the press or in Congress, that the Cubans had any right or reason to be hostile toward the United States. Yet they had a number of reasons, some of them good, and their feelings were sincerely held and not the result of perverseness, ingratitude or Communism.

Cubans, for their part, forget that the United States had kept its enemies away from the Western Hemisphere since 1815. Unlike the British or the Europeans, Americans are not psychologically adjusted to having formidable enemies across a river, a channel or a boundary line.

To blame everything on the United States—from Cuba's corruption to her distorted economy and rural poverty—has been a Cuban custom since the mid-nineteenth century. There we were—the "formidable neighbor," as José Martí called the American colossus—overpowering, looking out for our own interests and not giving a damn about Cubans as Cubans.

The importance of this feeling as a background to the Cuban Revolution can never be overlooked, but Cubans have only themselves to blame for much of what has been wrong in their country. They did not have to have corrupt governments, or to accept Yankee culture, or to permeate business with graft and nepotism, or to practice racial discrimination, or to permit such a socially unjust society.

They could have changed some or all of that without an upheaval. Now the changes are being made by means of a revolution. Washington is still the object of unending abuse. If the United States had not existed, as Jean-Paul Sartre wrote, Fidel Castro would have had to invent it. This has been the case with generations of Cubans.

United States policies in the latest postwar period toward Latin America in general, as well as toward Cuba in particular, played an indirect role in shaping Fidel Castro's ideas. This was true of other Cubans of his generation, and it helped to build up the anti-Yankeeism that was to characterize the Cuban Revolution.

The Cold War brought on an exaggerated—one can almost say hysterical—American attitude toward Communism. The consistent, traditional United States policy of seeking order and stability in Latin America was given a special coloration—anti-Communism. Thus, when the Guatemalan Government of President Jácobo Arbenz became Communist-influenced, Washington arranged, through the instrument of the Central Intelligence Agency, to overthrow the Arbenz regime. In that same year of 1954, Secretary of State John Foster Dulles concentrated his activities at the Tenth Inter-American Conference in Caracas, Venezuela, almost exclusively on getting an anti-Communist resolution passed.

The Latin countries were not interested in Communism, which, except in Guatemala, was no danger to any of them at the time. They were interested in solving economic and financial problems. The real threat to stability in Latin America lay in economic difficulties and in social imbalances and pressures. The United States not only went on neglecting these vital fields but actively favored reactionary regimes and unsavory dictators, including General Batista in Cuba, partly because they made believe that they were anti-Communist.

In 1959, President Dwight D. Eisenhower moved belatedly, at a hemispheric financial conference in Bogotá, Colombia, to lay stress on social reforms. Two years later, President John F. Kennedy launched the Alliance for Progress, a hemispheric program in which social justice was given equal prominence with economic reforms. The Alliance was so obviously an answer to the Cuban Revolution that all Latin Americans knew they had Fidel Castro to thank for it.

So far as Cuba was concerned, the damage had been done. Castro and the "Generation of '53"—as it is called from the date of the Moncada attack—had an inherited distrust for and antagonism toward the American Government and toward American business that acquired a burning, emotional quality as a result of

United States favoritism toward Batista. This had started, after all, in 1933 when Fidel was seven years old, so that he grew up amidst the nationalistic resentment toward "the formidable neighbor."

According to Draper, in his book *Castroism* (page 116):

> If anyone was responsible for opening the way to Castro's capture of power, that man was Fulgencio Batista. If there were grave-diggers of the former social order in Cuba, they were all those, Cubans and Americans, who condoned the coup [of March 1952] and supported the regime that came out of it. . . . Cuba was full of revolutionary conspiracies against Batista rather than with Castro; Batista, not Castro, was the indispensable revolutionary ingredient.

This kind of argument—a frequent one among those seeking to belittle Castro's role—overlooks the fact that Batista's coup was a natural, almost normal action within the framework of Cuban and Latin American history, whereas Fidel Castro was a unique phenomenon. One could use exactly the same words about Machado as Draper used about Batista—but there was no Fidel Castro in 1933 and hence there was no Cuban Revolution, although the nation was just as ripe for it then as it was a quarter of a century later.

Batista's coup provided Fidel with an excuse for action, but anyone who was in Cuba at the time, as I was, could not help being struck by the fact that those who felt disgust and anger were a minority with no possibility or intention of revolting. The vast majority of Cubans shrugged their shoulders and took the *cuartelazo,* or garrison revolt, philosophically: "There's that man again!"

Only one Cuban felt strongly enough and had the leadership qualities to do something about it. What he did—the Moncada Barracks attack on July 26, 1953—seemed futile at the time and it was rash to the point of madness, but that is how the man of destiny makes history.

Fidel Castro was rebelling against a system, a society, a corrupt and rotten state of affairs that spawned men like Fulgencio Batista. He was rebelling, too, against an economic structure run largely by foreigners, against income inequalities and high and growing unemployment. Deep inside of him and of all Cubans was a revolutionary tradition inherited from the decades of struggle against Spain, nourished in this century by continual United States military interventions.

There were reasons enough for a revolution whether Batista had come along or not. What was needed was the man to make the revolution.

Socially and economically, Cubans could be divided into "upper" and "lower" classes before the revolution. There was no "middle class" in the British or European sense; or else one must say that there was no upper class, only middle and lower classes. A true aristocratic upper class of Spanish descent existed, but it became small and unimportant as the decades of independence passed.

Families that were actually or relatively well-to-do represented the upper stratum of society. They were the big landowners, businessmen, high government officials, high military officers (colonels and generals), the top-ranking politicians, the successful lawyers, doctors, engineers and other professionals. These elements were overwhelmingly white—allowing for the Latin American attitude that a man or woman with a preponderance of white blood is white.

The attitude toward colored people—Negro and mulatto, who made up from a quarter to a third of the population—never approached the separatism or social ostracism that is found in the United States and to a great extent in Britain.

However, it was exceptional for Negroes and mulattos to achieve high positions in government, army, business and the professions. They were excluded from upper-class society. This occurred despite the fact that they played such an important and even heroic role in the wars of independence against Spain. There were many social and sports clubs, private schools and new residential areas from which Negroes were barred. They could, and did, go to the universities if their families could afford to send them there, but since the colored element consisted almost entirely of "hewers of wood and drawers of water," farm laborers and manual workers in industry, and hence were poor and unemployed for months in the year, their economic status acted to keep them down. All this has now changed.

The "rich" were the rulers, the bosses, the owners, the employers. They never worked with their hands. The wives had servants for the housework and nurses for their children. The office worker considered himself superior to the peasant, even though the latter might have owned a small farm and made more money. He also considered himself superior to the skilled industrial worker whose income also might well have been higher. In a practical sense this, too, has ceased to exist in revolutionary Cuba.

The "poor" in Cuba had its elements who lived decently and could give their children some schooling, but the great majority in the rural areas—*guajiros* or *campesinos*—lived in misery at a bare subsistence level. Their houses were miserable huts with thatched roofs to which the original Indian word of *bohíos* was still aptly applied.

One of the best succinct descriptions of the prerevolutionary situation in Cuba—and still one of the best studies of the Revolution itself—was edited and partly written by the English economist, Dudley Seers, then a visiting professor at Yale University. His analysis, and that of his associates, especially Richard Jolly who did a valuable paper on Cuban education, was published in book form by the University of North Carolina Press in 1964 under the title *Cuba: The Economic and Social Revolution*. The following passages from Professor Seers's paper are quoted from pages 13 to 19:

> Slowing down of economic growth to a virtual standstill [in 1958] was matched by a similar halt in progress in social fields. Illiteracy, after falling to relatively low levels in the first quarter of the century, failed to decline further. In fact, the proportion of children of school age attending primary school in the 1950's was lower than in the 1920's.
>
> Cuba in the 35 years from 1923 to 1958 showed little progress. The stagnation was more serious and lasted longer than in any other Latin American economy—excepting perhaps the economies of one or two very small and poor nations such as Bolivia and Haiti. . . .

If further progress was almost impossible to achieve, the status quo in 1958 was intolerable, especially for a country so close to Florida and receiving through many channels an imposing (perhaps exaggerated) picture of North American levels of living. Income per capita per year averaged about $500 or one-fifth as much as the average in the United States (far lower even than in any Southern state there). Yet by international standards this was not so bad. Only Venezuela and Argentina, of the larger Latin American countries, had a higher average income. What was intolerable was, first, a level of unemployment some three times as high as in the United States. In few families were all the male adults steadily employed. . . .

Second, in the countryside social conditions were very bad. About a third of the nation existed in squalor, eating rice, beans, bananas, and root vegetables (with hardly any meat, fish, eggs, or milk), living in huts, usually without electricity or toilet facilities, suffering from parasitic diseases and lacking access to health services, denied education (their children received only a first-grade education, if that). Particularly distressing was the lot of the *precaristas,* those squatting in makeshift quarters on public land.

A substantial fraction of the town population was also very poor. Here, too, there were squatters living in shacks, and of course there were slum tenements. In 1953 no less than one-fifth of families lived in single rooms, and the average size of these families was 5, according to the census. Taking the urban and the rural population together, 62 percent of the economically active population had incomes of less than $75 a month. . . .

The existing state of affairs—in which people were short of food and work but land lay idle and factories were not built—could not continue.

For those who knew Cuba in prerevolutionary years this was a true picture, and Seers is not by any means the only authority to make these points. During and after the especially difficult and floundering early years of the revolution, the United States State Department and critical scholars like Theodore Draper, Boris Goldenberg and Andrés Suárez, were to draw relatively rosy pictures of the prerevolutionary economic and social conditions, basing them on the same statistics that Dudley Seers used, but interpreting them in a more favorable light.

However, man does not live by statistics alone. There was no use telling millions of *guajiros* and city slum dwellers that Cuba's per capita income was the third highest in Latin America. Their misery was no less. They had the best-developed transportation system in Latin America, for instance, but they could not afford to use it and anyway it was inadequate.

To be sure, they—the masses—did not make the Cuban Revolution. The leadership and the effective forces came out of what is aptly called "the middle sectors."

In a valuable study, *Twentieth Century Cuba,* published in 1962 and written by Wyatt MacGaffey and others, it is pointed out (page 38) that:

> In every historical period since the late eighteenth century, there has been a middle sector definable in political terms, consisting of a sharply divided aggregate of self-seeking factions, drawn from a wide range of occupations and income groups, including notably the better educated and more prosperous elements of the lower class and the younger generation of the upper class.

It was out of this "middle sector" that Fidel Castro and most of his associates in rebellion came. For those who feel the need of historic "causes" General Fulgencio Batista and his 1952–58 dictatorship are convenient pegs upon which to hang the revolution. As has been seen, the true causes are complex, widespread and deeply rooted in Cuban history.

In 1944, having finished an elected term of office, General Batista retired to the luxurious Florida estate he had bought with his ill-gotten gains. The two succeeding Presidents—Ramón Grau San Martín and Carlos Prío Socarrás—belonged to the Cuban Revolutionary Party (PRC), better known as the Auténtico. It had come into power riding a wave of enthusiastic public hopefulness, and there were a number of important economic, social and institutional reforms. Moreover, the Auténtico governments were relatively democratic.

However, the promised agrarian reform was not made and—the most bitter disappointment of all—graft and corruption actually increased in those eight years. Mainly in reaction to the utter rottenness of the political structure, a dissident group of Auténticos, led by a dynamic reformer named Eduardo Chibás, formed the Party of the Cuban People in 1946. It was better known as the Ortodoxo party, and by 1951 it had become a powerful political force.

In that year, "Eddy" Chibás made the despairing gesture of committing suicide at the end of a radio tirade. The party held together, and it was as an Ortodoxo candidate that Fidel Castro ran for Congress in the 1952 elections. He told me once that he had felt certain of more than enough votes to be elected on June 1, 1952.

On March 10, Batista struck. In a well-organized palace revolt, he seized the main garrison of Havana; President Prío gave up tamely; other garrisons got into line; Washington was mildly upset; a benumbed majority accepted its fate—and a tiny minority of young men decided that something violent had to be done. The young and completely unknown lawyer, Fidel Castro, after making a gesture through the courts which he knew would be ignored, set about organizing the quixotic attack on the Moncada Barracks in Santiago de Cuba.

# 3  FROM MONCADA TO THE SIERRA

THE ATTACK led by Fidel Castro on the Moncada Barracks in Santiago de Cuba on July 26, 1953, has a similar significance for the Cuban Revolution as the fall of the Bastille eventually had for the French Revolution. In both cases, their significance was symbolic, not practical, and they were made important by the events that came after.

"Because you see Moncada as we all see it—as the commencement of the struggle," Celia Sánchez is quoted as saying to Haydée Santamaría in Carlos Franqui's work, *Book of the Twelve* (page 68 of the French edition). "Moncada—it was the mother of the revolution."

"It was at Moncada that we were forged," Haydée adds, "where we got used to the sight of blood, to men suffering, to the struggle."

Faustino Pérez, a young medical doctor who has gone through all stages of the revolution, also had a good phrase: "The combatants of Moncada did not achieve their military objectives," he said in 1966, "but they did achieve their revolutionary objectives."

Violence was endemic in the 1940s and 1950s in Cuba. It was

certainly as bad under the "liberal" governments of Grau San Martín (1944–48) and Prío Socarrás (1948–52) as it was under the Batista dictatorship from 1952 to 1959. Fidel Castro's period at the University of Havana, it will be remembered, was spent amidst murderous violence. Cuban politics, at every level from Federal government to local, was aflame with gangsterism.

In such an atmosphere, the use of violence would have seemed normal and natural. I remember thinking, on visits to Cuba in the 1950s, that of all the countries around the world in which I had worked during my career, there was none where life was so cheap as it was in Cuba.

Cubans have a Spanish preoccupation with death. "To die is nothing," wrote José Martí; "to die is to live; to die is to plant. He who dies, if he dies where he should die, lives."

The first stanza of the Cuban national anthem, *La Bayamesa,* written by Pedro Figueredo on the saddle of his horse before the "Liberating Army" took Bayamo from the Spaniards in 1868, says: "To die for the fatherland is to live."

Conte Agüero in his *Fidel Castro: Vida y Obra* (page 263) quotes Castro as having written on the margin of a page of the *Poesías Completas* of Martí: "I prefer to die riddled with bullets than to live humiliated."

The now familiar slogan of the Cuban Revolution is *Patria o Muerte!* (Fatherland or Death!), to which was added the more positive sentiment: *Venceremos* (We Shall Conquer).

Such slogans have a great appeal to Cubans—and they are not rhetoric. Cubans are willing to die. So when the time came that Fidel and the companions grouped around him decided that the only answer to the Batista dictatorship was revolt, they took to violence and faced death in typical Cuban fashion.

Fidel became the leader of the group through meeting Abel Santamaría, an employee in a sugar refinery, and Jesús Montané, an accountant for the Cuban branch of General Motors. The two young men had published a subversive pamphlet, and in Fidel Castro they found not only a kindred soul but a leader. Moncada was, in fact, to serve as a symbol of Fidel's heroic, revolutionary leadership.

It took more than a year to organize what at the time—and even in retrospect—looked like a mad, hopeless, suicidal adventure. Secret meetings, surreptitious arms purchases, a little training, an elaborate plan of attack—much too elaborate, as Fidel conceded later—these went on around the island. One hundred and sixty-five men were gathered for the attack, and two women: Haydée Santamaría (Abel's sister), and Melba Hernández, who was to become, and is now, the wife of Jesús Montané. None of them was as much as thirty years old; most were university graduates. They gave everything they owned or could scrape up to buy the arms and automobiles needed; and, of course, all gave up what jobs they had. Half of them were to die, and die after bestial torture, while many others went to prison.

It was madness, but there was idealism, self-sacrifice, heroism, patriotism of the purest sort. And no Communism! There was an epic quality about Moncada, as there was to be about the Sierra Maestra, and when all passions are spent, future generations of Cubans will recognize this fact and feel some pride, however bitterly some of them may condemn the revolution that followed.

Amidst the feverish preparations for the attack, Fidel took time off to prepare a "Manifesto of the Revolutionaries of Moncada to the Nation." It was dated July 23, 1953, and was not destined to have any effect, since the attack failed. However, three of the numbered paragraphs foreshadow the ideas to be expressed in "History Will Absolve Me." The text of the manifesto is printed in Luis Conte Agüero's *Vida y Obra* (pages 68–71):

2) The Revolution declares itself to be free of any links to foreign nations and also free of the influence and appetites of politicians and particular personages. The men who have organized it and represent it dedicate themselves to the sacred will of the people in conquering the future that they deserve. The revolution is the decisive struggle of the people against those who have betrayed them. . . .

6) The Revolution declares its respect for the workers and students and, as true elements defending the legitimate rights of the people throughout all its history, assures them and all the people of the introduction of a complete and definitive social justice based on economic and industrial advancement under a timely and perfect plan, the fruit of laborious and meditated study. . . .

9) The Revolution declares its absolute and reverent respect for the Constitution given to the people in 1940, which will be restored as the Official Code.

The language was turgid, the ideas were vague and a bit childish; and the pledge about the 1940 Constitution—to be made often in the next six years—made no sense. The 1940 Constitution—one of the longest in the world—was a hodgepodge of good, bad and indifferent ideas, some contradictory, some impractical, some impossible. It was never put into effect, but because of its liberal provisions it was a symbol of democracy and freedom and hence a rallying cry for oppositionists and revolutionaries.

All the same, the Moncada manifesto hinted at the sort of revolution Fidel Castro always had in mind. It was in its embryonic state in 1953.

Men and arms gathered at a chicken farm near Siboney, on the outskirts of Santiago de Cuba. Twenty-seven men had been detached to attack the smaller garrison at Bayamo, on the main highway west of Santiago along the Cauto River.

The plan was to take the sentry post at the entrance to the complex of buildings in the center of the city that made up the Moncada Barracks and then occupy the Civil Hospital (Abel Santamaría's job) and the Palace of Justice (Raúl Castro's assignment). Fidel was leading the main attack on the troops. If there had been any hope of success, two mishaps doomed the attack.

A patrol came out of the guard building at the exact moment that Fidel's contingent arrived, and its resistance alerted the whole garrison. An even worse misfortune occurred when the second half of the attacking force—and the more heavily armed—lost its way in the unfamiliar streets of Santiago and could not arrive in time to help in the fight. The unequal struggle ended quickly. Fidel ordered his followers to retreat. Raúl Castro and his small group got away, but the nineteen men and two women in the hospital were caught.

The attack against the Bayamo garrison was also a failure. According to Robert Merle's meticulous investigation, three *Fidel-*

*istas* were killed in the attack (not eight, as had been believed); sixty-eight were executed after capture—and generally after torture; thirty-two ended up in prison; and fifty got away. All the leaders of the still-unnamed movement were killed or imprisoned. "The Movement had been decapitated," Merle wrote; but as Fidel said when Merle interviewed him about Moncada, "The second phase of the revolution had begun."

> After the attack on the Moncada barracks in 1953 [Theodore Draper writes in his book *Castroism* (page 26)], the Partido Socialista Popular (PSP), as the official Cuban Communist Party was called, issued a statement that said in part: "We repudiate the putschist methods, peculiar to bourgeois political factions, of the action in Santiago de Cuba and Bayamo, which was an adventuristic attempt to take both military headquarters. The heroism displayed by the participants in this action is false and sterile, as it is guided by mistaken bourgeois conceptions."

The surviving rebels scattered in every direction. Many escaped but many others were captured. The methodic and horrible process of torture and killing of the prisoners under Colonel del Río Chaviano's orders and, certainly, with General Batista's approval, went on for days. It is a black page in Cuban history. Santiagüeros were horrified, and called upon the Archbishop of Santiago, Monsignor Enrique Pérez Serantes, for help. He was a saintly person, Spanish-born, about seventy years old. He told me and my wife once that he knew the Castro family well and we had the impression that he liked them, especially Raúl.

I induced him to tell me the story of what he really did after the Moncada attack and what role he played, if any, in saving Fidel's life. This was in 1963 in his episcopal palace, where my wife and I went to pay a friendly visit. He was then eighty years old, almost immobile because of his badly crippled legs, but cheerful as ever. I made a note of what he said immediately afterward:

> After the attack, eighty or a hundred of the boys were killed by the soldiers and Santiago was very disturbed. A delegation of magistrates and other leading citizens came to see me and they asked me to go with them to see the commander of the garrison, Colonel del Río Chaviano. "We must do something," they said. I replied that I could not agree more, so we all went immediately to

see Río Chaviano. He listened; was polite. I said nothing, but afterwards I realized that nothing was going to be done.

So I got into my little auto and drove to his office. This time I spoke to him, as we Catholics say, dogmatically. "You must stop this killing," I said, "and you must issue a proclamation saying that no more of the youths are to be killed. I will do the same." Río Chaviano was taken aback but said, "All right, I will do it." I returned immediately to this office, sat down at my typewriter and put the message down on one small sheet of paper. Just as I finished, an officer came from Río's office and asked to see what I had written. I showed it to him and he said it was fine, and could he take it to his commander? I said go ahead. He did so, and the next day my message was printed in all the newspapers. This committed Río Chaviano, although he did not issue a statement himself.

After the letter had been circulated, I went out to the edge of the woods, where it was known that a number of students were hiding, and showed myself and called for them to come out. A number of them began to do so. When they got into the clear, a rural guard or some other soldier began shooting at them and they started to run back. I am not a hero or a bold man, but I could not contain myself and instinctively ran toward them, shouting and waving to the soldiers that the firing must stop. It did, and seeing me standing there in my white cassock, the youths came toward me and surrendered.

About that time a man came to my office and said that he lived in the *lomas* [the foothills] of the Sierra and knew that Fidel was staying in a certain house belonging to a relative of his. I drove out to the spot with the man and a magistrate. We stood in sight of the house and shouted, "Fidel! Fidel!"—but nothing happened. Perhaps Fidel was suspicious when he saw the group of us and I never saw him again until after 1959. He and two others stayed in the woods until they were captured by Lieutenant Sarría. However, since the orders were already out that the students of the Moncada attack were not to be killed, Fidel was not shot when captured as this would have been disobeying orders.

Monsignor Pérez Serantes never claimed that he had made any special plea for Fidel's life. He did not know that despite the general order not to kill any more students, there had been a special order to kill any rebels caught with arms. Fidel presumed that he would not be taken alive, and while he counseled the other rebels with him to surrender, he was determined to keep trying to escape.

What has every earmark of being the true story of his capture is related by Robert Merle in *Moncada* (pages 305-17). Merle interviewed not only Fidel himself but every one of the sixty-one survivors of the plot and the attacks in Santiago de Cuba and Bayamo. He also spoke at length with the Cuban officer who saved Castro's life.

Fidel and two companions were sleeping, exhausted, in the *bohío* of a friendly mulatto worker on the night of July 31–August 1. The authorities had got wind of the fact that some of the Fidelistas were in the neighborhood of a farm owned by a man named Sotelo. A patrol was sent out under the command of Negro lieutenant, Pedro Sarría. He was fifty-three years old—a humane man of moral principles and moral courage. He had previously saved two young rebels whom excited soldiers had wanted to kill in the Moncada "calaboose," and he obviously disapproved of the wanton torturing and killing of the prisoners by Río Chaviano's soldiers. Although he did not have specific instructions to kill Fidel if he captured him, there was the order that rebels caught with arms were to be liquidated.

Men of destiny, like successful generals, need luck. Fidel had it that morning before dawn when Sarría's patrol came upon his *bohío* and the soldiers rushed in to find the sleeping men. They would have been killed then but for Sarría's intervention, although the lieutenant had recognized Fidel. Later, in Santiago, Castro was spared from torture and death because the lieutenant insisted that the three men were to be put in the safety of the civil prison and not taken to Moncada Barracks, where Colonel del Río Chaviano wanted them.

Monsignor Pérez Serantes tried to help, but Fidel proudly insisted that he had been taken prisoner by Lieutenant Sarría. According to Merle, Castro "wanted to avoid what the government propaganda was claiming—that he had surrendered to the authorities through the mediation of the archbishop. Fidel's reaction was political. He was sure that he would be executed and he wanted to safeguard the prestige of the Movement for the future."

Nevertheless, the story was put out, and is generally believed even to this day, that Fidel was saved by Monsignor Pérez Serantes. The archbishop, as I have stated, did not claim to have done so, and Fidel, some years ago, told me that the generally accepted story was not true.

All the prisoners were at first tried in the courthouse of Santiago de Cuba. Fidel had been in solitary confinement in the provincial jail at Boniato along with some of his companions. Haydée Santamaría and Melba Hernández were also at Boniato. All of them had been transferred from the *vivac,* or civil prison, where the two women did not see Fidel when he was brought in after his capture.

Fidel insisted on acting as his own lawyer, which he had a right to do, when the trial began on September 21, 1953. Perhaps because of the fact that his sharp questioning and aggressive attitude were embarrassing to the authorities, Colonel del Río Chaviano concocted a story that Fidel was ill.

Although Castro smuggled out a paper through Melba Hernández denying that there was anything the matter with him, he was prevented from appearing at the trial.

Instead, he was given a special trial in the nurses' lounge at the Civil Hospital. To insure secrecy, the only persons admitted inside the lounge, aside from the three judges and a heavily armed guard, were six reporters and two attorneys. Since there was a nationwide censorship at the time, nothing could be published and no photographers were allowed in.

Out of this hopeless situation, Fidel Castro was in the course of time to get the most famous document and the most effective piece of propaganda of the Cuban Revolution. It is the defense speech that he is supposed to have made on October 16, 1953, known for its concluding sentence as "La Historia me absolverá" (History Will Absolve Me). One must use the word "supposed" because the now historic text is a reconstruction, expansion and rewriting of the address made by Fidel the following year while in prison on the Isle of Pines. But as the Italians would say, *Se non è vero è ben trovato*—which roughly means "Even if it isn't true it is well put."

One of the six reporters present was a young Cuban woman who took notes for the magazine *Bohemia*. Marta Rojas Rodríguez later used the notes—which were not published by *Bohemia*—for a book whose definitive edition was published in Havana in 1964: *La Generación del Centenario en el Moncada*. Although completely Fidelista, it is valuable for many descriptive passages and for her coverage of the trials of minor figures in the episode as well as Castro's trial.

She describes how Fidel was brought from Boniato Prison into the "little nurses' room" of the hospital. It was a stiflingly hot day and the room must have steamed. Fidel prepared for his big speech:

> The staff of the hospital and his escort guard began to occupy positions from which they could see and hear. At the beginning they did so out of mere curiosity; then his address began arousing so much interest that they kept changing places among themselves so that everybody could hear something. Thus began his historic affirmations, and as his speech went on, the impatience grew to hear more. He spoke in clear tones.

Marta Rojas then gives the complete text of "History Will Absolve Me," as printed in 1954, although she was in the best position to know that it had been expanded by Fidel in prison. However, she gives herself away a little by saying that they had been listening to Fidel for "more than two hours." Had they listened to every word of the printed text it would have been more like four or five hours.

She also reproduces a famous passage which has become one of the enduring myths of the Moncada episode. In it, a sergeant, accompanied by other soldiers of the garrison, appears before Haydée Santamaría and shows her a bleeding eye. The sergeant says, "This is your brother's eye; if you do not tell us what he refuses to say, we will tear out his other eye." Haydée is supposed to have answered, "If you tore out one eye and he would say nothing, much less would *I* tell you."

Fidel wrote the passage in prison, having heard the tale; only on his release did he learn that it was not true. However, the story has never been expunged from the text as it continues to circulate. Robert Merle, in *Moncada*, carefully omits any mention of such an incident. This being said, it should be added that Haydée and also Melba Hernández did act throughout with extraordinary courage and dignity. There is nothing mythical about that. It should also be added that the true and unvarnished stories of the tortures and wanton killing of the helpless prisoners were horrible enough.

The history of "History Will Absolve Me" was slow to come out and hard to confirm. The first account of how it was issued in pamphlet form appeared in the Havana Communist newspaper *Hoy*, on July 21, 1963. Melba Hernández, who with Haydée Santamaría did much work preparing the text, told me that she had given the information to *Hoy* and that the article was essentially accurate.

She and Haydée began working for the Movement (which did not yet have a name) after being released from the women's prison of Guanajay on February 20, 1954, where they had served six of their seven-month sentence. Lidia Castro, Fidel's sister, acted as a go-between since she could visit him as a relative. Fidel at first told them, as *Hoy* writes, that "he was preparing a work that would contain the program of the Movement. This work was a reconstruction of the defense speech made at the Moncada trial."

Actually, the first reference to "La Historia me absolverá," according to Melba, was in Letter IV of the *Cartas del Presidio*: a letter addressed to her. In it Fidel said: "Mirta [his wife] will speak to you of a pamphlet of decisive importance for its ideological content and its tremendous accusations and I would like you to give it your closest care (*al que quiero le prestes el mayor interés*)."

"Fidel," continues *Hoy*, "was reconstructing the address little by little—writing it with lime juice which makes an invisible ink. In that way the opening paragraphs of the historic document started coming out of the prison."

At first Fidel smuggled out sentences, in matchboxes. Then he hit upon the idea of writing banal letters of greetings to fore-warned friends, and to some who had not been warned, in which the lime-juice words were traced between the ink lines. Melba Hernández told me it was a great problem collecting the letters, but that the words came out clearly enough when Lidia used a hot iron on the sheets. According to Melba and her husband, Jesús Montané, who was in the prison, Fidel went on giving instructions about the contents and the format down to the minutest detail.

Fidel had asked for 100,000 copies, but there were time and money to do only 20,000, according to *Hoy*. These copies, Melba's story continues, were all piled into one old car, which was so loaded down that the springs almost touched the ground. Two brothers from the Movement, Gustavo and Machaco Almeyeiras, were given five pesos—all the money that could be raised. They started out from Havana, stopping in every town to leave copies for distribution and to eat, sleep and get gasoline where they could—until they ended up in Santiago de Cuba at the other end of the island and distributed the last copies.

Fidel's instinct was right. As he wrote in the letter to Melba, "Propaganda must not be abandoned for a minute, for it is the soul of every struggle." However, the timing could not have been propitious. The pamphlet hardly made a ripple and, in fact, disappeared from circulation until Castro shrewdly resurrected it for the fifth anniversary of the Moncada attack in 1958. That was a well-chosen moment, and the document immediately became famous and very effective—as propaganda. It is now a vital part of the "mythology" of the Cuban Revolution. At the same time, there is no reason to doubt that Fidel's speech at his trial was, generally speaking, along the lines of "History Will Absolve Me."

Because of the emphasis he placed on its propaganda value, one must suppose that he expanded the section explaining the reforms he planned to make. The pamphlet certainly was used as a programmatic guide for the revolution. Similar ideas had been put forward by Cuban leftists and oppositionists from the time of the fall of Machado. This time they were to be put into effect.

There was a romantic revolutionary fervor in the words and ideas which was to give the pamphlet a great spiritual and political value. As with so much else about Fidel Castro and the Cuban Revolution, a cold, literal analysis would be misleading. Feelings and emotions are better guides to the importance of "La Historia me absolverá" than the words.

It is customary for sympathizers and supporters of Fidel Castro to claim that "La Historia me absolverá" contains the gist of his future revolutionary program.

"These pages pulsate with the essence of the revolutionary leader's thinking," Luís Conte Agüero wrote in an introduction he did for the English translation published during Castro's trip to the United States in April 1959. "They proclaim all the reform programs that he was to put into effect later, when he accepted office: agrarian reform, fifty-percent reduction of all rents, industrial development, elimination of unemployment, modernization of the educational system, conversion of the military headquarters, Camp Columbia, into a scholastic institution."

Conte Agüero could have added public housing, public health, nationalization of gas, electricity and telephones, and an end to the embezzlement of government funds. In one form or another, all these reforms were to be carried out by the revolutionary Government.

However, Castro also promised a number of other reforms in his speech that were never fulfilled—precisely the democratic and liberal promises which led his opponents to say that he "betrayed the revolution." Restoration of the Constitution of 1940, elections, free press, free speech, an independent judiciary—these and similar pledges went into oblivion. He who was to make Cuba the most powerfully armed nation in Latin America talked in his speech of no longer buying arms.

Taking it all in all, what may have sounded like rhetoric on October 16, 1953, now reads like judgment and prophecy.

"The future of the nation, and the solution of its problems," a typical passage says, "cannot continue to depend on the egoistic interests of a dozen financiers, nor on the cold calculation of profits drawn up in air-conditioned offices by ten or twelve magnates."

Fidel insisted in his speech (and insists to this day) that the plan of attack on Moncada was a good one and had excellent chances of success:

The Señor Prosecutor was very interested in knowing our possibilities of success. These possibilities were based on reasons of a technical, military and social order. An attempt has been made to propagate the myth that modern arms supposedly make impossible an open frontal attack by the people against tyranny. . . . No weapon, no force, is capable of overcoming a people that decides to fight for its rights.

This is what Fidel Castro was to prove—with help from the people—in 1957 and 1958.

There were other prophetic touches.

"Our plans," he said, "were to continue the struggle in the mountains in case the attack on the regiment failed." This shows that he had the idea of guerrilla warfare even then, and he naturally turned to it when the *Granma* invasion failed.

Here is another passage that pointed to the future:

As soon as Santiago de Cuba was in our hands, we would immediately have put the people of Oriente Province on a war footing. Bayamo was attacked precisely in order to place our advance forces along the Cauto River. It can never be forgotten that this province, which today contains 1,500,000 inhabitants, is without doubt the most warlike and patriotic in Cuba. It was this province that kept the struggle for independence burning during thirty years and that gave the greatest tribute of blood, sacrifice and heroism. In Oriente, you can still breathe the air of that glorious epic.

And so it was to Oriente again that he went in the *Granma* in December 1956.

In the concluding passage of his Moncada defense Fidel developed the idea of the right to rebel against tyranny. This right is contained in the Constitution of 1940 and was cited by Judge Manuel Urrutia during the trial in 1957 of some of the *Granma* prisoners. Urrutia's refusal to vote to condemn the youths led to the end of his career as a judge, but it laid the groundwork for his being chosen by Fidel Castro in 1958 as the future President of Cuba.

I have reached the end of my defense [Fidel says in the text as printed], but I will not do what all lawyers do, asking freedom for the accused. I cannot ask that, when my companions are already suffering in the ignominious prison of the Isle of Pines. Send me to join them and to share their fate. It is understandable that men of honor should be dead or prisoners in a Republic whose President is a criminal and a thief. . . .

As for me, I know that imprisonment will be harder for me than it ever has been for anybody, filled with threats, ruin and cowardly deeds of rage, but I do not fear it, as I do not fear the fury of the wretched tyrant who snuffed out the lives of seventy brothers of mine. CONDEMN ME. IT DOES NOT MATTER. HISTORY WILL ABSOLVE ME.*

That Fidel should have published such a revolutionary and abusive pamphlet while still in jail and open to further punishment shows his courage and, possibly, Batista's contempt, or perhaps ignorance of the existence of the pamphlet. It also shows Castro's shrewd sense of publicity, although in this case it was premature, partly through an exaggerated sense of his, and his Movement's, importance in that period. The reissue of the pamphlet in the summer of 1958 was a stroke of genius. It helped to establish the leadership of Fidel Castro and the 26th of July Movement in the rebellion.

One cannot make sense out of the Cuban Revolution without keeping in mind at all times the personal supremacy—at first potential and then real—of Fidel Castro. This predominance can be seen in its embryonic stage in the fervent response of the young men and women who surrounded him, or who were drawn toward him by his magnetic personality.

When it comes to a mass following, the adoration is almost impersonal—somewhat like the emotional response to the flag of one's country. What is most impressive in studying Fidel Castro is that those who have known him intimately since 1952 or 1953 and who followed him through Moncada, the *Granma* expedition, the Sierra Maestra and the difficult early years of the revolution when he led them—among other things—into Communism should have stuck to him so loyally. Not one of the survivors of the Moncada

* The last words are printed in capitals in the various Spanish editions. I have used the second edition, printed on the fifth anniversary of the July 26, 1953, attack. There are no variations in any of the Spanish texts.

Barracks attack and the *Granma* expedition—so far as is known—
has defected.

In the September 9, 1966, edition of the Havana magazine
*Bohemia* there is an interview by Lisandro Otero with Haydée
Santamaría and Melba Hernández, the two heroines of the Mon-
cada attack. The interview had originally appeared in *Juventud
Rebelde*. The young women described a desperate moment in the
military hospital where they had gone and where Haydée's brother
Abel was to be tortured and killed. Her fiancé also lost his life in
the Moncada adventure.

Here are some excerpts from the recorded conversation:

MELBA HERNÁNDEZ: The life of Fidel was the preoccupation of all of
us. . . .

HAYDÉE SANTAMARÍA: Then I said to him [Abel], "But this cannot be,
they can't kill you, Abel. You don't know if Fidel is alive." Then he
stood still, rigid, and said, "Yes! Fidel must be alive. Where is he?"

LISANDRO OTERO: At that moment you didn't know what had happened
to the other comrades? You were completely out of touch?

MELBA HERNÁNDEZ: Yes, we knew about Abel, because we lived
through that, but we did not know the fate of Fidel, because the obsession of all of us was to know the fate of Fidel. . . .

[Fidel Castro was at first taken to the same jail in Santiago, but the
girls did not see him until they were all put in the prison at Boniato.]

HAYDÉE SANTAMARÍA: First I saw his feet. Those are the feet of Fidel.
Then something happened. It was when I saw the face of Fidel that
I broke down, because I thought, "Can it be true? Is it a lie?" That
was when I really broke down, I broke down, I broke down, and for
a whole night. . . .

MELBA HERNÁNDEZ: I didn't think Haydée would live through that
night.

HAYDÉE SANTAMARÍA: But it was when I saw Fidel. Until I had seen
Fidel I had little feeling—a little but not entirely. I didn't feel or
suffer much of anything."

[They have a meeting with Fidel and he asks Haydée about her
brother Abel.]

HAYDÉE SANTAMARÍA: I said to him, "Abel is dead," but I said it very
naturally, as if Abel were there. "Ah, yes." Fidel bowed his head and
stood stock-still. But I said to him, "Never mind, Fidel, you are
alive!"

At another point Haydée says, "In the hospital Abel said, 'Yes. They are going to kill us here, but Fidel must not be allowed to die.' He groaned. 'Why didn't I go with Fidel? Will they know, those who are with him, that Fidel must not die?' Abel knew that he was going to be killed, but his obsession was that nothing should happen to Fidel."

In his chapter on Celia Sánchez and Haydée Santamaría in *El Libro de los Doce* (Book of the Twelve), Carlos Franqui quotes Haydée as using much the same language and exactly the same sentiments. After telling about the tragic scenes in the hospital and of later seeing Fidel, Haydée says (page 58, French edition):

> Those are the facts that remain in my memory. I don't recall anything else precisely, but from that moment on I thought of nobody but Fidel. All of us thought only of Fidel; of Fidel who could not be allowed to die; of Fidel who had to remain alive to make the revolution; of Fidel's life, which was the lives of all of us. So long as Fidel was alive, Abel, Boris [her fiancé], Renato [Guitart] and the others were not dead. They would live in the person of Fidel who would make the Cuban Revolution and who would lead the Cuban people toward their destiny.

Fidel spent three and a half months in Boniato Prison outside of Santiago de Cuba awaiting his trial. Lieutenant Jesús Yanés Pelletier, military supervisor of the jail, later said that one of Río Chaviano's aides ordered him to poison Castro's food and that he refused. He was rewarded with a position of minor importance in 1959, but he was to be a premature case of the *dolce vita* disease that attacked a number of the young rebels and he was quietly pushed into the background.

After Boniato, Fidel was sent to the prison on the Isle of Pines (where, incidentally, he himself was to send thousands of political prisoners in time). It was an outwardly uneventful sojourn, although, with hindsight, one can see that it was an important period of gestation for the revolution to come. The letters that Conte Agüero published early in 1959 (*Cartas del Presidio*), some other letters that Robert Merle used as an appendix to his book *Moncada* (I believe they were written to Naty Revuelta) and—most important of all—the pamphlet "La Historia me absolverá" show

how his mind was continually working on what he was going to do when he got out of jail.

For example, in a letter dated January 1, 1954, quoted by Merle (page 342— I must translate from the already translated French text), Fidel wrote:

> Everything that could be done in the field of technique and the organization of the schools would be of no use if one did not overturn the economic status of the nation from top to bottom— that is to say, the status of the mass of the people, for it is there that one finds the root of the tragedy.
>
> What a formidable school prison is! [he writes in another letter]. Here I have succeeded in forging my vision of the world and finding the direction my life will take. Will it be long or short? I do not know. Fruitful or sterile? But there is one thing that I feel to be taking form within myself: my passionate desire for sacrifice and struggle. I have nothing but scorn for an existence attached to the wretched bagatelles of comfort and self-interest.
>
> Above everything [he writes in August 1954 when he was in solitary confinement] I see our road and our goal more clearly than ever. Another time, perhaps, I will tell you other aspects of my thoughts. For today, it will suffice that you know that I have not wasted my time in prison. I have studied, observed, analyzed, made plans, forged a following of men. I know where to find the best of Cuba, and how to seek it out. When I began, I was alone; now we are many. The good men will unite and will be invincible.
>
> I never stop thinking of things [he writes in the last of the letters that Robert Merle publishes, which is dated April 15, 1954], for sincerely, what joy I would have in revolutionizing this country from top to bottom! I am convinced that every inhabitant can be made happy. I would be prepared to bring down upon myself the hatred and ill-will of one or two thousand men, among them some relations, half of my friends, two-thirds of my colleagues, and four-fifths of my old college classmates. . . . Have you noticed the number of invisible links that a man must break who is determined to live in accord with his ideas?

He had his moments of discouragement, of course. For someone of his temperament, imprisonment—and especially solitary imprisonment—must have been a torment.

I live because I believe I have tasks to accomplish [he writes to Luis Conte Agüero on July 31, 1954, in Letter IX of *Cartas del Presidio*]. In many of the terrible moments that I have had to suffer during the past year I have thought how much better it would be to be dead.

In a letter (Number XII) to his sister Lidia three months later he says:

It isn't always easy for someone who is out in the street to understand the feelings of a prisoner; the weeks are long and only a pleasant book makes them shorter for us.

He read voraciously while he was on the Isle of Pines. In fact, he always was an omnivorous reader, which is surprising for a man of action. In prison, his tastes were eclectic. The citations in "History Will Absolve Me" indicate the variety of books he was devouring—on ancient China, India, Greece and Rome, John of Salisbury, St. Thomas Aquinas, Martin Luther, François Kotman, John Knox, John Milton, John Locke, Jean Jacques Rousseau, Thomas Paine, and so on. He does not mention Lenin, but he read a bit of Lenin and Marx—not much, according to his brother Raúl.

It is not being suggested here that Fidel Castro is a scholar—far from it. He was a dilettante until, in recent years, he became a diligent reader of books on agriculture, in which he is now an expert.

It is not claimed, either, that his letters from the Presidio of the Isle of Pines were entirely prophetic. For instance, he had the impossible idea that he could submerge himself or stay in the background of the revolutionary events he planned.

I have repeatedly told you [he writes to Conte Agüero (page 60)] that I do not harbor the slightest personal ambition, nor do my comrades, and that our only aim is to serve Cuba and to make worthwhile the sacrifice of our dead companions.

Curiously, he had this same idea when he came down from the Sierra Maestra in triumph and entered Havana. He did not take the premiership at first. I remember a conversation my wife and I had with him at the time in which he insisted that he would be content temporarily heading the armed forces and that then he would like to retire to the Sierra Maestra to develop it and to teach. This made no sense, but I do not believe these statements of his were motivated by guile. Perhaps his intelligence was telling him that *caudillismo* and dictatorship ought to be avoided, although events and his own dominating character were to nullify this possibility.

At least, in the letter to Conte Agüero (Number XI), which is an important document, he does forecast what is to be one of the key features of his administration—a strong emphasis on the need for unity. He compares his ideas to José Martí's efforts to unify all Cubans: "The pages of the history of Cuba that I most admire are not so much the valorous deeds on the fields of battle as that gigantic, heroic and silent struggle to unify Cubans for the conflict." This obsession about unity was an important factor in Fidel's insistence, in 1959 and 1960, on including the Cuban Communists in every development of the revolution.

That same letter speaks of the necessity of "organizing the men of the July 26th and uniting in an unbreakable sheaf all the combatants—those in exile, in prison and in the street."

When Fidel and his fellow prisoners were released from the Isle of Pines on May 15, 1955, there was much enthusiasm among relatives and friends, and some public interest. However, Fidelista historians exaggerate his popularity and importance at that time. He was still a minor figure—an agitator who was not well known to the people of Cuba as a whole and who appeared to the Batista Government to be simply a nuisance.

True, he was the most famous of the prisoners, since he had led the attack on the Moncada Barracks twenty-two months before. But President Batista would not have granted Castro and his group an amnesty if he had thought they were dangerous revolutionaries.

The inception of the 26th of July Movement and its name—according to Haydée Santamaría and Melba Hernández, who have the best reasons to know—occurred on the ferryboat *Pinero* between the Isle of Pines and the main island when Fidel and his comrades were released from prison. Many of his companions from the Moncada days had gathered to greet the amnestied prisoners.

In the interview with Lisandro Otero for *Bohemia,* part of which has already been quoted, Otero asked when the Movement was conceived and Haydée answered that it was on the boat. There had been some discussion about whether to call it the "Moncada" Movement or the "26th of July." The vote was for the latter.

On that channel passage Fidel had insisted, according to Haydée, that "we must first exhaust every political means so that it is seen that we do not desire a war." However, even then he had no hope of a peaceful solution and talked of demonstrating to the people in this manner "that there was no other way out than an armed struggle."

It was characteristic of him—and of Cuban traditions—that one of the first things he did was to issue still another manifesto. It seems to have gone unnoticed (the quotation is from *Vida y Obra,* page 233):

> Our freedom will not be a fiesta or a rest, but a struggle and a duty, fighting ardently from the first day without respite for a country free of despotism and misery, whose better destiny nothing and nobody will be able to change.

The 26th of July Movement did not take official and public form until Fidel, in Mexico preparing for the *Granma* expedition, wrote and published a letter dated March 19, 1956, breaking his links with the Ortodoxo party. (It is published in Gregorio Selser's book, *La Revolución Cubana,* pages 102–18.)

The Ortodoxos, it will be recalled, were followers of "Eddy" Chibás, whose vain effort to arouse the Cuban people against the prevailing corruption ended in suicide. Fidel for years presented his ideas and aims as a form of *Chibasismo.* In August 1955, he defined the 26th of July Movement as "the revolutionary apparatus of *Chibasismo,*" and even in his letter separating the Movement from the Ortodoxo party (whose leaders he bitterly criticizes for their collaboration with the Batista regime) he claims that his group is the true expression of Chibás's ideals.

However, he now announces that "the 26th of July Movement is the revolutionary organization of the humble, by the humble and for the humble." He calls upon all Cuban revolutionaries to join this "struggle of the people."

As with all the early Fidelista pronouncements, there are no programs, simply the vague—but firm—intention to bring about a social revolution on behalf of the Cuban people—or, in the word he used here, for the *humildes*. Later—in the Sierra Maestra— more detailed programs were to come out, but as the revolution unfolded, Fidel did what he thought was best, or thought he had to do at a given time, regardless of promises and programs. Certainly he was more idealistic before he assumed power than after, but this is true of every candidate for power or for elected office, whether the system is democratic, authoritarian or revolutionary.

As Andrés Suárez correctly states in his book *Cuba* (page 32):

> Each time Castro was asked to produce a statement of doctrine he replied . . . that it would emerge from the depth of the events, since tying oneself down to inflexible theories in advance would restrict one within excessively dogmatic limits and would obstruct the necessary dynamism of the revolution.

In Havana, in 1955, Fidel became a nonviolent agitator against the Batista Government, but he could get nowhere. His attacks on the regime in the Havana journal, *La Calle,* and his radical ideas led to the newspaper's being closed down and to his being banned from talking on the radio or at public meetings. Anyone referring to him or quoting what he said would have a program or a meeting suspended. It became impossible for him to work as he wanted to work.

While Castro's ideas were revolutionary, he had come out of prison hoping that he could achieve them through peaceful, civic channels. He could not do so.

It was in that period that he decided on a renewal of violence in the form of an "invasion" or expedition from Mexico. Raúl Castro and a few others went ahead to prepare the way. Fidel left Havana on July 7, 1955. Just before that time he wrote for the magazine *Bohemia* (*Vida y Obra,* page 265):

We will return when we can bring to our people the liberty and the right to live decently without despotism and without hunger. . . . Since all doors to a civic struggle are closed to the people, no other solution remains but that of '68 and '95.

In Mexico—as before in Cuba, and as was to be the case often during the two years in the Sierra Maestra—there is a plethora of articles, speeches, letters and two formal documents called "Manifestos of the July 26th Movement." Scholars may have to wade through them at the expense of much confusion and weariness, but those looking for systematic ideas or for an ideology waste their time. Fidel was years away from Communism or Marxism-Leninism in Mexico and the Sierra Maestra. A generalized embryonic form of socialism can be extracted from the documentation—but that is true of all modern revolutions, even the Fascist or National Socialist (Nazi) types.

The premature charges of Communism against Castro began in Mexico. In an article he wrote for *Bohemia* (July 9, 1956) entitled "Basta de Mentiras" (Enough of Lies), he angrily denounced the Cuban Embassy in Mexico for giving out information, which the newspapers published, that "Seven Cuban Communists were arrested for conspiring against Batista." He called this charge absurd and stated that everybody in Cuba knew that he had no connections with the Communist party. He also offered as proof a report from the Mexican Federal Security Police "stating emphatically that the 26th of July group has no links with the Communists and is receiving no help from the Communists." It is an ironic feature of Fidel Castro's career that until he decided to carry his revolution into the Communist camp—which was not before the middle of 1960—he was sincerely indignant when the accusation of Communism was leveled against him.

As has been stated before, the vital factor to keep in mind was Castro's determination to make a radical social revolution. He proclaimed that fact on many occasions before 1959—and then astounded and horrified innumerable Cubans and foreigners by doing it. One can quarrel with the way he did it, but there was an unswerving consistency in the goals that he always had in mind.

Reading, for instance, an article headed "El Movimiento 26 de Julio," which appeared on February 3, 1957 in an ephemeral Cuban emigré publication in New York called *Patria*, one comes across this typical Fidelista passage. (It is typical, incidentally, in the length of the sentence and its involutions.)

> To be a noncomformist who would not resign himself to the political fatalism with which we have lived until now, to desire a better destiny for my country, a more worthy public life, a higher collective morality, to believe that a nation does not exist for the exclusive enjoyment and privilege of a few but that it belongs to all, and that each and every one of its six million inhabitants and the millions who will people it in the future have the right to a decent life and to justice, jobs and well-being, to struggle for this ideal without shrinking from any risk or sacrifice, without hesitating to devote the best years of one's youth and life, which hundreds of men of our generation are doing with incomparable disinterestedness, it little matters that people should try to present us before public opinion as social reprobates or capricious upholders of a conduct that is the most honest, loyal and patriotic of our times.

Boiling this rhetoric down, Fidel was simply saying that he wanted to make a revolution for the benefit of all Cubans and to put an end to the privileges of an exclusive few.

His second idea of how to overthrow the Batista Government was even more elaborate than and almost as completely disastrous as the Moncada attack. He would invade Cuba with his faithful fighting companions while at the same time other members of the 26th of July Movement on the island—and especially in Santiago de Cuba—would rise. A general strike would be called. They would then start a rebellion on the order of the uprising of 1895.

This was in the Cuban tradition—so much so that counter-revolutionaries kept trying the same method, until the resounding fiasco of the Bay of Pigs in 1961 discouraged the American Government and most Cuban refugees.

Fidel and his companions had no wealthy and powerful American Government to provide arms, training and millions of dollars,

nor did they have friendly Central American countries like Guatemala and Nicaragua to furnish bases for training and takeoff, as
was the case with the Cuban refugees. Least of all (perhaps in this
case one should say fortunately) did they have the immense and
eager Central Intelligence Agency to supervise the invading force,
make plans, pick leaders and give advice.

On the contrary, Castro and his group worked in a hostile
country—Mexico—whose police and Foreign Ministry kept seizing the few arms that they could collect, and whenever possible
throwing the plotters into jail. In a long interview published in the
Mexican magazine *Sucesos* on September 10, 1966, and reprinted
in the Havana *Bohemia* six weeks later, Fidel credited the ex-
President of Mexico, Lázaro Cárdenas, with interceding to prevent
him and his followers from being expelled.

In all, he and his group were in Mexico for about a year and a
half. It was a lean time for Fidel. In a letter to Melba Hernández,
written on July 24, 1955, he says that in order to pay for the
printing of the first "Manifesto of the 26th of July Movement" he
pawned his coat. When he decided to go to the United States to
raise funds for the Movement in October 1955, he was so short of
money that someone had to lend him the price of his rail fare from
Mexico. He would accept only enough for one way. In all, he
stayed seven weeks, visiting New York, Philadelphia and Miami,
holding meetings, making speeches and raising some thousands of
dollars that he would not touch himself; for another year he went
on living from hand to mouth.

Money was being collected also in Cuba by members of the
Movement who raised $8,000 by February 1956. For the sanguine
Fidel Castro this was enough to conquer a world of Cubas—but,
of course, it wasn't. However, from that month onward the preparations for the invasion got seriously underway—purchase of a
farm (Rancho La Rosa) outside of Mexico City, the buying of
arms (some were smuggled in from Cuba), and training of the
expeditionaries under the expert direction of a former Spanish
officer, Colonel Alberto Bayo, who had learned his trade at first
under General Franco in Spanish Morocco and then with the
Loyalists in the Spanish Civil War.

Unfortunately, as stated before, the Mexican police stepped in and broke up the entire plot, seizing the arms. A new start had to be made, this time in the greatest secrecy. Final encampments and training places were set up in Tamaulipas, Jalapa and Veracruz.

Faustino Pérez wrote in his article for *Cuba Socialista,* "Ten Years After the *Granma,"* which I have mentioned:

> The time was short, and an intensive program of training was prepared. The conditions were purposely made hard so that no one would be unprepared for what he was going to face in Cuba— shooting practice, marches, maneuvers, river crossings, mountain climbing, long marches in silence, living in the open, rudimentary food, and, along with all that, the spiny cactuses and the rattlesnakes constantly waiting in ambush.

One of the men taking the training and preparing to accompany the Cubans was a young Argentine doctor, Ernesto Guevara Lynch, who was always called by his Argentine nickname of "Che." He and his name—now so famous—were, for the rest of his short life and even in death, to be intimately linked by bonds of friendship and unfailing loyalty to Fidel Castro, the Cuban Revolution, and the ambitious Castroite plans to revolutionize all of Latin America through guerrilla warfare.

Che Guevara came of an upper-class Argentine family; he had a good education; he could have lived a quiet and prosperous life— but, like Fidel Castro, Che was a born revolutionary. He had within him that flame of rebelliousness which is sweeping over our contemporary world and so deeply affecting the youth, the colored races, the unprivileged masses and all those whom the powerful emotion of nationalism is driving toward the mirage of independence from the great powers.

A spate of books about Guevara has already appeared, inspired by his dramatic end in Bolivia. He became associated with Fidel Castro in Mexico after traveling a long route of anti-Perónism in Argentina and lone, searching, restless journeys up the length of South America and, at one stage, into Guatemala.

There he tried to help the embattled Arbenz Government in a very modest way. Highly exaggerated stories were written about this episode later, but in reality Che had simply put his medical experience and revolutionary sympathies at the disposal of the Arbenz regime—mainly because of his not uncommon anti-Yankeeism. He did not even meet Arbenz until the deposed President of Guatemala showed up in Cuba in 1959.

Che Guevara was not a Communist in Guatemala, nor later in Mexico, where he took refuge after the overthrow of the Arbenz regime. In fact, he never joined any Communist party until the entire Cuban leadership followed Castro into his Marxist-Leninist stage. The American CIA tried its best, of course, to find evidence of Che's Communism and had there been any proofs they would have been published eagerly in the bitter years of 1959 and 1960. But there was no evidence to be found.

It will be necessary to come back often to Che Guevara in this book, because of his importance to Fidel Castro and the Cuban Revolution.

I knew him fairly well. He once wrote of me as *amigo de siempre a pesar de diferencias ideológicas* (always a friend despite ideological differences). Our conversations, usually held after midnight for he worked nights and slept days, were largely arguments about politics. He was—far more even than Fidel—a man who surrounded himself with a wall that very few intimates could penetrate. It was as if he bristled, even when being friendly. There was an aura of mystery about him because he was such an unusual person—a passion held in leash, an almost missionary dedication to revolution, an exceptionally keen intellect with a tongue and pen that slashed at his own as well as the regime's errors.

Perhaps one key to his nature was the distressing physical handicap that he overcame with an almost unbelievable effort of will, for he was chronically asthmatic from childhood and must have suffered agonies in the soaking, chilly jungles of the Sierra Maestra. Yet he became one of the leaders and, as Fidel said to me when Che was killed, he was "too rash, too brave."

He felt no allegiance to any country, which was why he could leave the island of Cuba that had adopted him. He had no ideology in the sense of devotion to the Communist party, or any party. He left his first wife and child to marry a Cuban girl and then left her and their four children to pursue the will-o'-the-wisp of revolution to an almost certain death.

I said of this strange young man early in the revolution that he had only one loyalty—to Fidel Castro. I still believe that. When Che disappeared from Cuba in April 1965, many foolish and malicious stories were put out and printed in the best newspapers and taught in the best universities.

Yet those who knew Fidel and Che knew that they could never be separated in spirit while they lived. They never lost touch with each other. Che was a disciple who had gone out into the wilderness bearing Fidel's message, and there he died.

Castro himself did not take part in the guerrilla training. He was in Mexico City, preparing for the expedition. In fact, he once denied to me rather emphatically that he owed anything to Colonel Bayo in the way of guerrilla knowledge. After my interview with Fidel appeared in *The New York Times,* Bayo came to see me in my office. He told me what he had taught the group in Mexico—the classic rules of guerrilla warfare—and expressed great anxiety as to whether Fidel was following the rules.

Castro was following his own rules, as usual, but guerrilla fighting is much the same wherever it is waged. Many people thought later that the Cubans were following Mao Tse-tung's teachings, but the Cubans knew nothing about the Chinese until near the end. They were simply doing what came naturally to guerrilla fighters.

Régis Debray, the French writer whose fate became linked to Che Guevara's in Bolivia, wrote in his pamphlet "Revolution Within the Revolution?" that Mao Tse-tung's *Strategic Problems of the Anti-Japanese War* "fell into the hands of Fidel and Che after the [Batista] summer offensive of 1958. Much to their surprise, they read in that book what they had been doing under the pressure of necessity!"

Frank País, the 26th of July's leader on the island, went twice to Mexico to plan for the proposed uprising and the general strike that were to coincide with the landing. He appears to have been against Fidel's plans for the Cuban part of the plot, being realistic about the chances of getting either a popular uprising or trade-union support, but he yielded to Fidel's always sanguine and im-

petuous temperament. Frank País was one of the most able and
gifted men of the 26th of July Movement and it was a great loss to
the insurrection when he was killed by the Batista police in 1957.

Melba Hernández, Teresa Casuso writes in her book (page
116), also traveled up and back from Cuba and she likewise tried
to persuade Fidel, in vain, that he would get no help from the
island.

Fidel upset Bayo very much by telling the world that he was
going to land in Cuba before December 31, 1956. Jules Dubois
(page 138) has Bayo asking Castro, "Don't you know that a
cardinal military principle is to keep your intentions secret from
your enemy?" "It is a peculiarity all my own," Fidel is supposed to
have answered, "although I know that militarily it might be harmful. It is psychological warfare."

One announcement came in a letter Fidel wrote to Miguel Ángel
Quevedo, director of the magazine *Bohemia,* on August 26, 1956
(the text is in Selser's book, pages 112–18):

> The campaign of infamies and calumnies [against me] will have
> a perfect answer soon in the fulfillment of the promise we have
> made that in 1956 we will be free or we will be martyrs.

Hopes of buying a large boat had to be abandoned for lack of
resources. Fidel had noticed a beaten-up yacht undergoing repairs
on the Tuxpan River in the state of Veracruz, and decided that it
would serve his purposes. Small though it was, the Movement had
no money to buy it, so he went to a source that has been an
embarrassment to him every since—ex-President Prío Socarrás
(1948–52), for whom Fidel had had such contempt and whose
regime exemplified much that he was revolting against.

When I was in Havana in October 1967, I asked Fidel whether
it was really true, as many had said and written, that he accepted
money from Prío in order to buy the *Granma* in Mexico. He
frankly said that he had.

"It was a desperately difficult time for us," he told me. "Our
consideration was to make the revolution, and the only way we
could raise the money was from Prío. It was only forty or fifty
thousand dollars. We knew what we were doing. The money meant
nothing to him. Anyway, the 26th of July had a policy that it was

willing to wipe the slate clean so far as events before March 10, 1952 [when Batista staged his *coup d'état*] were concerned. We made no concessions to Prío afterwards. He hung around for a year in Cuba and then left. I have no regrets about it. We were willing to do anything for the revolution."

As the preparations were nearing their end, an informer in their midst—they were sure it was Rafael del Pino, who had been with Fidel in Bogotá in 1948—notified the Mexican police. Three caches of important arms were seized. Two of their men—one of them Pedro Miret, who was at Moncada and was to play an important role in the revolution, as he still does—were arrested and imprisoned. Miret was a sort of armorer for the expedition, as he had been for Moncada, where he was gravely wounded. He had been an engineering student at Havana University before joining the Movement.

Fidel ordered an immediate mobilization of his men. The *Granma,* still not completely repaired, could have held a dozen men in only mild discomfort. Eighty-two were packed into it, with insufficient food and water. The time was November 25, 1956, with rough seas and stormy weather all the way across. The yacht shipped water; the men were seasick, hungry and thirsty; and, worst of all, what with a bad engine and a contrary wind the yacht was delayed.

The uprising that was to coincide with the landing was set for November 30, and for a brief period Frank País and his comrades almost held control of Santiago de Cuba. Batista's forces had little trouble in suppressing the revolt.

On December 2 the *Granma* finally reached the western coast of Oriente Province between Niquero and Cabo Cruz. It was a marshy spot. The yacht could not be beached; the auxiliary boat shipped water and sank, so that the men had to jump into the water and flounder ashore, losing much of their equipment, arms and food in the process. They all had a hard time struggling through the interminable loam and vegetation of the swampy shore so that when they finally reached firm ground they were exhausted, hungry, thirsty, covered with mud. The spot where they landed was called Las Coloradas de Belic.

Batista's forces had been forewarned both by Castro from

Mexico and by the abortive uprising of November 30. A frigate came up and started shooting at the abandoned *Granma*. Planes began searching overhead. Francis L. McCarthy, correspondent of the United Press International in Havana, gave out a widely printed story that air and naval forces had intercepted the *Granma* expeditionaries and that Fidel and Raúl Castro and thirty-eight companions had been killed.

Fidel Castro was doubtless disconcerted, but he was not at all discouraged. As promised, he had landed in Cuba before the end of 1956 and, at that moment, he still had eighty-two men with him.

By normal standards—which, to be sure, can rarely be applied to Fidel Castro—the expedition had been a disaster. Yet, as Faustino Pérez was to write a decade later, "The *Granma* was a prolongation and development of the Moncada attack."

# 4 SIERRA MAESTRA

"IN TRUTH," Fidel Castro was to say in a speech on July 26, 1966, "we can affirm that our revolution began under incredible conditions." Indeed it did!

Although all eighty-two of the men of the *Granma* got ashore on December 2, 1956, some lost their way in the swamp and it was a few days before the expeditionary force—such as it was—could get together. They struggled inland to a place called Alegría de Pío, to which two peasants had directed them, and where they were foolish enough to rest in a sugarcane brake. It was December 5th. More than likely, the peasants had informed on them.

> There we were surprised by the troops and planes of the tyranny [in Faustino Pérez's words], and in that terrible and unequal battle in the midst of the burning cane it was impossible to avoid dispersion and disaster. . . . The fate of the small and scattered groups who tried to get away from that unlucky spot was varied. Some were ambushed in the gulleys lined with soldiers; many were captured and immediately killed; other more fortunate ones landed in jail. . . .

But the most extraordinary lesson of those days of bitterness and defeat was that of the faith which we derived from them. Without knowing the fate of the rest of our companions, and amidst the grief for those who had fallen and the improbability of his own survival, Fidel remained confident that he would encounter many companions in the mountains and felt sure that the struggle could go on and be developed.

Faustino Pérez and Universo Sánchez—the two men who were alone with Fidel in the first agonizing days (and who, incidentally, are still with him in the Cuban Government), are the best possible witnesses of the "incredible" beginning of the Sierra Maestra saga. Faustino, as was mentioned before, was a medico just out of training.

Universo was one of the few peasants in that early stage of the revolution. He told his story to Carlos Franqui, the newspaperman who had been a Communist agitator since the age of fifteen and who has become one of the leading "intellectuals" of the revolution. Ever since the Sierra days he has been an intimate associate of Castro's. He is the one who put together the "autobiography" of Fidel Castro that one of these days will get into print. Like so many of the remarkable young men and women who have made the Cuban Revolution, the gentle, humorous, dedicated Carlos Franqui deserves a book to himself.

Universo Sánchez's story is the second chapter of Franqui's *El Libro de los Doce*. The conversations were taped and published without alteration, Franqui asserts. In the wild scramble at Alegría de Pío, Universo was at first alone with Fidel, but as night was falling they saw someone approaching who turned out to be Faustino Pérez.

"Fidel," Universo said, "wanted at all costs to go back and regroup his men. I and Faustino persuaded him to stay where he was because God knows where our comrades had been scattered to. And after all, if there was one person about whom to be anxious it was he, who would lead the revolution and who would overthrow Batista. He should not risk falling into the hands of the soldiers. Those were my very words."

They stayed put for three days, consumed by hunger and most of all by thirst which they assuaged a little by sucking pieces of sugarcane. Then they moved through the plantation and were lucky enough not to stumble on the soldiers who were still searching and killing. After several days they came upon a peasant's hut where they were fed and treated kindly, but Fidel was suspicious because he realized he had been recognized. Only days later did they learn that the peasant was Guillermo García's father; this was during their struggle toward the Sierra Maestra, when Guillermo joined them, carrying two rifles that had been abandoned at the tragic cane field of Alegría de Pío. García had been advised that the landing was being made.

Guillermo led them to the farmer who was to be the guerrillas' guardian angel and who had joined the 26th of July Movement before the landing—Crescencio Pérez. Crescencio conducted them to the house in the Sierra of his brother Ramón—"a good revolutionary," said Universo—and Ramón hid them in a canebrake for a few days while a search was made for other survivors about whom they began to hear. The plantation was called El Purial de Vicana. One of the survivors, they heard, was wounded in the neck and was asthmatic. They knew this was Che Guevara, who had, indeed, been gravely wounded at Alegría de Pío.

"Fidel sent out for the comrades, who came along in groups," Universo continues. "We saw arriving Raúl [Castro], Che, Almeida, Julio Díaz, Ciro Redondo, Camilo [Cienfuegos], Calixto García, [Efigenio] Almeijeiras, Luis Crespo. Everyone had his gun, although with hardly any bullets. Fidel, happy, said, 'We will win the war! We are now going to start the struggle!' "

Raúl Castro told me, when I saw him in October 1967, of how, when they were dispersed after the *Granma* landing and then finally got together, Fidel embraced him and the others. They had to crouch down because there were Batista soldiers all around them, and as they crawled upward Fidel whispered in Raúl's ear, "Now, when we get clear and organize ourselves, we can start our campaign."

Faustino Pérez once told Carlos Rafael Rodríguez and confirmed to me an even better example of Fidel's incorrigible optimism and fighting spirit. He, Universo Sánchez and Fidel had moved inland at nights, resting during the days, and still with nothing to eat except the sugar they sucked from the then just-ripened canes. At one point Fidel looked up at the hills and mountains of the Sierra Maestra ahead. Evidently he was working out in his mind the plan of guerrilla fighting that he was to follow now that his original plan had failed.

"Ah!" said Fidel to his companions. "Now Batista will be defeated!"

Faustino confessed to me that he and Universo Sánchez thought Fidel must have become light-headed. In reality, Castro was just being himself. There had been guerrilla training in Mexico, and to Cubans, with their historic background, guerrilla tactics came naturally. In any case, as has been remarked before, Fidel never loses his self-confidence and fighting spirit. One of the best stories of all about him in those first hopeless (to anyone but him) days is given in Lee Lockwood's book, *Castro's Cuba, Cuba's Fidel* (page 52). He is writing about a sojourn spent with Castro and some of the revolutionary leaders in El Uvero, on the Oriente coast:

> After breakfast, I have a chat with Guillermo García. He is a hero of the Revolution, the first peasant to join Fidel's forces in the Sierra Maestra. Today he is commander in chief of the armies of the three western provinces and a charter member of Cuba's eleven-man Politburo. . . . He had been a simple *campesino* who traveled through the mountains buying cattle from other peasants for one of the rich landowners.
>
> "I met Fidel for the first time on the twelfth of December, ten days after he landed in the *Granma*. I remember the moment very well. We were walking through a field of *plátanos* [bananas]. Fidel said, 'Are we already in the Sierra Maestra?' I said, 'Yes.' 'Then the Revolution has triumphed!' he said.
>
> "At that moment we were four men, with two rifles and one hundred and twenty-seven bullets." Guillermo's barely visible smile indicates that he is tremendously amused.
>
> "And did you believe him?" I asked.
>
> "Did I believe him? . . . If I didn't believe him I wouldn't be here now, *chico*," he says softly. . . .
>
> "You know, Fidel spoke with such emotion—you had to believe him. . . . And now, look where we are."

Although there are so many differences in the two men, Fidel Castro was like Lenin in having the gift of inspiring all those around him by his faith in himself and in what he was doing. He had the same galvanic quality that Lenin possessed, and in both cases it showed up best in the worst and apparently most hopeless periods.

The survivors reached a place of safety. Universo Sánchez's account to Franqui concluded with these words:

> It was a few days before Christmas. Mongo [Ignacio] Pérez's father-in-law, a friendly peasant, cooked two suckling pigs and we celebrated the commencement of the victory of the revolution.

It is a legend of the Cuban Revolution that the insurrection in the Sierra Maestra began with twelve men. That depends on just what day is chosen and who is counted, but for historic purposes it is an acceptable figure. There is a curious parallel in Cuban history. Carlos Manuel de Céspedes, who raised the standard of revolt against Spain in 1868 with the *Grito de Yara* in Oriente Province, said after his first defeat, "Twelve men suffice to conquer the freedom of a people."

Fidel Castro has spoken often—privately to friends and publicly in speeches—of those first days near Pico Turquino, the highest mountain of the Sierra Maestra, where the seemingly pathetic little band of isolated men set up a base from which—against any possibility of belief at the time—they were two years later to march into Havana in a wild triumph.

Here is a passage chosen from many, in which Fidel discusses the beginnings in the Sierra Maestra. It is from the speech he made on July 26, 1966:

"But our eighty-two men again became practically nothing because of lack of experience, because we must add to all this that none of those men had been trained in a military academy and none of those men really knew very much about war. It is a fact that seven weapons were collected again, seven weapons of the eighty-two weapons with which we had landed. Then we had to begin that struggle with seven weapons. The setback was very great. It is possible that very few people would believe that seven weapons, seven men who had regrouped with their arms, could attempt to organize an army. Nonetheless, despite such adverse conditions the effort was made; we made the effort. We began to pick up more weapons, and with nineteen armed men we waged our first small but victorious battle [at La Plata, January 17, 1957]. . . .

"However, this did not mean that from then on all would go well. We had yet to learn very bitter lessons in the months to come. We had to suffer the effects of the enemy's infiltration tactics. We had to suffer the consequences of treason and on more than one occasion our enemies were on the verge of exterminating us. It was a bitter apprenticeship, but it was a very useful apprenticeship."

Régis Debray (whose famous *Revolution in the Revolution?* is almost entirely a rationalization of Che Guevara's writings, which in turn come from Fidel Castro's experiences and ideas), writes (page 23) shrewdly: "For a revolutionary, failure is a springboard. As a source of theory it is richer than victory; it accumulates experience and knowledge."

As Debray points out, it was valuable for Fidel to learn his own lessons from hard and dangerous experience in the region where he was going to have to fight for two years. Mao Tse-tung's *Strategic Problems* would not have helped him even if he had read it. However, if he had paid more attention to Colonel Bayo's teachings in Mexico he would have avoided some elementary errors. It is an incorrigible feature of Fidel Castro's character, as I have remarked before, that he takes no advice and has to learn by trial and error.

This trait in his character was to lead to fantastically costly mistakes in the first years of the revolution. It was characteristic of him that he had made a plan in Mexico, insisted on it against the advice of his own lieutenants on the island, saw it turn into a complete fiasco—and then used his defeat to create a victory. And not only did he retain his supreme self-confidence after the disaster of the *Granma,* as he did after Moncada, but all the men and women who followed him—those who survived—retained their loyalty and faith in him.

Castro, in effect [Draper writes of the *Granma* expedition in his book *Castroism* (page 24)], backed into guerrilla warfare after all his other plans had failed. Yet this is what set him apart from the other anti-Batista conspirators. They would have withdrawn from Cuba to prepare another invasion or uprising. Castro and a few of his most trusted men went into the mountains to suffer privation and danger, slowly building up a small guerrilla force.

This much is well put, but then Draper falls into a too frequent error of taking a Castro document literally and basing a positive, long-range thesis on it:

> In 1957 and the first months of 1958, however, no one, *not even Castro* [the italics are Draper's] thought that Batista could be overthrown by guerrilla warfare. In February 1957, the pro-Castro, urban-based Resistencia Cívica was organized, and victory seemed so far away in the Sierra Maestra that Castro expected the main blow to come from the urban resistance in the form of a general strike.

Draper gives as his authority the 26th of July Manifesto issued by Fidel from the Sierra on March 12, 1958. (The text is given in Selser's book.) As it happens, this was simply a tactical document aimed to help the general strike which was imminent and which was attempted, with disastrous results, on April 9. It was a very serious setback for Fidel, but only because of the bad publicity.

Régis Debray, who was given access to much unpublished material from the guerrilla years, quotes a letter that Fidel wrote to a certain Nasín on March 23, 1958, before the attempted strike (page 77):

> If he [Batista] succeeds in crushing the strike, nothing would be resolved. We would continue to struggle, and within six months his situation would be worse. . . .

Moreover, Debray was convinced from his talks and studies in Cuba that Fidel, as well as Che Guevara, had counted on winning the struggle against Batista in the mountains and not in the cities. (There was much discussion in those two years of the relative strength of the *sierra,* where the guerrilla forces were engaged, and the *llano,* the plain where the civic resistance operated.)

"The city is a cemetery of revolutionaries and resources,"

Debray quotes Fidel as having said. He points out that Castro sent Faustino Pérez to Havana to reorganize the Movement in January 1957, with orders to send every gun he could lay his hands on up to the Sierra Maestra. Fidel, according to Debray, went along with the general strike in a skeptical mood, feeling that the men down on "the plain" would know the situation in the cities better than he.

I find it impossible to believe Draper's conclusion that "Thus, until the failure of the general strike, Castro himself believed that guerrilla warfare was a subordinate, if indispensable, tactic."

While Fidel did make an elaborate plan for an uprising in the cities, and sabotage and strikes to coincide with his landing, the eighty-two men in Mexico were trained exclusively for guerrilla fighting in mountain and jungle terrain.

Far more important than this is the testimony, some of which I have quoted, of Fidel's companions as they struggled up to the Sierra Maestra in the first catastrophic weeks. I know and have talked to most of the men involved—Faustino Pérez, Universo Sánchez, Raúl Castro, Che Guevara, Juan Almeida, Calixto García, Camilo Cienfuegos, René Rodríguez, Ramiro Valdés, and others who arrived a little later, including the three outstanding women of the insurrection in the Sierra—Celia Sánchez, Haydée Santamaría and Vilma Espín. For all of them, there never was any question of the supremacy of the *sierra,* which is to say of Fidel Castro's guerrilla fighters.

One would have to believe that all these young men and women concocted stories about Fidel's fighting spirit and confidence in *his*—not anybody else's, not some amorphous and still nonexistent civic resistance's—ultimate victory. In those early days there was only that handful of men in the Sierra Maestra and the 26th of July Movement in Santiago de Cuba and Havana, which Fidel immediately subordinated to his command up in the mountains.

I have the best of reasons to know this personally, since my trip to the Sierra Maestra—to get the first interview with Fidel, on February 17, 1957—coincided with a gathering of the 26th of July leaders from all over the island, summoned by Castro. He was to them what he later became to Cuba—the *Jefe Máximo,* or Chief Leader.

To think, as Draper implies, that Castro would have allowed

"an urban-based Resistencia Cívica" to take any authority away from him at any time is sadly to misjudge Fidel's character. It is also beyond me to understand how Draper could have believed that "victory seemed so far away in the Sierra Maestra" that Castro was relying on civic resistance and a general strike as early as February 1957—which was the month I went up to see him. His supreme self-confidence and his faith in his own fighting force—small though it was at the time—was so genuine that it was inescapably convincing. The Resistencia Cívica had just been formed in Santiago de Cuba and, anyway, Fidel Castro never—not even to this day—has been willing to grant the importance of the role played by the urban resistance movement.

These are points that, I believe, must be insisted upon, because they are basic to an understanding of the Cuban Revolution. It is a peculiarity of the three major scholars' writings on the revolution—Theodore Draper, Boris Goldenberg and Andrés Suárez—that unconsciously or deliberately their unquestioned erudition and overwhelming documentation are aimed at belittling Fidel Castro and his role in the Cuban Revolution. This is a variation of playing Hamlet without the Dane. To be fair to Draper, whose work is always very distinguished, he does bring out the fact that the Cuban Revolution is essentially Fidel Castro's revolution, but the massive documentation he supplies manages to distort and depreciate Fidel's role.

Haydée Santamaría, in her taped interview for Carlos Franqui's book, tells how Frank País suggested that they try to persuade Fidel to leave for a Latin-American country to reorganize the Movement. "He could be killed and we cannot afford that luxury," País said to Haydée. They went up to the Sierra for the meeting at the time I was there, and before they had a chance to say anything, Fidel, as Haydée quotes him, said, "Look, the soldiers are firing down below us but they don't dare to climb up here. If you bring me [20 rifles and the ammunition for them] I promise you that I will launch a real battle in two months."

"Neither Frank nor I had anything more to say," Haydée continues. "Fidel had such conviction."

"And at the time," Celia added, "there were only eighteen partisans in the Sierra!"

No one has written more vividly about the great and terrible days in the Sierra Maestra than the gifted Che Guevara in his *Pasajes de la Guerra Revolucionaria* (Reminiscences of the Cuban Revolutionary War), a series of articles first published in the magazine *Verde Olivo,* and put out as a book in Cuba in 1963. It has now been published in an English translation. Che's more famous work, *La Guerra de Guerrillas* (Guerrilla Warfare) became a textbook for the American counterinsurgency Special Forces. His greatest book came out after his death—the serenely tragic *Diary of Che in Bolivia.*

The unending danger of treachery can be seen in this episode from Che's *Pasajes* (page 32) about the traitor Eutimio Guerra, whom I have mentioned. Eutimio had already informed on them twice, but they still did not suspect him.

> One of the last nights before we learned about his treachery, Eutimio said that he had no blanket and he asked Fidel if he would lend him one. On the crest of the hills, in that month of February, it was cold. Fidel said that if he did that both of them would suffer from the cold and that they should sleep under the same blanket and with the two overcoats it would serve the better for both of them. They did this. Eutimio Guerra spent the night next to Fidel, with a .45-caliber pistol that Casillas [one of Batista's officers] had entrusted to him in order to kill Fidel, and with a pair of hand grenades with which to protect his [Eutimio's] retreat down from the hills. . . . Thus, Eutimio passed that night next to the leader of the revolution, holding his life at the muzzle of a pistol, hoping for an opportunity to assassinate him, and not having the courage to do it. All night a good part of the Cuban Revolution hung on the mental obstacles [*vericuetos*], on the sums and fractions of courage, fear, terror and, at moments, scruples of conscience, ambitions for power and money, of a traitor. However, fortunately for us, the sum of inhibiting factors was the greater, and daylight came without anything happening.

They paid dearly for their trust in Eutimio, because several days later their encampment was attacked by the soldiers and they lost one man and some precious matériel. However, Fidel's suspicions had earlier been aroused and he had hustled his men out just in time. This was February 9, 1957.

Eutimio must have been stupid and greedy, for he tried once more, on the very day—February 17—that I was in the Sierra with Fidel and his comrades. Che tells about his execution in a chapter of the same book called "Fin de un Traidor" (End of a Traitor): "He fell on his knees before Fidel, and simply asked that he be killed. He said he knew he deserved to die."

He did die—although not before being bitterly reproached by Fidel and Ciro Frías, one of the guerrillas, whose brother had been killed because of Eutimio's treachery. When asked if he had any last wish, Eutimio begged the group to look after his children.

"The revolution complied," Che ends. Eutimio's children "are going to school and receiving the same treatment as all other children and preparing themselves for a better life, because some day they will have to learn that their father was put to death by the revolutionary authority because of his treachery."

Many other traitors were mercilessly executed when they were caught. The story of Eutimio Guerra is told here because it is one that made the deepest impression on the little guerrilla force. Yet the incident was typical of the hazardous life that the guerrillas led, and it was a lesson they never forgot—that the most precious of all revolutionary qualities, loyalty, has its inescapable counterpart in treachery.

Those first months in the Sierra Maestra were the hardest. By no means all who joined "the Twelve" could stand the life there, and some who were not at all traitors left the group. Fidel, according to Che, announced very early in the game that three offenses would be punished with death: insubordination, desertion and defeatism. (He did not have to say what would happen to traitors.)

There was a picturesque flowering to be noted at that time. The famous beards of the guerrillas, which led them to be called *los barbudos,* was an early and natural development. Manuel Fajardo, one of the first two peasants to join Fidel in the mountains, gave his version of the phenomenon to Carlos Franqui (page 81, French edition):

I never shaved. [Luis] Crespo and I were the first. I stopped shaving on the 6th of December [1956]. And from May 1957 I didn't cut my hair any more.

Fidel began to wear a beard about the same time that we did. He was among the first. But he never stopped having his hair cut. Luis Crespo was the first combatant to let his hair grow long. Che shaved his head. As for a beard—he didn't have one. Raúl even less. . . . When we were at the Second Front, Raúl got us together and told us that our beards and our hair no longer belonged to us since they belonged to the revolution.

The photograph of Fidel that was taken when I saw him in the Sierra shows him with the same kind of beard and short haircut that he has to this day. Aside from its being a convenience not to shave in the Sierra, Fidel shrewdly realized that it was a picturesque trademark for the rebels. Besides, he knew he looked better, since even when much younger, and in spite of his superb physical condition, he has had a little double chin that the beard hides.

Guevara, whose frankness was one of his many engaging characteristics, conceded that morale was very poor in the early weeks and they had to get rid of some men. There had been the devastating baptism of fire at Alegría de Pío, then the unending exhaustion, hunger, thirst, drenching rain and a deadly peril that never left them from the ubiquitous soldiers of Batista.

Only men with the stoutest hearts and a blind faith could have borne such hardships, but those who did and who survived are the men who today surround Fidel Castro, and under him run the Government and the Cuban Revolution. Loyalty is the number-one requisite in a revolution. Everything is forgiven to the loyal, but those whose loyalty falters, or is lost, commit the unforgivable revolutionary sin. This, among other things, explains the unhappy fate of Major Hubert Matos in the first year of the revolution.

The law of revolution is not unlike the law of the jungle. The morality of a normal society cannot be applied, because a revolutionary process is abnormal and has its own "laws." Those who reject them reject revolution; those who accept revolution must accept its rules or perish.

Fidel Castro is what they used to call in the American West a "tough hombre." He had to be tough; he had to hold his own and other lives cheaply; he had to make superhuman demands on himself and his followers; he had to be and do these things to survive those two grueling years of insurrection in the Sierra Maestra.

I never claimed more for myself in the interview I had with Castro in the Sierra Maestra on February 17, 1957, than that I recognized *his* quality and, joining it to the countrywide antagonism to the Batista regime which existed at the time, forecast the role that he was to play. I could not realize then how much danger and hardship he and his followers had yet to survive, or I might not have been so confident.

I did not know how small a force Fidel had at that time—eighteen men with rifles—but I doubt that this would have made any difference in the story I wrote for *The New York Times,* which was published on Sunday, February 24. The dangerous position we were in during my interview was perfectly obvious. In fact, all through the morning we had to talk in whispers and every one of the group was under orders not to speak in a normal voice. We were surrounded by Batista's soldiers. One of my most vivid recollections of the incident is of Fidel crouching on the ground next to me and of his hoarse, impassioned whisper in my left ear as he poured his youthful, revolutionary heart out into my old and somewhat war-weary soul. (I was fifty-seven and he was thirty.) For I had seen much of wars and revolutions, starting before Fidel Castro was born.

That group of eighteen men was enough for the purpose of the moment in the struggle. Reinforcements were to come soon. The guerrillas were nearer to defeat in the summer of 1958 when they had hundreds of well-armed and experienced men fighting against Batista's last all-out offensive. Anyway, what Fidel did not seem to realize was the extent to which he had already become a symbol of resistance for the youth of Cuba, and that he would become *the* symbol of revolution after my story was published in *The New York Times.*

He knew he needed publicity; he always had a keen eye for that, and inviting a newspaperman was one of his most brilliant strokes. All Fidel had to do, to put it in common terms, was to sell himself to me—and being the man he was, he simply had to be himself to do that.

For an island-wide conference of the 26th of July Movement and for the meeting place with me, Fidel's group of eighteen men came part way down from the mountains while the men and women of the 26th went up from Santiago de Cuba and Manzanillo. Some, like myself and my wife (who waited in Manzanillo) had come from Havana. That my trip should have coincided with the 26th of July meeting—the first held since the *Granma* landing—was, of course, pure coincidence. The place, Che wrote in his book, was not far from a hamlet named La Montería, "a little ridge of the mountains near a stream."

I have told the complete story of the interview with Fidel in my book *The Cuban Story,* written in 1961. As I have mentioned, the word had gone out that Castro was killed at the time of the *Granma* landing. Fidel wanted to prove that he was alive and fighting. Faustino Pérez was then in Havana, organizing the underground resistance of the 26th of July Movement. Fidel sent one of his men, René Rodríguez, to Havana to find out whether a newspaperman would make the journey to the Sierra Maestra through the Batista lines and do a story about him and the guerrillas.

No Cuban journalist offered to go. The father of one of the July 26th members, Felipe Pazos, a well-known economist, was approached by his son Javier. Felipe Pazos knew the *New York Times* correspondent in Havana well. Mrs. Ruby Hart Phillips, just at that time, heard that my wife and I were going to Cuba for a holiday. When I arrived and the proposition was put to me I, of course, jumped at it.

My wife Nancie joined in order to provide an innocent-looking cover for the trip to Manzanillo, and it was she who smuggled out the highly subversive (for Batista) notes that I had made. We were driven on the long—overnight and morning—journey to Oriente Province by Javier Pazos, Faustino Pérez and a young society woman named Liliam Mesa who was a member of the Movement.

Faustino went into the hills to prepare for my visit and also to join all the others from the Movement who were gathering for their conference. Javier Pazos was delegated to go up with me and then go back to Havana with us. We slipped through the Batista patrols in a jeep driven by Guerrito Sánchez (who has a government position now) and then, when the climb had to be made, Universo Sánchez acted as a guide. Fidel joined the group I was with at dawn and we talked through much of the morning, or, rather, Fidel talked in answer to my questions. Then I was guided down to a peasant's house where Guerrito Sánchez again picked me up to rejoin my wife in Manzanillo.

The interview had to be written in New York. When it appeared the following Sunday as a leading news story, with a photograph of Fidel holding his precious rifle with the telescopic sight, it created a tremendous sensation in Cuba and throughout Latin America. The story had come at the ebb tide of Fidel's fortunes and there is no use speculating how much longer it would have taken him to consolidate himself in the Sierra Maestra and arouse the wide-spread civic resistance which played such a great role in defeating General Batista.

The *New York Times* story made him a hero and a symbol for the resistance. He had been thought to be dead—and Batista's Minister of National Defense, Santiago Verdeja, issued a statement saying that my story could "be considered as a chapter in a fantastic novel" and "at no time did the said correspondent have an interview" with Fidel Castro. My newspaper thereupon published a photograph of Fidel and me together in the Sierra.

After his flight from Cuba, General Batista wrote in his book *Respuesta* (page 52), which was published in an English edition as *Cuba Betrayed:*

> The military chiefs of the province told the General Staff so emphatically that no such interview had taken place that the Minister of Defense publicly denied it had occurred. And even I, influenced by the reports of the General Staff, doubted it. The interview had, in fact, taken place and its publication was of considerable propaganda value to the rebels. Castro was to begin his era as a legendary figure, and end as a monster of terror.

Santiago Verdeja referred in his statement to "the pro-Communist insurgent, Fidel Castro." At no time in the two years of the Sierra Maestra struggle was Castro or the 26th of July Movement pro-Communist.

"It is a revolutionary movement that calls itself socialistic," I wrote in my interview. "It is also nationalistic, which generally in Latin America means anti-Yankee.

"The program is vague and couched in generalities, but it amounts to a new deal for Cuba, radical, democratic and therefore anti-Communist."

This statement and more that I wrote in the interview are typical of the confusion that was to reign during the insurrection and in the early period of the revolution. At the time of my interview, the Cuban Communists were out of the picture and were, in fact, disapproving. Fidel naïvely (to use his own word to me) believed that the rebels could make a radical social revolution democratically. Since his basic aim was revolution, and democracy was simply the method that he thought he could use, when the crunch came he changed his method, not his goal.

There was no error in writing what I did in my story about the "democratic" ideals of the guerrillas because the statements accurately reflected what Fidel said and—in my opinion—believed. There was a decided error in my understanding of the size of the forces that Castro then had under his command. To give him credit, Fidel merely said—as I quoted him—"I will not tell you how many [men] we have for obvious reasons."

It has become a standard source of glee among the Cuban rebels who were there, from Fidel and Raúl Castro down, that they had fooled me into believing that they were a larger and stronger force than they really were. Fidel himself, with a slightly malicious gleam in his eyes, later broke the news that he had had only eighteen armed men. This was at a huge luncheon of the Overseas Press Club which I helped to arrange in New York in April 1959. In Carlos Franqui's book on "The Twelve," Celia Sánchez, Guillermo García, Manuel Fajardo, Efigenio Almeijeiras and Vilma Espín all talk about their ruses. When I saw Raúl Castro in Havana in October 1967, he chortled about it once again.

In Celia's words: "We prepared everything so that Matthews would get a good impression and believe that Fidel was in another camp." It seems that Raúl "passed up and back always with the same men." He is supposed to have told Fidel about news from "another column," and so forth. These tactics are as old as the history of warfare.

It was all interesting as showing how anxious they were to make "a good impression" and get effective publicity—but if these things took place they made no impression of any kind on me. Fidel did spend the night somewhere else. Che Guevara and Calixto García —original members of "the Twelve"—told me later that they were elsewhere in the Sierra when I went up. I know from my own observations in Manzanillo that dozens of July 26th members were close to me in the Sierra on that same day. Since we had to whisper, I would not have been able to hear Raúl tell his brother about "another column."

There were three things that, fortunately for the rebels, did impress me. One, which antedated my trip, was the conviction I had that Cuba was in a suppressed state of ferment and of widespread hostility to the Batista regime. We had published an editorial in *The New York Times* on January 31, headed WHAT IS WRONG WITH CUBA? which described the terrorism and counter-terrorism, and the tight censorship, and expressed puzzlement at "the extent and intensity of the anti-Batista feeling compared to a year or two ago."

A second impression was that so long as Castro fought the way he did in that trackless mountain jungle, Batista's troops could not destroy his guerrillas. The great risk was that Fidel would be killed while leading his men—and he always did lead them in those early months.

I expressed the final, and most important, impression in these words:

> The personality of the man [Fidel Castro] is overpowering. It was easy to see that his men adored him and also to see why he has caught the imagination of the youth of Cuba all over the island. Here was an educated, dedicated fanatic, a man of ideals, of courage and of remarkable qualities of leadership.

This was why my interview, with its mistakes and misconceptions along with its accuracies, was to prove prophetic. No amount of sensational publicity would have meant anything in the course of a short time if Fidel Castro had not been just as I described him.

When the 26th of July meeting in the Sierra broke up, Frank País promised to send reinforcements—and he was as good as his word. The intervening weeks were extraordinarily difficult for the constantly moving, always soaked, hungry and exhausted band. Che Guevara's asthma almost killed him. On March 7 General Francisco Tabernilla, Batista's Chief of Staff, announced that Castro's forces had been "completely defeated."

With the arrival of the fifty or so men that País sent up in March (thirty of them armed), a turning point came. The men were green, soft, and at first overwhelmed by the hardships. A few turned back, but most stuck it out and a number of them died fighting.

At the time they came along, Efigenio Almeijeiras, in Franqui's book (page 132), has Fidel say:

> Che, we must immediately deal a great blow against the tyranny to make them understand that they can no longer hide from the Cuban people that we are in the Sierra Maestra, now that our number has grown, and above all, now that Batista denies our interview with Matthews.

It was not until May 28, after a fresh shipment of arms arrived, that the garrison at El Uvero was successfully attacked. A long stalemate had then been reached, during which the rebels were too strong to be attacked and too weak to do more than carry out raids and sabotage from which they returned to their safe haven in the Sierra Maestra.

On March 13, 1957, a group of daring students from Havana University's Directorio Estudiantil attacked the Presidential Palace in Havana and almost succeeded in their objective of killing

General Batista. The plan failed because there was treachery or cowardice on the part of two groups of students who should have joined the attack. Those who got into the palace fought bravely and some got away alive. One of them was Fauré Chomón, who later set up a guerrilla front of the Directorio Estudiantil in the Sierra de Trinidad. One who died was the leader, José Antonio Echevarría, whom I had interviewed secretly after my return from the Sierra.

In April 1957, a Columbia Broadcasting System team of Robert Taber and a photographer went up to the Pico Turquino and made a remarkable documentary which gave Castro and his guerrillas some wonderful publicity. Taber later had to leave CBS because of his emotional involvement with the revolution.

He wrote what is still the most complete and accurate history of the Sierra Maestra insurrection. It is called *M-26: The Biography of a Revolution* (1961). The book made little impact, since by that time Castro was anathema in the United States, but the television documentary was a great contribution to the romantic image of Fidel that existed in the United States—until another television correspondent, also with CBS, Stuart Novins, rescued his outfit by doing a documentary on May 3, 1959, in which he prematurely, but effectively, put a Communist label on the Castro regime.

On September 5, in that same year of 1957, there was a naval revolt in the southern port of Cienfuegos. The city was held for the day but was mercilessly bombed into defeat by Batista's air force.

Thus the year had brought three failures, so far as popular resistance outside of the Sierra Maestra was concerned. There had been no general uprising when the *Granma* was arriving; the attack on the Presidential Palace had failed; so had the naval revolt. On April 9, 1958, an attempted general strike was to prove a resounding and dangerous failure for the resistance.

For Fidel Castro, the lessons were inescapably clear—the decisive push that could overthrow the Batista regime had to come from his guerrilla warfare, starting where he was—in the Sierra Maestra—and spreading to the rest of the island. It was his dogged and dramatic struggle alone that permitted the urban resistance to keep going, and it was a combination of this resistance and the

Rebel Army's growing strength and invincibility that undermined the morale of Batista's army.

The transformation in Fidel Castro's image in the United States was an extraordinary feature of his revolutionary career, but while he was in the Sierra Maestra the publicity was highly favorable. The mountains became a Mecca to which a stream of newspapermen, magazine writers, broadcasters and news photographers went.

Fidel was too busy running his little guerrilla army and the 26th of July Movement in the cities to think much about politics or ideology. He had none of either in those days, although this did not inhibit his flow of language. He was, for the most part, repeating what he had said in "History Will Absolve Me" and in his previous manifestos, without realizing the extent to which he was promising to do the impossible.

Put in another way, many thousands of Cubans in the resistance movement around the island (and many Americans, too) believed that Castro's victory would result in drastic reforms and a much-needed cleanup within the traditional pseudo-democratic system that Cuba had known since the Republic was founded.

Fidel, for his part, had never hidden the fact that he was going to make a revolution. As he confessed later, he did not specify—while he was up in the Sierra Maestra—how drastic that revolution was going to be if he had his way.

Celia Sánchez once made a revealing remark to me concerning the promises made in the Sierra:

> We could not know during that period that when victory came we and the 26th of July Movement would be so strong and so popular. We thought we would have to form a government with Auténticos, Ortodoxos, and so forth. Instead we found that we could be the masters of Cuba. That [in 1959] was when we began to put policies into effect that we always had in mind but thought would have to be postponed. There was no need to lose any time.

Régis Debray, in *Revolution in the Revolution,* provided another justification. "Strategically," he wrote of the guerrillas in the Sierra, "they risked everything to win everything; at the end, they deserved to get everything."

It is true that for Castro and the guerrillas it was a fight to the finish—victory or death. For many of the young resistance fighters of the Movement in the cities it was also a desperate risk, but for most it was not too dangerous to be in the opposition. This is aside from the fact that the *barbudos* suffered terrible privations and hardships in the jungles of the Sierra Maestra.

No one thought that Fidel would do what he said he would do: make a social revolution. But he himself thought that he would be able to make his revolution without going the way of dictatorship and, ultimately, Communism. This was the clash of contradictory ideas, pledges and hopes that led to the charge that "Fidel Castro betrayed the revolution."

For Cubans and Americans it all began in the Sierra Maestra. Castro, by his actions and his words, led, expressed, and symbolized the powerful emotional forces that existed throughout Cuba in mounting degrees as the Batista regime went on toward its climax of sadism and corruption.

President Batista, to whom I spoke about the popular hostility to his regime in the summer of 1957, naturally, and no doubt sincerely, denied that any such hostility existed. So did the unfortunate American ambassador, Arthur Gardner, who considered Fulgencia Batista the United States's "best friend." Yet my interview would not have created such a sensation in Cuba if overwhelming numbers of citizens had not been waiting for some word or rallying point around which to focus their opposition to the Batista Government.

There was a trial in May 1957 of the twenty-two captives from the *Granma* expedition and about a hundred actual and alleged participants in the Santiago de Cuba uprising on November 30, 1956, which was to have coincided with the landing. It was at this trial that Dr. Manuel Urrutia, one of the three magistrates of the Santiago Urgency Court, voted against his colleagues to free the prisoners on the grounds of their constitutional right to oppose tyranny.

Among the Santiagüeros who were acquitted was the young schoolmaster who was the leader of the 26th of July Movement, Frank País. He immediately went underground after the trial, got in touch with Fidel as soon as it became possible, and for the few remaining months of his life continued to be Castro's most valued lieutenant.

But he was more than that. Frank País—"the unforgettable Frank País," as his comrades called him—was a rare soul. He was a man whose life was a sacrifice to idealism. His personality, capacities and courage made a profound impression on his companions, and those who knew him retain a sense of something precious that has been lost. I met him only once, at a hideout in Santiago de Cuba in July 1957, the month in which he was killed. Like Che Guevara, who also met him only once, at the February meeting of the 26th of July in the Sierra, Frank País was truly "unforgettable"—a superior human being, whose death was the greatest single loss during the prerevolutionary struggle.

On the afternoon of July 30 he was tracked down on the Calle Germán in Santiago during an intensive security search and shot to death. All Santiago mourned, and most of all Fidel Castro and the rebels in the Sierra Maestra. The road to revolution is strewn with the bodies of the young.

Frank País, Camilo Cienfuegos, Che Guevara—all three were remarkable human beings destined to sacrifice themselves. Che, at least, lived to serve the revolution until it became too staid for him.

In the last chapter of his book (*Pasajes,* pages 122–26), which is about the death of a Guatemalan guerrilla friend, El Patojo, Che synthesizes all he learned of guerrilla warfare in a brief passage:

I limited myself to recommending emphatically three points: constant mobility, constant distrust, constant vigilance. Mobility means never to stay in the same place; not to spend two nights at the same spot; never to stop marching from one place to another.

Distrust—from the very beginning distrust your own shadow, your peasant friends, your informers, your guides, your contacts; distrust everything until you have established a free zone. Vigilance—sentry posts at all times, constant patrols, encampments only in a secure place and, above all these things, never sleep under a roof, never sleep in a house that can be surrounded.

This is how Fidel Castro and his guerrillas learned to live in the Sierra Maestra.

Guevara's lament for his friend El Patojo reads strangely now like a mournful echo from the past which was taken up sorrowfully by Che's own friends in Cuba when the news came from Bolivia that he, too, had been killed in the dangerous game that guerrillas play. Che grieved that El Patojo had not taken his advice fully to heart. Fidel too said to me sadly, "Che was too rash!" Yet, in Bolivia, Che had taken all the precautions he outlined to his friend, as his diary showed when it was published in July 1968. They were not enough.

The events from Moncada onwards and the wonderful, agonizing months in the Sierra Maestra were the fire that forged the men and women who made the Cuban Revolution and who run Cuba today. No individuals in the train of social revolutions that began in France in 1789—except for the Chinese Communists—had to pass such a test of character, stamina, morale and loyalty as the group that fought with Fidel Castro for two years in the mountains. It was his leadership, his personality, faith and courage that kept them together and built up the hard core of the Rebel Army, which explains why—now that ten years have passed—the Cuban Revolution is still going strong.

It is again to Che Guevara, the most thoughtful and the most "literary" exponent (Castro is an orator, not a writer) of the revolution, that one turns. Che sent a long letter in 1965 to Carlos Guijano, editor of the Montevideo (Uruguay) weekly *Marcha,* which was published in Havana as a booklet in English: "Man and Socialism in Cuba." In it he writes (pages 12–13):

In this process [the Moncada attack], which contained only the first seeds of socialism, man was a basic factor. Man—individualized, specific, named—was trusted, and the triumph or failure of the task entrusted to him depended on his capacity for action.

Then came the stage of guerrilla warfare. It was carried out in two different environments: the people, an as yet unawakened mass that had to be mobilized, and its vanguard, the guerrilla, the thrusting engine of mobilization, the generator of revolutionary awareness and militant enthusiasm. This vanguard was the catalyst which created the subjective condition necessary for victory. The individual was also the basic factor in the guerrilla, in the framework of the gradual proletarianization of our thinking, in the revolution taking place in our habits and in our minds. Each and every one of the Sierra Maestra fighters who achieved a high rank in the revolutionary forces has to his credit a list of noteworthy deeds. It was on the basis of such deeds that they earned their rank.

No individual in the Cuban Revolution, which is so rich in its list of outstanding figures, was more remarkable than Celia Sánchez. Celia is the daughter of a physician of Pilón, which is outside Manzanillo in Oriente Province. She is a slight, wiry and attractive woman, of great simplicity, dignity and poise—a very warm personality with those whom she knows and likes. She dresses fastidiously and elegantly. And this is the same young woman who lived in soiled military fatigues and fought with the guerillas in the Sierra Maestra for almost the whole dangerous and grueling period. She developed the habit there of eating only when hungry and sleeping only when tired, regardless of the time. Courage, brains, idealism, dedication to the revolution, and passionate, absorbing loyalty to Fidel Castro to whom she is *alter ego,* serving as confidante, housekeeper, and a Cabinet Minister with great responsibilities—this is Celia Sánchez.

She had belonged to the Movement since 1954, the year after Moncada, and had wanted to go to Mexico to take part in the *Granma* expedition. Haydée Santamaría and Frank País dissuaded her, and, anyway, Fidel in Mexico said, "No women!" What was decisive was País's argument that Celia would be more valuable at home in Oriente because she knew the region so well. In fact, she and Frank País did the never-to-be-used organizing for the landing, and if the *Granma* had come ashore farther north where it was expected, there would have been jeeps, trucks, gasoline, food and medicines awaiting the rebels.

As soon as Celia learned where Fidel and "the Twelve" were hiding, she went up to join them. This was at the end of December 1956. For a while she acted as a courier to Frank País and the 26th of July in Santiago de Cuba, but shortly after the February meeting in the Sierra, in Che Guevara's words, "Celia was definitely incorporated into the guerrilla force, never to leave us any more."

It was Celia Sánchez who gave me an eyewitness account of Fidel's first important victory. This was the battle on May 28, 1957, at El Uvero, on the southern coast of Oriente Province, where the rebels overwhelmed the garrison, seized their arms and melted back into the Sierra. With that feat, as Che wrote in *Pasajes* (page 82):

> Our guerrilla force came of age. From the time of that combat, our morale rose enormously, our determination and our hopes of triumph also grew with that victory, and although the succeeding months were a hard trial, we were already in possession of the secret of victory over the enemy.

The many battles, skirmishes, raids and forays of the next year and a half do not need retelling here. By August 1957, as Che Guevara wrote (page 121), "the Batistiano troops left the Sierra once and for all." However, they kept up their incursions and made one all-out offensive in the summer of 1958 that almost overwhelmed the bulk of the Rebel Army which Fidel Castro commanded.

On March 1, 1958, Raúl Castro had set off with a column of fifty-three men. He cut across the eastern end of the island and set up a second front in the Sierra de Cristal. Che Guevara, Juan Almeida and Camilo Cienfuegos were leading other columns on long raids. Fidel had his headquarters safe in the mountains up above the village of La Plata, with quick access to Cuba's highest mountain, Pico Turquino. Aside from entertaining visiting journalists, he was issuing statements over the radio and, in a confused and confusing fashion, arranging for what was to be a definitive manifesto outlining the program of the rebels, their allies in the resistance, and the emigrés in New York, Miami, and Caracas, Venezuela.

Meanwhile small and separated nuclei of guerrillas established themselves in the hills nearer Havana. One was headed by Eloy Gutiérrez Menoyo, a survivor of the attack on the Presidential Palace. His force was trained by a young American adventurer, William Morgan. They held out in the Sierra de Escambray. In February 1958, Fauré Chomón, another survivor of the March 13, 1957, attack, landed with a small force from the Directorio Estudiantil and went up into the Sierra de Trinidad. Under the different demands of the revolution, Morgan at first worked with Fidel, then plotted against him and was caught and executed. Gutiérrez defected to Florida, led CIA-sponsored raids into Cuba, was caught and is now serving a long prison sentence. Chomón, after an initial attempt to assert himself, worked with the regime and, after serving as Ambassador to Moscow, became a valued Cabinet Minister.

In *Revolution in the Revolution?* Debray writes (pages 60–61):

> The meticulous and almost obsessive attention Fidel paid to the smallest concrete detail of preparation for the most minor action, until the last day of the war, was amazing. His war correspondence makes this abundantly clear: the placing of fighters in an ambush operation; the number of bullets issued to each one; the path to be taken; the preparation and testing of mines; the inspection of provisions, etc. An excellent lesson in strict efficiency.

In the conversation, already mentioned, between Lee Lockwood and Guillermo García, the former peasant of the Sierra Maestra, there is another revealing and characteristic aspect of Castro.

"Fidel had never been in these mountains before," García says to Lockwood (page 53):

> But in six months he knew the whole Sierra better than any *guajiro* who was born here. He never forgot a place that he went to. He

remembered everything—the soil, the trees, who lived in each house. In those days I was a cattle buyer. I used to go all over the mountains. But in six months Fidel knew the Sierra better than I did, and I was born and raised here.

Two aspects of the latter months of the insurrection were of vital importance—the attitude toward the United States and the political pronouncements that Fidel Castro was making.

The rebels were at all times deeply resentful of the fact that Batista was using American arms, although fresh shipments were cut off, perhaps not completely, in March 1958. The United States refused to withdraw the military, naval and air-force missions, which went on advising the Batistianos until Castro sent them packing as soon as he reached Havana in January 1959. As he sardonically remarked, if they had not been able to teach Batista's troops to fight any better than they did, he had no use for them. The Pentagon also foolishly went on wining, dining, decorating and praising Batista generals when things were at their worst in the mountains.

The Government in Washington had reasons to worry. Although the CIA, FBI and the military intelligence were naturally at work thoughout the insurrection, they could find no evidence that Fidel or any of the men who fought with him were Communist. To be sure, Raúl Castro, as a student, had gone to Eastern Europe for a conference and had made trips to several Iron Curtain capitals. Che Guevara had played a very minor role in the pro-Communist Arbenz Government in Guatemala. However, the Cuban Communists, whose party was then called the Partido Socialista Popular (PSP), were openly and officially critical of the Castroites. The Communists had also condemned the student attack on the Presidential Palace. All this, to them, was "putschism"—until they saw in the late summer of 1958 that Fidel was going to win.

Nevertheless, the anxious Americans were aware of the often-expressed anti-Yankeeism of the rebels plus the radical implications of Fidel Castro's revolutionary ideas. Washington would have liked Batista to depart or, failing that, for him to set up a "liberal" reform government, but the General was as tough as

Castro, and in any event Fidel had no intention of stopping. He had learned from the failure of the general strike on April 9, 1958, that he could not count on the urban resistance to overthrow the regime. His strength, following and confidence were growing. It had to be a fight to the finish.

The United States Government was especially alarmed when Raúl Castro's detached Second Front forces invaded the American-owned Moa Bay Mining Company's property on June 26th and kidnapped twelve engineers, ten of them Americans. Two days later, thirty United States soldiers and marines, driving between the Guantánamo naval base and the city of the same name, were seized and held captive. Other raids were made until the rebels held about fifty hostages.

They were all treated with courtesy and even bonhommie but were made to realize that they had better not try to escape.

Manuel Fajardo, one of the peasant rebels and by then an "officer" with Raúl's column, told Carlos Franqui for his book on "The Twelve" (page 83) that one of the marines asked him how he could prevent him from escaping. Fajardo said he simply replied that if the marine tried to get away he would shoot him.

The State Department had to negotiate with the rebels, and the hostages were all released by July 18. It had been a successful, although dangerous, operation that brought tremendous publicity in the United States and an enforced truce by the Batistianos, who did not dare to attack for fear of harming the hostages. The captives, with few exceptions, took the adventure with good grace and later told how well they had been treated.

Fidel, his brother Raúl said to me, was always clever in recognizing the limitations of his power at any given time. Raúl told of how, in late 1957 or early 1958, a group of American journalists went up to the Sierra. (The rebels were sure, incidentally, that two members of the group were not really journalists—in other words, they were CIA or the equivalent.)

Fidel was cautious in his claims to the newspapermen, and Raúl taxed him with it afterwards. "Now we have eighty men," his brother said. "When we have five hundred we can do a lot more; when we have five thousand we can conquer Cuba, and when we have fifty thousand we can stand up to the United States."

The basic, unending antagonism toward the "Yankees" was always there. Fidel Castro went out of his way recently to show that his resentment had begun early and never ceased. At the Salón de Mayo in Havana, during a conference of the Organization of Latin American Solidarity (OLAS), in July 1967, a greatly enlarged reproduction of a handwritten letter from Fidel to Celia Sánchez, dated June 1958, was hung prominently on the wall. It read:

DEAR CELIA:

When I saw rockets firing at Mario's house, I swore to myself that the Americans were going to pay dearly for what they were doing. When this war is over, a much wider and bigger war will begin for me: the war that I am going to launch against them. I am saying to myself [*me doy cuenta*] that this is my true destiny.

The Mario mentioned was a peasant in the Sierra Maestra. The rockets came from a Batista plane but, of course, had been bought in the United States. When I asked Fidel about the letter, in October 1967, he laughed. "You see, Draper was wrong. I haven't changed," he said.

The reference to Theodore Draper was caused by my having reminded him earlier in our conversation of Draper's well-known dictum that Fidel "promised one kind of revolution and made another." This, of course, was not only Draper's judgment but that of the numerous Cuban refugees, the U.S. State Department and the American press. It was based to a large degree on a choice of certain pledges made by Castro while he was still in the Sierra Maestra, plus misjudgments and misconceptions on the part of many Cubans and Americans whose wishes, as well as sincere beliefs, fathered the thought that Fidel would and could make a democratic revolution—or not make a revolution at all.

Contacts with Cuban Communists began in 1958. By July, when one of the veteran leaders, Carlos Rafael Rodríguez, joined the rebels in the Sierra Maestra, there was mutual acceptance between the PSP and the 26th of July Movement as well as with other parties and movements. To call this a "Castro-Communist Alliance," as Draper does in his book *Castroism,* is misleading. Fidel was never anti-Communist, but welcomed support from all quarters, right and left, as far back as Mexico.

In 1958 the Cuban Communists became his followers; they never, despite the widespread belief, became his masters. The picture that was invariably drawn in the United States in the early years of the revolution was of a naïve Fidel Castro being swallowed up by the clever, experienced Cuban Reds directed from Moscow. It was false. In reality, those who believed this were naïve. They did not know Castro or they would have realized that nobody, in or out of Cuba, was ever going to swallow him alive. This, incidentally, could also be said of his brother Raúl, and of Che Guevara. Fidel embraced the Communists, but as events proved, he was at all times the master in the Cuban house.

In *Revolution in the Revolution?* Régis Debray puts forward an interesting thesis (pages 105–06). He points out, correctly, that at no time in the Sierra did the rebels try to form a political party:

> It has been said with dismay that the party, the usual instrument for the seizure of power, was developed *after* the conquest of power. But no, it already existed in embryo—in the form of the Rebel Army. . . .
> Under certain conditions . . . the guerrilla force is the party in embryo.
> This is the staggering novelty introduced by the Cuban Revolution.

The important point about this is that Fidel Castro and his followers were not interested in politics when they were in the Sierra; they were concerned with fighting, surviving and winning the war. The Cuban politicians, the professionals, the emigrés in Miami and Caracas, quarreling, arguing, drawing up plans for the future government, sending representatives up to the Sierra Maestra, were bewildering and extraneous factors for the rebels. They were a burden that had to be accepted in the circumstances, from Fidel's point of view—people and parties with whom he would have to get along after victory. At that period, accepting what he accepted and promising what he promised, Fidel truly was naïve—as he conceded in conversations I had with him years later.

There was a stream of manifestos, platforms, programs, pamphlets, talks on the radio and so forth coming out of the Sierra from Fidel Castro in 1957 and 1958. These, Draper argues in his book *Castroism,* were what the Cuban people thought Castroism to be. This is debatable. What "Cuban people"? How could anyone make a coherent program out of the confusions and contradictions flowing out of the Sierra? And here is Draper himself saying (page 52): "There is no such thing as Castroism per se. . . . The inspiration and source of authority of the Castroite tendency is Fidel Castro, not the Soviet leadership, Mao or anyone else."

This is true. Analyzing the documentation of the Sierra Maestra is frustrating and—what is worse—a futile exercise in scholarship.

It is legitimate to sketch out some broad lines of policy that recur often and that give a general tone to what Castro thought, or said, he would do. The promise of popular elections, for instance, was a reiterated pledge. A general sense of a revolution to be made in a democratic way—free press, free speech, return to constitutionalism, and so forth—also emerges from the flood of words. At the same time, there were clear enough indications that Castro's aims could not be achieved without a genuine revolution.

It can be argued that he should have realized what would have to be done to make the kind of revolution he always had in mind—and so should the Cubans and all of us. However, of all the revolutionary leaders of modern times, only Hitler outlined his program and stuck to it. Lenin did not know how he was going to make his revolution, and neither did Mussolini. As Fidel once said to me, "The same things happened in the French, Russian and Mexican revolutions."

Mao Tse-tung was a Communist when he led the Chinese

Revolution and he had a party line to follow. Fidel Castro was not a Communist when he fought for and began his revolution, and he simply did not know how he was going to do it. At times, up in the Sierra, he thought he knew, but operating as he did without an ideology, without the assurance of unhampered power when the time came, without experience of any kind—political, economic, administrative—how could he have been expected to create a coherent system labeled "Castroism," and then follow it through after achieving power?

In the military field he used what strategy and tactics he could in achieving his goal of defeating Batista. In the political field he also used what strategy and tactics he could in achieving his goal of social revolution. But in neither case was his goal hidden.

There were many leaders in the civic resistance movement who, for their part, thought that they could dominate a post-Batista government and in that respect they were being no more honest toward Fidel Castro than he was toward them. It is always forgotten by Castro's critics that a struggle went on within the anti-Batista movement and that Fidel maneuvered for power against those supporting him in the resistance and in exile, just as they maneuvered for positions from which they could restrict, or even control, Fidel and his 26th of July followers.

Men like the economist Felipe Pazos, the educator Raúl Chibás of the Ortodoxo party, ex-President Prío Socarrás, Antonio de Varona of the Auténtico party, the lawyer Dr. Miró Cardona, and others surely realized that Fidel's ideas were more radical than theirs and that he was going to be a hard man to dictate to. He proved that much when he was still in the Sierra Maestra. In the struggle for power and position, Fidel Castro was cleverer, stronger and shrewder than they were, although they were experienced politicians and men of affairs and he was a young amateur in every respect.

It should not be forgotten, either, that in referring to the urban resistance as if it were entirely composed of middle-class citizens now in exile, anti-Fidelistas are talking and writing nonsense. The most daring leaders—Armando Hart, Faustino Pérez, Haydée Santamaría, Melba Hernández, Fauré Chomón, José Llanusa and many others in Havana and Santiago de Cuba—were middle class Fidelistas of the 26th of July Movement; and they have not defected.

Batista's counter-terrorism made the last year or more of the insurrection a horrifying passage in Cuban history. Boris Goldenberg, who is very anti-Fidelista and has the extraordinary idea that the revolutionary aims were "primarily political and not social," puts what happened succinctly (page 144): "The police tortured and murdered, the army competed with the police, and pro-Batista armed bands like Senator Masferrer's 'Tigers' vied with both."

Fidel Castro's worst enemies have to admit that in the Sierra Maestra his guerrilla force at all times acted with humanity. The prisoners he took were well treated, their wounds attended to, and they were then released or turned over to the International Red Cross. The rebel prisoners taken by Batista's troops were, with few exceptions, killed, and generally after torture. The same was true of the young people caught by Batista's brutal police, even before the *Granma* landing. The rebels treated the peasants of the Sierra, and later elsewhere, with respect and kindness and always paid for the food and other things they took.

All this is on record. The cynical can argue that Fidel Castro gave these orders so as to present to the nation a contrast to the brutality, torture and killings of Batista's counter-terrorism. Knowing Fidel, I find it much more plausible that, aside from his shrewd calculation of the publicity and morale value of such behavior, he was responding to the genuine and typical Spanish *caballería* of his character. He is very tough, as I have said, and he can be hard, fierce and unforgiving, but there is not an iota in his character of the cruelty that Spaniards have often displayed in history.

This is equally true of the later revolutionary period. The executions that so horrified Americans were never preceded by torture as in the Batista regime. Fidel has been harsh and unrelenting about political prisoners, but they are treated decently and there has been an elaborate "rehabilitation" system in recent years.

This is not offered as an excuse for holding thousands of political prisoners—which is an abhorrent policy in any country and the ugliest feature of the Cuban Revolution—but simply to keep the record straight and also to throw another beam of light on Fidel's character.

President Batista made one last and determined offensive to wipe out the Rebel Army starting on May 24, 1958. Considering the overwhelming superiority of his forces in men, arms of all kinds, airplanes and even his navy, which landed a battalion on the southern coast on June 15 behind the rebel lines, he should have succeeded—and probably almost did—in gaining his objective. It was by far the biggest and hardest-fought campaign of the war, and those who have written blandly—as almost all the American commentators have—of the collapse of morale and the undermining of the Batista army from within conveniently overlook this very desperate period for Castro's force of about three hundred armed men. Had Batista won, there would have been no talk of his army's morale and, of course, no Cuban Revolution.

In this campaign, as at the Bay of Pigs invasion, Fidel Castro was to show a capacity for military leadership of a high order. He had, of course, seen the preparations for the offensive and pulled in all his rebel columns from the south and center of Oriente Province to the zone surrounding Pico Turquino. In all, he had six of his eight columns with him, Number One directed by himself as the overall commander, and the others by his trusted *comandantes,* or majors, who were then hard-bitten and experienced fighters: Juan Almeida, Camilo Cienfuegos, Che Guevara, Ramiro Valdés and Crescencio Pérez. They set up a thirty-kilometer perimeter.

Batista's forces started moving in from the plains in two columns about five miles apart. They had to climb over the foothills and through narrow valleys, deep gorges and roadless jungle. Small rebel detachments were able to harass them all along. However, with the landing on the coast, the Batistianos closed in on Castro's forces near a village on the western slopes of Pico Turquino called Santo Domingo.

On June 19 they attacked at several points in what was to prove the decisive battle of the insurrection. The key objective was Santo Domingo. From what I heard from some who fought there, it was nip and tuck for three or four days, but the rebel lines held. On June 29 Fidel launched a counterattack which shattered the force of the most hated Batistiano officer, Lieutenant Colonel Ángel Sánchez Mósquera, who was wounded but escaped with most of his two battalions.

The fighting went on through July, but Castro was growing stronger every day, using his interior lines of communication and his knowledge of the enemy's plans. The Batista forces were too extended; the planes could help little; casualties mounted, along with exhaustion and discouragement. By mid-August it was all over. Fidel had 443 prisoners, whom he turned over to the International Red Cross, many captured tanks, mortars, bazookas, rifles, machine guns and a great deal of ammunition.

Clearly, Batista and his regime were finished. At least it should have been clear; but, amazingly, it was not to the stubborn and amateurish American ambassador, Earl E. T. Smith, and therefore to the Government in Washington, which did not understand the situation. Smith had two well-informed, intelligent and experienced staff members in Havana, whose advice he ignored—John Topping, the political counselor; and Richard Cushing, the public-affairs officer. They had kept Smith informed of the true state of affairs—as they had his predecessor, Arthur Gardner—but neither ambassador would pay any attention.

The Cuban Communists were not that stupid. They saw the writing on the wall and began their moves to get on the Fidelista bandwagon.


Castro lost no time. On August 21, 1958, he signed a general order detailing Che Guevara to lead two columns of seventy to eighty men each across to Las Villas Province in the center of the island. Camilo Cienfuegos commanded the second column under Che. It was an adventure of extraordinary hardships and danger, dogged by treachery and carried through only because of Che's

indomitable will and courage and the support, under equally difficult conditions, that Camilo gave him. In a dispatch to Fidel that
tells simply and vividly of their trek, Cienfuegos wrote that in
thirty-one days they had eaten eleven times, once "a mare, raw
and without salt."

It was a bedraggled, exhausted and reduced rebel force that
reached the Sierra de Escambray on October 6. (Che and Camilo,
incidentally, had retraced the march of Generals Gómez and
Maceo in 1895 during the War of Independence.) There they were
joined by the small and sometimes mutually contending forces of
the other little guerrilla groups who had been operating in those
mountains, and it was from this base that Che Guevara was to lead
the rebels to their final victory.

On November 3 Batista held a farcical Presidential election in
which one of his men, Dr. Andrés Rivero Agüero, was "elected."
The United States Government accepted the results. Neither Fidel
Castro nor the by then overwhelming civic resistance movement in
the cities paid any attention. One of our more egregious Congressmen, Senator Ellender of Louisiana, was quoted by newspapermen
in Havana as saying on December 12, 1958, "Is there a revolution
here? I hadn't noticed any trouble."

Fidel, incidentally, as late as 1966, insisted to me that "the
Havana resistance hardly helped me at all." It did help, as a matter
of fact, with money, arms and—most of all—in the myriad ways
in which it undermined the morale of the armed forces and the
Government. However, Fidel is undoubtedly right in contending
that the resistance was inspired and sustained by the guerrillas and
that nothing done by the civic opposition could ever have sufficed
to overthrow the Batista regime.

This is especially true because the powerful industrial unions of
the Confederation of Cuban Workers (CTC) were led by men
chosen, paid and bribed by General Batista. The head of the CTC,
Eusebio Mujal, an ex-Communist turned Auténtico and then
Batistiano, became a millionaire during Batista's regime. Naturally, he and his cronies who headed the federations and unions
had no sympathy with the rebels in the Sierra or the resistance in
the cities. Therefore, there could be no general strike until those

who could do so (Mujal was one of them) had fled from Cuba with Batista.

Fidel and his brother Raúl began an offensive toward Santiago de Cuba on November 7. There was no collapse of the Batista forces at that end of the island.

The push that sent Batista flying came from Guevara and Cienfuegos, who began to move toward Sancti Spiritus on December 20, capturing it on the 24th. Then they drove on to Santa Clara, which fell on the 29th. This was the deciding blow for General Fulgencio Batista. At 2 A.M., January 1, 1959, he and those he wanted to save from certain death flew to the Dominican Republic, where they were by no means welcome to the worst dictator of them all, Generalísimo Trujillo. Shortly before he left, Batista had made a last effort—which American Ambassador Smith backed—to turn over the armed forces to Major General Eulogio Cantillo, but nothing could stop Fidel Castro. Cuba was at his feet.

All that has happened since has temporarily blurred the memory of Fidel Castro's extraordinary accomplishment and has tarnished his image in the eyes of many Cubans and Americans. Yet his feat was a true epic, without parallel in the Western Hemisphere. The civic resistance, granting the vital role it played, was based on *his* resistance in the Sierra Maestra; on his symbolic figure of courage, endurance and faith; on his agonizing struggle which started with a dozen men and ended with no more than eight hundred guerrillas.

There was a remarkable intelligence behind the insurrection in the Sierra, a capacity for leadership, a flair for publicity, a toughness and an unassailable self-assurance that should have forewarned friend and foe alike.

Such a man was not going to be just another Latin American *caudillo,* another Fulgencio Batista, a compliant tool or partner of the colossus 90 miles away, or a puppet of Moscow. Fidel Castro had lived and fought all his adult life for a true social revolution and nothing would shake his determination or deny him his goal if he lived. All that could change was the way the revolution would be made under the bruising pressures of Cuban and foreign realities.

I saw Fidel in January and February of 1959 and it was so obvious that he missed the Sierra Maestra, its camaraderie, its simplicity, its clear-cut daily problems! In 1965, Lee Lockwood was with the revolutionary leaders at El Uvero and an evening was spent during which all of them reminisced about the Sierra Maestra. As he wrote in *Castro's Cuba* (page 80):

After a round of tales had extracted its last chuckle, there was a lull, and then I heard Celia say, her low, husky voice throbbing in the darkness as though in reverie: "Ah, but those were the best times, weren't they? . . . We will never be so happy again, will we? *Never. . . .*"

# 5 THE REVOLUTION BEGINS

A HUMAN being and a nation making a revolution go through a process that is the reverse of mechanical. It is necessarily dynamic, opportunistic, a course of trials and errors. A social revolution is a gradual and very painful development, which over a long period of time loses its impetus, slows down, gradually starts a new process, loses its dynamism, its extremism, its spirit, its early leadership. There is, finally, a new stability, and the revolution is over—but in all true modern social revolutions the cycle takes a great many years.

The process transforms the country in which the revolution occurs. In a great many fundamental ways, Cuba will never again be what it was in the first six decades of the Republic. For good or ill, Fidel Castro has revolutionized Cuba.

These simple facts—which are really truisms—are stated here because so many Cuban exiles, for understandable, emotional reasons, do not accept them, and also because the United States State Department, for political reasons, chooses to ignore them.

As the Oxford dictionary states, a revolution comprehends

"complete change, turning upside down, great reversal of conditions, fundamental reconstruction, especially forcible substitution by subjects of a new ruler or policy for the old."

"It is a quality of revolutions," Abraham Lincoln said in a speech in 1848 when he was a Whig Representative, "not to go by old lines, or old laws; but to break up both, and make new ones." But how?

A library of books, articles, pamphlets, speeches, white papers and the like was built up in the early years of the Cuban Revolution, telling Fidel Castro how he could and/or should have made his revolution. But it was *his* revolution, and he—with his loyal associates—had to make the formidable adjustments and changes in the face of enormous and unceasing obstacles and under fierce pressures that came within Cuba and from across the Florida Straits.

At the same time—I mean, from Fidel Castro's point of view, of course—he had to consolidate power for himself and the group of young men and women who had fought with him and whom, alone, he could trust. And he and those around him were very young (at thirty-two Fidel was one of the oldest) and completely inexperienced in every aspect of government administration, economics and finance.

In the course of doing all this, he had to hold the Cuban people together in support of him and his revolutionary program. Of all the things Fidel Castro has had to do, perhaps this was the hardest, for by character, traditions and history Cubans were never united, never in favor of their governments, an individualistic, emotional, refractory people whose great virtues did not include civic responsibility.

Lee Lockwood, in his book (page 141), quotes Castro as saying:

In Cuba, people had been talking so long about revolution and revolutionary programs that the ruling classes paid no attention. They believed that ours was simply one more program; that all revolutionaries change and become conservatives with the passage of time. As a matter of fact, the opposite has happened to me. With the passing of time my thought has become more and more radical.

"There is something strange in revolutionary processes," Castro was to say on August 30, 1966, in a speech to the Confederation of Cuban Workers (CTC):

"Revolutionary processes have two facets: one is the theoretical facet and the other is the practical facet. One is revolutionary theory, which inspires and guides the struggle of the oppressed, and the other is what revolutionaries practice. It is the task of making the revolution from the seat of power.

"When one agitates from a barricade, when one issues a revolutionary proclamation, it all looks easy from afar. . . . Yet the most difficult task is the task of creating a new society. The most difficult task is to convert ideas into realities. Ideas have countless interpretations, a number of overtones. And stop to think what a revolution is at the outset. . . . It is a struggling, working beehive of men who, though filled with good intentions, lack experience, lack knowledge, lack training. And suddenly, there is thrust on the shoulders of these men the task of making the nation move forward, administering everything. . . .

"And if I were asked what was the principal merit of a generation that undertakes a revolution, my reply would be: having made the revolution and having marched forward despite their great ignorance. . . .

"All revolutions are very complex processes, very complex. . . .

"I have no objections to repeating today what I said when I was nothing more than an ignorant man on January 8, 1959—an ignorant man with an enormous responsibility on my shoulders, with enormous authority in my hands—when we descended, victorious, from the mountains."

These words of Fidel Castro were wisdom after the event. When he found himself catapulted into power in January 1959, he was consumed by his customary euphoria, his unbounded assurance and confidence. I remember a conversation I had with him soon after his triumph. We were strolling in the grounds of a villa he had taken over for himself at the little fishing port of Cojímar (the scene of Hemingway's *The Old Man and the Sea*). When I remarked to him that the tasks he was going to take over now were infinitely more difficult than anything he had faced in the Sierra Maestra and that the power he held could do great harm as well as great good to Cuba, he stopped, turned to face me, put his hands on my shoulders and in an almost bewildered fashion asked, "But how could *I* do harm? We have the most wonderful plans for Cuba!"

Alas! as Jean-Paul Sartre was to write, it was a case of *"les enfants au pouvoir."* They were all so young, so "ignorant," as Fidel was later to confess.

Revolutions invariably change character as they take hold. "The most awe-inspiring lesson of the French Revolution," Professor J. L. Talmon wrote in his book *Political Messianism* (page 295), "is not that men with their deliberating reason can make a revolution, but that the revolution plays havoc with men." As he rightly pointed out, Robespierre, Barère, Danton, Marat, Saint-Just—the Jacobins—were driven into the Reign of Terror "irresistibly like sonambulists."

Hannah Arendt, in her book *On Revolution* (page 44), puts the problem well:

> What appeared to be most manifest in this spectacle [of the French Revolution] was that none of its actors could control the course of events, that this course took a direction which had little if anything to do with the willful aims and purposes of men, who, on the contrary, must subject their will and purpose to the anonymous force of the revolution if they wanted to survive at all. This sounds commonplace to us today, and we probably find it hard to understand that anything but banalities could have been derived from it.

"Commonplace," indeed! Perhaps to scholars like Hannah Arendt, but not to the numerically small but qualitatively powerful Cuban "middle class" whose members soon became victims of the Castro Revolution; or to the American press, the American public which it misinformed, the American State Department which naturally reacted in alarm and resentment against what was happening, or, of course, to the American business and financial world that saw some $800,000,000 or more in investments in Cuba going down the drain.

So, the loud cry was "The revolution has been betrayed!" No one asked, "Which revolution? Whose revolution? Who was betrayed?"

It may be useful, at this point, to call attention again to the situation in Cuba at the end of the Batista dictatorship, because of the great emphasis placed by the hostile American critics on what a "prosperous" country Cuba was. No one was in a better position to know the true facts than Rufo López-Fresquet, Castro's first Minister of the Treasury. His book *My 14 Months with Castro* was written in exile and is critical of the Castro regime. He writes (page 10):

> When Batista fled in January 1959, seven years after his seizure of power, social and economic conditions had worsened. The rural per capita annual income $91.25. Of the rural families only 11 percent drank milk and only 4 percent ate meat. Thirty-six percent of the country people suffered from intestinal parasites and 14 percent from tuberculosis. Forty-three percent were illiterate, and 88 percent of those who had gone to school had not passed the third grade. Sixty-six percent of the rural houses had dirt floors; only 2.3 percent had running water, and only 9.1 percent electricity.
>
> In May 1956, only 62.2 percent of the labor force was totally employed.

Fidel Castro had to do a lot of things in those early months of the revolution, but it is obvious that from his point of view he had to consolidate power for himself and his like-minded associates if he was to make the kind of revolution that he had in mind. The first Government, which he once claimed to me he had no part in choosing, was composed of moderate, middle-class, liberal—all, incidentally, middle-aged—men of exemplary character and patriotism and all with an immaculate anti-Batista record.

To mention some, there were the first Prime Minister, Dr. José Miró Cardona; the Minister of Foreign Affairs, Roberto Agramonte; the Minister of the Treasury, Rufo López-Fresquet; the Minister of Public Works, Manuel Ray. There were other officials like Felipe Pazos, president of the National Bank of Cuba; businessmen like José M. Bosch of the Bacardí firm, and publicists like Miguel Ángel Quevedo of the magazine *Bohemia,* all of whom were among the best types of Cubans and who nevertheless had to go.

Castro told me that he disapproved of some of the government members but he, personally, had chosen the President, Dr. Manuel Urrutia, of whom he later disapproved most of all.

It was obvious to anyone in Havana in the early weeks—and I was there—that Fidel could not keep his anomalous position outside of the Government, merely "reorganizing the armed forces." I will always remain puzzled as to whether he really thought he could be a Cuban Cincinnatus, as he earnestly told my wife and me one day, but it is not beyond reason. He did not at first enjoy the bewildering, utterly strange mass of problems that was dumped into his lap.

"Fidel was not at all happy about it," Teresa Casuso wrote in her book (page 167). "In my presence he reminded Celia [Sánchez] that it was she who had insisted on his accepting the post. He went through with it, but unwillingly, for it brought more responsibility and restricted even further his cherished sense of personal freedom."

Fidel does have a convenient—almost innocent—capacity for self-deception. He was quite capable, with one side of his nature, of feeling that he should stand aside and, with another side, of being driven to seek and hold the primary place of power. It was typical of him that, once having taken the premiership, he should have had the most wildly optimistic ideas about what he was going to achieve.

"If we go ahead with the plans that we have made," he said in his television speech on the night of February 16 (quoted in Selser's book, page 252), "and we will carry out all these plans if traps are not laid for us, I am sure that in a few years we will raise the Cuban standard of living above that of the United States and Russia, because those countries invest the greater part of their economic resources in making war matériel. . . ."

In any event—and of this there can be no question—Fidel had no choice but to take over the premiership. Everyone turned to him with every kind of problem. There were two governments in Cuba, one centered in the President and the Cabinet, and the other wherever Fidel Castro happened to be—and he never was in the same place any given day or night.

The situation became so impossible for Prime Minister Miró Cardona that he resigned on February 13. Fidel Castro was sworn in on February 16 as Prime Minister, and from then on—whatever he might have thought before—he set out to eliminate every member of the Government and to replace each with a man of his own. It took fourteen months, at which time Treasury Minister López-Fresquet finally resigned.

> Pe.haps no man has ever reached the Presidency under circumstances more difficult than mine [Dr. Urrutia lamented in the book he wrote afterwards, *Fidel Castro and Company, Inc.* (page 31)]. I had only nominal power; all real power, political and military, was in the hands of Fidel Castro. He was supported not only by his personal prestige but by his revolutionary organization, by the Rebel Army, and by popular fervor. Nevertheless, I was ready to collaborate loyalty with the Revolution and with Fidel Castro in accomplishing everything he had pledged to the people.

However, according to Treasury Minister López-Fresquet, Urrutia was sabotaging the revolution long before he was forced out. For one thing, he delayed signing bills. "His conduct disrupted the functioning of the Government," so that on July 17, when he was forced out, the Cabinet "offered no opposition to his overthrow [page 48]."

The thesis of "betrayal of the revolution," put forward by Cuban liberals and exiles, by the United States Government, and by scholars like Draper, is based on the assertion that Castro failed to deliver—in Dr. Urrutia's phrase—*"everything* he had pledged to the people."

That phrase is reached by choosing from Castro's pledges those that referred to liberal and democratic policies—elections, free press and speech, free judiciary, the Constitution of 1940, and so on. It is a formidable list which, taken by itself, would have given Cuba a reform government of a democratic type.

During the long and valuable series of interviews with Castro reproduced in his book, Lee Lockwood asked Fidel (pages 144–

45) about his having gone back on his promises of many "democratic reforms." Fidel replied:

> Yes, that is true, and that was our program at that moment. Every revolutionary movement, in every historical epoch, proposes the greatest number of achievements possible. If you read the history of the French Revolution, you will find that the first aspirations of the revolutionaries were very limited. They even thought they would maintain the monarchy, but in the course of the revolutionary process they did away with it.
>
> If you study the history of the Russian Revolution, you will find that the first programs of the Bolshevik party were not strictly socialist programs. . . .
>
> No program implies the renunciation of new revolutionary stages, of new objectives. . . .
>
> I told no lies in the Moncada speech ["History Will Absolve Me"]. That was how we thought at the moment. . . .

Fidel had also—and always—pledged himself to other than liberal democratic policies. These included the basis of a real social revolution: redistribution of wealth, equality of opportunity for all citizens, agrarian reform, independence from foreign domination—a revolution, above all, for the workers and peasants. He did not "betray" this revolution; he made it.

It would have been hard, in February 1959, to find anybody of importance in either Cuba or the United States who believed that Fidel Castro would become a dictator. He surely did not think so himself—as either a possibility or a necessity. However, once Castro became Prime Minister, it is true that President Urrutia's powers, which were never great, dwindled into insignificance except for the opportunity his position gave him to play an uncooperative and, at times, negative role. He had been caught in a revolutionary torrent in which he could only be carried along until the time came to be tossed ashore, high and dry.

When Dr. Urrutia realized his predicament, his only explanation was that the Communists—and he later included Fidel Castro in that category—were to blame. He never grasped the fact that he was involved in a drastic and radical social revolution in which Communism was one casual and by no means deciding factor.

First came the revolution; then came Communism, but Communism in the service of the Cuban Revolution.

Men like Manuel Urrutia—high-minded, sincere, honest, patriotic—could not serve Cuba because they could not serve the kind of revolution Fidel Castro was determined to make. It was, in fact, impossible for these men to accept it and be themselves. As a journalist, I can understand their dilemma and their personal tragedy. I could not work at my profession in a country which did not have freedom of the press. Cuba was not my country, but it was theirs. So Cuba lost their services and, as the months passed, the services of many thousands of civil servants, businessmen, bankers, managers, technicians, teachers, doctors, lawyers, and the like. It was a grievous loss from which Cuba has not yet recovered, but no one can doubt that, in accepting this loss, Fidel Castro saved his revolution.

He had spent his last days in the Sierra Maestra feverishly preparing for an assault on Santiago de Cuba, where Major General Elogio Cantillo commanded the garrison. The General agreed in a parley on Christmas Eve to deliver the garrisons of Santiago and Bayamo, but instead flew to Havana. Fidel was to hear the news of President Batista's flight on New Year's morning over Radio Rebelde. His forces immediately moved into Santiago de Cuba, where there was virtually no resistance.


On Jan. 2, 1959, Fidel began a slow, wildly triumphant and joyous procession across the length of Cuba to Havana. It set the whole island aflame with a fervor which he was to use with extraordinary skill in making his revolution.

Meanwhile, law and order were being restored by members of the 26th of July Movement and the Rebel Army. There was no mob vengeance, as there had been after Machado's flight in 1933 or as had taken place in Caracas, Venezuela, a year before, when the hated dictator, General Marcos Pérez Jiménez, was overthrown. The explanation in Cuba was that Fidel had pleaded on the radio for restraint, and promised that justice would be meted out to "war criminals" by revolutionary tribunals.

One of the telltale signs that Castro was intending to take power for his own 26th of July group was his refusal to recognize or even confer with Colonel Ramón Barquín who, with other political prisoners, had been released from the Isle of Pines prison and gone to Havana. Barquín had headed a military plot against Batista in April 1956, well before the *Granma* landing, and he was the most respected figure in the regular armed forces opposed to the Batista regime. Fidel, instead, put Che Guevara and Camilo Cienfuegos in charge of Havana pending his arrival. Barquín soon faded into insignificance and later joined the militant exiles.

What then happened was within the pattern, or "anatomy," of that kind of revolution and also within the framework of all Latin American history. Fidel instinctively and naturally followed what has been called "the Jacobin tradition" of creating a centrally governed, unitary nation.

I had flown to Camagüey in central Cuba with my wife to meet Fidel as he made his slow journey in a popular delirium westward to Havana. We had experienced the wild joy and barely restrained ferocity against Batistianos in the capital after the General fled. In Camagüey and along the highway we were to sense the over-whelming surge of popular emotion that was going to leave Fidel Castro no choice but to become his country's *Jefe Máximo*. No other man, no other party or movement, could hold any leading place in Cuban hearts and minds in those early days and weeks. Power—absolute power—was forced upon Castro.

Professor Richard Lowenthal, the British journalist, in an article on the Russian Revolution of 1917 published by *Encounter* in October 1967, points out that as early as the October Revolution Lenin realized the necessity of rejecting "any legal limitations on the revolutionary power."

> Yet after victory, and especially with the spread of civil war, the creation of a new, revolutionary army, police, and bureaucracy became imperative if the Soviet regime was not to follow the Paris Commune also on the road to defeat. The new, professional state machine had to be staffed with reliable cadres at least in the key positions; and in the conditions of party dictatorship, reliable cadres could only mean Bolsheviks.

Fidel was never—not even in 1968—to permit a "party dictatorship"; but substitute his own tried and trusted *barbudos* for Lenin's Bolsheviks and the situation was almost exactly parallel in Cuba, both in the problem faced and in Castro's reaction to it. Yet I doubt very much that Fidel Castro gave a thought to Lenin in the process. He was following a natural revolutionary procedure, adapted to his personal position and to Cuban conditions.

In a paper on Castro published by the *Political Science Quarterly* of June 1962, Professor Frank Tannenbaum of Columbia University, one of the best-known Latin-Americanists in the United States, discussed the Cuban and Latin-American attitude toward the political leader:

> The leader has exclusive power of government. All the power had belonged to Batista, and when he was gone there was no army, no police, no judiciary, no congress, no one and nothing to substitute for the government that had vanished like a dream—evaporated like a fog. There was only Castro, the new leader, coming out of the mountains, who suddenly found himself possessed of all the authority formerly exercised by Batista.

This is an oversimplification, and it was by no means as easy as that for Fidel Castro, but the Latin-American tradition of "personalism" certainly operated in his behalf. One has to understand that tradition to grasp the extraordinary appeal that Fidel has in Cuba. I wrote about it in my book *Cuba* (page 29):

> The leader, the dictator, the military chieftain (the Spanish word is *caudillo*) does not have to be, and rarely is, the embodiment of ideal qualities like a George Washington or an Abraham Lincoln. He is different, unique, special, commanding. For his followers, his right to rule is in his stature as a "hero," and he may even attain that stature by defying the law and the constitution of his country. A leader whose supreme virtue is to be like a vast majority of the population has no attraction for Latins.

Since Fidel Castro is such an outstanding example of the charismatic leader, I cannot resist one other quotation, which comes from Reinhard Bendix's book *Max Weber* (page 303):

> Since charismatic leadership occurs most frequently in emergencies, it is associated with a collective excitement through which

masses of people respond to some extraordinary experience and by virtue of which they surrender themselves to a heroic leader. . . . The charismatic leader is always a radical who challenges established practice by going to "the root of the matter." He dominates men by virtue of qualities inaccessible to others and incompatible with the rules of thought and action that govern everyday life. People surrender themselves to such a leader because they are carried away by a belief in the manifestations that authenticate him. They turn away from established rules and submit to the unprecedented order that the leader proclaims.

It would be hard to find a more apt description of Fidel Castro. The man was like that, and the Cuban people "turned away from established rules"—but by no means all of them, and not without much travail and agony. What can now be expressed in philosophical terms was then the birth pangs of a new society.

The degree of disorganization in Cuba at the beginning of 1959 and all through that year was almost unbelievable.

In a letter I wrote to my wife from Havana, on July 4–5, 1959, I said:

The whole trouble, to simplify it, is disorganization, amateurishness and incompetence and it all centers around Fidel and his character. Like everybody, Rufo [López-Fresquet] stresses how good a man Fidel is, how good his intentions are, how much he wants to do what is right, etc. However, he is too untrained, inexpert and impractical to grasp what has to be done and how to do it. He thinks that when he signs a decree the thing is done. He is so disorganized that there are, said Rufo, 800 to 1,000 decrees lying in his office, piling up daily, that he can't even be induced to sit down and sign. When Rufo [who was Treasury Minister] got his tax reform all worked out it took him twenty days to get to see Fidel to present it! Moreover, if Fidel wants something he is convinced he knows more than the experts or he feels the experts should work things out willy-nilly the way he wants them. The young men are all yes men. . . .

There is no question of Fidel's enormous popularity, as I felt and kept on feeling all day yesterday. I was at the Ambassador's [Philip W. Bonsal] 4th of July reception and met at least fifty people, mostly Cubans and important ones whom we know, and their pride, joy and adoration of Fidel are just unbounded.

On July 7 I wrote about speaking to the director of Ambar Motors, the largest automobile import firm in Cuba. He told of the Castro Government's ordering 150 Japanese jeeps and paying for them immediately.

> He said in wonder, "And it did not cost us a cent." In other words, no bribes, no graft. This is the first time in Cuban history such things are happening—but who tells the American public anything good?
>
> I'll try to work that into a piece, as it is typical, and also mention the virtual end of gambling, hoodlums, the efforts to suppress the drug traffic, the school building program.
>
> The American colony . . . is incredibly bitter about this setup, but they were Batistiano and I suppose it is not incredible. However, it is doing Fidel a lot of harm in the United States. They will never become reconciled.
>
> I am making progress, but Fidel has not been in Havana since I arrived. He is gadding about the country on the agrarian reform. . . .

(I have seen Fidel Castro often since writing that letter and the last time—in October 1967—I could still write that "he is gadding about the country on the agrarian reform.")

Incidentally, in my letters on that trip I told how the wives of political prisoners in Havana came to see me about husbands who were in jail for six months without trial—and no civil courts to try them. Also about a landowner we knew in Oriente who had been outrageously treated. In fact, we knew of many such cases in those early months.

> They say [I wrote] that Oriente, outside Santiago, is being mismanaged by ruffians, bandits and in some cases Reds, and I believe them. They agree that the young people we all see and hear about, Fidel included, mean well, and want to clean up such situations, but they can't get to them; they have so many other things to

do. This is the typical disorganization of a revolution, and I am sure that in time it will be cleaned up since it is contrary to what all the leaders want, but how long will it take and how much damage will be done beforehand?

Revolutions break lots of hearts that don't deserve to be broken.

The lack of technicians is a most serious feature of the Cuban situation [I wrote in my notes on a trip to Cuba in November 1959]. There are so many amateurs at work everywhere in Cuba and at all levels—inexperienced, untrained but enthusiastic, honest, patriotic and hardworking. . . . The new men have a basic distrust of existing interests, a suspiciousness toward advice from interested quarters, an approach that is more theoretical than practical, a disdain for orthodoxy, an indifference to individual suffering or injustice if it is for what they consider the good of Cuba.

I spoke to Fidel about the injustices on a trip I made to Cuba in March 1960. He replied, "I know that there have been abuses. I know that properties have been seized without inventories and in some cases without proper justice. This comes from the fact that we have had to use young, inexperienced men. We have had to improvise, to learn as we go along by trial and error. This is true of our whole revolutionary process. There are many amateurs in the Institute of Agrarian Reform lacking efficiency and with too much zeal. I try to do as much as I can, but I have innumerable things to do. I cannot do everything. I cannot watch everything."

The Sierra Maestra crowd, in those months, was irritated by the growing influence of the Cuban Communists who had sabotaged them most of the time during the fighting days and at best had been unhelpful. However, Fidel already had his convictions about the need for "unity" and he found the PSP men, with their experience and discipline, to be useful.

What I did not fully realize in that first year or two (I know of no one who did) was that Castro was using the Communists; he was not being victimized or taken over by them, nor was he taking orders or even advice from Moscow. That became clear later on, but since it suited Fidel's purposes to give the Cuban "Old Guard" Communists considerable leeway and since his international policies were linked to the Communist bloc, the picture was befogged and distorted for years.

A development that was to damage Fidel Castro's image in the United States came at the beginning. It was the execution, after the most summary trials by revolutionary courts, of some six hundred so-called "war criminals." These were men who were attested, by previous open knowledge or by families of the victims, to have been torturers, killers and brutal persecutors on behalf of the Batista regime.

"The foreigner, especially the North American," wrote López-Fresquet (page 68), "put his emphasis on the legal aspects of the revolutionary trials. The Cuban was interested in moral justice."

I know of no cases where innocent men were executed, but the rough, swift justice that violated every Anglo-Saxon idea of fair trial outraged the American public and press. For Americans, without too much exaggeration, the history of Cuba began on January 1, 1959. Batistianos had killed—generally after torture—to a horrifying extent for two or three years, but there had been no American protests.

Even if the then popularly accepted figure of twenty thousand victims of the Batista regime was greatly exaggerated, the fact that *Bohemia* could publish the names of more than a thousand persons assassinated by Batista was bad enough. Many gruesome photographs were also published. There certainly were many more than a thousand victims.

An overwhelming majority of the Cuban people approved of the trials and executions. Even President Urrutia, a former judge and a stern critic of Fidel Castro, approved (page 215 of his book). The executions, as I stated before, fulfilled a pledge that there would be justice, and it is for that reason, I am sure, that there was no mob vengeance.

Fidel was so sure that Americans, like Cubans, would understand the reasons for what he was doing that he invited American journalists to come to see a trial and execution—only to get the worst possible publicity in the United States. It showed his naïveté, and it also made him bitter against American newspapermen—a bitterness that he never lost. I would be the last to blame him for the way he feels, since I started saying in January 1959 that the coverage of the Cuban Revolution was the worst example of American journalism I had seen in my long career; but Fidel's attitude and his inability to understand how American journalism really works has done him and his revolution a great deal of harm.

The executions were based on a "law" Castro signed on February 11, 1958, in the Sierra Maestra. It was in the tradition of the Cuban wars of independence. What happened was understandable in terms of Cuban feelings at the time, as well as Cuban temperament, character and concepts of justice.

An attempt on my part to get *The New York Times* to publish an editorial that I cabled from Havana trying to explain the reasons for the summary trials and executions was rejected with great indignation by the publisher and editor. There was no question in my mind of excusing the methods being used, which were obviously open to the strongest criticism, but of trying to get Americans to understand.

That failure—which happened to be my first—was to prove typical. A lack of understanding then and there became a permanent feature of Cuban-American relations on both sides. Fidel's references to the United States in his speeches at the time were vitriolic, and American spokesmen, journalists and radio commentators replied in kind. A vicious circle of recrimination and counter-recrimination—and soon, of deed and answering deed—had been set in motion, never to cease.

The executions; the often harsh prison sentences, not only for Batistianos but for all "counterrevolutionaries"; the ruthless way in which those who lost or faltered in their loyalty to Fidel Castro were treated—these things show how tough the *Jefe Máximo,* as he began to be called, really was. Since very few Cubans and still fewer Americans knew him as an individual, this came as a shock. It should also have been a warning to the Cuban people and to the United States State Department.

*"Ceux qui font des révolutions à demi,"* said Saint-Just, one of the toughest of the French revolutionaries, *"ne font que se creuser un tombeau."* (Those who make revolutions by half measures are only digging a grave for themselves.) Fidel Castro did not make

that mistake. It was not because he was consciously being a Cuban Jacobin, or because he had read Mao Tse-tung's "thoughts" about a revolution not being "a dinner party." He was just doing what came naturally to him.

"There were individuals," he said in a speech at Havana University on March 13, 1966, "who took part in the revolutionary action about whom one wonders: when they were carrying out a revolution, what idea of revolution did they have? . . . Perhaps they wanted the country to go on as before."

In what I would consider much the best piece of work he has done on the Cuban Revolution—an article "Runaway Revolution" for *The Reporter* of May 12, 1960, written after the only trip he has been able to make to Cuba—Theodore Draper said: "When Fidel Castro entered Havana a conquering hero on January 8 last year, no one knew what he was going to do. It is doubtful that he himself knew, except in the most general terms."

This is true, but those "general terms" included a determination to make radical, structural social and economic changes in Cuba— in short, a revolution. Considering the heterogeneous composition of the mostly middle-class elements who made up the bulk of the civic resistance to Batista, some people, some interests, some classes had to be "betrayed." Even if Fidel had wanted to satisfy that vague, nebulous and mixed-up middle class, there was no conceivable revolution that could have avoided a "betrayal."

In the process, Fidel Castro would have truly betrayed the men and women who fought and suffered with him in the Sierra Maestra and the 26th of July Movement in the cities. He would have betrayed the peasants of the Sierra Maestra who helped him. He would have broken many promises he made other than those pledging a liberal democracy. He would have repudiated the ideals that he had held most deeply since his university days.

One of the greatest misconceptions about the Cuban Revolution is contained in the thesis postulated by Draper, the State Department and the Cuban exiles that it was "a basically middle-class revolution." It was not a middle-class revolution. It was not a proletarian revolution, because the workers were either passive or helped Batista. It was not a peasant revolution because the peasants of the Sierra Maestra—the only ones who took part—were not typical of the more sophisticated, better-off and partly industrialized peasants of the plain.

It was a social revolution of the type initiated by France in 1789. It was created, shaped and directed by Fidel Castro. The primary beneficiaries have been—in uneven degree—the peasants, the workers, the youth, the Negroes and mulattoes, the poor. The primary victims have, indeed, been the great bulk of the middle class which lost privileges, wealth, property, and saw their incomes and standard of living fall heavily if they stayed in Cuba.

And, of course, every Cuban lost his freedom—not only the middle class.

The revolution came in on a flood of talk. Those who laughed at Castro's ceaseless torrents of oratory were North Americans, not Cubans. Rhetorical skill was an important part of Cuban education and it is a greatly admired trait in public figures. Castro's marathon speeches were listened to, and they were effective. They were, in fact, a frightening reminder of Big Brother in Orwell's *1984*.

The television brought his glowing, bearded and tousled head and his hoarse, impassioned voice into every city, town and hamlet of Cuba. Oratory was an instrument of major importance to him. He exhorted, explained, reasoned, aroused and excited Cuba's millions. At the time I called it "government by television."

Fidel is a natural orator, a truly gifted one who eschews the tricks of rhetoric. There is no organization to his speeches, no structure, no text. He knows what he wants to say and improvises as he goes along, relying on his easy command and flow of language and on his magnetic personality to hold his audience and convey his message. Between television and radio he was reaching 90 to 95 percent of the Cuban people.

There are mannerisms, but they come naturally from his character. He can be—and often is—a rabble-rouser. Sometimes he is so carried away by his own eloquence that he makes promises and predicts accomplishments that are beyond the possibility of being realized.

His problem was not to win popularity—he had it to an incredible, almost hysterical, degree; it was to keep that popularity with one of the most fickle and individualistic people on earth, and to hold them at fever pitch so that they would accept his revolutionary policies and sustain the impetus that a revolution needs.

His first test—and he botched it badly—was with the agrarian reform of May 1959. This affected sugar, the basis of Cuban economy; the landowners, Cuban and American; the peasants and the semi-industrialized workers in the sugar mills and ports. In the economic field, agrarian reform was—and still is—the most important feature of the Cuban Revolution.

One could wonder that the Castro regime survived its errors in this field if it were not for the fact that this was a *social* revolution. Economics was not the primary factor in the early years; the social changes were.

Thus Fidel could—and did—slash rents 50 percent, ruining a relatively small number of real estate owners while rejoicing the hearts of their many tenants. Of course, the building industry was destroyed until the state could step in with public construction.

This is not the place to go into the details of what a mess Fidel Castro, Che Guevara and their associates made of Cuba's economy in the first years of the revolution. Draper, Goldenberg, Suárez, the U.S. State Department, and many other sources have done a thorough, fully documented and generally accurate job in this field. Their work is a vital part of the early history of the Cuban Revolution, although a less important part than they have believed.

Fidel knew—and I remember his agreeing with me several times in the first few years—that in the long run the success or failure of his revolution was going to rest on its economic performance. However, in those early years there was fat to live on—the huge value of expropriated properties and businesses, the accumulated inventories, and a certain amount of credits such as the $50,000,-000 or so he owed Standard Oil (Creole) in Venezuela and Royal Dutch Shell in 1960 when he took over their refineries in Cuba

because they would not (on Washington's advice) refine the
cheaper Soviet oil that Cuba was importing.

No one has described the major economic errors better than the
keen-minded and always frank Che Guevara. In his article in *International Affairs,* October 1964, Che wrote:

In its agricultural policy the Revolution represented the antithesis
of what had existed during the years of dependence on imperialism
and exploitation by the land-owning class. Diversification versus
monoculture; full employment versus idle hands; these were the
major transformations in the rural areas during those years. . . .

Our first error was the way in which we carried out diversification. Instead of embarking on diversification by degrees we attempted too much at once. The sugar cane areas were reduced and
the land thus made available was used for the cultivation of new
crops. But this meant a general decline in agricultural production.
The entire economic history of Cuba has demonstrated that no
other agricultural activity would give such returns as those yielded
by the cultivation of the sugar cane. At the outset of the Revolution
many of us were not aware of this basic economic fact, because a
fetishistic idea connected sugar with our dependence on imperialism
and with the misery in the rural areas, without analyzing the real
causes: the relation to the uneven trade balance.

Unfortunately, whatever measures are taken in agriculture do not
become apparent until months, sometimes years, afterwards. This is
particularly true as regards sugar cane production. . . .

The second mistake was, in our opinion, that of dispersing our
resources over a great number of agricultural products, all in the
name of diversification. . . .

Only a very solid productive organization could have resisted
such rapid change. In an underdeveloped country, in particular, the
structure of agriculture remains very inflexible and its organization
rests on extremely weak and subjective foundations. . . .

I have spoken of certain achievements in the industrial field
during the first years, but it is only just that I should also mention
the errors made. Fundamentally, these were caused by a lack of
precise understanding of the technological and economic elements
necessary in the new industries installed during those years. Influenced by existing unemployment and by the pressure exerted by the
problems in our foreign trade, we acquired a great number of
factories with the dual purpose of substituting imports and provid-

ing employment for an appreciable number of urban workers. Later
we found that in many of these plants the technical efficiency was
insufficient when measured by international standards, and that the
net result of the substitution of imports was very limited, because
the necessary raw materials were not nationally produced.

These errors were so elementary that one could gasp in wonder
that grown-up and well-educated men could have made them,
however economically inexperienced they were. But one has to
keep in mind the extent to which Castro and his associates dis-
trusted what they called imperialism and what they thought capitalism was. They had rejected the old world to create a new one. It
seemed so simple. In this respect they were children playing in a
grown-up world.

The critics, the victims and all those who longed to see Fidel
Castro driven out of power failed to take into account that however amateurishly he acted, this was a most formidable young man
with a keen intelligence and widespread popular support even
when things were at their worst. Besides, among his first acts had
been the creation of his own Rebel Army to replace the regular
forces that he destroyed; his own police force under a remarkable
companion who had been with him from Moncada days and who
is still Minister of the Interior—Ramiro Valdés; his own huge
militia; and a ubiquitous civic defense force that in the dangerous
early years provided delators to guard against counterrevolution.

No autocratic government, possessing such power *and willing to
use it,* can be overthrown except, perhaps, by the most massive
sort of popular opposition. This never existed, although Cuban
exiles and United States Government officials, especially members
of the misguided—so far as Cuba was concerned—Central Intelligence Agency, thought that it did.

Fidel Castro has to learn by trial and error—but he does learn.
His early, loyal and constant associates know that once Fidel has
developed a firm conviction on any subject, even if they know it is
a wrong or bad judgment, they had better go along with him at the
time and either try to talk him out of his position gradually or let

him change his own mind when he sees that he was wrong to begin with. In the latter case, someone else may get the blame, but the situation is rectified.

There was a civic resistance against Fidel Castro in the first few years until the Bay of Pigs disaster wiped it out once and for all. Small—but for months ineradicable—peasant and middle-class guerrilla forces of counterrevolutionaries operated in the Sierra de Escambray and in Las Villas and Pinar del Río provinces. The CIA arranged for the landing of some of these forces, and, as former Ambassador Bonsal wrote in his article for *Foreign Affairs,* ". . . anti-Castro guerrillas were receiving arms-drops from a source generally assumed to be a United States agency." The source could not have been anything else. It took what Fidel called a "systematic campaign" using peasant militiamen and the Rebel Army to check and then eradicate these counterrevolutionaries.

Moreover, Florida air bases were for a while being used freely by anti-Fidelista refugees, thus contributing to the mounting bitterness between Cuba and the United States. One incident in particular aroused a furor.

In June 1959, the first head of the Cuban Air Force, Major Pedro Díaz Lanz, defected and fled to the United States, where the witch-hunting Senate Internal Security Subcommittee gave him a public hearing so that he could tell the world that Cuba was being taken over by Communists. On October 21, having been furnished with a plane, he flew over Havana dropping leaflets calling Castro a Communist. Cuban antiaircraft batteries vainly opened fire, and, in all likelihood, it was their shells falling in the streets of Havana that killed two people and wounded forty-five.

The Government announced that Díaz Lanz had bombed Havana from an American air base, and on October 26 Fidel delivered a furious attack on the United States before a huge crowd.

This attack coincided with two other developments that had a profound effect on the revolution—a temporary one, in my opinion, but some authorities believe that those late October days represented a crisis and a turning point for Castro and the revolution.

Díaz Lanz had been a minor figure in the Sierra Maestra. Major Hubert Matos played a more important role as a column leader toward the end of the insurrection. Neither man belonged to the original close-knit group of youths who had been with Fidel Castro from Moncada and *Granma* days. This was of basic importance—and it was not understood in the United States or by the Cuban exiles. After the Matos affair, all the important appointments made in government, diplomacy and the economy were Fidel Castro's men, loyal to him, and they were his choices, not even those of his brother Raúl or of Che Guevara.

Major Hubert Matos had been made Commander of the Rebel Army in Camagüey Province. Matos had been one of the many middle-class Cubans (he had been a teacher before the revolution) who disapproved of the growing influence of the Communists. He said so openly in a speech on June 8, which had the approval of President Urrutia. Matos lumped the Moncada-Sierra group with the PSP Communists, although not one of the Castro group had been or was a Communist.

When Raúl Castro was named Minister of the Armed Forces in October, Matos offered his resignation. As Suárez says in his book *Cuba* (page 76):

> We know very little about the real aims of this [Matos] resignation. What we do know is that Fidel and his associates were certain that Matos was engineering a plot that would have taken most of his provincial military staff officers with him. Camagüey was a very sensitive region at the time, and Matos had made his move at a dangerous moment, before Fidel's power had been fully consolidated. Moreover, Castro was then working out his policy of "unity," which was neither pro- nor anti-Communist but which included the Communists in the power structure. Fidel, suspicious as always of the United States, feared that Matos was getting encouragement from the Americans. Anyway, as Castro said at the trial, Matos was "a false revolutionary."

In the circumstances, it was logical that Castro should strike and strike hard. He thought his revolution and his power were endangered—and they might well have been. At a trial in December that had more emotion than legality in it, Hubert Matos was condemned to twenty years' imprisonment, which he is now serving in the same Isle of Pines Presidio where Fidel went after Moncada.

The fierceness, implacability and disdain for impartial legality that Castro displayed in the Matos affair were characteristic of him, but it has to be recognized that in the Hubert Matos case, and always, a revolution makes its own laws.

October and November had been very difficult months for Fidel. On October 19 he lost one of his most trusted, loyal and cherished companions—Camilo Cienfuegos, whose airplane disappeared with him in it on a flight from Camagüey to Havana. Because neither the plane nor the body were ever found, Castro's enemies had the chance—and they still use it, as Andrés Suárez and Dr. Urrutia do, for instance, in their books—to hint at some sinister machination on Fidel's part.

Camilo Cienfuegos was one of the most colorful and popular of the Cuban revolutionaries. He was the son of exiles from the Spanish Civil War. His father had been an anarcho-syndicalist in Spain. His brother Osmani, according to López-Fresquet, was a "card-carrying Communist." After his brother's death, Osmani was named Minister of Public Works, succeeding the far more able Manuel Ray, who went into exile and plotted against the regime.

> Camilo became the spoiled darling of the masses [López-Fresquet wrote in his book (page 58)]. Power delighted him; he loved women, songs and wine. He had a charming personality and was too popular for Fidel's peace of mind. Fidel became increasingly suspicious of Camilo's loyalty.
>
> Camilo began to visit the fashionable clubs and became increasingly friendly with the wealthy playboys of Havana. I do not believe he had played a significant political role. . . . But his disappearance and presumed death made him a great martyr of the revolution.

In other words, Camilo Cienfuegos was an early example of the *dolce vita* disease which became so serious by 1966 that Fidel Castro cracked down and punished even so close and valuable a friend as Efigenio Almeijeiras, whose Sierra Maestra record, like Camilo's, was of the first order.

I saw Fidel in November 1959, and found him very much upset about the Matos affair, but, as I wrote in my notes at the time, "He is more depressed about Camilo than anything else that has happened."

Hubert Matos was one of two disastrous choices—from Fidel

Castro's point of view—that he himself had made. The other was Dr. Manuel Urrutia, the first President. He was eliminated from office by a demagogic stunt of which Machiavelli would have approved. I do not know that Fidel's reading included *The Prince* and the *Discourses,* but as Professor Richard M. Morse of Yale University wrote in an article for the *Journal of the History of Ideas* of January 1954: "On nearly every page of Machiavelli appears practical advice which almost seems distilled from the careers of scores of Spanish American *caudillos."*

The last straw for Fidel, so far as Dr. Urrutia was concerned, came in a television interview that the President gave to Luis Conte Agüero of the CMQ station on July 13, 1959. In it, Dr. Urrutia said that the Communists had done "horrible damage" to Cuba. He praised Castro, which implied that the Prime Minister was anti-Communist. Moreover, Dr. Urrutia made no secret of the fact that in his speech at the forthcoming July 26th celebration he was going to make another attack on "the sinister Red doctrine."

Early in the morning of July 17—on the television, of course—Fidel announced his resignation as Prime Minister. The reaction—both spontaneous and organized—was naturally pro-Castro and anti-Urrutia. That night the President naïvely hoped he could go on the national television to defend and explain himself. Instead, it was Castro who appeared once more.

In his book, Dr. Urrutia claims that he had offered three times to resign. A Cabinet Minister with whom I discussed this snorted in disdain and asked, if that were so, why it had been necessary to call a special meeting of the Cabinet on July 17 to demand the President's resignation. López-Fresquet mentions only one resignation—on the last day.

Dr. Urrutia, however, concludes his chapter on "The *Coup d'État* of July 17th" with these words:

> I asked protection from no one; it was granted me [in the Venezuelan Embassy] only because it suited Castro's purposes. I limited myself to presenting my fourth resignation, and left the Presidential Palace, in effect a prisoner.

A bulletin issued a week later by the Information Office of the Presidential Palace asserted that it had become necessary to effect social and economic adjustments "for which the President would not have been suitable." The President, it continued, had "become a dead weight on undertakings which the Government had to carry out."

This was true, simply because Dr. Urrutia, however honorable and patriotic his intentions were, neither understood nor approved of the revolution as Fidel Castro was making it. In a phrase I have heard Castro use about a number of similar cases, Dr. Urrutia was "not a revolutionary."

When Fidel announced in the Sierra Maestra his impulsive choice of Judge Urrutia for provisional President, he made an error. On the other hand, Castro never made a better choice in the whole course of the revolution than in his second candidate—Osvaldo Dorticós Torrado.

It was immediately pointed out by critics that Dorticós, as a law student, had been a PSP (Communist party) organization secretary in his home town of Cienfuegos. He was not a party member, so far as anyone has been able to find out, and he certainly was not a Communist when he became President. Like Fidel, for whom he has worked so effectively and brilliantly, he had nothing for or against Communists or Communism as such, and he agreed with Castro's policy of bringing the Cuban Communists into the whole structure of the revolution.

This included the Confederation of Cuban Workers (CTC), founded in 1939 under Communist leadership. However, the Communists were forced out during the Presidencies of Grau San Martín and Prío Socarrás, so that when the Castroites took power and the Batista leaders fled or went to prison, the CTC was non-Communist.

In a book called *Elites in Latin America,* edited by Seymour Martin Lipset and Aldo Solari, there is a description by Henry A. Landsberger (page 271) of what happened:

> If there ever was a test case of what labor's allegiance would be under genuinely free conditions, it was probably in Cuba in the eleven months following the fall of Batista on December 31, 1958. Despite the superior experience of the Communist leadership, the *Frente Obrero Humanista,* the labor sector of Castro's 26th of July movement, which was radical but anti-Communist, gained the vast

majority of the union elections held in 1959. The anti-Communist Castro groups were in solid control of the CTC by the time its Tenth Congress was called in November 1959. A "unity" slate containing the names of the three Communists was rejected by the Congress; a second one, with no Communists, approved. The later purge of anti-Communist leaders was a government inspired activity, not a spontaneous move on the part of labor.

Fidel had personally intervened at that November Congress to urge that the "unity slate" be elected. He was not concerned about what the trade union leaders wanted; he was determined to "unify" all phases of the revolutionary structure—and, of course, he got his way. When the Communists, in their turn, went too far and tried to monopolize the whole CTC, they were slapped down. Trade union officials in Latin America are almost always the equivalent of government officials.

Fidel Castro, in any event, was reaching for the mass of the industrial workers, not union leaders who could be hired and fired, or even—as happened to Fidel's first choice as head of the CTC, David Salvador—thrown into jail. In the same way he was reaching for, and getting, peasant support.

Professor Zeitlin, in *Revolutionary Politics and the Cuban Working Class* (page 277), concluded after his impressive personal interrogation of many industrial workers all around Cuba that: "The workers' active and armed support of the Revolutionary Government has been decisive in the consolidation and defense of its power."

So far as the peasants are concerned, I would agree with the conclusions in *Elites in Latin America* (page 334):

> The Cuban experience, like that of China and Vietnam, shows clearly that under revolutionary and very coherent ideological direction, or under international circumstances which encourage the expansion of the objectives of the revolution initiated for more limited purposes, that the peasant class can become a genuine ally and most rigorous supporter of a deep and total revolution.

The process of consolidating power in the hands of Fidel Castro and his loyal revolutionary supporters went on through 1959 and 1960. The primary emphasis was on loyalty in order to have the power to make the revolution. Thus, in November 1959, Fidel ousted the expert Felipe Pazos as head of the National Bank of Cuba and supplanted him by the utterly amateurish Che Guevara. Bankers, after all, are not revolutionaries; Che was a revolutionary, and he was loyal to Fidel.

There was method in this madness. When Fidel Castro and his even younger associates came into power, they looked around and then back at their history. They saw the social imbalances—the few wealthy and the many poor; the unending, shameless corruption; the tragic farce that their Cuban variety of democracy and their so-called democratic elections represented; the capitalism that enriched a small minority and left the majority in misery; the domination of their economy and their very system of life by the United States, a foreign power; and they said, "If this is democracy and capitalism, we don't want them."

Of course, it really was not democracy and it was not capitalism as it exists in the United States, Great Britain or Western Europe. But it was too late to argue.

There was a built-in antagonism to the United States. The Cuban rebels came down from the Sierra Maestra with their special resentment against the United States for having helped Batista and sold him the arms that were used against them. There was a powerful nationalism which—as in all of Latin America—took a xenophobic, anti-Yankee form.

From the beginning, from the hostile American reaction to the execution of "war criminals," and especially after the agrarian reform law of May 7, 1959, Fidel and his associates were convinced that the United States was determined to frustrate and, very soon, to destroy their revolution.

In reality, Washington tried to be forbearing and patient in the early months under great provocations. As former Ambassador Bonsal wrote in the *Foreign Affairs* article:

> The American reaction [to the agrarian reform] was friendly and understanding. Our legitimate preoccupation with the compensation of our citizens was reflected in discussions with Cuban officials over a period of months, during which the possibility of long-term bonds was contemplated. Most of the confiscation and other arbitrary actions of the Cuban authorities regarding the agricultural property of foreigners and Cubans had no sanction in the law.

This was the rub. The agrarian law was considered Communistic, but, in reality, the Cuban Communists had opposed anything so radical and impractical.

Professor Ernst Halperin, in his foreword to Andrés Suárez's book (page vii) correctly points out that the author's

> documentation shows that all the measures that were decisive in transforming Cuba's capitalist, free-enterprise system into a Communist command economy—agrarian reform, urban reform, nationalization of foreign and domestic enterprises—were taken without consulting or even informing the PSP; that in each case the PSP leadership was caught by surprise and hurriedly had to adjust its policy to the new situation.

Castro's obsession with "unity" did not mean that the Cuban Communists had any role in making government decisions.

The agrarian reform law was what Fidel Castro wanted it to be, and since it did not work, he changed it, and then changed it again, and in 1968 he was still refashioning details. This is how Fidel Castro works. How were Americans, with their Anglo-Saxon, orthodox, democratic mentality, supposed to understand a Fidel Castro or approve of a revolution that did them and the United States so much harm? A drastic revolution in Cuba was inevitably going to damage American property and business interests in Cuba, and American influence in the Western Hemisphere.

"An important element in the United States reaction to Fidel Castro was his attack on America's illusions of her innocence and omnipotence," Professor Robert F. Smith of the University of Rhode Island wrote.

North Americans are always pained and indignant when the historic, all-pervading, never-ending emotion of anti-Yankeeism manifests itself in Latin America. They thereupon take refuge in the thought that the Communists are to blame. This is a dangerous delusion. Fidel Castro was anti-Yankee long before he became a Communist.

The question of whether the situation had to deteriorate to the point of irreconcilable conflict is a complicated one, incapable of proof and, in any event, academic.

The intensity of American hostility toward Fidel Castro and the Cuba he represented reached and sustained a pitch of emotionalism which was without parallel in American history in peacetime. It is still an extraordinary phenomenon that cannot fully be explained by the obvious facts, or the dangers, or the element of Communism. Certainly, the attitude of the United States Government, Congress, the press, business interests and public opinion—after the brief honeymoon in early 1959—drove the Cubans farther away.

"We did not force them into the arms of the Soviets," Philip Bonsal writes in his *Foreign Affairs* article, "but we were, in my judgment, unwisely cooperative in removing the obstacles in their chosen path." That is a good way of expressing it.

In Alexander Werth's biography of de Gaulle (Penguin edition, page 340), after referring to the sweeping nationalizations and expropriations of the newly independent Algeria, he says that "the French Government showed striking patience and restraint—which produced from Fidel Castro the remark to Ben Bella: 'How lucky you are! If only *we* had a de Gaulle in the United States.' " He could also have written a Franklin D. Roosevelt, who took the Mexican oil expropriations with good grace. Fidel had Dwight D. Eisenhower and his big-business Administration. He also had American hysteria about Communism.

Fidel Castro made his one and only—and rather famous—trip to the United States while Premier in April 1959, at the invitation of the American Society of Newspaper Editors. As it happened, the visit was fated to have no effect on either side. President Eisenhower pointedly went off to Georgia to play golf before Castro arrived, but it was not an official visit. I do know (as I saw Fidel in Washington and New York) that he was satisfied with the non-results and the extraordinary public interest he aroused.

He had instructed his Treasury Minister López-Fresquet, and Felipe Pazos, president of the National Bank, not to ask for a loan or to seek a trade agreement.

When Castro finally told us that we were not to ask for aid [Treasury Minister López-Fresquet wrote in his book (page 106)], we were indeed surprised. I asked him why he was giving us an order that would take away the reason for our presence on the trip.

"Look, Rufo," he said, "I don't want this trip to be like that of other new Latin American leaders who always come to the U.S. to ask for money, I want this to be a good-will trip. Besides, the Americans will be surprised. And when we go back to Cuba, they will offer us aid without our asking for it. Consequently, we will be in a better bargaining position."

It was a period of uncertainty in Cuba and a time when his policies were in flux.

"We want to establish in Cuba a true democracy, without any trace of Fascism, Peronism or Communism," he said in a press conference in New York on April 23. "We are against every kind of totalitarianism."

This was naturally interpreted at the time as anti-Communism. As later events proved, it simply meant that he was not going to let the Cuban PSP take power away from him, and that he had not, in April 1959, decided to make a government that was both Communist and totalitarian. He was seeking solutions and, in fact, he still is.

In that period, Fidel and the 26th of July Movement hit upon an idea and a word that seemed to them to embody what they had in mind: humanism. It was too vague a concept to be formalized. Castro was using phrases like "bread and liberty" and "liberty with bread and without terror." These, in retrospect, were an ironic reminder of the question asked by the Grand Inquisitor in Dostoevski's *The Brothers Karamazov*: "Why must man choose between freedom and bread?" The answer is that mankind "will understand at last that freedom and bread enough for all are inconceivable together."

An oft-quoted remark of Castro's, published in the Havana *Revolución* on May 22, 1959, was that "capitalism can kill man with hunger, while Communism kills man by destroying his freedom." However, since "humanism" was linked to liberal, democratic, non-Communist policies, it could not long survive the steady drift toward authoritarianism.

It was in 1960 that the Eisenhower Administration wrote off Fidel Castro and his revolution as hopeless. It was not known until

General Eisenhower admitted it later that in March 1960 he had authorized the training of a Cuban exile invasion force. On July 6 of that year, President Eisenhower suspended the Cuban sugar quota, and on December 19 he cut it off permanently. In retaliation, Castro nationalized the American sugar mills in Cuba in August 1960, and within three months he had expropriated what was left of American investments. Something like $800,000,000 or $900,000,000 had been swallowed up, and there has not been a cent of compensation paid to date.

It will be recalled that sugar is the mainstay of the Cuban economy. The United States bought 40 to 60 percent of its sugar from Cuba under a quota system which fixed amounts and prices —prices generally a few cents above the world market so as to protect American sugar producers and also to receive Cuban tariff preferments for American goods. Financially, it worked well for Cuba—and for the great American sugar interests in Cuba—but it is understandable why Che Guevara should have said that the system "amounted to slavery."

On August 7, 1960, the U.S. Department of State issued a 78-page White Paper on "Responsibility of the Cuban Government for Increased International Tension in the Hemisphere." It listed all the "democratic" promises that Castro had made in the Sierra Maestra—separation of powers, free elections, individual freedom, free trade unions, free press and radio, a free judiciary, and the like. It then detailed the growing Communist power, the closer relations with the Soviet bloc, "the interventionist activities in the hemisphere," the military buildup and "economic discrimination and aggression."

The State Department staff must have had an easy time preparing this long arraignment, which was mostly true so far as it went. However, it was a polemical document, selective in its choice of material, misleading in many ways, and a distortion of the true picture. Such documents, and books of a similar nature, served at the time as sticks with which to beat a regime that was an obvious danger and nuisance to the United States and to the governments of Latin American countries. Moreover, the Cuban regime was an offense to all who believed in democracy and feared Communism.

There were—and are—aspects of the Cuban Government and

the revolution that are utterly distasteful to a liberal who believes in individual and civic liberties, who dislikes dictatorship and any kind of totalitarianism. It was a bitter disappointment to all of us who hoped that Fidel Castro would and could work out his problems in a more or less democratic way without a break with the United States, when we saw him take the road of Marxism-Leninism.

Like so many Cuban and American well-wishers in the first year of the revolution, I spent much wasted time and breath arguing with Fidel against Communism as a system and against allowing the Cuban Communists and Moscow to become such strong factors in his regime.

Rufo López-Fresquet, Fidel's Minister of the Treasury, quotes Fidel as saying of me in July 1959, "I am sick and tired of that old man who thinks he is my father. He is always giving me advice."

Of how many people he must have said that in the first few years! He rarely took advice, as I have remarked before, but this did not become quite clear until the end of 1959. American Ambassador Philip W. Bonsal had to learn that lesson. So did the Russian ambassador, and Moscow, too. And so did experts like Colonel Bayo, who gave guerrilla lessons in Mexico, and the French agrarian specialist, Professor René Dumont, whom Fidel called on—and then paid no attention to his advice. At least, one has to say that Fidel Castro makes his own mistakes.

I was in Cuba in August 1960, at which time I found Ambassador Bonsal convinced that Fidel had every intention of provoking the United States to the limit—and beyond. As 1961 was beginning, he demanded that the United States reduce the embassy staff in Havana to the same number that Cuba had in her embassy in Washington—eleven. Within a few days, President Eisenhower broke diplomatic relations with Cuba. One can safely say that they will not be resumed so long as Fidel Castro is Prime Minister of Cuba.

On that trip to Cuba I wrote in my notes:

Those struggling here with this revolution are like a man buffeting the waves. He cannot see the ocean. He struggles with daily reality; the tide of history sweeps him along but he is not conscious of it. The last thing he can be is detached, objective, unemotional, academic, history-minded.

A revolution is an ugly thing, like a civil war or a surgical operation. It must keep going, must have dynamism, can never stop. It is like a fire. It blazes so long as there is something to feed on, but sooner or later it must go out. In the meantime, Fidel has to keep throwing things on the fire to make a good blaze, and nothing is so inflammable as Yankee imperialism.

# 6 THE ROAD TO MARXISM

COMMUNISM WAS not a cause of the Cuban Revolution; it was a result. More foolishness was said and written along Fidel Castro's path to Marxism-Leninism by ill-informed journalists, demagogic Congressmen, angry and myopic United States Government officials and ponderous scholars than about any other phase of the Cuban Revolution.

The critics were right in saying that Marxism-Leninism was forced upon the Cuban people. There were enough Cubans in favor of it—or indifferent, ignorant or powerless—so that it could be done. Communism would never have been voted in, nor would the trade union leadership or other elements have become Communist by choice. Most Cubans followed Fidel Castro and trusted him.

Cuba was the first—and is thus far the only—country in the world to become Communist of its own accord after its leaders had taken power. In all the others—Russia, the countries of Eastern Europe, China—the governments were taken over by men who were already Communists. Cuba is also the only Communist nation detached from the geographically solid Sino-Soviet bloc, and she is, of course, the only Communist country in the Western Hemisphere.

It was the pressure of problems and events, not the inept, small and bungling Cuban Partido Socialista Popular, nor the cautious, diffident but generally contented Soviet Union, that brought Castroite Cuba into the Communist camp.

"People who say that Fidel and the others must be Communist because of what they are doing," I wrote on a trip to Cuba in November 1959, "overlook the fact that whether they are Communists, anti-Communists, fellow travelers or pro-Communists, they would be doing exactly the same things."

However, on this aspect of the Cuban Revolution as on all others, the decisive factor was Fidel Castro—his character, his ideas, his development, his actions. He became a Marxist-Leninist of a special Cuban, Fidelista type; therefore the revolution became Marxist-Leninist.

At the beginning, appearing on the American television program *Meet the Press* during his trip to the United States in April 1959, Castro could honestly say, "I am not a Communist, nor do I agree with Communism." But he could have added something very significant: "Nor do I disagree with Communism."

Fidel went to Buenos Aires from the United States to attend a session of the Economic Assembly of the twenty Latin-American countries plus the United States. At this meeting, on May 2, 1959, he made a characteristically long speech which, if taken literally, offered the last chance for the United States and Latin-American Governments to keep Castro within a more or less democratic, certainly non-Communist, hemispheric framework.

The address, at least, was that of a democratic leader. In it he made two striking proposals.

In one of them he pointed out that the United States, thanks to its powerful economy, could aid the Latin American countries far more than it was doing.

"If we can solve our economic problems," he said, "we will have established the basis for a future, humanistic democracy on the basis of liberty with bread for all peoples, which is the highest aspiration to which men can aspire. . . . The experts of the

Cuban delegation have calculated that the economic development of Latin America will require a financing totaling thirty billion dollars over a period of ten years."

A figurative roar of laughter went up in all communications media from the Canadian border southward. The American delegation dismissed the idea with amused contempt. But less than two years later, President Kennedy put forward the proposal for his Alliance for Progress, pledging $10 billion for the first ten years. Later President Johnson promised another $10 billion to continue the program.

The second important idea that Castro advanced was to point out that in Latin America "many industries cannot be established for lack of a market or because the market is insufficient. Therefore we arrived at the conclusion that it is necessary to amplify our market. How? Why, by selling in a Latin-American common market."

The suggestion was ignored—but in the spring of 1967 a hemispheric economic conference was held in Uruguay where the big decision made was precisely to create a Latin-American common market—without Cuba, of course. (The text of Castro's speech is to be found in Selser, pages 307–23).

It is futile to speculate on what might have happened if Fidel Castro had been taken seriously at Buenos Aires, but it is worthwhile to note that Castro's suggestion for huge United States financing implied an appeal to Washington for economic aid— something he avoided doing while in the United States.

Moreover, Javier Pazos, then in the Cuban Ministry of Economics and a member of the delegation to Buenos Aires, later wrote (in *The New Republic,* January 12, 1963) that Fidel

> was very mad at the [Cuban] Communists because they had brought out their militia in the May Day celebrations. He expressed himself in very strong words about them in his rooms at the Alvear in front of Celia Sánchez—his most trusted confidante—Botí [Ambassador to the United Nations] and myself. At one point he said that if they kept on pushing him, he would take a plane to Havana and finish them off before public opinion, his most effective weapon at that time.

When Fidel Castro got back to Havana from Argentina, he may have dealt with the Communists on the quiet. Outsiders, especially North Americans, thought that the Cuban Communists were manipulating him.

Milorad M. Drachovitch of the Hoover Institute in California edited a book on *Marxism in the Modern World* for which he wrote an introduction. Two references to Cuba appeared apt to me (pages xii–xiii):

> China and Cuba never entered the minds of any nineteenth-century Marxists—and of very few in the first half of this century—as candidates for socialist preeminence, and the success of Communism in these two countries is hardly conceivable without the voluntarism of Mao Tse-tung and Fidel Castro. One could therefore say that the destiny of Marxism in our century is easier to explain in terms of Thomas Carlyle and his heroes than in terms of Karl Marx and his economic laws. . . .
>
> The originality of Fidel Castro lies in the fact that he, a non-Communist at the moment of seizing power, has hurriedly pushed Cuba along one of the most militant Communist paths while eliminating one after another, the Communist old guard. . . . Every Communist "ism" discussed in the following pages represents a huge effort made in the name of Marx but certainly not according to Marx.

"We began to construct socialism without knowing how socialism should be constructed," Castro said on September 8, 1964. "We knew what we wanted but we did not know how to get it." (This is quoted in Draper's *Castroism*, page 214.)

Fidel's words could, in fact, be applied to just about everything he did from 1959 onwards. He knew that he wanted to make a radical social revolution but he did not know "how to get it." His experiences gradually convinced him that the way to "get it" was to employ the Communist method.

One of the most often-quoted American official pronouncements on Fidel Castro's non-Communism in the first year of the revolution (I used it in my book *"The Cuban Story,"* and so did every-

body else) came from General C. P. Cabell, Deputy Director of
the United States Central Intelligence Agency in testimony before
the Senate Internal Security subcommittee in November 1959:

> We know that the Communists consider Castro as a representa-
> tive of the bourgeoisie and were unable to gain public recognition or
> commitments from him during the course of the revolution. . . .
> We believe that Castro is not a member of the Communist Party,
> and does not consider himself a Communist.

The CIA—which was soon to blunder so gravely on the Bay of
Pigs invasion—was right. It was courageous of General Cabell to
say it at a time when the hostility toward Castro in the United
States was at fever pitch and when nearly all Congressmen be-
lieved that Fidel was either a Communist or a prisoner of the
Cuban Communists.

Of the meeting of President Kennedy and Chairman Khrushchev
in Vienna on June 3, 1961, Arthur M. Schlesinger, Jr., in *A
Thousand Days* (pages 362–63) writes:

> Kennedy restated his thesis: change was inevitable, but war could
> be catastrophic in the nuclear age; both sides must therefore take
> care to avoid situations which might lead to war. As for miscalcula-
> tion, every leader had to make judgments; he himself had miscalcu-
> lated about the Bay of Pigs. . . .
> All right, said Khrushchev, but how could we work anything out
> when the United States regarded revolution anywhere as the result
> of Communist machinations? It was really the United States which
> caused revolution by backing reactionary governments: look at
> Iran, look at Cuba. Fidel Castro was not a Communist, but Ameri-
> can policy was making him one.

Khrushchev had said the same thing in September 1960 at the
United Nations General Assembly to an Indian journalist: "Fidel
Castro is not a Communist now, but United States policies will
make him one within two years."

It took less than two years though the United States did not
deserve all the blame. Yet Fidel could truly say, as he did in his
speech to the General Assembly on September 26, 1960: "On our
honor we swear that up to that time [1959] we had not had the
opportunity even to exchange letters with the distinguished Prime

Minister of the Soviet Union, Nikita Khrushchev. That is to say that when, for the North American press and the international news agencies who supply information to the world, Cuba was already a Communist government, a Red peril 90 miles from the United States, with a government dominated by Communists, the Revolutionary Government had not even had the opportunity of establishing diplomatic or commercial relations with the Soviet Union."

On February 4, 1960, Deputy Prime Minister Anastas Mikoyan had opened a Soviet trade mission in Havana, and before he left he signed a trade agreement with the Cuban Government whereby Moscow undertook to buy Cuban sugar for the next five years and extended a $100,000,000 credit at 2½ percent for the purchase of industrial plants, machinery and the cost of technical aid. Raúl Castro told me years later that the Russians also agreed at the time to supply Cuba with arms.

A whole series of relationships was set up by Cuba with the Communist countries during 1960 and the first part of 1961. In July 1960, for instance, there was a trade agreement with Communist China, and in September Cuba became the first Latin-American country to open diplomatic relations with Peking. By mid-1961 there were diplomatic and trade relations with every Iron Curtain country plus, for good measure, North Korea, North Vietnam and even the ephemeral communistic government of Gizenga in the Congo.

Every one of these moves plucked a feather from the American eagle's tail, as Churchill would have said. They were understandable and consistent policies within the Fidelista framework, but there was also an element of defiance and provocation on Castro's part.

The United States tried, at conferences and by using diplomatic pressures, to stir up all of Latin America against Cuba, but—except for frightened Central America—the attempt had little success. Most of the countries enjoyed seeing the Cuban David using his slingshot against the Yankee Goliath. It took the missile crisis to jolt them all into line—and even then Mexico refused to stay there.

The extent to which the Russians may have thought that Fidel

Castro and his Government would take orders or even advice from them cannot be known. Until recent years the Soviet-bloc countries were satellites of Russia. All the Communist parties were directed from Moscow until the split with Peking. Yet Castro could never have had any intention of letting the Cuban PSP or the Kremlin dictate to him—and they were not able to do so. Moscow made the best of a good enough bargain. The Cuban Communists took back seats and watched their Partido Socialista Popular melt away.

In a sensational dispatch to *The New York Times* on November 25, 1960, Max Frankel began by writing:

> The leaders of Cuba's Communist movement are confident that they have won the battle for Fidel Castro's mind and are striving, under his protection, to convert the Cuban people to their ideology.

The long article—whose information, according to Frankel, primarily came from Carlos Rafael Rodríguez—was undoubtedly a faithful reflection of how the Cuban Communists felt at the time, but it was completely misleading so far as Fidel Castro was concerned. Rodríguez, who was then director of the Havana Communist newspaper *Hoy,* quickly and frantically published a denial of the Frankel article. He said that it was the other way round—the Communists were following Castro.

I saw an American report written in April 1960, which still seems to me to have been a reasonably close description of the situation at that time:

> Communist adherents and sympathizers now occupy positions throughout the Cuban revolutionary government, many of them positions of great responsibility, and exercise significant influence on the course of Cuba's destiny. They have effectively made themselves felt at all levels of the Government and in the Cuban social structure as a whole. Following their traditional pattern, they are gradually gaining control in strategic areas such as public communications media, the armed forces, labor organizations and the national economy. Most of Cuba's top young revolutionary leaders, if not Communist adherents themselves, are at least sympathetically inclined toward Communism. . . .
>
> Up to now there are few signs, however, that the leaders actually fall within the Soviet discipline, that is that they receive and accept directives from the Soviet Union. They may, therefore, retain the

power to free themselves if they so wish. To date there has been no indication that such an effort will be made. On the contrary, an objective prognosis points to increasing Communist influence.

The phenomenon in Cuba of a large body of young, intelligent, able, strong-minded men and women—in no sense captured by their preexisting Communist party or by Moscow—turning toward Communism is one of the most interesting political and human aspects of the Cuban Revolution, particularly as it encompasses men and women of very different characters, temperament, education and careers.

Faustino Pérez, for instance, during a conversation in October 1967, told me he could not say when he decided that Fidel was right and that the Communist course was the one to take. Although he had worked as close to Castro, since Mexico, as anyone in the ruling clique, he said it was impossible for him to say when any phase of Fidel's thinking coalesced. He stressed how slowly Fidel's ideas developed—and this is something that Castro says of himself. There were no sudden conversions, so far as I know, among the Cuban leadership, and there was certainly no question of orders—sudden or otherwise—from Moscow. The drift into Communism, like the whole Cuban Revolution, was a process.

An American, a Briton, or a Western European of liberal mold has no difficulty in understanding why a Communist turns anti-Communist. One wonders how many have stopped to think why anti-Communists sometimes become Communists. Cuba would be fertile ground for such a study.

None of the leaders of the Cuban Revolution was Communist in the Sierra Maestra or at the beginning of the revolution. Men like Armando Hart, for years Minister of Education and now organizer of the Communist party of Cuba; Faustino Pérez, a very religious Catholic who left the government in distress in December 1959 because of its Communist trend and who came back to his present high position in the economy; Raúl Roa, who became Foreign Minister in the spring of 1959 and still has that post—these men were all anti-Communist. So was Celia Sánchez.

Many—like Fidel Castro, his brother Raúl, Che Guevara and President Dorticós—were non-Communist even though a few had had Communist links or Marxist ideas before the revolution. I know that in the spring of 1960 President Dorticós privately told an officer in the American Embassy that, "having been exposed to Communism, I now understand it and am firmly opposed to it."

The case of Raúl Castro needs explanation. I might first state that I have questioned Raúl about the Communist accusations half a dozen times. He always denied emphatically that he was, or ever had been, a party member. He repeated this to me as late as October 1967, when I last saw him.

I believe him, but Raúl's denials have to be taken in the strict sense of the word "Communist." Robert Merle, in *Moncada* (pages 119–22) claims that Raúl told him that for a month and a half in 1953 he did belong to the Socialista Universitario and, as such, was a party member.

According to Merle, this was after the famous trip Raúl made as a student to the Communist Youth Congress in Vienna in February 1953. He then went to Bucharest, Budapest and Prague. From the point of view of the Castro regime's enemies and of American propaganda this made Raúl at the least an ex-Communist, which was nonsense. Like innumerable youths from a great many countries, Raúl Castro accepted an invitation to go behind the Iron Curtain as an adventure.

Lee Lockwood questioned Fidel Castro about this matter and has the following passage in his book (page 144). It should be kept in mind that the words of Fidel in the book were taped and later checked by Castro for accuracy.

"You must remember, of course, that when I was in the mountains I was not a member of any Marxist party . . . ," Fidel says. "Neither was Che, whom I met in Mexico about a year and a half before the *Granma* landing, a member of any Communist party."

"Nor your brother Raúl, either?" Lockwood asks.

"Raúl, yes," Fidel answers. "Raúl, completely on his own, while he was a student at the university, had joined the Communist Youth. But it should be said that when he went to the Moncada attack, he was not behaving in a completely disciplined way, properly speaking."

"You mean he broke party discipline?" Lockwood asks.

"Exactly," Castro replies.

The question of Raúl Castro's "Communism" can, I believe, be disposed of once and for all. As a young student he had a very brief fling as a member of the Juventud Socialista (Socialist Youth), which was an affiliate of the Partido Socialista Popular, the Cuban Communists. But in a matter of weeks he had left them to join his brother's 26th of July Movement and he did not again become Communist until the entire Fidelista leadership moved into the Marxist-Leninist camp. However, it is doubtless correct to add that Raúl Castro had a tendency or urge to be pro-Communist where his brother was neither pro- nor anti-Communist.

Che Guevara's Communism was never more than formal, even at the end. As he said to me once, "I have no political coloration; I do not like to think in ideological terms, either Marxist or Communist." This, also, cannot be taken at face value. As Fidel said, Che never was a member of any Communist party. I am sure he had not bothered to study the writings of Marx or Lenin or anyone else. However, his revolutionary ideas placed him in a leftist position where he had to be socialistic and—in a popular sense of the word—Marxist. He did not influence Fidel Castro in an ideological sense, as was widely believed. His interest, in the Havana government, was to make a radical social revolution in the teeth of "Yankee imperialism"—but Fidel had those same ideas before Che Guevara.

"I have not been able to find a single document showing that Guevara was familiar with the classics of Marxism or could be identified completely with any Communist position before the summer of 1960," Andrés Suárez wrote in his book (page 39). He might have added, "And neither could the CIA."

The role of Che Guevara was greatly exaggerated in the formative years of the Cuban Revolution, even by such authorities as Theodore Draper. Che was not "the ideologist-in-chief"; he was not responsible for Cuba's economic policies; he was not the brain directing Cuban affairs; he was not an *éminence grise* or a power behind the throne.

Guevara was a loyal follower and intimate friend of Fidel

Castro. He had a keen intelligence, a sharp tongue and pen, and he often acted as spokesman for revolutionary policies. His mind was quick and he frequently foresaw developments and assumed, or was given, the task of foretelling what was going to happen.

Of course, he did influence Fidel, but this was because he was a close, respected companion, whose heart, mind and soul were dedicated to making a success of the revolution. At the height of his influence, Che was playing a secondary role in Cuba. There were times when Raúl Castro and, later, President Dorticós were more important figures than Ernesto Che Guevara.

The way Che faded out of the Cuban picture in April 1965, without any effect on the course of the revolution, was the best possible proof that he was neither dominant nor indispensable.

A typical American misunderstanding of Che's place in the Cuban Revolution can be found in Draper's book *Castroism* (pages 197–98):

> The relationship of Fidel Castro and Ernesto Che Guevara is one of the main keys that unlock the innermost secrets of this Cuban revolution. The personal impress of Guevara on the revolution may prove in some respects to be the equal of Castro's, despite the fact that Castro alone can carry the burden of making the final decisions. . . . Guevara has devoted himself to the deadly game of infighting for the levers of power and to the elaboration of a theoretical mold for the unfolding revolution.

In the autumn of 1964—months before this was written by Draper—Fidel and Che began working out the elaborate plans for guerrilla warfare in Bolivia. Che Guevara was bored and restless with desk work. He wanted to leave, and he did so in April 1965.

It is true that the similarity of ideas between Fidel and Che was always so great that one could not help wondering who was influencing whom. I believe one answer is to be found in the fact that Guevara's ideas on guerrilla warfare, expressed in his book on the subject, were merely a theoretical formulation of what Castro had done in the Sierra Maestra. Moreover, it is absurd to think of Che's doing any "infighting for the levers of power"—and least of all against Fidel Castro whom he worshiped.

Fidel's policy of "unity" meant that the Cuban Communists had to be included in every phase of the revolution. By extension, this implied that there should be no anti-Communism and, as a corollary, that anti-Communism represented counterrevolution. This development led to much internal ferment, the flight of many middle-class and anti-Communist Cubans (which brought about the Díaz Lanz case), and the dismissal or even arrest—as happened with Major Hubert Matos—of those who actively opposed the Communists.

Andrés Suárez, in his *Cuba* (page 55) gives as the first sign of Fidel Castro's policy a quotation from a television appearance that the Communist newspaper *Hoy* printed on July 4, 1959. On this occasion Castro said:

> Our position in regard to this problem of the Communists is very clear. It is that in my opinion it is hardly honorable for us to start campaigns and attacks against them just in order to prevent people from accusing us of being Communists ourselves.

Juan Marinello, nominal leader of the PSP, had said on the television as early as February 8, 1959: "Whoever raises the flag of anti-Communism is a traitor to the revolution." By the end of the year, Fidel had taken the same position, although his interest was in "unity," whereas the PSP rashly sought power for the Cuban Communists.

As Suárez writes (page 80): " 'Unity' in the Communist sense, that is, any type of collaboration with Castro that allowed the PSP to take part in decisionmaking, made no progress at all."

In fact, Carlos Rafael Rodríguez told me once that the Cuban Communists and Fidel Castro came very close to a break in relationship in the early months when they tried to persuade Castro to do things against his better judgment. This was especially true, as I have indicated, on the occasions when Fidel visited the United States and made his speech at the Buenos Aires economic conference. Rodríguez claims that he realized the danger and argued with his fellow party members that the revolution was going to be run by Fidel and that the PSP must go along with him—not vice versa.

One of the curious features of the early stage of the revolution was that *Fidelismo* was more radical than *Comunismo*. In the so-called "May Conclusions" reached by a plenum of the Central Committee of the PSP on May 25, 1959, there was this passage (cited by Suárez, page 61):

> We are a small country, situated only a very short distance away from the United States. The deformation of our economy through imperialist influence has made us very dependent on imports, even for the most basic foodstuffs of the people. In view of this, any leftist extremist tendency, any exaggerated measures . . . to be applied or implemented by the revolution, and any attempt to disregard the realities and the concrete difficulties confronting the Cuban revolution must be rejected.

The Communists "rejected" but Fidel Castro went right ahead. His agrarian reform of that same month was decidedly more radical than the program the Communists had advised. He was, indeed, a "leftist extremist."

Fidel, after working hard to get complete power, asked me wonderingly in reference to the American and the Cuban opposition accusations, "How can anybody believe that I will divide my power with the Communists?"

Of course, his Cuban enemies and many in Washington who should have known better believed that the reality was worse than a division of power; they thought that the Cuban Communists and Moscow were taking Fidel Castro captive. The ones who made the greatest mistake of all were the Cuban Communists, who believed that they were permanently gaining power at Fidel Castro's expense and that they would be running the government one day.

Blas Roca had less understanding of Fidel Castro than Carlos Rafael, as everyone calls Rodríguez in Cuba, but Roca kept enough detachment to save his skin and his position for the future. Both men were early "Old Guard" Communists, and, ironically, Rodríguez was a Cabinet Minister in Batista's 1940–44 Government. Both now have high posts in the Castro Government.

Carlos Rafael, who is personally very fond of Fidel Castro and has the highest opinion of his abilities, is especially close to the Prime Minister. He is a rare type for Cuba, a Communist intellectual familiar with the writings of Marx and Lenin. As a corollary, it can be added that Rodríguez and Blas Roca are also especially valuable to the Cuban Communists and to Moscow. They represent two big party feet still in the Castro camp.

It was impractical, on the part of Americans, to have expected Castro to turn on the Cuban Communists when they were supporting him and now approved of the Revolution. Fidel understandably was in a clash with the Cuban non-Communist moderates and the forces on the extreme right. The Communists were natural allies, useful and well-trained, and were the only political party— the PSP—that remained intact after the flight of Batista. All the other parties had been discredited, either by their collaboration with the Batista regime or by their internal dissensions.

It was clear to those who knew Fidel Castro and the situation in Cuba that he was in a position to crush, or chastise, the Cuban Communists any time he wanted to do so and that he would do it if they threatened his personal power, or if they got in the way of *his* revolution which was not *their* revolution. In fact, he was to slap them down hard in March 1962, and to do so again even harder early in 1968. However, he was certainly not going to turn on them in those early years when it would have seemed that he was doing so in response to United States criticism, threats or pressures.

A Cuban Cabinet Minister, still in office, told me during a visit to Cuba in November 1959 that Raúl Castro was fed up with the Cuban Communists. At a Ministerial Council, my informant asserted, Raúl had said that if the Reds got in the way of the revolution "he would slit their throats."

This did not mean—the distinction must always be made—that Raúl was being anti-Communist. He was furious with a specific group of PSP men who were trying to take the revolution away from Fidel and, by the same process, away from Raúl, Che Guevara and the Sierra Maestra group. What he said at the Cabinet meeting, however, does show that Raúl was not a crypto-PSP-Communist.

On returning from a brief trip to Cuba, March 6–13, 1960, I wrote a long, confidential memorandum, as I always did, for the publisher and the editors of *The New York Times*. Among other things I said:

I would like first to note the really burning resentment in Cuba against the bombing which takes place almost daily from the United States. . . . Every Cuban from Fidel downward is convinced that the United States is not making the efforts that should be made to prevent these bombings. I agree entirely with the Cubans on this point. . . .

"Put yourself in our place," Fidel said to me. "Suppose planes based on Cuba went over and dropped leaflets or even bombs on Washington. Suppose they bombed farms in Florida. Suppose we harbored men in our country and had elements in our Government who encouraged criminals and revolutionaries plotting to overthrow the United States Government. Suppose Cuban diplomats went around urging and even plotting to prevent other countries from selling arms that you feel you need for your defense. Suppose your economy was completely dependent on the unilateral decision of the Cuban Congress, swayed in some respects by forces hostile to your Government. How would you feel? How do you think Cubans feel?" . . .

In talking to Che, he argued that what we really feared is that Cuba should be completely independent of the United States economically as well as politically. I said no, that what we really feared was a drift toward Communism which would in time lead to a military alliance, a Red base or something approaching this, perhaps even a Communist government in Cuba.

"How is it that you do not fear Yugoslavia; and, in fact, help her?" Che asked. "She is a Communist country." I explained that Yugoslavia is far away and Cuba very near and also that we were helping Yugoslavia because she was against Russia.

"In other words," Che retorted, "you look upon Cuba as a pawn in the military game between Russia and the United States. We do not want to be that. It is independence that you fear. This would be the worst thing for the United States."

To come back to Fidel, he asserted that there are no Communists of any importance in the government. There are a few Communists in the army, he said, but none in important posts. "You know them all," he went on. "They are the same men who have been with me from the beginning. You know that I would not take any Communists with me on the *Granma*."

The French ship *La Coubre*, carrying a load of munitions, blew up in Havana harbor, on March 4, 1960, just before my wife and I arrived in Cuba. Many Cubans were killed and wounded. We went down to the dock and heard some bitter remarks about Americans from dock workers and repairmen.

As I wrote in my notes:

Fidel has the absolute conviction that it was sabotage, and so have all the others. I have no doubt of the sincerity of their belief but I argued with all of them against the injustice of accusing the United States without any proof. On that score, Fidel pointed out that he had publicly admitted he had no proof, but that they were going on the basis of the fact that if there had been sabotage, as they believed, it would have come from people representing those who most opposed them.

When I argued with Che on this point and said that the saboteurs might have been Dominicans or Batistianos, he said, "But where would they have come from? And if you shelter such people, or help them, would that not mean a moral responsibility?"

In his book (page 83), López-Fresquet wrote that a Belgian expert arrived the day after the explosion and "ruled out the possibilities of improper handling, heat, and all other accidental causes. He maintained that it was sabotage but could not determine whether the action took place in port, during the trip, or while loading." The arms in the vessel had been bought from Belgium.

As time passed, Fidel became more and more emphatic about American responsibility for the *Coubre* disaster. It has become a permanent part of the mythology of the Cuban Revolution but, of course, one cannot rule out a CIA operation.*

* While on the subject of my March 1960 trip, I find this in the conclusion of my memorandum: "Ernest Hemingway is still the great hero of the Cuban people. He is staying at his home and working as a deliberate gesture to show his sympathy and support for the Castro Revolution. He knows

One of the keys to the Marxist evolution lay in Fidel's obsession with "unity." This was not a Communist conception in Cuba. For Communists, "unity" means an authoritarian system run by the Communist party. For Castro, it was an all-embracing governmental structure in which the Communists are one element, while the power remained in his hands. Only later, and very gradually, were all the movements, parties and other elements brought together in a new political framework which is now called the "Communist Party of Cuba" but has nothing directly to do with the old Partido Socialista Popular (PSP).

The best political description of what has happened that I have seen is quoted in an article by Professor Richard F. Fagen for the *Journal of International Affairs,* No. 2, 1966. It comes from the book *Political Religion in the New Nations* by David E. Apter (page 78). As Fagen points out, it is confusing simply to label the Castro Government as a Communist regime. The most useful concept, he argues, is what Apter calls "the mobilization system":

> Harmony in the political sphere derives from the messianic leader who points out the dangers and noxious poisons of faction. Many such leaders are charismatic who represent the "one." They personify the monistic quality of the system.
>
> To achieve such oneness, mobilization systems begin by politicizing all political life. As a result, politics as such disappears. This is in keeping with monistic political belief. Conflict is not only bad but also is counterrevolutionary. It runs counter to the natural evolution of human society, and ideas of opposition downgrade and confuse the power of positive thinking. . . .
>
> Mobilization systems are characterized by what Durkheim called repressive law. Punitive and symbolic, it is political crimes which are punished with great severity. Such regimes are humorless. Their model of society is an organic one. Although it does not fit exactly, Marxism or some variant thereof is appealing because it satisfies these conditions theoretically and Leninism supports them organiza-

---

Cuba and the Cuban people as well as any American citizen. I was glad to find that his ideas on Fidel Castro and the Cuban Revolution are the same as mine."

tionally. Such systems represent the new puritanism. Progress is its faith. Industrialization is its vision. Harmony is its goal.

The emotional and simplistic attitude of Americans toward Communism and Cuba has blinded them to the fact that Fidel Castro's greatest difficulties in the field of "counterrevolution" (once he mastered or drove out the middle-class moderates) lay with the Cuban Communists. He had to make his Marxist-Leninist "mobilization system" with them and with the vital Soviet-bloc economic and military support, but without permitting the PSP to control his government and without permitting Moscow to control his international policies.

His two well-timed and effective moves in the early years came with the first "Escalante Affair" in March 1962, and his use of the high-handed way Khrushchev treated him in the missile crisis.

No effort will be made here to follow Cuba's slow and not very meaningful political evolution. Suárez, among others, has covered the tortuous field in his book *Cuba*. For present purposes, the development to be noted is that Aníbal Escalante made the mistake of putting his own henchmen in many key positions in the Organizaciones Revolucionarias Integradas (ORI). He made a similar, and even greater, mistake in 1968 and is now in jail. (Details of both Escalante affairs are set forth in Chapter 10.)

The first affair came to a head at a difficult time for Castro. The economic situation was very bad. The 1962 sugar crop was 1,000,000 tons short of its goal. In that same month of March 1962, rice, beans, meat, chicken, fish, eggs, milk, potatoes and soap had to be rationed.

Fidel moved gradually and then, on March 26 in one of his four-hour television appearances, blasted Aníbal Escalante ferociously and in the process crushed the Communist "Old Guard."

The attack was not aimed against Cuban or Russian Communism, but against certain Cuban Communists who had overestimated their strength and underestimated Fidel Castro.

There had been many signs throughout 1961 of Fidel's intentions to move openly and doctrinally into Communism. The "socialist" nature of the revolution was officially proclaimed on April 16, the day after the preliminary air raids of what was to be the Bay of Pigs invasion (of which more later). In his May 1 speech he spoke of "our socialist revolution."

His language—and his ideas—obviously had changed since the Sierra Maestra and the beginnings of the revolution. To use his own word, he had been going through a "process."

Fidel's change was that of the amateur theorist facing realities. When he came to put his ideas and hopes into practice, he found himself driven, as he thought, into the Communist position. The temptations that an authoritarian solution offers are great, and to one of Castro's temperament they were irresistible. He said to me often, as he did to others, that a radical revolution can be made only under a strong centralized government. Liberal democracy is a luxury that can come afterwards.

Thus, he was convinced that he could not hold elections without interrupting the revolutionary process and then dividing authority with Congress and with competing political parties and leaders. In his position and with his aims, he was being logical—aside from the fact that elections in Cuba were never models of democracy. Fidel can be criticized for not having thought of this sooner, but the frank answer from him and his associates is that the promises were made in the Sierra Maestra and at the beginning of the revolution when he and the 26th of July Movement could not know that they would have enough power to dispense with elections.

The same was true of a free press. A weak government, such as Fidel had in 1959, was in danger from newspaper attacks—usually vitriolic in the Latin way. Moreover, Havana, for instance, had eighteen newspapers when four or five would have been ample, and all but one or two had been kept going by subsidies from the preceding Governments, including Batista's.

One can go down the line on all the civic freedoms—freedom of speech and of assembly, trade unionism, property rights, inviolability of the home, and so on—and see the logical answers from Fidel's point of view. This is not to offer an excuse for what he did, but an explanation. There is no question that in Cuba, and in making the kind of revolution he had in mind, Fidel Castro had no choice.

The great problem that kept forcing itself on his mind and his policies was how to carry through his revolution while a propertied class was being despoiled of its property and wealth, a middle class was being deprived of its liberties, privileges and income, and a hostile United States was out to destroy him and his Government for economic, political and strategic reasons.

He could not take the Fascist solution since that is linked to military-landowning-big business-church interests. His was, perforce, a leftist revolution. As between extremes, the obvious solution was the Communist—or, as he came to call it, the Marxist-Leninist—method.

By the end of 1961, it seemed necessary to Fidel Castro not only to proclaim his Marxism-Leninism, but to make believe that he had always been a Marxist at heart or, as he is fond of putting it, in embryo. Historically and factually speaking, this was nonsense, but politically and tactically it was logical for him to take the public position that he did take in speeches spread over December 1961 to March 1962.

In the process he presented himself as deliberately deceitful, cunning and scheming—all of which has permanently damaged his moral standing in the non-Communist world. In the long run the speeches have harmed his own cherished freedom of maneuver because he put a straitjacket on himself labeled "Marxism-Leninism"—an international Communist philosophy—whereas his hopes and determination are to make a Cuban revolution. He apparently did not foresee that his nationalism and personalism would put him in conflict with Moscow and Peking, even while he remained within the Communist camp.

The revolution really had been Cuban in the sense that it had no help from outside in its triumph. In fact, it had been hindered by the Cuban Communists until the last months. To begin with, therefore, Fidel Castro had made a purely indigenous revolution. He seemed—but only seemed—to have thrown away this autochthonous quality as the year 1961 ended.

It is always necessary, in dealing with Castro's career, to keep in mind his capacity for self-deception: his sincere convictions of one day that can change to equally sincere and quite different convictions another day, and his shrewd sense of timing. When he is speaking publicly or for publication he will, like all politicians and statesmen since the dawn of government, say what he wants to be believed. The problem for the historian or biographer is to try to capture the essence, which, in Fidel's case, I would define as his determination, from his university days, to make a radical, populist social revolution.

When he set about making it and found himself, as he thought, forced into a Marxist-Leninist position which placed Cuba in the Socialist-Communist camp, he proceeded to rationalize the process by which he, and the Cuban revolutionary leadership that followed, became Marxist-Leninist. His description is pure rationalization after the event; it is an autopsy performed on himself and the Cuban body politic.

To try to draw a consistent pattern or line is, for a biographer, an exercise in futility, because there was no consistency. Draper, in the foreword to his book *Castroism,* detects a "red thread or threads that run through the entire development of Castroism, before and after taking power, in revolutionary tactics and in economic policies." If there was such a thread it was part of "a coat of many colors."

The results of a rebellious character are traceable, politically or socially, but there is nothing inevitable about the process; no "thread or threads" lead without break to a specific philosophy. Communism is a political system which may be adopted by a man or a woman; it is not a part of one's character.

I have discussed with Fidel on several occasions the process by which he became a Marxist-Leninist. In the quiet of his study, or over the dining table, one hears and sees him groping for the explanation—trying to satisfy himself. He can never do so clearly because he is not a trained, systematic thinker.

After one such occasion—on October 29, 1963—I made notes of what he said which later appeared in a paper I wrote for the *Hispanic American Report* of Stanford University in California. The gist was that he had a predisposition for Marxism; it was in his nature. He felt that he always was a potential Marxist—"a utopian Marxist"—although he did not become one in reality until well after the revolution started. I quoted him as follows:

> I entered college with the ideas of my birth and upbringing, the son of a landowner educated by Jesuits. In the third year of univer-

sity I started reading Marxist literature and it impressed me intellectually, although not to the extent of wanting to join the Communist Party or to embrace Marxism formally. . . .

In the 1952 electoral campaign I was sure of getting elected a deputy. . . . Once in Congress I planned to introduce a very radical reform program, not Marxist and within the normal political framework.

At the time of Moncada I was a pure revolutionary but not a Marxist revolutionary. In my defense at the trial ["History Will Absolve Me"] I outlined a very radical revolution, but I thought then that it could be done under the Constitution of 1940 and within a democratic system. That was the time when I was a utopian Marxist. During my time in prison I could not do much. In the Sierra I was still at the early stage of the process, still thinking in utopian terms. This was the state of affairs when the insurrection triumphed.

It was a gradual process, a dynamic process in which the pressure of events forced me to accept Marxism as the answer to what I was seeking. . . .

The PSP had men who were truly revolutionary, loyal, honest and trained. I needed them. Moreover, the 26th of July Movement and the country as a whole had divided into Left and Right, and soon much of the Right moved into counterrevolution and exile. It was necessary to insist on unity, a unity that included the Cuban Communists. . . .

So, as events developed, I gradually moved into a Marxist-Leninist position. I cannot tell you just when; the process was so gradual and so natural. [However, answering a question, he agreed that it could well have been mid-1960.]

With my ideas and my temperament, even in my school and university days, I could not have been a capitalist, a democrat, a liberal. I always had it in me to be a radical, a revolutionary, a reformer, and through that instinctive preparation it was easy for me to move into Marxism-Leninism.

That was his story—and he stuck to it. A few years later, speaking to Lee Lockwood in one of the taped interviews (pages 138–43), Fidel expatiated at considerable length on the same ideas.

At Havana University, he told Lockwood:

I had not read *The Communist Manifesto*. I had read hardly anything by Karl Marx. . . . Later on, I read *The Communist Manifesto* of Marx and Engels, which made a deep impression on me. For the first time I saw a historical, systematic explanation of the problem, phrased in a very militant way, which captivated me completely. . . .

This encounter with revolutionary ideas helped me to orient myself politically. But there is a big difference between having a theoretical knowledge and considering oneself a Marxist revolutionary. . . .

The conflicts between all that the Revolution stands for and everything the United States stands for became clear immediately when they gave asylum to the worst criminals, individuals who had murdered hundreds of Cuban people. . . .

And when I looked a little further, I saw what imperialism stands for in the rest of the world, that we were entangled in the same problem that peoples of other continents are entangled in. . . . And we all had occasion to learn of the solidarity of the Soviet Union and the Socialist camp, who were the only true allies of the effort to make a revolution within our country.

I have had a very interesting and very effective schooling. That is simply, more or less in general lines, the process which, from my first questionings until the present moment, made me into a Marxist revolutionary, which is what I consider myself today.

Some of this is true. Much of it—with all due respect to Fidel Castro—is pure hokum.

When I was in Cuba in October 1967, I talked to Raúl Castro about Cuban Communism. I asked him about something that Carlos Rafael Rodríguez had said to me on two different visits— that it was Fidel who had induced Raúl to read Marx and Lenin and encouraged him to become a Communist. It was true, Raúl said, that when they were in the same cell together on the Isle of Pines in 1954–55, Fidel gave him some books by Marx and Lenin and told him to read them. But Raúl laughed heartily about *Das Kapital*. "We read about three chapters of it," he said, "and then threw it aside, and I am certain that Fidel never looked at it again." He did say that they were impressed—he more than his brother—by socialism.

Fidel never embraced any ideology, Raúl said—not until the present Marxism-Leninism. When I interjected that "for me, *Marxismo-Leninismo* is *Fidelismo*," Raúl laughed and replied, "It was *you* who said that!"

Whatever its definition—or whether it is even capable of definition—Fidel Castro's Marxism-Leninism must be taken in all seriousness. Those two words mean that Fidel, his associates, the Cuban Revolution and Cuba herself are in the Communist camp.

Insofar as the process was a public one, it came to a head in the famous speech of December 1–2, 1961, in which Fidel thumped the table in front of him and shouted, "I am a Marxist-Leninist and I shall be a Marxist-Leninist until the last day of my life."

The speech was a concoction, a composition, a political construction, engineered to fit the particular moment and Fidel's aims. It was what he wanted everyone to believe.

The length (it spread over five hours of the late night and early morning), the rambling, confused and almost contradictory wording, probably were calculated. Fidel wanted to put over the idea that in his heart, or in embryo, during his early career and in the Sierra Maestra he had been a Marxist. At the same time he knew that he could present no convincing evidence, for the simple reason that he had not been a Marxist.

The speech was therefore so lacking in precision that those who wanted to believe that he had been a Communist since his university days could pick passages out of context to prove their point. This resulted in the second great bloomer that the United Press International was to commit with regard to Fidel Castro—the first being the report of his death in the *Granma* landing.

An excited Cuban exile, monitoring the speech in Florida for the UPI in the early morning of December 2, jubilantly sent on to New York a rather inaccurate version of the passages that rejoiced the listener's heart. By the time the Havana newspaper *Revolución* was available in the United States with the full text, it was too late to change the impression given by the incorrect UPI story. The CIA's Federal Broadcast Information Service published a translation of the text within a few days.

But a myth had been created. Three high officials of the State Department and United States diplomatic service, to my knowledge, believed even months later that Castro had confessed to having been a Communist from his university days. For years after, when I lectured on Cuba at some American college or at a conference, I would be asked how I could say that Fidel Castro had not been a Communist in 1959 when he had himself confessed to being one.

The irony of the situation was that a careful reading of the complete text made it clear that far from admitting that he had been a Communist all along, Fidel was apologizing because in his university days and in the Sierra Maestra he had not seen the light, appreciated the great virtues of Marxism and become a Communist. The only "confession" in his speech was his regret and humility that his conversion had taken so long. Even this was phony, because if there is anything foreign to Fidel Castro's character it is humility.

Correct analyses of the speech soon came out. The *Hispanic American Report* of Stanford University, Columbia University School of Journalism's quarterly review, and the writings of Theodore Draper and other careful students of the Cuban Revolution set the record straight for scholars and for history—but the myth lives on.

The true importance of the December 1961 speech lay in its political significance, and above all in that defiant proclamation about being a Marxist-Leninist "until the last day of my life." Fidel hung an albatross around his own neck. However, one can say of his Marxism-Leninism what Humpty Dumpty said to Alice: "When *I* use a word it means just what I choose it to mean— neither more nor less." And to make one more literary reference— Fidel Castro was like Molière's *Bourgeois Gentilhomme* who discovered with pleasure that all his life he had been talking prose. Fidel now discovered that—although he evidently had not known it—he had been a Marxist-Leninist all his life.

One thing was certain for anyone knowing Fidel Castro: His Marxism-Leninism was going to be something such as Moscow and Peking never dreamed of.

The Cuban Communists, throughout the early years of the revolution, sought power, positions and an ultimately exclusive Communist structure for the nation. They now find themselves with a Marxist-Leninist structure in which they—as orthodox, Muscovite Communists—have no more power than when they started. Power still lies in the hands of Fidel Castro and the small group of men and women he trusts.

All are nominally Communist now. A few are from the "Old Guard" Stalinists and are the genuine article; most of the leaders are Fidelistas disguised as Communists; the rank and file are a part of a Communist structure that is Cuban first and foremost but belongs in what Castro calls "the socialist world."

The distinctions may be too subtle for the American public and press and for the purposes of the United States State Department propaganda, but they are real and they are vital to an understanding of what is happening in Cuba.

The "Old Guard" again and again found itself out of line with the revolution as Castro was making it. Blas Roca, the PSP leader, as Moscow's representative was continually outmaneuvered while the more astute—or more Cuban and more Fidelista, as well as younger—Carlos Rafael Rodríguez gained authority. Nevertheless, when the "Old Guard" was smashed at the time of the Escalante affair, Blas Roca saved himself, along with Rodríguez, and continued to have an important place in the Castro Government. Roca must have been more astute behind the scenes than he appeared to be in public. At least, he was never disloyal to Fidel, never indiscreet and always compliant—which neutralized the negative effects of his Moscow orthodoxy.

Che Guevara was interviewed by the late Lisa Howard of the American Broadcasting Company which televised the conversation on March 22, 1964. In it, Miss Howard asked, "Major Guevara, when you were fighting in the hills of the Sierra Maestra did you foresee that the revolution would take so radical a turn?"

"Intuitively, I felt it," Che answered. "Of course, the course and the very violent development of the revolution couldn't be foreseen. Nor was the Marxist-Leninist formulation of the revolution foreseeable. That was the result of a very long process, and you know

it very well. We had a more or less vague idea of solving the problems which we clearly saw affected the peasants who fought with
us, and the problems we saw in the lives of the workers. But it
would be very long to recount the whole process of the transformation of our ideas."

Suárez believes (page 111) that Che Guevara "began to famil-
iarize himself with Marxist thought in the middle of 1960." I do
not believe that Che ever acquired more than a superficial knowledge of scientific Marxism. He had no time for it. The Castroites
played their Communist music by ear.

In the spring of 1961 I referred to the Castro regime as
"communistic but not Communist." Fidel could apply to himself a
statement that the late John Strachey made to United States immigration authorities who tried to deport him in 1935 as an alien
Communist while he was on a lecture tour.

"I do not deny I am a Communist," Strachey said, "but I do
deny that I am a member of the Communist party, and therein lies
a great difference."

For practical reasons Castro felt the need of proclaiming an
ideology and then building a party to provide an instrument and
framework for his revolution. It seemed as if he was going through
a process of institutionalizing the revolution—but the years pass,
and the process seems unending.

Fidel did not at the beginning, I am sure, realize the extent to
which his early tolerance and then embrace of Communism was
going to upset Americans and the United States Government. In
the first place, however, the very deep and bitter resentment of the
revolutionaries led them to blame the United States for leaving
them no alternative, and in the second place it gave them a certain
satisfaction to hit back hard against blows that they asserted came
first from the American side. Che Guevara—and not only he—
argued with me that if a weak party is hit, he must try to strike
back just as hard.

I can offer a typical high-level Cuban opinion on Communism
from a note I made in August 1960, after a conversation with
Armando Hart, who was the Minister of Education.

"United States policy," he said, "is forcing us to make our

revolution much faster than we wanted to. It is a stupid policy, because the reaction is always the contrary of what the United States wants.

"Communism was no problem here. If it is now, you created it by forcing us into policies for which we had no other choice. It would have taken a genius greater than Franklin D. Roosevelt to have handled the Cuban situation. The inevitable should have been recognized from the beginning. The revolution never could be defeated or destroyed. Fidel's victory, Fidel's stature and what he was going to do should have been understood and the policy made to conform. The United States is losing a billion dollars here. That is a great deal, but it is not enough to make it worth what you are now going to pay. If you keep on with your policies you will lose everything. There are only two ways in which empires are lost. One is the voluntary way, as the British have been doing, or else there is a dissolution, a breaking away, a rebellion.

"In a struggle for our national existence we will seek and take help where we can get it."

"All of them blame us," I wrote in my notes a few days later, "and say no other choice was left to Cuba except the one they are following, which is acceptance of Soviet support, economic aid and a growth of Communism internally. All deny that Communism has any control or that any of the leaders are Red.

"It seems obvious that they will not change their present policies even if they could. They are going to make their revolution and since they are convinced that the United States is trying to destroy it and the Soviet bloc is trying to help it along, they will continue to accept Soviet aid. This aid, by the nature of things, not only comprehends acceptance of help but—as part of their defense as they see it—it must comprehend partnership in anti-Yankeeism in the hemisphere."

On that same trip I had a talk with Che Guevara at one o'clock in the morning at the National Bank where the subject of Communism came up. I remarked to him that when, during the Spanish Civil War, the Republicans had to accept help from the Russians, the Spanish Communist party gained great strength and went on growing, and that I was afraid this would happen in Cuba. He agreed almost emphatically. "But that is your fault," he said. "The more we are forced to deal with the Soviet bloc the stronger the [Cuban] Communists will become."

A story had been published in the United States quoting Che Guevara as saying that Cuba—in August 1960—was Marxist. I asked him about that. He got out the text of his speech and read me what he had said. I then paraphrased the passage for him as follows: "This is not Marxism. If it seems so, it is an accident of history. Cuba did not choose a Marxist line. If we seem now to be Marxist, or to be doing what Marxists would be doing, that is simply because in carrying out our revolution in our own way we did things that paralleled Marxism."

He said, "Yes, that is the meaning of what I had stated. Marxism, anyway, is a vague philosophical concept of a hundred years ago. One might as well talk of Newtonism. Today a nation faced with certain problems follows certain lines which often parallel previous situations. If we did some things like the Chinese Communists in our agrarian reform, that did not mean the Chinese had sent advisers to tell us what to do, as all your newspapers wrote. It was an accident of history."

The hardheaded President Dorticós, when I saw him on August 15, assured me that "there is no danger of the regime going Communist." That proved wrong, but he was right when he added that he could not "possibly conceive of the Reds taking over Cuba or even dominating policy and the government because we won't let them." This was true, of both the Cuban and the Russian Communists. "The Russians offered us valuable aid on excellent terms when we needed it most and when the United States had barred aid," he added.

All of them argued that while the Communist bloc bought their sugar, supplied arms and gave technical advice, neither the Soviet Union nor Communist China acquired or wanted any Cuban property. They had no material foothold, and insofar as there was a Russian presence, it was limited to technical advisers in the economic and military fields. The economic advice was disregarded as often as it was accepted.

At that time I was making the point to Fidel, Dorticós, Che Guevara and others that they must realize that Cuba was "expendable" so far as Moscow was concerned. (Curiously, there is no good Spanish word to convey the exact meaning of "expendable" and the idea was hard to put over.) At the time of the nuclear crisis Fidel Castro learned how expendable Cuba was.

For the sophisticated minority in the United States and for just about everyone in other Western nations, Communism is simply another and different political, economic and social system. For most Americans, Communism is a sin, a moral evil, a heresy; there must be a crusade against it. This of course explains to some degree the ghastly blunder of the Vietnam War. Similarly it also explains the shock of anger, dismay, disgust, even fear, that gripped nearly all Americans when Cuba turned Marxist-Leninist.

There was no use arguing, as some of us did, that there are no dogmatic truths in politics; there are not even scientific truths. The primary analytical instrument in the Cuban case should not have been faith or morals or ethics. Of course, American business and financial interests had their material reasons for hostility, and the Pentagon had its strategic reasons. I am arguing, simply, that but for Communism the American attitude toward Fidel Castro and his revolution might have been much more patient, tolerant and understanding.

President Eisenhower said in July 1960 that the United States would not "tolerate the establishment of a regime dominated by international Communism in the Western Hemisphere." President Kennedy, in his first State of the Union Message on January 30, 1961, declared that "Communist domination in this hemisphere can never be negotiated." On a number of occasions, Secretary of State Dean Rusk was to make it clear that the United States would not "negotiate" with Fidel Castro.

Statesmen should never use the word "never." As it happened, the Castro regime was not "dominated" by the Communists, Cuban or international, but Washington was not well enough informed in those days to understand this. The situation, in that respect, has been clear to the American Government for several years—which nevertheless has not reconciled Washington to the existence of a Communist government in the Western Hemisphere.

That Fidel Castro was the most dangerous enemy of the United States ever to arise in Latin America became obvious even before he turned Marxist-Leninist. The missile crisis later provided shocking proof of that. However, at the beginning, the Soviet Union and Communist China (less at odds then than they became) displayed caution and not much interest in Fidel Castro and his doings. Peking did not have the means or the logistic and economic possibilities of being an important factor in helping Cuba, but Moscow was in a different position. For the first time in modern history, Russia saw a chance to play a power role in Latin America, one that would compensate a little for the encirclement by the American containment policy.

Fidel Castro was not at first contemplating a 180-degree turn from dependence on the United States to dependence on the Communist bloc. He and his companions had not fought so hard for "independence" from the Yankees to want to lose it to the Russians. But in the two-power world that was then operative, a developing nonindustrialized country in a highly strategic position would be forced to make a choice between the two world-power giants.

Fidel, it can be argued, slammed the door leading to the United States. Washington thereupon turned the key, feeling sure that the locked-in and isolated Cuban Government would break down and that popular discontent would then lead to the overthrow of Castro. This was one of the major mistakes in the long history of Cuban-American relations, and it showed how badly informed the CIA, FBI and the State Department were. Castro was allowed no way out.

A measure of Fidel's naïveté about the way the world goes can be guessed from an answer he gave to Lee Lockwood (page 186) about the United States attitude:

> What we didn't see completely clearly was that the North American interests affected by the Revolution possessed the means to bring about a change of opinion in the United States and to distort everything that was happening in Cuba and present it to the United States public in the worst form.

The lack of sophistication involved would be astonishing if it were not for the fact that Fidel Castro was so completely inexperienced. Except for brief trips to the United States and his sojourn in Mexico, he had never left Cuba. To this day, his ignorance of the United States and of the psychology and temperament of North Americans is enormous. He should have known that when he started expropriating American properties worth hundreds of millions of dollars, the most powerful kind of pressures would immediately be brought to bear in Washington on the American Government. This was especially true of a government like President Eisenhower's in which business and financial interests played so great a role. Congressmen would be subjected to the same pressures, and the mass media of communications would go along.

With the first hint of Communism, even though it came to the United States very early and prematurely, the whole vast mechanism of vested interests and government would inevitably be set in motion. Although it irritated Castro to get warnings and advice, he should have listened to those of us who were telling him about the extraordinary sensitivity and emotionalism of Americans when it came to Communism. He would not—and probably could not—have changed his policies in the long run, but he could have put them in a more understanding framework, less extreme, less hasty, less insulting and less rash.

He admitted to Lockwood that when he seized the Texaco and Shell oil refineries he did not know whether the Russians would supply Cuba with oil or not. This was typical of Castro's gambling spirit, which was to reach its breathtaking apogee in 1962 when he gave a welcome to Khrushchev's nuclear missiles. Fidel seems to glory in taking desperate chances and is at his best in moments of disaster. He instinctively believes in the slogan Mussolini popularized: "Live dangerously."

I made up my mind early in the revolution, on the basis of many talks with all the top Cuban leaders, that their greatest preoccupation was the conviction that the United States was determined to overthrow the Castro regime and, in the process, destroy the revolution. American self-righteousness in the first few years was ridiculous, because there always were powerful interests in government, business and finance which certainly wanted to do just that. It stood to reason that the United States would not want to see a radical revolution in Cuba. The highly favorable publicity that greeted Fidel Castro's descent in triumph from the Sierra Maestra was short-lived. It was based on a mistaken conception of what sort of man he was and what kind of revolution he intended to make.

In any event, at some point in the first period of the revolution, United States policy toward Cuba certainly was based on an effort to drive Fidel Castro from power and put an end to his revolution. The history of the Cuban Revolution could be written in figurative terms as one vicious circle after another. Americans felt that they had to destroy the Castro regime because of its Communism; Cubans felt that they had to be Communists to protect themselves against the Americans. The Cubans saw Russia as a friend; because the Soviet Union was a friend to Cuba, United States enmity and fear grew. And so it went.

Another conviction the Cuban leaders entertained was that the United States had lost ground politically everywhere in the world, would continue to lose more ground, and could not possibly recover what had been lost. They convinced themselves of the reality of American "imperialism" and considered that the United States had an empire in the British and French sense. They felt sure that the American empire would go the way of the other empires and that there would be more revolutions in Latin America.

As Che Guevara put it to me, "Cuba is just a small incident. You will lose everywhere in the world."

These hopes (which the Vietnam War revived) helped to sustain Fidel Castro and his associates in those difficult years. It was Fidel's equivalent of the Trotskyite belief in the world revolution of the Western proletariat. As a general proposition, Marxism-Leninism has given up that hope, but the Fidelista variation of Latin-American revolution lingers on.

In the first flush of victory, Fidel and his followers foresaw the doom of the dictatorships of the Dominican Republic, Nicaragua and Haiti. Exiles were welcomed in Cuba, allowed to acquire arms and training, and threats were launched daily over the air.

The hopes were soon dashed, and the efforts—insofar as they were encouraged by the Castro Government—were temporarily abandoned. Of the so-called invasions from Cuba in 1959, only one—the two groups that entered the Dominican Republic in June—had official Cuban backing. Fidel told me about the Dominican involvement and it was a shock to him that it failed so quickly and disastrously.

The other "invasions" were made either by adventurers and mercenaries, like the landings in Panama in April and Haiti in August, or by groups that evaded Cuban vigilance. The State Department must have known these facts but chose to make a big propaganda issue against Fidel Castro for policy reasons.

On more than one occasion Fidel Castro made the point to me that while it was true that Cuba was trying subversion in other Latin-American countries, the United States was trying subversion in Cuba.

"You Americans keep saying that Cuba is ninety miles from the United States," Fidel said to me once. "I say that the United States is ninety miles from Cuba, and for us that is worse."

In the summer of 1960 he asked me whether the United States was preparing an invasion of Cuba. I said I was sure it was not. Fidel knew better; we were doing just that.

# 7 PIGS AND MISSILES

▓▓▓ IN THE life of Fidel Castro and the history of the first decade of the Cuban Revolution, the Bay of Pigs invasion of 1961 was more important than the nuclear missile crisis of 1962. The former profoundly affected the internal Cuban situation, finally consolidated Castro's power and led to an intensification of the socialist trend and the proclamation at the end of the same year of the Marxist-Leninist line.

The latter was an incident—of supreme importance to the Cold War, the world balance of power, the relations between the United States and the Soviet Union, but it had no internal effects in Cuba. It did, however, confirm and crystallize Fidel Castro's ideas about going his own way in the field of international politics. This led to a serious clash with Moscow which is still reverberating. Fidel felt a sense of betrayal on Russia's part which led him to assert his political independence of Moscow while retaining his economic dependence. The event was a lesson in power politics which he needed. He has by no means, even now, shaken off what he calls his "utopian Marxism."

Both events showed that Castro and his revolution had more than adequate popular support against an American-directed invasion or the threat of one. The Bay of Pigs provided Fidel with the opportunity to display his remarkable qualities of leadership in time of danger. There he could be—and he was—the charismatic hero.

The missile crisis, on the other hand, was a humiliation for which the Russians will never be forgiven. For the first, and thus far only, time in his career, Fidel Castro allowed the power of decision to lie in other hands. What was worse, it lay in Russian, which is to say foreign, hands.

The "crisis of the Caribbean," as the Cubans call it, was a shocking experience for Castro, but I have a suspicion that he took a certain satisfaction and pride that he, Fidel Castro, a Cuban, could have brought the world to the brink of nuclear holocaust. I do not mean that he wanted or expected a nuclear war. He was thinking in terms of the defense of Cuba and the defensive relationship of the "socialist world" toward American "imperialism." Yet, it was within his power—one young Cuban's power—to permit Khrushchev to install the missiles, or to refuse to permit the Russians to do so. No Latin American had ever had such power. Let us hope that none will ever have such power again.

No one in 1960 and 1961 dreamed of nuclear missiles, but the United States had grown very anxious about the way the Castro regime had armed itself. Raúl Castro told me in 1967 that on the very day the Rebel Army entered Havana—January 8, 1959—Fidel gave orders that 50,000 rifles and machine guns should be bought abroad. They were ordered from Belgium, which, however, could sell the Cubans only 40,000. Part of that shipment was on *La Coubre,* which helps to explain why Fidel Castro felt sure that American sabotage was involved. One of the ships carrying arms, Raúl and Fidel both told me, was mysteriously rammed when coming out of its Belgian harbor. I also heard that the United States consul in Antwerp tried to prevent the *Coubre* from sailing.

Castro tried to buy the other 10,000 small arms he wanted in Italy or England, but, the Cubans say, the United States protested and blocked the sales. However, as I have stated, when Mikoyan paid his visit to Havana in February 1960, the Russians started selling arms to Cuba. Then they gave the arms and provided the technicians to teach the Cubans how to use them; and they also trained in Russia hundreds of young Cubans destined to be officers in Fidel's Rebel Army.

Within a matter of three or four years, Cuba was the most heavily armed country of Latin America—and it has remained so. The strain on the economy was always great, even when the arms cost Cuba no more than a bookkeeping debt to Moscow. Castro felt the need to build up and maintain a large regular army, which in time got its rank and file from a national draft. (Incidentally, Fidel had strongly criticized his predecessors' system of drafting soldiers and had pledged his Movement to dispense with anything but volunteers. In this, as in so many other ways, he found that his "utopian" ideas did not satisfy his real needs.)

Batista's regular army and police force were, naturally, replaced immediately by the Rebel Army in 1959. The top posts of the navy and air force were then filled by loyal revolutionaries. A civilian worker-peasant-student militia was set up toward the end of 1959 as a paramilitary organization. In September 1960, it was turned into a reserve military organization. The wisdom of doing this was shown at the time of the Bay of Pigs invasion when it was the militia that first attacked the exile force until the regular army's tank, artillery units and more heavily armed soldiers could get down to the battlefield and finish the job.

After disbanding Batista's brutal and corrupt police force and putting his own men in, Fidel moved in June 1961 to establish a Ministry of the Interior with responsibility to maintain public order. His remarkable young police chief, Ramiro Valdés, was by then thoroughly experienced, and he continued to have Russian police advisers behind the scenes. The Ministry also supervised the already existing "Committees for the Defense of the Revolution," whose original purpose was to inform the authorities of counter-revolutionary activities and to keep an eye on the immediate neighborhoods in which they worked. In 1963, there were reputed to be 1,500,000 members in offices, factories, schools, churches, cooperatives, farms and residential areas. They now do more social work than informing.

These committees proved valuable, and even indispensable, to

Fidel Castro. At the time of the Bay of Pigs invasion they and the militia rounded up several hundreds of thousands of suspects. They later helped Valdés's police organization to foil plots against the regime and to capture would-be assassins of Castro, generally sent in by the Cuban-exile organizations, with (the Castro revolutionaries are certain) CIA tolerance if not active help.

My own theory throughout the years has been that the CIA did not want Fidel Castro to be assassinated because of the political repercussions that would follow in Cuba and Latin America. It would have made a martyr of Fidel and would have led to a bloodbath and chaos in Cuba. This is an opinion which, emphatically, is not shared by Fidel Castro and his associates.

In May 1966, when I was in Cuba, they were all still talking about the plot by which Major Rolando Cubelas, a Sierra Maestra man who had proved incompetent and emotionally unstable and hence was given less and less important posts, was to kill Fidel. This plot, the Cubans knew, followed a conference in Madrid with Manuel Artime, the young exile chosen by the CIA to lead the Bay of Pigs invasion.

Due to clever work by Ramiro Valdés, the plot was foiled and Cubelas arrested and imprisoned. Because he had been "one of the boys," Fidel and the others felt rather sorry for Cubelas, who received a relatively light sentence. While I was in Havana, Fidel sent him some books to read in prison.

With such plots happening—including intermittent landings by saboteurs and would-be assassins from a "mother ship" presumably furnished by the CIA—I found myself unable to convince the Cuban leaders that Washington (or, more particularly, the CIA) did not want to have Fidel Castro killed, even if it could be done without seeming to involve the United States.

In such matters, laymen like myself can only guess. When it came to the Bay of Pigs there was no need to guess. It was a CIA affair, bungled so completely and ridiculously that the organization temporarily became a worldwide laughingstock.

The CIA's clumsiness with regard to Cuba did not begin in April 1961. In a book published in 1963 by Christopher Felix, a former American secret service officer, called *A Short Course in the Secret War*, there is a revealing quotation (page 107). It comes from an article by Thayer Waldo of the San Francisco *Chronicle:*

> This reporter spent the first half of last year [1960] in Cuba. At that time, with the Embassy still in operation and fully staffed, eight of the personnel were CIA agents, three worked for the FBI, and each of the Armed Services had from one to five operatives assigned to intelligence work. . . . In addition to the Embassy staffers, the CIA had a number of operatives (I knew fourteen, but am satisfied there were more) among the large colony of resident U.S. businessmen.

With the embassy staff and the American business community gone, the CIA-FBI operations had to be handled through the Cuban counterrevolutionaries and contacts with friendly foreign diplomats. This made the information scarcer and less trustworthy, but it did not make headquarters in Washington or the American operators any the less sure of themselves.

*The New York Times* published a series of articles on the CIA written by members of the staff. One article, printed on April 28, 1966, dealt with Cuba:

> At the Bay of Pigs, just after President Kennedy took office in 1961, the worst finally happened; all the fears expressed through the years came true.
>
> The Bay of Pigs must take its place in history as a classic example of the disaster that can occur when a major international operation is undertaken in deepest secrecy, is politically approved on the basis of "facts" provided by those who most fervently advocated it, is carried out by the same advocates, and ultimately acquires a momentum of its own beyond anything contemplated either by the advocates or those who supposedly "controlled" them.

Ironically, the only secrecy in the operation involved men in the United States Government who should have been kept informed: not only the State Department Cuban desk officers and the United Nations staff of the United States, but also the intelligence branch of the CIA itself. Many American newspapermen began to learn about the preparations in October and November 1960 and knew a great deal about the plan by January 1961. Several thousand Cuban exiles were directly involved and many more thousands learned by word of mouth that an invasion was planned.

It stood to reason that Fidel Castro and his associates also knew whatever was to be known. Shortly before the attack, he had his Foreign Minister, Raúl Roa, protest to the United Nations General Assembly against United States "aggression." Castro renewed his warnings to the Cuban people and kept his militia on the alert— but there had been incessant warnings before and no invasion had taken place. Fidel's most effective move was to mass his Soviet-built tanks and mobile artillery near Havana, whence they could be moved swiftly to the point of attack.

He knew roughly when the invasion was coming, but he could not know where, and—the most important factor of all to him—he could not know just what the United States would do and how far it would go to help the force it had armed, trained and would escort to Cuba. Neither the Cuban exiles nor the Cuban revolutionaries could believe President Kennedy when he said, publicly as well as privately, that "in no circumstances" would United States armed forces be used to overthrow the Cuban Government.


The long and ridiculous—or sad—story of the Bay of Pigs fiasco is too well known to need more than the briefest summary. Arthur M. Schlesinger, Jr., tells it brilliantly and frankly from the Kennedy and United States viewpoint in two chapters of his book *A Thousand Days* (pages 233–97). The Cuban Government issued a long White Paper afterwards, and four of the young exile leaders who took part told their emotional and exaggerated, but moving, story to Haynes Johnson for his book *The Bay of Pigs*. Two expert American reporters—Tad Szulc of *The New York Times* and Karl E. Meyer of the Washington *Post*—wrote a quick and superficial but generally accurate account called *The Cuban Invasion: The Chronicle of a Disaster*. Ted Sorensen, Roger Hilsman, Theodore Draper and others wrote articles and parts of books on the incident which overshadowed every act of foreign policy by President Kennedy until his brilliant handling of the missile crisis redeemed him and erased a good deal of the shattering effect on the Administration and on United States hemispheric policy of the Bay of Pigs fiasco.

A year afterwards Szulc and Meyer could write (page 8): "No melodramatic and tragicomical touch was missing in the hours that Operation Pluto [its cloak-and-dagger name] lived its short life as the strangest tragedy of errors in which the United States was ever involved."

The invasion was, of course, Washington's clumsy attempt to answer what was seen as the provocations and the dangers that the Cuban Revolution represented. The Eisenhower-Nixon reaction of 1959–60 was based more than anything else on the radical nature of Castro's acts and the unindemnified expropriations of American properties by the Castro regime. At the time that Vice President Nixon said he wanted to arm Cuban exiles and send them in, the only men available were Batistianos. Fidel will now wonder whether Nixon, as President, will now seek a delayed satisfaction.

Later, the waves of middle-class, moderate and in many cases anti-Batista refugees flowed into Florida and made it possible to form a respectable, although still prerevolutionary and hence *ancien régime* leadership for an exile force. This element was moved strongly by the growing Communistic trend of the Castro Revolution.

The same factor of Communism was a basic motive for Eisenhower and, when he became President, for Kennedy. The latter, with his keen and subtle intelligence and his sophistication, would surely have understood the true relationship of Fidel Castro to the Cuban Communists and to Moscow if he had been properly informed.

Just before the attack Kennedy asked Arthur Schlesinger, then an aide in the White House, to prepare a White Paper explaining to Cubans and all Latin Americans why the United States was going to support the still-secret invasion. Schlesinger quotes the President as saying, "Our objection isn't to the Cuban Revolution; it is to the fact that Castro has turned it over to the Communists."

Castro had done nothing of the sort. This is surely obvious to every student of the revolution by now—but it should have been sensed, at least, in 1960 and 1961. In April 1961, as Suárez wrote (page 127), "The PSP was not represented in the Cuban government or in the leadership of the Rebel Army or of the mass organizations." American policy was based on a mistaken understanding.

Castro, it is true, was acting just as the Communists would have liked to see him act. In practical terms it could be argued that there was no difference. However, *he* was the master, not the Cuban Communists or Russia. He had not yet openly embraced "socialism"; he was to do this on April 16, 1961, the day after the first air strike by the Cuban exile force.

The erroneous belief that Fidel was a puppet and Cuba a satellite played into the hands of the Cuban Communists. With better understanding, Kennedy's Cuban policy could have been more intelligent and probably wiser and more effective.

The CIA had no doubts or qualms. Its mind was on the easy but very different case of Guatemala in July 1954. At that time the CIA, strongly backed by Secretary of State John Foster Dulles, whose brother Allen was head of the intelligence organization, put a pliable Guatemalan colonel named Carlos Castillo Armas at the head of an insignificant force which had only to step across the Honduran frontier for the Arbenz regime to collapse. The Americans had a "pistol-packin' " ambassador in Guatemala City, John Puerifoy, who directed the rebellion from inside. The Guatemalan army leaders—who were never on Arbenz's side and who could intelligently have been used to stage a palace revolt—did not support the President.

The aftermath was a weak, corrupt, reactionary, pro-Yankee regime that had foreseeable results—the assassination of Castillo Armas, the election of a President, Miguel Ydígoras Fuentes, who became a millionaire in office and turned his country over to the CIA for the Bay of Pigs preparations, and who was succeeded by a well-meaning but guerrilla-burdened Administration. However, for Allen Dulles and the CIA it was their one great "victory" in Latin America and they were sure that they could repeat it in Cuba. The situation in Cuba, of course, was entirely different in every respect and, most of all, in that Fidel Castro was not Jacobo Arbenz.

Guatemala has to be recalled not only because it misled the Americans but because Castro sensed very soon that the United States would think it could achieve "another Guatemala" in Cuba. He warned in his speeches against our trying it. It was ironical that the CIA, in fact, used Guatemala as the training base for the 1,400 Cuban exiles who made up the expedition.

The President of Nicaragua, Luis Somoza, son of the dictator and himself a dictator, happily put the harbor and airfield of Puerto Cabeza at the disposal of the exile force. The first move was a tricky but clumsy idea which boomeranged: bombing the Havana military airport in order to destroy Fidel's small air force. The deceit lay in our claiming that the Cuban pilots were defectors from Castro's air force in Cuba. The trick was quickly detected, but not before one of the United States's most precious human assets—Ambassador Adlai Stevenson—was permitted to lie to the UN General Assembly, much to his later bitterness and dismay.

Only a few of Castro's planes were destroyed. He later claimed that they had been hidden and dispersed, and that when the land attack came, he had more planes than pilots to fly them. Schlesinger's information was that Fidel still had two T-33 jet fighters—which did the most deadly work—some Sea Furies (fighters) and several B-26 bombers. Against the T-33s, the invaders' slow, heavy B-26 bombers, which the United States had furnished, were like sitting ducks. A T-33 hit the ammunition and communications ship, the *Houston,* and blew it up at the beginning of the fight. As Schlesinger wrote, Castro's air force "reacted with unexpected vigor." With Castro, the unexpected is what usually can be expected.

He made a televised speech at the funeral for the victims of the air strike the next day in which he predicted that it was a prelude to invasion. "If President Kennedy has one atom of decency," he cried, "he will present the planes and pilots before the United Nations. If not, then the world has a right to call him a liar." Of course, Kennedy was lying. In fact, there was an astonishing amount of American lying before and during the invasion, which was understandable, but it did not help the American image.

The landing on April 17, 1961, is called the Bay of Pigs invasion by Americans from the Spanish name of the inlet—Bahía de Cochinos. Cubans always refer to the affair by the name of the

beach where the first and main body of the invaders landed—
Playa Girón, which is on the eastern side of the bay. Another
beach—Playa Larga—on the western side played a less important
role. Beyond Playa Larga is the great swamp known as the Cién-
aga de Zapata.

The plan from the military point of view, as Castro said later,
and as I discovered on a visit, would have been feasible had it been
carried out properly. Playa Girón is a horseshoe-shaped beach
about a mile wide. For about 100 yards the water is quite shallow;
then it shelves suddenly and steeply. Ships can come close to shore
and the men can get out and wade onto land. Along the beach and
close to the water, across to Playa Larga, is an excellent paved
road running east and west. From there the only road goes due
north. A small but adequate airfield was just across the road from
Playa Girón.

The idea was to establish a beachhead that should have been
easy to defend because there were only those two roads at right
angles and swamp all around. The defenders could come down
only on the north-south road to Playa Larga. If the beachhead had
been established, the Americans could have flown in the pseudo-
government they had formed, which would have asked for recognition and help.

The invaders began coming ashore at two in the morning of
April 17, and it was ironical that the first frogman to touch land
was an American. President Kennedy had given strict orders that
Americans were not to take part. One hundred and seventy-five
paratroopers were dropped inland to secure the access roads, but
they were not put down far enough from the shore to perform their
task of cutting the communications.

The invading force struggled some miles inland, but by then
Fidel's army began to close in. He had used his tiny air force
skillfully; his militia had been called up; the tanks and artillery,
which had been held in readiness near Havana, were sent down;
and a huge roundup of possible suspects filled Havana jails,
stadiums and even theaters with 200,000 men and women. This
was a measure of how large he thought the active opposition to be,
although his greatest danger would have been from the armed
underground resistance if it had been mobilized and warned. The

ugly system of delation by the Committees of Defense paid off from the Castro side in this crisis. Nearly all those sequestered when the attack began were quickly released.

Castro set up his own headquarters just north of the battle area and directed the operations from the beginning. The exiles fought as well as they could, but they never had the slightest chance. As Fidel said later; "We attacked them incessantly." The government forces gradually closed in on the beachhead and with ammunition exhausted and no possibility of help or reinforcements, there was nothing for the invaders to do but surrender. Playa Girón fell at five-thirty in the afternoon of April 19, 1961.

"The invaders have been annihilated," Fidel announced over the radio with understandable jubilation. "The revolution has emerged victorious. It destroyed in less than seventy-two hours the army organized during many months by the imperialistic Government of the United States."

Schlesinger quotes President Kennedy as saying after the debacle; "The test had always been whether the Cuban people would back a revolt against Castro." Everyone in the United States Government should have known that the "people" would not do so and that the Cuban underground and the disaffected would have no chance.

One of the many miscalculations made by the Americans—and of course the Cuban exiles shared it—was to underrate Fidel Castro, his followers, and the strength of the popular following he had among the Cuban people.

Military technicians in the United States went on speculating about what would have happened if President Kennedy had not canceled the second air strike, or if he had allowed the American marines and pilots to do more than they did, but this was typical military nonsense.

It was exactly the type of mechanical thinking that led the United States deeper and deeper into the quicksand of the Vietnamese War. On paper, in the Pentagon, North Vietnam and the Vietcong should have been defeated once the Americans put their immensely superior power and wealth into the conflict. However, the Vietnamese—in the North and in the Vietcong—had something that military minds find it impossible to gauge: spirit. They fought for their country, their race, their traditions, their freedom as they saw it, their dignity as human beings having a right to settle their own affairs. They were not—and are not—fighting for international Communism or for the Communist party of North Vietnam as such.

The same thing happened in Cuba at the time of the Bay of Pigs invasion. It would have happened later if the missile crisis had led to armed conflict. It will happen again if the United States, for any reason, leads another "crusade" against Communism in Cuba or against the Castro regime, or against any regime that has been chosen and set up by Cubans themselves.

The folly of the American Government in believing that 1,400 Cuban exiles, armed, trained, supported and guided by the United States, could have held a beachhead in Cuba against the Castro forces was beyond belief at the time. This is not wisdom after the event. Those who knew anything about Fidel Castro and the internal situation in Cuba were saying before the invasion started that it was certainly doomed to failure if President Kennedy carried out his public pledge not to use American armed forces to support the attack.

When we heard at *The New York Times* that Kennedy had given the orders to go ahead, I, for one, simply took it for granted that once he saw the invasion by Cubans alone could not succeed, he would throw American planes and warships into the conflict and either brazen it out with lies or plead the same necessity to defeat Communism at all costs that was the major reason for the Vietnam conflict.

The President told one *New York Times* editor the day before the landing that he felt very doubtful, but he thought the invasion had "a fifty-fifty chance." This shows how badly informed he was; the invasion had no chance whatever of success.

The military editor of *The New York Times,* Hanson Baldwin, knew very little about Castro or Cuba and he shared the generally accepted Pentagon belief that the invasion, as he wrote, "was lost in Washington." It was lost in Cuba, but Baldwin was right in saying that "use of the United States armed forces was the one factor that could absolutely ensure success."

Roger Hilsman, who was then Director of the Bureau of Intelligence and Research of the State Department, disposes of the Cuban exile and American military belief that cancelation of the second air strike made all the difference. In his book *To Move a Nation* (page 33) he writes:

A second air strike, twenty-four hours later, when the planes have been dispersed, hidden, and protected, has no hope at all of achieving such total surprise. And the overwhelming point is that if Castro's air attacks on the beachhead had not crushed the one-thousand-man landing force, the two-hundred-thousand-man army of militiamen that followed would certainly have done so.

The cancellation of the "second strike" did not doom the Bay of Pigs operation. It was doomed from the beginning, and the true failure was in not seeing this when the decision was made.

Hilsman does not explain why the invasion "was doomed from the beginning." Arthur Schlesinger, in *A Thousand Days,* gives one good reason: "The reality was that Fidel Castro turned out to be a far more formidable foe and in command of a far better organized regime than anyone had supposed."

This was true, but the key to the failure—and to its inexcusable character—lies in the phrases Schlesinger used: "turned out to be" and "than anyone had supposed." "Anyone" really knowing Fidel Castro and Cuba could feel only despair that as late as April 1961 the CIA, the State Department, the Pentagon and the White House did not know Fidel Castro's capacities, how well organized his regime was for defense and how great his popular support was. As Schlesinger says:

His patrols spotted the invasion at almost the first possible moment. His planes reacted with speed and vigor. His police eliminated any chance of sabotage or rebellion behind the lines. His soldiers stayed loyal and fought hard. He himself never panicked; and, if faults were chargeable to him, they were his overestimate of the strength of the invasion and undue caution in pressing the ground attack against the beachhead. His performance was impressive.

What Schlesinger did not know—in fact, I have not seen a reference to it in anything written about the Bay of Pigs—was that the United States Navy carried out a feint off the western coast of Pinar del Rio. Fidel told me about it later. The navy had escorted the ships with the Cuban invasion force, and the Americans were at all times keeping an eye on what happened. The aircraft carrier *Essex* hove to close to the Cuban shore, lowered a number of boats and had marines descend and get into them in sight of land.

Fidel, who naturally expected the Americans to take part and was always suspicious of them, took it for granted that the marines were preparing to land on the west coast of Cuba. He told me that he sent a considerable force there, led by Che Guevara, to defend the shore, diverting that many troops from the Bay of Pigs. This was what the Americans intended to happen. It was clever and it helped the Cuban exiles, but not nearly enough.

> One reason Washington miscalculated Castro, of course [Schlesinger continues], was a series of failures in our own intelligence. We regarded him as an hysteric.

This from Schlesinger is a revealing confession of ignorance, not only of Fidel Castro but of the Latin—in this case Spanish-Cuban—temperament. Fidel is a lot of things, but he could never be accused of being "an hysteric." He does not behave or talk like an Anglo-Saxon, which evidently was the yardstick Washington used.

Only one American officer, of those I have read, grasped the lesson in human and psychological terms that was to be learned by the invasion fiasco. He was Rear Admiral H. E. Eccles, Retired, who wrote a paper called "Notes on the Cuban Crisis" which Hanson Baldwin cited in the *New York Times* article of August 1, 1961.

The Cuban venture, Admiral Eccles stated, emphasizes that

> in the protracted conflict with the totalitarian concept, the fate of the free society will be determined much more by the understanding of human emotion and the exercise of intellectual power and moral value than by technological factors.

The lesson obviously was not learned in Washington; otherwise the United States would not have been so blind to the consequences of getting deeply involved in Vietnam. When the Cuban missile crisis came along a year and a half after the Bay of Pigs, the Kennedy triumph was against Khrushchev and had nothing to do with moral values or Fidel Castro's emotions. Kennedy, sensibly, did not care how Castro and the Cubans felt; the power of decision and the technological factors were out of Castro's control. This was not the case at the Bay of Pigs.

There were at least a dozen good reasons for the American disaster at the Bay of Pigs. Even when Kennedy relented on the second day and ordered six United States jet fighters from the carrier *Essex* to provide cover for two B-26 bombers coming from Nicaragua, someone neglected to tell the Americans that there was an hour's difference in time, so that the lumbering B-26s had no protection and were shot down. Since the weary Cuban pilots had refused to fly them and four American pilots working for the CIA volunteered to do so, this meant four American deaths.

United States destroyers, with air cover, searched the offshore waters for survivors and picked up some. In a number of small ways, therefore, the Americans did take part. Washington's chief responsibility, however, lay in the fact that the invasion was planned and the invaders were trained, armed, provided with planes and ships and other matériel by the United States.

Fidel Castro, therefore, could legitimately claim a victory against the "Colossus of the North." He could also claim a victory for his revolution. Many Cubans in those days would have been— as many are now—unhappy about the revolution and the hardships and dictatorial regime it brought to Cuba, but only a tiny fraction of older, prosperous, reactionary Cubans would have wanted to turn the clock back to 1958. Yet this is what the CIA tried to do. Even those Cubans who were bitterly unhappy at the way the revolution went rebelled against the past just as strongly as Castro and his associates.

President Kennedy did not want a "Batistiano" victory and had made that clear, but the CIA had its own ideas of what was good for the United States. There were guerrilla units operating inside

Cuba, of which the most effective was the Movimiento Revolucionario del Pueblo (MRP) directed by ex-Minister of Public Works Manuel Ray. Frank Bender, the CIA operator, refused to give Ray and his associates money and help, and before the landing he had arranged to get Ray removed from the picture. The MRP—the only really efficient underground movement in Cuba—was not notified of the invasion date, and hence did not rise when the exiles landed. The organization was permanently smashed by Castro and many of its members imprisoned in the immediate cleanup.

Bender, and the type of Cubans he preferred, had never forgiven Ray and his associates for having worked with Castro in the first months of the revolution. The MRP men were all anti-Communist, liberal, democratic and slightly left of center. Evidently that was considered a dangerous position by the CIA. It was called "Fidelismo without Fidel."

Batistiano military officers were placed in some command positions. On the political side, help was given to the Frente Revolucionario Democrático, composed of worthy, but pre-Batista conservative men with no popular following in Cuba.

A "Revolutionary Liberation Committee" was formed, but it was put under virtual arrest at the time of the landing and held incommunicado. The supreme military command of the invasion was given to a brash, compliant young exile who had joined the Rebel Army in the last week of the insurrection, and whom Goldenberg calls, with considerable understatement, "inexperienced and unpopular"—Manuel Artime.

One could go on almost indefinitely with the distressing (from the United States point of view) details of this almost incredible adventure. Theodore Draper's pithy characterization in his book *Castro's Revolution* (page 59) has become the classic summary: "The ill-fated invasion of Cuba in April, 1961, was one of those rare politico-military events—a perfect failure." From Fidel Castro's side it was an almost perfect success. It was the best thing that has happened to him in the ten years of the revolution.

President Kennedy gallantly took the blame for the fiasco and, at least, he learned a lot of lessons from it. Unfortunately, his Vice President, Lyndon B. Johnson, did not learn what, in retrospect and for historians, may well have been the most important lesson of them all: that nationalistic peoples will fight fanatically against foreigners on their own soil.

Fidel Castro was not a Marxist-Leninist or any kind of Communist on April 17, 1961, but even if he had been, the result would have been the same. He was a Cuban defending his country. The invaders were also Cubans, but they were fighting with foreign help under foreign orders, and Fidel could call them "mercenaries"—even though they were not.

Anyone familiar with the psychology of nations under dictatorships, and with their exiles, knows that those who stay at home and stick it out are the ones the country turns to when the change comes. They do not want exiles to return to run the country which they have left—and particularly a country which will have changed enormously during their absence. The pathetic Cuban Revolutionary Council that Washington set up to form a provisional government in Cuba would not have been welcomed by the Cuban people, not even by the enemies of the Castro regime.

This is a point that needs emphasizing. Fidel Castro can be overthrown by the United States; he cannot be overthrown by Cuban exiles. His danger at the Bay of Pigs was that President Kennedy would change his mind and throw American planes, ships and marines into the conflict. The decision not to do so doomed the invasion.

This was something that Kennedy did not regret; he had always been determined not to allow American armed forces to take part in the invasion. As he said on April 21, while the bitter taste of defeat and humiliation was at its strongest, "Any unilateral American intervention in the absence of an external attack upon ourselves or an ally would have been contrary to our traditions and to our international obligations. But let the record show that our restraint is not inexhaustible."

To be sure, he and the United States had violated the Charter of Bogotá, the hemispheric treaty that bans direct or indirect intervention by one American state against another. However, as President Johnson showed when he sent marines into the Dominican Republic in 1965, this clause of the Bogotá Charter is not—and never has been—operative.

There is a clash in this hemispheric pact with the Monroe Doctrine. Fidel Castro knows this even though Khrushchev, when he was Premier, announced the demise of the historic American document on July 14, 1960. The State Department's reply was a virtual rewording of the prophetic and important speech by the late Assistant Secretary of State Edward G. Miller, Jr., on April 26, 1950: "The Monroe Doctrine has not lost its meaning with the passage of a century and a quarter, for today we consider any attempt to extend the Communist system to any portions of this hemisphere as dangerous to our peace and safety."

In a response to a request of mine, the then Assistant Secretary for Latin American Affairs, Roy R. Rubottom, Jr., wrote to me on June 23, 1959, that: "The United States considers the Monroe Doctrine to be a valid *unilateral* statement even though our position vis-à-vis the other world powers, including the Latin American states, has changed considerably since 1823."

The emphasis is on the security of the United States, and this is the factor that comes into play in our relations with Castro's Cuba. Fidel's Communism was seen as a potential threat to American security. The missile crisis of October 1962 was to show how great a threat it could be.

The same fear was a prime motive in the decision to help the Cuban exiles in the Bay of Pigs invasion. This is not meant to deprecate the genuine and perennial American desire to "make the world safe for democracy." A great deal about the American role in the Cuban invasion was immoral, but not the intention to help men who were willing to risk their lives to free their country from, as they saw it, a foreign-dominated tyranny. It is more than doubtful that given a choice the Cuban people would have voted for the invaders against the Castro regime. The way Fidel Castro was supported is evidence to the contrary. In that sense, the United States policy was at least misguided.

"Afterward," Schlesinger writes, "Kennedy would sometimes recur incredulously to the Bay of Pigs, wondering how a rational and responsible government could ever have become involved in so ill-starred an adventure."

Rather astonishingly, the only people whom President Kennedy reproached publicly were the newspapermen. Actually, all of us knew more or less what was happening from October 1960 onwards. *The New York Times* was one of many responsible organs that withheld a great deal of information out of a misguided sense of patriotism or—in a few cases—by request. Fidel Castro learned nothing from the American press that he did not already know. In fact, his intelligence within the Cuban exile community is fairly complete at all times.

The role of President Kennedy in the two climactic Cuban events of his all-too-brief term in office—the Bay of Pigs and the missile crisis—was decisive for Cuba and therefore for Fidel Castro. I had a long talk with the President between the two events—on July 3, 1962. Since it throws some light on Kennedy's ideas about Fidel Castro and the Cuban Revolution, I am giving the pertinent passages here from my notes, without change. In these paragraphs I was answering the President's questions, which explains the one-sided form of the notes:

> Halfway through he [Kennedy] suddenly asked: "What do you think of the Cuban situation?"
>
> I went into a long speech on their being in a state of transition now; that they may have touched bottom. I explained how Fidel and the others came into power completely untrained, without experience of any kind and without any ideology, because Fidel was not a Communist then, despite the belief here. I went on to say that Fidel and the others were determined to make a very radical revolution and they were extremely nationalistic—determined to break the domination of the United States, to whom they were an economic satellite. A conflict with the United States, I said, was built into the situation and was inevitable.
>
> He said it seems like a Greek tragedy, once it got started. I said once the break came with the United States, Fidel had no other choice than to turn to the Soviet bloc, but that I was not one of those who believed that we drove him into the arms of the Reds— he rushed in. However, we were unable to roll with the punch or take the punishment. I said it was frightening that Fidel chose Marxism-Leninism and this is something that might happen elsewhere in Latin America. I gave him my theory that the totalitarian

method has a great appeal in these underdeveloped countries. Anyway, that Fidel turned things more and more over to the Reds.

He broke in to ask why I thought Fidel made that December 2 speech. I had no good explanation—just thought it fitted his mood and the way he was going then. However, I went on, Fidel realized early this year that the Reds had made an awful mess—that he had agreed all along his revolution would succeed or fail on the economic results. So he began kicking out some of the Reds in March and bringing in loyal followers.

"You don't believe that Fidel, Raúl, Che were Communists?" he asked. I said no, in the sense of belonging to the Party and being under Party discipline. They were never under any discipline, and the Cuban people were completely incapable ever of achieving the discipline that a Communist regime demanded.

At one time Kennedy asked what we could do. I said nothing else than we are doing now, but I said I thought it was a mistake not to allow Fidel a line of retreat. I had to agree several times, in arguing this matter, that Fidel could not possibly change his policies now, but I argued that if his economic situation improved in the next few years perhaps he might want to, or be willing to.

"You mean turn Tito?" Kennedy asked. I said, maybe. Kennedy said, "You are like Fitzroy MacLean who predicted that Tito would break with Moscow."

I developed the idea of Fidel's character—wild, undisciplined, rash, tough. I had earlier expounded my idea that the impact of the French Revolution lay in its extremism, contrasting it to our Revolution.

I argued that we don't have to fear Communism in Latin America. The parties and movements are weak, with no good leaders. He seemed to agree. But I argued that we do have to fear the attraction of the totalitarian method in underdeveloped countries. I again stressed how bad it is that the gap between the United States and Latin America is widening. He took up some paper he had and made some notes—said he would ask Kenneth Galbraith to make a study of the problems of the underdeveloped countries and would also have a study made as to why or how our methods could be better in solving their problems. I reminded him of his speech about "our unfulfilled task."

He was much interested in my forthcoming trip to Cuba and asked me to come and tell him about it when I got back.

He was obviously much intrigued with the idea that Fidel might change and came back to it several times. However, he kept pointing to the climate of opinion here and the problems with Congress.

"What else could we do but give them a sugar quota—that's all they have to sell—and how could we get that out of Congress? Even if we wanted to give him an out, how could we?"

I said one possibility might be to allow a back door to be opened by one of the Latin American countries—Brazil wanted to try to mediate at one time. And I returned to my idea that if the economic situation in Cuba improved enough, Fidel might feel strong enough to make a change.

I told him how I had argued often with Fidel about Communism and how I had reminded him of Palmerston's dictum about nations having only permanent interests and that Cuba's interests had to be with us. I agreed it was hopeless now to expect any change. I said when I saw Fidel I was going to say [apropos of the Cuban Communists], "I told you so."

Kennedy said Fidel could do himself a lot of good by releasing those [Bay of Pigs] prisoners. I told him I had written Fidel telling him that, but not to forget that Fidel is pure Spanish and very revengeful.

"He ought to be grateful to us," Kennedy said. "He gave us a kick in the ass and it made him stronger than ever. However, that invasion did some good. If it wasn't for that we would be in Laos now—or perhaps unleashing Chiang."*

I said at one point that we could not count on a collapse and I didn't think there would be one. I pointed to Spain after the war. Fidel, I said, has been doing some good work on education and is now training thousands of young men as technicians, engineers, etc., and if he has five more years he will be able to replace many of the technicians who went into exile.

Kennedy talked a good deal of the Alliance. I said that if I were a betting man I would give him ten to one it would fail, at least in the ten-year period, but I agreed that it was an excellent plan and the only answer we could give, and I called attention to the way in

---

* His reference to Laos concerned the fact that the situation there came to a crisis at the same time as the Bay of Pigs incident. Kennedy was in delicate negotiations with the Russians which would have failed, with certainty, if the Cuban-exile invasion had succeeded. As it was, Khrushchev waited to protest to Washington until Castro clearly had the situation in hand. Kennedy referred to Marshal Chiang Kai-shek because he was under pressure to lift the ban against the Nationalist Chinese trying to invade the mainland.

which we always boosted it editorially—at which he nodded agreement. He spoke primarily from the angle of winning support in Congress and the United States. Also of the vastness and cost of the problem, which obviously has impressed him enormously. He has a remarkable grasp of the problems involved in Latin America, but was certainly weak on Cuba.

I kept insisting on the extent to which it is Fidel's revolution.

I several times stressed that Fidel is very intelligent—much more so than Americans believed. I said that giving Cubans no line of retreat and demanding unconditional surrender, they would fight to the death. Also, that Fidel, for all his mistakes, was sincere and patriotic and wanted to do what was best for Cuba and the Cubans. He isn't evil—he is bad for the United States. When I said that Fidel still had a big following in Cuba he nodded assent.

He was very surprised to hear how young Fidel was—when I told him he is ten years younger than he.

In explaining how it is Fidel's revolution, I said, You have to put up with a legislature, a press, a judiciary even when they run counter to your policies. When Fidel came to power and found that these were impediments and even dangers to his revolution, he simply abolished the legislature, suppressed free press, changed the judges. This is the way things are done in Latin America.

He said Khrushchev told him in Vienna that Fidel was not a Communist. This was apropos of my saying that Fidel must be a headache to Moscow.

I said that I am heretical enough to feel that we would all be worse off if Fidel were killed.

His last words when we shook hands were to request that I should come in and see him after I got back from Cuba.

The trip had to be postponed because of the missile crisis. President Kennedy was dead when I returned from my long journey to Latin America in 1963.

The political and revolutionary results of the thwarted invasion were exemplified by the leadership on the two Cuban sides. Nearly all the Cubans accepted or chosen by the Eisenhower-Nixon regime, and used with some misgivings by the Kennedy Government in the leading positions at the time of the exile invasion, were what

Schlesinger aptly called men who "stood for the Cuba of the past."
The respected members of the Liberation Committee would indignantly deny this characterization, but in the revolutionary—not
communistic—sense, this was true.

Fidel Castro represents the Cuba of the future, and he will do so
when his Marxism-Leninism has ceased to have any meaning in
Cuba. The Cuban people—represented militarily by his militia of
200,000 or 250,000 men and women—rallied to his side in the
Bay of Pigs invasion because of his revolution, not because of his
Communism, which, as I have made clear, had not publicly been
formulated in April 1961. It was the vast opportunities opened to
him by his triumph against the invaders and against the United
States that permitted Castro to carry his communistic policies to
their climax.

The Bay of Pigs represented a political watershed for the Cuban
Revolution. Fidel first proclaimed his "socialism" the day after the
air strike from Guatemala which signaled the commencement of
the invasion. Before the end of 1961 he had made his "I am a
Marxist-Leninist" speech.

I am convinced that Fidel Castro does not himself know when
he decided that a socialistic-communistic system was best suited to
the revolution that he was making. However, it is obvious that his
victory at the Bay of Pigs presented him with opportunities and
possibilities which did not exist before. He took advantage of them
with skill, intelligence and forcefulness.

As Schlesinger wrote, his performance at the time of the invasion had been "impressive." Fidel Castro is always at his best in
moments of crisis. This is one of the keys to his hold over the
Cuban people, and it will be one of his claims to an outstanding
position in the history of our times.

He came out of the invasion crisis with his charisma—his heroic
stature—greatly enhanced in the eyes of the Cuban people.

Moreover, Castro had 1,100 Cuban-exile prisoners for whom
President Kennedy personally, and the United States in general,
had a heavy moral responsibility. The Americans had sent a
number of Cubans to their death and the rest into the always harsh
conditions of a Latin-American—in this case Cuban—prison. In
the Isle of Pines Presidio they were a burden and expense to the

Castro Government. While they had been humiliated by defeat, they had fought well as long as they could and were heroes in the eyes of the Americans and their Cuban-exile relatives.

Fidel knew that Kennedy had these men on his conscience and would do what he could to get them released. From Castro's point of view, the prisoners were at best mercenaries, as he called them, and at worst criminals and traitors. The Government in Washington and the relatives in Miami at first feared that they might be executed, but there was never any chance of that.

Since he considered himself the aggrieved party and the United States the major culprit, Fidel could not see why the Americans should not ransom the prisoners. He therefore at first asked a price of 500 bulldozers for them. As the American Government had never officially conceded the role that it had played in the invasion, it could not pay for the captives' release. For private citizens or organizations, the price was too high. Vice President Nixon, whose role from the beginning was a devious one, sententiously remarked that human beings ought not be bartered.

Negotiations dragged on for months. Fidel was persuaded to accept his ransom in $53,000,000 worth of food and medicines, which were privately donated. Without waiting to get the full amount, he released the prisoners in time to let them get home for Christmas, 1962. He got no credit for clemency and seems to have been cheated on the amount of food and medicines promised to him.

The aftermath of the invasion was a bitter one for the Cuban exiles. They were enormously cheered when President Kennedy went down to Miami on December 29, 1962, and said to the released prisoners after they presented the Brigade flag to him; "I can assure you that this flag will be returned to this Brigade in a free Havana." Mrs. Kennedy spoke emotionally in Spanish. Kennedy had promised more than he could fulfill. His Administration—and Johnson's after his—clearly abandoned any idea of using either an American or Cuban-exile force against the Castro regime. The exile organizations broke up; the leaders went their separate ways; and Washington contented itself with the belief that Castroite Cuba had been "contained" and would not be a bother any more.

Kennedy's policy of isolating and ignoring Castro worked well [Schlesinger wrote in *A Thousand Days* (page 999)]. By 1963 he was hardly even a thorn in the flesh. Once his influence in Latin America was destroyed, the survival of a mendicant Communist regime in the Caribbean was not important.

Fidel was not unhappy about being "isolated" from the United States. The survival of his revolution and his hopes of achieving economic viability depend on Cuba's being left alone and in peace to work out her problems. So far as being a "mendicant" is concerned, the Cubans figure that Moscow is more than getting its money's worth by having a Communist regime on the doorstep of the United States.

And if "Castro's influence in Latin America was destroyed," why did a panicky President Johnson feel constrained to pour 30,000 United States Marines into the Dominican Republic in April 1965, at the mere hint of a threat of "another Cuba"?

The Bay of Pigs fiasco insured the survival of the Castro regime by showing Fidel's capacity for leadership, the military and police power of his regime, and its popular following. It might all have gone down under a deluge of American bombs at the time of the missile crisis, but this would have been the destruction of Cuba—not just of the Cuban Revolution—and it might have been the opening blasts of a nuclear world war. The issue there was not Castro or Cuba; it was the struggle of the United States against the Soviet Union. The security of the United States was at stake, and Cuba was literally just a pawn in that game.

The decision to permit Soviet nuclear missiles to be installed in Cuba was the greatest act of folly in Fidel Castro's hectic career. Nikita Khrushchev received and deserved universal condemnation for bringing the world to the edge of the most horrible abyss into which humanity can fall—a nuclear war. But he could not have done it without Castro's enthusiastic cooperation.

The first victim of a confrontation, if the Russians had not pulled back in time, would have been Cuba. A great American army was poised across the Florida Straits ready to move into

Cuba. The enormous resources of the American air force were in place and prepared in a matter of moments to devastate every part of Cuba where the bomb sites were known or suspected to be, and where the Soviet Ilyushin-28 bombers had been spotted.

Fidel Castro, in short, almost brought about the destruction of his country. In that case, his revolution would have gone up in smoke—and perhaps in radioactive smoke. The measure of his daring, if it be measurable, was shown by this amazing performance. The extent of his good fortune was shown by the fact that the crisis was resolved peacefully and that Castro's position in Cuba was, if anything, fortified. However, in the process he was deeply humiliated, and the humiliation still rankles.

Yet it still has to be said that in the way the "crisis of the Caribbean" worked out, it became a mere incident in the course of the Cuban Revolution. It was as if Fidel Castro had been halted in his stride, given a hard jolt, and then continued on his way. The Cuban people seemed never to have grasped the enormity of the peril they had escaped. In a short time, it was as good as forgotten.

I wish it were possible to state with any confidence whether it was Castro or Khrushchev who conceived the idea of installing the missiles. Naturally, the decision to provide the weapons had to be made in the Kremlin. Arthur Schlesinger, who devotes two chapters (pages 794–841) to the missile crisis in *A Thousand Days,* summarizes on page 795 what was known in 1965:

> The Soviet Union had never before placed nuclear missiles in any other country. . . . Why should it now send nuclear missiles to a country thousands of miles away, lying within the zone of vital interest of their main adversary, a land, moreover, headed by a willful leader of, from the Russian viewpoint, somewhat less than total reliability? Castro, with characteristic loquacity, later produced a confusion of explanations. He told a Cuban audience in January 1963 that sending the missiles was a Soviet idea; he repeated this to Claude Julien of *Le Monde* in March 1963; in May he described it to Lisa Howard of the American Broadcasting Company as "simultaneous action on the part of both governments"; then in October he told Herbert Matthews of the *New York Times* that it was a Cuban idea, only to tell Jean Daniel of *L'Express* in November that it was a Soviet idea; in January 1964, when Matthews called him

about the Daniel story, Castro claimed again that it was a Cuban idea; and, when Cyrus Sulzberger of the *New York Times* asked him in October 1964, Castro, pleading that the question raised security problems, said cagily, "Both Russia and Cuba participated."

As for the Russians, Khrushchev told the Supreme Soviet in December 1962, "We carried weapons there at the request of the Cuban government."

In that speech he mentioned an agreement to install "a few dozen ballistic rockets of medium range" in Cuba.

I can add another piece of confusion to this bewildering compilation. At the end of October 1967, in a conversation with Fidel Castro, I asked him once again whether it was his idea or Khrushchev's to install the nuclear missiles in Cuba.

This time [I wrote in my notes], although Fidel thought he was repeating what he told us [my wife and myself] in 1963, he gave a different—and I now believe true—explanation.

"It was a time when we felt ourselves in danger from the United States," he said. "We consulted with the Russians—which is to say, Nikita Khrushchev—on what could be done. When they suggested the missiles, we immediately said, 'Yes, by all means, we are completely in accord; this satisfies our desires 100 percent.' We also felt that we were in duty bound to agree out of solidarity for the Socialist bloc. In the crisis, Khrushchev was clumsy [Fidel used the word *torpe* several times]. Moreover [this was in answer to my prompting] it is true that he was acting solely in Russian interests and not in Cuban interests. We were acting both in our own interests and in the interests of the Soviet bloc. This was the simple truth. I think that Khrushchev did it entirely on his own without consulting other members of the Politburo. I also think that Kennedy acted as he did partly to save Khrushchev, out of fear that any successor would be tougher. Kennedy was willing to give up the Turkish and Greek bases. Khrushchev did not even make sure, as he could have, that Kennedy would give a firm promise not to attack Cuba."

The reference at the end is to the fact that Khrushchev accepted the Kennedy proviso that the United States would promise not to attack Cuba if a United Nations team was allowed to inspect the missile sites to make sure that they were clear. This Fidel refused to permit, and he was bitter against Khrushchev, among other reasons, because he was not consulted on this point. It was a case in which the Russians showed as great a failure to understand Fidel Castro as the Americans did. Khrushchev should have known that Fidel would never consent to a United Nations inspection—or perhaps the Russians did not care what happened at that stage. Fidel Castro was the least of their worries, and as I and no doubt others had warned Fidel all along, so far as the Russians were concerned, Cuba was always expendable.

In practice, it became of no importance whether or not there was an American promise. Aerial reconnaissance with U-2 planes provided a means of inspection. The United States has not contemplated invading Cuba, and there is no reason in present circumstances why it should do so. Fidel was at least able to show that so far as Cuban soil was concerned, he was the ruler, not Khrushchev and not Moscow.

On the question of who first had the idea of introducing the missiles into Cuba, my own tentative conclusion is that both Khrushchev and Castro wanted to do it for somewhat different reasons. For the Soviet Union, it offered the possibility of altering the world balance of power—or terror—and achieving a tremendous political victory in the eyes of the world over the United States. For Cuba, it offered the chance of strengthening the island's defensive posture to an enormous extent. The idea was clearly a dazzling one to Fidel.

One must suppose that neither Castro nor Khrushchev was insane enough to court a nuclear world war. The fact that they almost got it was due to an underestimation of President Kennedy's courage and the American willingness to go to the most extreme lengths in defense of United States security and its position in the world.

My conversations with Fidel on the subject convinced me that he was genuinely thinking in defensive, not offensive, terms. It has always been hard—or even impossible—for Americans to believe that Fidel Castro and all his associates in the ruling group are in constant fear of American aggression against them. This is not an excuse that they invent for their policies; it is an obsession, a firm belief.

In early July 1962, when Raúl Castro went to Moscow and is believed to have made the final arrangements for the nuclear missiles, the Cubans felt the menace strongly. It was not much more than a year after the Bay of Pigs invasion. The CIA was continually at work sending in saboteurs, guerrillas and counter-revolutionaries of all kinds. Fidel claimed to me, in November 1963, that on the basis of information they were getting early in 1962 from a number of sources, they felt almost sure that the United States was preparing a military invasion of Cuba.

They were strengthened in this belief [I wrote at the time in a paper for the *Hispanic American Report of* Stanford University] after Aleksei I. Adzhubei, Premier Khrushchev's son-in-law and editor of *Izvestia,* had an interview with President Kennedy early that year. The official report of the interview was conveyed to the Cubans who interpreted some of the things that President Kennedy said as confirmation of their belief in a planned invasion. [The State Department denied that President Kennedy was so threatening, or that the United States was planning an invasion.]

The Russians, Fidel Castro argued, were also persuaded that Cuba was going to be attacked. In these circumstances, he asserted, the nuclear weapons were "defensive"; they were intended to discourage the United States from going ahead with its plans.

"In the world today," he went on, "there are two war phobias, one of a nuclear war which can be ruled out because nobody wants it, and the other of local wars. The United States and Russia, in the crisis of the Caribbean, were facing a world war, but Cuba was facing a local war. She was going to be attacked by the United States. If Cuba were attacked, the Russians would have been drawn in because of their commitments to us."

Curiously, in a radio broadcast on April 2, 1959, Fidel brought up the subject of atomic bombs (Selser, page 291):

"People here talk of war," he said, "they talk of atomic war, and we don't have a rabbit's hole in which to put ourselves. I know what war is. At least, bombs of 500 and 1,000 pounds were dropped on us. I don't want to know what an atomic war is like. They talk of war as if they were in the age of Christopher Columbus and not the age of atomic bombs, and meanwhile nobody in Cuba has told the truth about our complete defenselessness in case of war."

He set about changing that state of affairs quickly—and in fact, large orders for conventional arms had already been given. However, the following year, Fidel was charmed when Khrushchev brought up the subject of missiles in a bellicose speech about Cuba.

"It should be borne in mind that the United States is now not at such an unattainable distance from the Soviet Union as formerly," the Soviet Premier said on July 9, 1960. "Figuratively speaking, if need be, Soviet artillerymen can support the Cuban people with their rocket fire, should the aggressive forces in the Pentagon dare to start intervention against Cuba."

The key words, of course, were "figuratively speaking"— meaning theoretically or symbolically or anything but a direct threat that the Soviet Union would use nuclear missiles if the United States intervened militarily in Cuba. I was in Havana in August 1960, and was told by a few government people that Khrushchev's statement came as a complete surprise to them. One of the top officials told me that they all learned about it from the American news agencies.

Fidel, perhaps knowing better, insisted for some time on taking Khrushchev's words literally and claiming that Cuba was being protected by Soviet missiles. The United States, for its part, was lulled by the knowledge that Russia did have nuclear-bomb missiles which could reach the United States. It therefore seemed to follow that the Russians had no need to install medium- and intermediate-range missiles in Cuba. As part of the deception, when the time came to install the missiles in Cuba, the Russians, on September 11, 1962, repeated that "there was no need to search for sites" outside the Soviet Union. However, this time they stated that an attack on Cuba would mean a nuclear war.

Four days before, President Kennedy, alarmed by the heavy buildup of Soviet arms, technicians and sophisticated surface-to-air antiaircraft missile bases (SAMS) in Cuba, had requested Congress for standby authority to call up reserve troops. On September 13 he issued a solemn warning:

"If at any time the Communist buildup in Cuba were to endanger or interfere with our security in any way . . . or if Cuba should ever attempt to export its aggressive purposes by force or the threat of force against any nation in this hemisphere, or become an offensive military base of significant capacity for the Soviet Union, then this country will do whatever must be done to protect its own security and that of its allies."

Since the first stage of the Russian program was to install SAM missile sites and place MIG fighters on Cuban air bases, the photographs from the U-2 planes still indicated only preparations for defense. Intelligence reports from Cuban refugees could not be trusted because past experience had shown that while some information proved correct, much the greater part was inaccurate. Reports from CIA agents took time and always needed checking.

The first verifiable U-2 photographs of missile sites were made on October 14. As Robert F. Kennedy's posthumous account stated, no proof was available of the missile sites until that date. The demagogic New York Senator Kenneth B. Keating claimed to have had the information and given public warning, but as Roger Hilsman conclusively demonstrated in *To Move a Nation* (pages 177–180), this was impossible. It was wild guessing which proved roughly true. When the U-2 films of October 14, 1962, were processed, they "clearly showed the erector-launches, missile-carrying trailers, fueling trucks, and radar vans of a battalion of soviet medium-range ballistic missiles" at San Cristóbal in western Cuba, Hilsman wrote.

Thus began what Americans call the missile crisis and Cubans *el crisis del Caribe*.

Hilsman believes (page 159) that the Soviet decision to deploy long-range nuclear missiles to Cuba must have been reached some time during the spring of 1962 and certainly no later than early summer. If so, Raúl Castro's trip to Moscow in July would have been primarily to arrange details. A major motive for Khrushchev's desperate gamble, Hilsman thinks, was that the Russians decided their "whole ICBM system was suddenly obsolescent."

For Schlesinger "one can only speculate as to what these Soviet reasons were," though they might have been "a probe of American intentions."

So far as Fidel Castro was concerned, the reasons were clearer, even though the conception of arranging for the introduction of the missiles is confused. It cannot be doubted that for Fidel's daring, gambling spirit and with his fear and antagonism where the United States was concerned, the idea was a splendid one. Of his closest associates, Raúl, his brother, and Che Guevara would have been equally thrilled. It is a good guess that the cautious and sensible President Dorticós was unhappy and worried. Celia Sánchez would play no role in such a decision and would walk into a fiery furnace with Fidel if this was his fate.

Theodore Draper, in an article "Castro and Communism" for *The Reporter* of January 17, 1963, guesses that the Bay of Pigs triumph "gave Castro and his ruling group the illusion that they could do anything."

The history of the missile crisis from the American side has been well told, especially by "insiders" like Schlesinger, Sorensen, Hilsman and Robert Kennedy after his brother's assassination. The Russian side is, as always, shrouded in the fog that envelops the Kremlin. The Cuban version has to be gleaned from speeches by Fidel, Raúl, Che and information published in the Havana newspaper *Revolución*. Theodore Draper, with customary thoroughness, did an excellent job on that material in the *Reporter* article just cited, with special emphasis on the aftermath.

The Russians set out to install four intermediate- and six medium-range nuclear missile sites in Cuba, according to Schlesinger. The process required an extraordinary degree of organization and technical proficiency, and the Americans were amazed by the secrecy and speed with which the Russians worked.

The Cubans did nothing. It was a Soviet job from beginning to end. Had the missiles been installed, Russians—not Cubans— would have manned and operated them. The same was true of the SAM sites, but after the crisis Cubans were trained in their use, and they are now part of Cuba's own military defense. SAMs are ground-to-air, with only a 25-mile range, so they are no threat to the Florida coast. The Russian ballistic missiles could easily have reached Washington and the Middle Western cities.

The presence of the missiles started President Kennedy on a process that Schlesinger describes with justice as a "combination of toughness and restraint, of will, nerve and wisdom, so brilliantly controlled, so matchlessly calibrated, that [it] dazzled the world."

The key points were the decision to blockade (for legal reasons it was called "quarantine") the Cuban coast so that the Soviet ships en route to Cuba would be stopped. It was made clear to Moscow that if Khrushchev did not agree to withdraw the missiles already in Cuba, destroy the missile sites and take out the IL-28 bombers, a large army massed in Florida would invade Cuba with air and naval support. Khrushchev quite simply gave in, with nothing to show for his breathtaking plan except an agreement by Kennedy that the United States would not invade Cuba, providing a United Nations inspection force verified the removal of the offensive weapons. Even that accord came to naught when Castro refused to permit a UN team or even a mission from the International Red Cross to enter Cuba. Effectively, the crisis ended on Sunday, October 28, 1962, when Khrushchev's letter announcing a willingness to withdraw the nuclear missile material reached Washington.

It was none too soon. As Secretary of State Rusk was to say later, the two giants were "eyeball to eyeball."

From the Cuban point of view, an important factor was that every member Government of the Organization of American States supported a United States resolution authorizing the use of force to carry out the "quarantine." The missile crisis was a severe setback for Fidel Castro in Latin America. It shocked every responsible Latin-American official into a realization of the mortal danger each of their countries faced because of policies that Fidel had pursued and might pursue again.

On the face of it, he seemed to be acting as a stooge of Moscow, introducing Communist power as well as Communist ideology into the Western Hemisphere. What he did was recognized as an act of inexcusable recklessness. Although Cuba and the Soviet Union were, in fact, following the same policy for different reasons in the missile adventure, and although Castro did not in the least consider himself as a tool of Moscow, appearances were against him.

The fact that the crisis was settled between Kennedy and Khrushchev, without Castro's being consulted at any stage, was a humiliation which demonstrated Fidel's and Cuba's weakness. In international terms, this was the lowest point that Fidel reached in his revolution. He knew it, and the knowledge rankled.

At the same time, Schlesinger's verdict, which was typical, was exaggerated. "The missile crisis," he wrote, "displayed him [Castro] as a rather impotent and ignominious Soviet tool." Fidel was "impotent" in the crisis because there could be no stage at which he controlled the missiles and pads being installed. Consequently, once the decision was made to withdraw them, he could do nothing. He was a "Soviet tool" only in the same sense. The crisis, in fact, taught him a lesson and started him on policies that are contrary to Russian desires.

Fidel Castro's image was fractured and reduced when the missile crisis ended. It is a tribute to his extraordinary resilience that he managed, after some floundering about, to recover much of the lost ground. Little, if any, ground had been lost within Cuba. Those outside the government were confused about what was happening and, because of the controlled and doctored news they were given, never understood clearly what it was all about.

On the popular side there was, from what I heard later, a truly impressive demonstration of support for Castro and the regime. Unlike the Bay of Pigs affair, there were no arrests of Cubans; there was no Fifth Column. That Cuba was endangered from the United States, which was the way it looked from the island, was enough to rally all but the diehard enemies of the revolution. The Cuban exiles briefly had their hopes raised. An American invasion would have meant the end of Fidel Castro, a return to live in what was left of Cuba, and a new life there. As it happened, the resolution of the missile crisis was to put an immediate end to any hopes of United States intervention without which the Castro regime could not be overthrown.

Fidel expressed his feelings well in an interview with the French journalist Claude Julien which *Le Monde* of Paris published on March 22 and 23, 1963:

> Cuba does not intend to be a pawn on the global chessboard. Cuban sovereignty is a reality; that is what we fought for. I cannot accept that Khrushchev should have promised Kennedy to withdraw his missiles without the slightest reference to an indispensable accord with the Cuban Government. To be sure, it was a case of Soviet missiles which were out of our direct control. But they were on Cuban territory and nothing should have been decided without consulting us. We are not a satellite. Obviously, the U.S.S.R. has global responsibilities which we do not have. Khrushchev wanted peace and we also wanted peace. Nobody has the right to dispose of Cuban sovereignty. That is why we proposed a five-point program which, alone, can guarantee peace in the Caribbean.

Fidel's five points were: (1) end of the economic embargo and all commercial pressures; (2) end of all subversive activities by the United States against Cuba; (3) end of "pirate attacks" from bases in the United States and Puerto Rico; (4) end of violations of Cuban air and naval space; and (5) United States withdrawal from Guantánamo naval base.

The program was, of course, quite unacceptable to the United States. In a conversation with a Cuban Cabinet Minister in 1966, I was told that the five points were simply "a declaration of independence" with the intention of showing that Cuba had a policy of her own and was not just a Russian satellite. There was no expectation, he said, that they would be carried out literally.

It was doubtful that they fulfilled any purpose except to give Castro an excuse to reject United Nations or any other international inspection of the withdrawal of the missiles from Cuba. This he did categorically in a television broadcast to the Cuban people on November 1. However, aerial inspection showed that the bases were being dismantled and shipped back to Russia. "The camera," President Kennedy said in December, "is going to be our best inspector." It still is.

In those days of crisis, while Fidel Castro was being completely ignored, the only balm came from Secretary General U Thant of the United Nations. He visited Havana on October 30 and 31, and while he could not induce Fidel to yield on the question of inspection he treated the Cuban Premier, with his customary courtesy, as the head of a member Government of the United Nations.

Aside from that, Fidel was able to take some of the anger out of his system when Mikoyan arrived in Havana on November 2. Castro would not receive him for nearly two weeks and the unfortunate Deputy Premier could not even get back home for the funeral of his wife, who died while he was in Cuba. It took Mikoyan three and a half weeks to get Fidel calmed down and somewhat pacified. At that, he left Fidel brooding, for it was a few months before Castro again made a public speech.

In the spring of 1963, the Cuban leader did accept an invitation to visit the Soviet Union, where he was given what probably was the warmest and most flattering reception ever accorded a foreign dignitary. I saw him not long after his return to Havana, and he positively glowed in talking about his Russian experience. As in Aesop's fable, the way to get Fidel Castro to take off his coat and relax is not to huff and puff at him, but to envelop him in sunny warmth. Besides, Moscow made a new and even more generous trade agreement with Cuba.

Fidel has never conceded, and never will, that the nuclear missile adventure was a mistake. He regretted that he became involved in something over which he had no control, but this is how he felt about the affair as late as March 13, 1965, in a speech at the University of Havana:

"They [the Cuban people] did not hesitate to face the dangers of thermonuclear war, of a nuclear attack against us, when in our country and our territory, with the full and absolute right which we have not given up, and in an absolutely legitimate act for which we will never be sorry, we agreed to the installation of strategic thermonuclear rockets on our territory. And in addition, not only were we in agreement that they should be brought here, but we disagreed that they should be taken away."

I have seen several references by students of Cuban affairs to what might be called a Samson complex in Fidel Castro's character—a willingness to pull down the pillars of the temple to destroy Cuba and himself if he feels driven to a point of desperation—or of exaltation. Perhaps, although I would say that this was more applicable to the younger Castro of the early years of the revolution than to the Castro of 1969 entering his middle age. The revolution has become more and more precious to him as the years pass. He says he is becoming more radical as he gets older. I think that he is getting less reckless.

One is left at the end of any contemplation of the nuclear missile crisis with a sense of wonder that Khrushchev and Castro did not know what the American response would be. Early in this book I described what Cuba meant to the United States historically, economically—and strategically. There were the American attitude toward Communism; the hostility toward the Castro regime; the shock that was bound to follow a nuclear-backed intrusion by the Soviet Union into the Western Hemisphere; the overwhelming military power that the United States possessed a few miles from Cuba while the Soviet Union was thousands of miles away; and the undiminished unilateral validity of the Monroe Doctrine to the United States. "We should consider any attempt on their [European powers] part to extend their system to any portion of this hemisphere as dangerous to our peace and safety," the Doctrine reads.

How could Khrushchev and Castro have expected the United States not to react with all its power even if the Russians had been able to complete the installation of their missiles and planes?

One is faced with something like the reverse of the questions asked about the Bay of Pigs. The fallibility of the leaders in both adventures is the most sobering of the thoughts stirred up by the events in Cuba. If a Bay of Pigs and a missile crisis can occur in Cuba, what might not happen in Vietnam, Korea, Berlin, the Middle East?

Yet President Kennedy did handle the missile crisis with extraordinary flair and brilliance. There were indications in the weeks before his assassination that he was rethinking his policy toward Cuba. However, there is nothing in what he is known to have said to his associates, or what he said publicly, to indicate that he was considering terms that Fidel Castro would have or could have accepted.

To the end, Kennedy considered Cuba a Soviet satellite. He wanted Fidel Castro to cease his economic and military dependence on the Soviet Union and to give up his policy of trying to subvert Latin American countries. From Fidel's point of view there would have been very little in the way of a *quid pro quo*.

The former United States Ambassador to Guinea, William Attwood, asserted in his book *The Reds and the Blacks* (pages 142–44) that he undertook to bring about negotiations in which Fidel might make "substantial concessions" and that he had made progress. Castro, according to Attwood, had agreed to conversations. His close associate and physician, Major René Vallejo, was the intermediary. However, Kennedy was killed before anything could be done.

The vagueness of the procedure, Attwood's lack of knowledge of what was happening in Cuba, and the skepticism at the White House made it unlikely that anything could have come of the attempt.

I do know that Fidel Castro was left wondering whether Kennedy was planning to change American policies toward Cuba. However, I know of no time when Fidel would have made "substantial concessions" to the United States. The year in which Kennedy was assassinated—1963—was economically a very bad one for Cuba. The revolution was still at ebb tide, and Fidel Castro would have been negotiating from weakness. This has never been his style.

# 8 THE ECONOMIC STRUGGLE

FIDEL'S WILDLY exaggerated hopes of a paradise in a New Cuba took a few years to fade into the hard world of economic realities. Economists cannot predict very much, but the consequences of certain unorthodox economic acts are predictable. It does not follow that Fidel Castro thereupon turned into a conservative and orthodox economist. His ebullient, supremely optimistic character and his fighting spirit were intact. In this as in other things, he will not accept defeat.

He still makes plans that are certainly beyond the range of probability—such as his goal of producing 10,000,000 tons of sugar by 1970. Some of his associates in government believe that he purposely aims higher than he can reach. It permits him to make great demands on peasants and workers so that they will produce more than they would otherwise do. It gives him a chance to exhort, to scold or praise, to be the *Jefe Máximo,* the Cuban Moses leading his people into the Promised Land.

All this, however, would be of no avail if Fidel Castro and his associates had not learned a great deal. If they still make some errors they can ask: Have the British and American leaders made none?

There is no way of rewriting the economic history of the first four or five years. The pictures of the wreckage—in words—are irrefutable in the books and articles by hostile or friendly critics and in speeches by Fidel Castro, Che Guevara and President Dorticós. Che, whom I have already quoted on this subject, was as frank and eloquent as any foreign critic. Fidel has had his personal problem of sustaining the faith, hope and spirits of the Cuban people during these years when life had been fairly grim for those whose living standards used to be relatively good. It would have been impractical for him to intone a *mea culpa* even if it were in his character to do so. The furthest he would go in his speeches was to say, *"We* have made mistakes."

He has been in a position to blame much of Cuban hardship on the American trade embargo, which Kennedy made complete on February 3, 1962. This has been an effective argument for Fidel, partly because the embargo and United States pressures on every non-Communist nation dealing or trying to deal with Cuba have hurt badly. The psychological effect of economic warfare on a proud and nationalistic people is to draw them together against the power or powers seeking to harm them. I saw that happen in Spain after the Second World War when a similar hostility of the Western nations strengthened Franco's political position inside of Spain.

"For over three years," wrote Theodore Draper in an article for *The New Leader* of April 13, 1964, "the Castro regime has fed its people far more fantasies than food."

This was true in the literal sense; the food situation was extremely bad and was still bad four years later. At the same time, no Cuban went hungry; children under seven received a quart of milk a day; thousands of students in the schools and universities received free or cheap meals; hundreds of thousands of civil servants and workers in all fields were able to get a solid midday meal free or cheaply. Taking the population of Cuba as a whole, it is arguable that Cubans have been better fed under the revolution than before 1959 although some hundreds of thousands of Cubans are much worse fed, especially in the cities.

Moreover, the truths that the critics have printed about the economic situation in Cuba—such as the Draper citation above— are really half-truths. They omit the fact that a social revolution provides benefits which are not measurable in terms of food or other statistics. It is true that a dismal failure was made of the Cuban economic structure for a number of years. It does not follow that the Cuban Revolution has been a failure; at least, not yet. It will fail *in the long run* if the Cuban economy is not put on a healthy, viable basis which, among other things, means plentiful and unrationed food supplies. Cuba is still far from realizing that goal.

One of the key speeches that Fidel Castro made on agriculture in the early years of groping for solutions was his talk of August 18, 1962, to the National Sugar Cooperatives Congress. This was the speech in which he announced the end of cooperatives:

"If there is one thing we must understand," he said, "it is the need to train men so that they will not make our mistakes. If you know that many mistakes have been made, what other way can there be to overcome these shortcomings? No one is born with knowledge. Many men who were suddenly called on to fill a post did not know how, and it cannot be said that it was their fault. But if, within some years, there are no men of complete ability and competence, then the blame will be ours. But we will not make that mistake.

"We know what we are doing. We know that in the future we will not have the shortcomings, nor will we lack the elements we lack today. Today is the bitter present of work, suffering and patience. We need all the devotion of the revolutionaries and the faith of the revolutionaries, encouraged by a tomorrow that we know will be very different when these masses of youths, properly trained, join in the task, in the effort.

"Tomorrow, the problems may be different, corresponding to new stages of progress. However, what is scarce today will abound tomorrow. And it is not a question of days, weeks, or months; it is a question of years. Of course, we would all like to be living in tomorrow; we would all like that right away. But that does not happen in life. Not even to the fastest-germinating seed. It always requires years."

What the sanguine Fidel Castro did not realize in August

1962—although he was a sadder and wiser leader than the one who produced the rash agrarian reform of May 1959—was how many years would be required. He faced reality in the speech quoted above. No one could have expressed better what these years of struggle have been than Fidel did in his sentence: "Today is the bitter present of work, suffering and patience."

The hopes that he held out would have been "fantasies" (in Draper's word) if they had not been accompanied by acts that have already improved agriculture and that may in time solve the problems Cuba has faced in the field of agrarian reform.

In that same speech Fidel was able to tell about the thousands of rural youths studying in vocational schools and universities and of others being sent to the Soviet Union "to take courses in administration, machinery and agricultural techniques."

These thousands are now in agricultural work and other thousands are now studying in the schools which have increased in number and efficiency. There is still a shortage of competent teachers, but they are coming along steadily.

Fidel Castro, in spite of what he says and believes, need not have made the serious mistakes that he did make for four or five years in agriculture and industry. However, he did correct some of them; he has studied a whole library of books by the outstanding experts in foreign countries on agrarian techniques. He himself by any standard, is now an expert in agriculture—and not a theoretical one. He is a practical farmer on a vast, national scale.

This does not mean that he will make no new mistakes. The socialist agriculture of the Communist bloc has been a failure when compared to the capitalist, developed countries of the West. Yet Castro is trying to make a success of a state-directed, socialistic system of agriculture. I have no competence to say whether he can succeed where his confrères have failed. I do know that agricultural production in Cuba has been improving, is better organized, and gives promise of further improvement in the coming years.

But Fidel has learned that he needs many more years than he thought he would need when he made that speech to the sugar workers in August 1962. Perfection will, of course, elude him as it does all leaders in all nations. In the years to come he will still be saying what he said in 1962 in a moment of truth:

"We know that there are many things to overcome, many shortcomings, many things we lack, many things that hurt us all, weaknesses which hurt us, errors which hurt us, carelessness that hurts us."

When the economy of any country is changed from a capitalistic structure—such as Cuba had—to a socialistic one, great difficulties are created. For one thing, the existing structure is destroyed; the new one has to be built up from the bottom. Every feature of the economy—administration, financing, entrepreneurial activities, pricing, marketing and labor—has to be adjusted to different conditions. Perhaps the greatest difficulty is to train and retain workers.

In the case of Cuba, one must add that she was a developing country, with a lopsided dependence on sugar exports, an unbalanced social structure and a virtually colonial relationship to the United States. Put a group of young and rash amateurs, headed by a Fidel Castro, in charge of the transformation, and one can wonder that the Cuban economy survived.

That it did so was due, in part, to the peculiarity that in a social revolution economic factors are secondary, at least in the early revolutionary stage. In addition, there was vital help from the Soviet bloc. And Cuba is richly endowed by nature.

Finally, there was the always sanguine, enthusiastic, tireless Fidel Castro, showing up everywhere, in person or on the television, carrying the nation with him on his shaky way. He retained the trust of most of the people and kept a restraining hand on those who felt rebellious. The authoritarian structure he quickly established—Rebel Army, police, delators and militia—gave him the power to prevent an uprising in the worst times of the revolution.

The stream of refugees going out to the United States, Central America, Puerto Rico and Venezuela had the effect on the Cuban body politic that bloodletting would have on a disordered human body. It was harmful to the economy because nearly all the refugees were middle-class and therefore included professional elements, technicians, managers, entrepreneurs—the very people who provide the motor force of a modern economic structure.

The exodus of doctors, dentists, teachers, engineers, lawyers and scientists also meant a serious loss to the social structure. The chief emphasis in the educational field has been on replacing such men. It is being done, but it takes years of schooling and then years of experience to make a competent professional.

However, while the flow of refugees hurt the revolution it also helped to save it. Fidel, the revolutionary, was glad to see them go. They were at best a burden to him and at worst a danger, since they would not have helped his sort of revolution; indeed they might actively have tried to sabotage and destroy it.

In addition, these refugees took their wives, children and old folk with them, which is to say nonproducers, consumers of scarce food and goods. The revolution, with its emphasis on and favoritism toward youth, meant earlier marriages, more births—a population explosion, in short. There has been no census, but it is a safe guess that where the Cuban population was about 7,000,000 in 1959, it must be well above 8,000,000 in 1969. Numerically, the refugees who probably total about 300,000 and may in time become as many as half a million, have been more than replaced. However, qualitatively, the Cuban exodus represented a grievous loss. Before the revolution, far more Cubans wanted to emigrate to the United States than our immigration laws would allow; now everybody who can reach Florida is welcome.

The flow continues and would be greater if more transport were available. Those leaving now have been a drain on the Cuban economy. They can take nothing with them and, hence, whatever they abandon becomes the property of the state. But many families leave one or two members behind so in that way they can keep their houses and other possessions within allowable real estate, rural landowning and income limits.

The public relations effect has not bothered Castro and his associates. They could not have a worse image so far as the United

States is concerned. The refugees are branded by the ugly word *gusanos* (worms). The first wave of Batistiano exiles might well have deserved some such appellation, but it has been disgraceful to apply the term indiscriminately to all Cuban exiles. However, for reasons of internal public relations and morale, it may pay the regime to use the epithet, at least with *hoi polloi*.

The class resentment of workers and peasants against the middle and upper classes who make up the great bulk of the refugees is there for Fidel Castro to manipulate—which he does whenever he can. The fact that he and most of the ruling clique are from the middle class is no handicap. They are "converts" to proletarianism and, anyway, the majority of Cuba's middle class has stayed in Cuba. This fact is often overlooked by foreign observers.

Once the government had expropriated and nationalized nearly every sector of the Cuban economy, it followed that there would have to be a centralized programming of production, supplies and investment. Every sector, such as agriculture, industry, labor, marketing and financing, had to be organized. Thus agriculture, the most important of all, was put under an administrative agency called the National Land Reform Institute (INRA). A supreme Central Planning Board (Junta Central de Planificación, or JUCE-PLAN) was placed in control of the whole vast network of agencies.

A council runs JUCEPLAN. It is headed by the Premier—in other words, Fidel Castro. This makes good revolutionary sense since it gives the *Líder Máximo* ultimate control over the vitally important structure of Cuba's economy. Moreover, Fidel has become an authority in the agricultural field and he has learned a great deal about other sectors of the economy.

Nevertheless, economic planning requires the greatest expertise and a training that he has never had. It is work for professionals. Fortunately for Castro, Carlos Rafael Rodríguez, who headed INRA for several years, has great capacities in that field and it has been his task as minister without portfolio to devote all his time to economic planning. There have been Iron Curtain experts working quietly behind the scenes as advisers whose advice may or may not be taken on decisions of national policy. And, of course, there are a great many Cubans at work—more and more as the years pass—who have been trained behind the Iron Curtain or in Cuba.

Fidel Castro is not inclined to take advice, as I have said, unless the advice agrees with his own ideas. He will never take orders if they come to him as orders. If the Russians want him to do something, they have to either let him make his own errors and correct them himself, or else embark on a careful process of suggestion and appeal.

Some such process may well have been operating to bring about the major economic shift of the revolution—back to a "sugar economy" after the overambitious efforts to industrialize and to diversify agriculture too quickly. Because this shift followed Fidel's long visit to Russia early in 1963, Theodore Draper believes that it was a case of Moscow ordering and Castro obeying. This is a *post hoc, ergo propter hoc* argument.

The switch was going to be necessary about that time in any case. The signs were all too clear. I have already cited Che Guevara's confession and how the leaders all realized that their policies were wrong. I suspect that it was simply a case of Fidel's recognizing the obvious.

> Castro's unconditional backing of Khrushchev was influenced by another and, according to Castro himself, the most important economic factor [Draper wrote in an article "Castro, Khrushchev, and Mao" for *The Reporter* of August 15, 1963]. From now on, the Cuban economy will be based on an "international division of labor" within the Soviet bloc. Castro agreed in Moscow that Cuba should specialize in certain fields of production for which the island is best fitted by nature.

The relations between Cuba and the Soviet Union in the last five years do not fit this picture of a chastened, servile Fidel Castro.

As a survey of the United Nations Economic Commission for Latin America, published in December 1964, says, "no real start" was made on long-term plans until 1964, except for a few sectors such as that of electric power. In a broad and general sense, Fidel Castro's economic program has not changed over the past five years. He seeks, first, to increase the volume of exports, which means primarily sugar but also tobacco, meat, fish, nickel, coffee and fruit. Secondly, his regime is once again—and much more widely—working to diversify the agricultural sector, with strong emphasis on stock farming. Fidel is no longer in a mad rush toward diversification; he sees it as a medium- and long-term goal. Finally comes industrialization, but not of an ambitious nature nor aimed so pointedly at import substitution. The program now is to create light industries producing consumer and intermediate goods from national resources and raw materials.

These generalized plans—which are sensible and are progressing at an uneven rate—cannot be immediate substitutes for the harsh realities of life in Cuba when it comes to food and clothes beyond the necessary and the adequate. Such simple consumer products as soap, toothpaste, electric light bulbs, matches, and detergents, are frequently unobtainable. Rationed products are often hard to get in the cities. Luxuries are out of the question. No new automobiles for personal use have been imported since 1959. What few new refrigerators and television and radio sets are available are fantastically high-priced.

Cuba's economy, in short, has been one of necessities, fairly distributed to all, while an infrastructure is being created which should gradually increase production. A little improvement has been visible each year for about three years, but the three preceding years were exceptionally grim.

What had been deliberately destroyed in the years 1959, 1960 and 1961 would have taken a very long time to reconstruct even if the Bay of Pigs invasion had succeeded and the economic clock had been set back to the more or less capitalistic system of pre-revolutionary days. In that case, the United States would not only have taken back what was expropriated, but would have given substantial economic aid. This would not have been a happy situation for the majority of Cubans who had benefited from the revolution, but the economy in general, and statistically, would have been improved—by capitalist standards—in fewer years than it is going to take Fidel Castro to create a flourishing socialistic economy.

A major reason is the paradoxical one that in ending the unemployment, which was one of the great weaknesses of the Cuban economy before the revolution, the Castro Government found that it could not quickly—or even yet—increase production to keep pace with the numbers who now have work but find little on which to spend the wages that they make. This has brought the classic inflationary situation, in Hugh Dalton's phrase which Fidel once cited to me, of "too much money chasing too few goods."

As a result, vast sums of money have been tied up in savings accounts. This has brought excessive liquidity and for the individual worker the feeling "Why should I work more than I have to when I would have nothing on which to spend the extra money I earn?" It also means that the Castro Government cannot effectively offer cash incentives to workers. One of the problems that have plagued the Castro regime, therefore, is absenteeism from work and nonfulfillment of norms or of normal production. Thus, there is a degree of invisible "unemployment" while everybody has work.

Fidel Castro and his associates try to combat the tendencies to go slow by appealing to revolutionary sentiments, "socialist emulation," patriotism—in other words, nonmaterialistic incentives. The results have been mixed, but in the circumstances it is remarkable that Fidel has been able to sustain the level of productivity that has been achieved over the years.

His exhortations, his appeals, his unflagging enthusiasm and optimism, his own indefatigable presence in one part of Cuba after another, on this state farm or in that factory or office—these have not only kept the economy going but instilled hope by demonstrating that effective measures are being taken.

In the first part of October 1963, eastern Cuba had the worst, the longest and the most destructive hurricane in Cuba's recorded history. The storm went in circles, out and back four times. Hundreds died; 1,000,000 cattle out of 6,000,000 were drowned; the ripening sugar crop was beaten to the ground; the entire coffee crop, whose beans were just ripe for picking, was lost. The three rivers of central Cuba overflowed and turned a great region into a lake.

Three weeks later, when my wife and I visited the region in an army helicopter, the waters were just receding and dead bodies—human and animal—were still being found.

Cuban exiles expressed hope today that Hurricane Flora would blow Fidel Castro off their island [an Associated Press dispatch from Miami of October 8 read]. Some believe she might. They said the hurricane may accomplish what anti-Castro saboteurs had been risking their lives to do—ruin Cuba's principal crops and thus devastate her economy. Some urged action.

"Now is the time to strike, because electric facilities will be out for a good time; bridges are out; rails are washed out, and the only communication in eastern Cuba is by radio," said the Reverend Germinal Rivas of Junta Revolucionaria.

A spokesman for another activist group, Commandos L, said: "It is a pity we were not prepared for this occasion on a large scale. Fidel's people might give a lot of thought now as to whether it is still worth while backing him. Many had been on the border line. . . ."

Rafael Fernández Dalmas, of the 30th of November Movement, said: "Now the people of Cuba will surely redouble their efforts to overthrow Communism. A hurricane, bad as it is, is not as bad as Communism."

These worthy gentlemen and their henchmen would not have been welcomed back in Cuba for a number of reasons, but none greater than the fact that Fidel Castro's behavior during Hurricane Flora increased his stature among all Cubans.

He was everywhere—first ordering every possible precaution as the storm approached. When it came, he was out in the midst of it, giving directions, comforting, sharing the dangers—so intrepidly that at one moment he was within an ace of being drowned. When the hurricane blew over, it was his indomitable spirit, his refusal to be discouraged or dismayed, that sustained the people. And he took practical measures—help for the homeless, aid for those who lost property, and orders that all Cubans must share the cost and the burdens of the hurricane equally.

Hurricane Flora set the economy back by at least a year. Fidel did not let this discourage him, either. When I saw him, he was full of plans for rehabilitating the economy. Those plans were carried out.

The Castro regime's economic mistakes cannot be excused by hard luck, but it is a fact that heavy hurricanes struck Cuba in six of the ten years of the revolution. There were two droughts that rank as the worst in the history of the Cuban weather records. In 1968, the sugar crop was badly hurt by drought. Stock production also suffers from hurricanes and droughts.

Although Cuba is one of the fairest lands on earth, as Christopher Columbus realized, the agricultural products by which she has always lived are vulnerable to the freakish weather patterns. The urban centers of Oriente Province lacked water for generations. No regime in Cuba did anything about the problem until the present one in which Fidel is carrying out an ambitious plan of hydroelectricity, flood control and irrigation. The program has for years been under the direction of Faustino Pérez, one of the men who were with Fidel in the *Granma* disaster and went up into the Sierra Maestra with him.

Against hurricanes there is no recourse. Better weather forecasts giving longer warning to prepare for a blow are now available in the Caribbean. The rest depends on luck. However, the sort of tragicomic error that kept happening in Cuba is shown by one incident connected with Hurricane Flora, which Raúl Castro mentioned in a speech he made in Santiago de Cuba on May 25, 1964. Among a long string of mistakes that were being made, a consignment of saddles was sent to Cayo Juan Claro where there were no horses.

There was too much of what Fidel called "theoretical radicalism in the field of practical accomplishment." There was also too much bureaucracy—a disease from which all modern nations suffer, but developing nations more than others.

"Each one organized his organization as he saw fit," Fidel said in a speech on October 26, 1964. "We then found towns where the stores began to disappear and offices began to appear."

In 1967, the situation was even worse. "Everybody's lifelong dream," he complained in a speech on February 20, 1967, "is to land an office job." Even the commissions he had set up to struggle against bureaucracy had themselves "become strongholds of bureaucracy," he said.

However, Fidel's greatest problem in the economic field was not bureaucracy, but the need to increase productivity, both of the individual and of the national product as a whole. Plans, labor measures, incentives, exhortations, scoldings day after day—there is an incessant stream flowing over the worker's consciousness.

The trade balance has been persistently and heavily negative. There is no knowing what the Cuban external debt is, since the figure is not available, but—on paper—it is probably well above the billion-dollar mark even though the Soviet Union canceled its charges for military supplies. Budgets are persistently unbalanced. That, in itself, would require rationing and higher prices to reduce consumption.

The rapid expansion of the social services, the great expenditures on education, the new schools, hospitals, housing, roads—all these are the glories of the revolution, but at the same time they are an almost unbearable economic burden. The technical problem of making a social revolution can almost be boiled down to balancing productivity against increased social expenditures. If this is not done, the Churchillian gibe at socialism is apt: an equality of misery.

The extreme lengths to which Castro is willing to go in socializing the economy and getting direct control of every facet of Cuban economic life was shown on March 13, 1968. He announced in a speech that all remaining private business activities, such as those of self-employed persons, artisans, street vendors, were to be eradicated. He called such private persons "counterrevolutionaries," and their activities were branded as amoral and antisocial. The process of nationalizing them began immediately.

This was evidence of discontent both in the few private sectors and in the government. It was the sort of impractical "utopianism" that frightens Fidel Castro's associates. Such an extreme type of socialism has not prospered in any of the Communist-bloc nations, and one wonders at Fidel's rashness in believing it will work in Cuba. It shows a supreme confidence in his regime's strength.

Meanwhile, wealth is being created in Cuba; this has been

especially true in the last four years. There has been a distribution of poverty, connected with the early, sharp drop in productivity. The improvement of recent years is significant and hopeful, but so much remains to be done that where Fidel Castro was talking of 1970 as a vital target date, he now talks of 1975 and 1980.

The already mentioned synopsis of the Cuban economy from 1959 through 1963, put out by the United Nations Economic Commission for Latin America, concluded with this paragraph:

> Development efforts have taken the form of an intensive investment and capital formation campaign, concentrated since 1961 on the directly productive sectors. This has made it possible to carry out projects which have increased agricultural production capacity, appreciably enlarged the amount of crop land available and added to the infrastructure works. At the same time, capital has been invested in numerous branches of industry, and will lead to a considerable expansion of installed capacity in the manufacturing sector in 1964–1966.

It did that, and, in fact, the increased rate of investment and capital formation in the last few years has brought a more noticeable rate of improvement in the economy than in the previous five years.

This is not statistically provable since so few statistics are published, and one hesitates to rely on the figures which are available, but anyone in close touch with Cuba and its rulers can see differences and know how much has been done. The money and effort invested in the infrastructure—especially in agriculture—simply must pay off.

In Cuba, from the time the Spaniards imported slaves, there was no shortage of labor on the sugar plantations. In prerevolutionary, capitalistic days, the Cuban and American owners could rely on the fact that the peasants had to have work, even though it kept them employed only four or at the most five months a year on low pay and no pay for the *tiempo muerto,* or dead months, when life was grim and the peasant often went into debt at the company stores to keep his family in enough food to subsist.

All that has been changed now. There is work for everybody all year round. Since cutting and loading sugarcane is hard, even exhausting work, the rural laborer has naturally sought other means of earning a livelihood.

"It is difficult to get a man to do pick-and-shovel work," Fidel complained in a speech on October 26, 1964. "Therefore, our demand for laborers has increased tremendously. . . . This kind of work still has to be done and is hard, because we have not achieved a sufficient level of mechanization. This is because they are paying more in other work, and thus competing for these workers."

Those who have studied the Caribbean islands have long noted that there is what Professor Thomas Mathews of the University of Puerto Rico called "a deep, almost psychological aversion to work in the cane fields."

"Such hard labor," he wrote in an article "Caribbean Kaleidoscope" for the January 1965 *Current History* magazine, "most inadequately reimbursed, is quickly shunned if there is an acceptable alternative."

Fidel found a revolutionary substitute which works much better than amused and contemptuous foreigners believe. It is to call upon hundreds of thousands of "volunteers" to go out into the cane fields during the *zafra* and help with the cutting and loading of cane. Of course, they do it in an amateurish and wasteful way and, of course, they are by no means all genuine volunteers.

There are social pressures on them to go out into the fields. For many, it would mean a handicap in their work or university careers to refuse to help. Many doubtless go along indifferently, because everyone around them goes. The leading officials of the country—political, diplomatic and military—set an example by getting out into the fields and doing their best for a few weeks. Fidel Castro cuts cane for at least two weeks in every harvest, taking along the President, the Cabinet and other close associates.

Those who scoff have never been out with officials or with youths and girls doing "voluntary" work in the fields, not only with sugarcane but with coffee, fruit, beans and other vegetables. Naturally a certain number are fed up, bored and resentful, but it is surprising how many make a sort of picnic or outing or camping trip of the task.

Cubans have a delightful gift, which operates spontaneously in such situations. Put a lot of Cubans together, and in no time you have a fiesta. They have a natural sense of comradeship and fun. This is especially true of the young people, but it has been remarkable to hear the older government officials express the feeling that the work is good for them—physically because it is healthy and gets them away from their desks, and socially because they learn what manual labor is like. They all participate in the revolution in a literal fashion.

Throughout Cuba's history the upper economic and social classes despised manual work and considered it completely *infra dig*. A Cuban never even cultivated his garden. His wife would not dream of caring for her own children if the family could afford servants. All this has changed. Former servants now work in factories or are taught professions like nursing. Former prostitutes are turned into seamstresses. Prostitution, incidentally, has not been entirely eliminated. After all, it is the "oldest profession" and revolutions do not change human nature. What Fidel Castro has done is virtually to eliminate streetwalking in the cities and to "rehabilitate" many of the professionals by training them for factories or hospital work.

Lee Lockwood, in *Castro's Cuba* (pages 123–124), asks Fidel about "that old Cuban institution, the *posada*." This, Lockwood explains,

> is slang for a motel-like place where couples go to make love, no questions asked. There are at least two or three dozen in Havana alone, former private enterprises which are now run by the Revolutionary Government.

> Traditions and customs can clash somewhat with new social realities [Castro observed], and the problems of sexual relations in youth will require more scientific attention. But the discussion of that problem has not yet been made the order of the day. . . . Naturally, those centers to which you refer have been in operation because they satisfy a social need. Closing them makes no sense. . . . But what has definitely been fought is prostitution. That is a vicious, corrupt, cruel thing, a dead weight that generally affects women of humble origin who, for an infinite number of economic and social reasons, wind up in that life. The Revolution has been eliminating it, not in an abrupt, drastic, radical way, but progres-

sively, trying to give employment and educational opportunities to the women so that they might learn other skills that would permit them to work and earn their living in a different manner.

Havana was a "wide-open city" before the revolution, with special emphasis on gambling and prostitution. It was a haven for the Las Vegas sharks who ran the gambling casinos. The big, new hotels were financed by a calculation of high gambling profits without which they could not repay their capital investment and upkeep.

Those days are gone. There has been a puritanical flavor to Castro's revolution. The lottery—one of the greatest sources of bribery and corruption from Presidents down to policemen on the beat—was turned into a bond system.

As for the ubiquitous corruption in Cuban government, business and finance before the revolution, there is nothing more extraordinary in revolutionary Cuba than the way it has been eliminated. As with prostitution, it would be asking too much of human nature to expect Cubans—for whom bribery, graft and corruption were a normal way of life since Columbus discovered the island—to be completely free of these vices. But corruption has gone completely in the upper echelons of government, the armed forces and the economy.

The former Treasury Minister, Rufo López-Fresquet, wrote in his book of "a phenomenon new to Cuban politics: administrative honesty." He also mentions "the new governmental probity." No one could have been in a better position to know than López-Fresquet, and when he wrote his book he was an anti-Fidelista exile.

The nearest thing to the old corrupt ways was what Fidel called the *dolce vita* in a speech he made on March 14, 1966. This disease attacked some well-known figures, such as Major Efigenio Almeijeiras and Raulito Roa, the son of Foreign Minister Raúl Roa, who despite his youth had been made an ambassador.

"The people well know those who have been working these seven years," Castro said, "and they know very well those who have been playing around these seven years. The people know very well who have been studying and improving themselves, and who have been flitting from party to party, from one drunken stupor to another. . . . I can assure you, they are not more than fifty and that is exaggerating a lot. . . . It is really a crime that when in the streets even empty containers are collected for economy's sake, there are individuals here who spend thousands of pesos on the *dolce vita.*"

Human nature was being counterrevolutionary. What happened was only too understandable. Almeijeiras, for instance, was one of Fidel's most valuable, trusted and loyal officers in the Sierra Maestra and in Havana. But he came of a very poor family, was uneducated, unsophisticated. One day he found himself head of the Cuban national police force, and later Vice Minister of the Armed Forces Ministry, with power and with money to spend on wine, women and song. Not only did he have a good time, but everybody in Havana knew about it. Fidel had warned him and punished him once; he relapsed, and this time Fidel made an example of him—gently, to be sure.

Almeijeiras, Raulito Roa and others worked their way back to grace in rehabilitation centers. They are not counterrevolutionaries and were not being subversive, as the American press said. Fidel started a cleanup of the Foreign Ministry, Diplomatic Corps, Ministry of Foreign Trade and a few government agencies.

The *dolce vita* flurry is worth mentioning only to show the close control that Fidel Castro keeps over every aspect of his revolution. It also shows the pride he takes in it, and his determination to keep it honest. Cuba is a more orderly and better-organized country today than it was in the first years of the revolution when local officials and commanders committed many disgraceful acts. Havana is a safer city to live in than New York.


"Everybody is a volunteer in the front rank in demanding things, but everybody hangs back when it comes to producing," Fidel complained on June 6, 1963. This has been his perennial nightmare.

One way to get cheap labor for the fields during harvests is to use soldiers. This is an old Latin-American custom. Since men are drafted, and there is no enemy to fight, why not put them to work? The trouble in Cuba was that Fidel Castro had been scornful of the draft, of the small amount that the soldiers earned, and of militarism in general. These were among the pledges that had to be forgotten.

"If Fidel Castro was on record unequivocally on any subject, it was on compulsory military service," Theodore Draper writes in *Castroism* (pages 173–74). "One of his first utterances after taking power had been: 'We will not establish military service because it is not right to force a man to put on a uniform and a helmet, to give him a rifle and force him to march.' "

On November 12, 1963, a compulsory three-year military service was put into law. It was announced that the draftees would spend three or four months a year cutting sugarcane, picking coffee beans and doing other agricultural work. Since a soldier earned only 7 pesos (nominally $7.00) a month, the new law provided a great many laborers at a cheap price.

They were needed primarily for the sugar crop—Cuba's mainstay. It had been foolish to think that the economy could be quickly diversified and industrialized. The switch back to a "sugar economy," which was announced in the autumn of 1963, did not mean that Castro was turning the clock back to prerevolutionary days, as Draper and other critics claimed.

"They [Yankee commentators] said that we were abandoning the aspiration to be a country that is industrially developed in order to become producers of agricultural articles," Fidel said in a speech on September 29, 1963. "Of course, that is very far from what our country intends to do. . . . Today we have a much clearer view of our possibilities and we know how to invest our resources much better. We know what sugar means to us as a source of foreign exchange. We know the extraordinary possibilities of our agriculture which, because of our climate, can surpass the agriculture of the most-developed countries."

This made—and still makes—sense. It was right to blame Castro for having thought that the Cuban economy could be changed abruptly from the so-called sugar monoculture, but to criticize him for having corrected his mistake is illogical. In fact, the "Yankee commentators" to whom Castro referred were also being misleading. The "sugar monoculture" to which the Castro regime returned in 1963 has a vital difference from that of pre-revolutionary days. Throughout Cuban history, sugar was produced on large plantations or on small farms bound to the great refineries. Ownership of the major plantations and refineries was mostly in Spanish hands in the nineteenth century and mostly in American hands for the first half of the twentieth century. At the time the Batista regime was overthrown, American ownership was about 40 percent—but this comprised the best land and the most modern refineries.

The situation today is entirely different. All the sugar-producing land has been expropriated and belongs to the state. This is also true of the refineries. Where previously the refineries had been established next to terrain owned or controlled by American and Cuban companies without reference to their contribution to the national production, a gradual reorganization is taking place to rationalize sugar refining.

There is a vital difference between, on the one hand, an industry owned to a considerable extent by foreigners—Americans—with Cubans producing for the benefit of a few absentee owners and shareholders, and, on the other hand, a sugar industry owned by the state and run by managers and technicians whom Havana controls. The Russians do not own one acre of Cuban sugar land—nor do any other foreigners.

"The Soviet Union did not have any sugar plantations in Cuba," Fidel pointed out in a speech he made in Havana on January 25, 1964. "It did not have any sugar mills in Cuba. It did not have any property in Cuba. The Soviet Union was not receiving foreign exchange from Cuba. The Soviet Union did not collect dividends. It did not collect interest. On the contrary, the Soviet Union was extending large loans to Cuba to allow us to cope with this situation."

Sugar is exported where Cuba can sell it, even though, through the agreements with the Soviet Union and Communist China, those countries absorb most of the crop. Russia does not need the sugar, and in years when it has been important to Cuba and when the crop is short, the Russians have released Havana from a portion of its obligation.

The most important change of all from the human point of view is that the vicious system of labor whereby the peasants who worked on the plantations were idle and getting no money for seven or eight months of the year has gone. There is work for all peasants all the year round.

Not only that; the government sees to it that the peasants' children go to school where they are decently fed and clothed, as well as taught. The wives can make extra money picking coffee beans or doing other work—and their children will be taken care of during the day. While rural housing is lagging far behind Fidel's early dreams, there has been much new building. Something is gradually being done to replace the wretched bohíos, or huts, in which rural laborers have lived throughout Cuban history. Side roads are being built; electricity is gradually reaching all corners of Cuba. All peasant families now get free medical care.

In the light of these ascertainable facts, how can the Cuban-exile and American critics like Draper blandly speak of the decision to return to a sugar economy as a return to prerevolutionary days?

To a considerable degree, Goldenberg's gibe in *The Cuban Revolution and Latin America* (page 301), paraphrasing Draper, is true: "Castro promised bread and freedom; he brought austerity and totalitarianism." He also brought adequate food to every Cuban on the island including, incidentally, bread. This was never the case before. He brought a quart of milk for every child under seven—and that was unheard of before. And he did this in the worst years of the economy.

Only the most stubborn and emotional critics of the Castro regime would argue that the Cuban peasants, taken as a whole and considering the "fringe benefits" in food, medical care, education and housing, are not better off today than ever before. The situation of the industrial worker is another and disputable matter. "In most parts of Cuba," Che Guevara wrote in an article for the magazine *Verde Olivo* which was reprinted in the *Monthly Review* of July–August 1961, "the country people had been proletarianized by operations of big capital, semi-mechanized forms of cultivation that gave it a stronger class consciousness."

Over a period of about twenty-five years, factory workers and the laborers connected with the sugar refineries, tobacco and the docks had strong unions which were favored by succeeding Presidents. The union leaders, chosen by the government, were supine creatures of the Presidents and were corrupt. The last head of the Cuban Confederation of Workers, Eusebio Mujal, as I have said, was a millionaire when he fled from Cuba with Batista. Incidentally, when Batista first took power in the 1930s he placed Communists at the head of the national labor confederation.

The workers were pampered, at least compared to rural labor. They insisted, for instance, that a large proportion of the refined sugar be loaded in bags by hand when machines could have been used. Tobacco workers forced the companies to have nearly all cigars rolled by hand although experts say machine-rolling produces equally good results.

One advantage of a totalitarian regime is that it can impose efficiency and mechanization and let the union workers grumble under their breath. The justifiable complaints now are that real wages are lower than before, that work norms are higher, that there is no freedom to move from job to job and place to place, and that there is precious little to spend extra money on.

Cubanologists, working at a distance, seeing evidence now and then of discontent—such as absenteeism and attempted strikes—and taking human nature into account, write that the Cuban industrial worker is an unhappy, perhaps potentially rebellious, member of the community.

This may be so, but once again the opinions do not take into account the advantages that the revolution has brought. The children of those workers can now go to vocational schools or universities and learn to be engineers or managers or for that matter become doctors or dentists. Workers could not afford to send their sons and daughters to higher schools in the past. There is no racial discrimination now in industry or anywhere else. The Negro worker before the revolution was on the whole in the lowest income brackets. He can now train himself for a better job while his children, too, have exactly the same educational privileges as the white children. Cubans are a superior people in terms of national sentiments, political consciousness and intelligence. While these traits—including a refractory individualism that all Cubans possess—may turn many workers against the revolutionary regime, they can equally provide an impulse to others.

My own personal judgment in this field is limited, as I can claim no academic competence in economics or sociology. However, I have seen and talked to a great many Cuban workers over the past ten years. I have often watched Fidel Castro addressing gatherings of workers or—better still—mingling with them as we went around. He does not overawe them; there is a genuine rapport, an easy relationship. I would say that a majority of the Cuban industrial workers support the revolution actively. Many more accept it and carry on with no thought of rebellion.

The only "scientific" on-the-spot sociological study in depth that I know of is the one I have already mentioned, made by Professor Maurice Zeitlin and published in book form under the title *Revolutionary Politics and the Cuban Working Class*. The material was gathered by Zeitlin and his wife in the summer of 1962 when the revolution was three and a half years old. They interviewed workers in twenty-one plants scattered over all six provinces of Cuba. The book is valuable because it is still, I believe (to quote Zeitlin's academic language on pages 3 and 4), the only

> study to utilize the empirical methods and theory of contemporary sociology for sustained and systematic inquiry into the causes of the differential response of the workers to a social revolution—while that revolution itself was still "young."
>
> The Cuban workers have played a decisive role in their revolution—the first socialist revolution in the Western Hemisphere, and the only [one] that has taken place in a capitalist country in which wage workers constituted the most numerous and perhaps most cohesive class in the population.

The following are extracts from Professor Zeitlin's concluding chapter (pages 277–95), in which he summarized the results of his investigations:

> The workers' active and armed support of the Revolutionary Government has been decisive in the consolidation and defense of

its power. Without their support the revolutionary leadership could not successfully have transformed the old order and created Cuban socialism. The revolution was not a workers' revolution in the classical Marxist sense, however. . . .

One could never have predicted the revolutionary potential of workers in this generation from a mere knowledge of their relative economic security in prerevolutionary Cuba—despite the vast importance economic insecurity had in generating revolutionary consciousness. . . . The majority of these workers, well paid and working regularly, and thus supposedly conservative in their politics, not only support the revolution but nearly a third of them were pro-Communist *before* [Zeitlin's italics] the revolution. . . .

The direct impact of nationalization on social relations in the plants was of profound importance to many workers. . . . Nearly three-quarters of the workers we interviewed who were dissatisfied with their work for one reason or another before the nationalization of industries told us their attitudes toward their work had been transformed since nationalization. . . .

This new sense of nationhood and their own emancipation were spontaneously linked by worker after worker in our interviews. Though we never asked a question in which the word "imperialism" appeared, and though we had no question on Cuban independence as such, the workers themselves raised the issue in one context or another. . . .

The Revolution had abolished their [the workers'] alienation from the means of production, from Government, and from nation.

Another thing that the revolution has done, economically and socially, is to offer work of all kinds to women. This is new in the history of Cuba where women formerly did menial, servant's labor and jobs like secretarial work in the cities, or peasants' work in the fields, or—in the case of all middle- and upper-class women—no wage work at all.

Now one sees women of all classes in nursing and medicine, as chemists and clerks, working during the days while their children are taken care of in the Círculos Infantiles. The revolution has opened up a new life for Cuban women and a new and valuable source of labor for the nation. Before the revolution, it was barmaids, cabaret girls, waitresses, prostitutes, and, as Fidel once put it, "whorehouses in every city."

No study comparable to Zeitlin's has been made in recent years about Cuban farm laborers. Before the revolution, except in the semi-industrialized fields such as sugar and tobacco, the workers had no trade unions. The only peasants directly linked to Castro's insurrection were those in the Sierra Maestra. These were among the poorest, most illiterate and least politically conscious peasants in Cuba. They were not typical.

Fidel had his problems winning them over, as he confessed to me in 1959. They had been treated too badly through the centuries to trust anyone. Che Guevara greatly exaggerated the role of the peasants in the Sierra Maestra. Castro learned to understand them and feel sorry for them, and there is no region of Cuba where a greater and more favorable transformation has taken place than in the Sierra Maestra. There are today roads, schools, hospitals and better working conditions and income for all.

The peasants elsewhere in Cuba had to be wooed and won—like other workers. This was not an easy or quick process. Too many mistakes were made. The agrarian reform of May 1959 has already been mentioned. It was ill-conceived and too radical. Fidel had a vague idea about the desirability of cooperatives and talked about them from his Moncada days.

"Agrarian reform," he said ruefully in one of his key speeches on the subject on August 18, 1962, "is one of the most complex tasks of a revolution, one of the most difficult. . . . The problem of distributing the land is quite clear. First of all, there is not enough land to go around."

Later in the same speech he explained what was wrong, from the revolutionary point of view, with cooperatives. "The cooperative is a collective center different from the people's farm," he said. "The people's farm is like a factory; its workers are equivalent to workers in a factory. The cooperative is similar to a group of workers who work for themselves, not for the nation."

He decided, as he told me in 1967 when I was interviewing him for *War/Peace Report,* that cooperatives belonged in a capitalistic, not a socialistic, system. So they were abolished for the *granja,* the state or people's farm.

A Second Agrarian Reform Law was promulgated on October 3, 1963. It was primarily aimed at breaking up and nationalizing a number of "medium"-sized landholdings that still existed, especially in Matanzas and Las Villas provinces. These ran up to 1,000 acres. Every farm of more than 165 acres was taken over by the state. It was more a political than an economic move. Fidel was finding that owners of even medium-sized properties were nonrevolutionary and, in many cases, counterrevolutionary. He claimed that the CIA had corrupted them. Certainly there was much peasant discontent in central Cuba.

About 30 percent of the farms remain in private hands, but even they are subject to government control. Owners produce what they are told to produce and sell at prices fixed by the government. Within such limits, there are privately owned farms in Cuba, and Castro promised that the proportion would not be reduced below the level existing in 1963. However, laws are flexible in revolutionary Cuba, and for all practical purposes the agricultural sector is under government control.

When one says "government control" in Cuban agriculture, one means, quite simply, Fidel Castro's control. This is his special province; it is the phase of the economy and the revolution to which he devotes most of his time, effort and thought—what he recently called "the central task of the Revolution."

There, as in all other industries, he keeps emphasizing production. His speeches to workers and peasants for years have harped on that theme.

"Señores," he said in an address to the Cuban Workers Organization on August 30, 1966, "there is something that must be quite clear: the Revolution is the abolition of the exploitation of human labor but not the abolition of human work."

The heavy reliance on sugar exports is a gamble, but Fidel Castro is a gambler. The price of sugar on the world markets has been very low for five years—so low that sugar cannot be produced profitably in a free-enterprise, profit-and-loss economy.

"Let us produce all the sugar we can," Castro said in a speech on January 25, 1964, "and if we have to get into a price war, then we will get into a price war, and we shall see who wins that battle. What is more, it is not the same for a socialist nation in a price war because all the bourgeois sugar producers will be ruined. What happens here is just what happened during the hurricane [Flora]; the entire nation took on the burden of the problem.

"We are going to produce without restrictions. It is clear that in proposing this we were contemplating the prospects of the market in the socialist camp, and the prospects of arriving at economic agreements with them which would allow us to sell them all our surplus sugar. Everything is now absolutely clear."

Cubans argue that the world situation essentially represents underconsumption of sugar, not overproduction, since many millions or hundreds of millions in the underdeveloped world do not eat sugar—or eat very little—because they cannot get it and cannot pay for it. India, China and Africa are potentially great markets. One Cuban official assured me that a study of world production in relation to population growth would show that per capita sugar production varies little from year to year.

For Fidel Castro, at any given moment, everything really is "absolutely clear." It was so when he was making his worst mistakes. A leader has to have such a temperament in order to carry on and to inspire those who are being led.

He also has enough shrewdness and common sense not to put all his eggs into that one basket. Agriculture is being diversified, especially in the notable increase of stock raising and fisheries, but also in the considerable effort to increase production of coffee and, to a lesser extent, fruits and vegetables. Artificial insemination, one of Fidel's pet projects, has brought the cattle population far above prerevolutionary days.

Cuba has not been called the "Pearl of the Antilles" for nothing. Fidel once referred to it as "a hothouse" where farm products grow all year round, and this is true, allowing for the hazards of hurricanes and intermittent droughts. Sugar has been grown in Cuba for centuries because the soil produces cane with a higher sucrose content than it has in other countries. The land has never been exploited as it could be, under any government or system.

There is no possibility of competing with Cuban cigars because the *vuelta abajo* tobacco is incomparable. One might as well talk of competing with French champagne. Incidentally, on a recent visit to Havana I noticed some pipes and a large can of American smoking tobacco next to Fidel's chair, showing that he can get tobacco from the United States although Americans cannot get cigars from Cuba.


In this summary discussion of Cuban—which is to say, Fidel Castro's—economic policies and problems, one cannot overlook minerals and especially nickel. Cuba has great potential wealth in its nickel reserves, which are second only to those of the United States in quantity. A foreign ambassador estimated that there were $4-billion worth of nickel in Cuban soil.

The two big mines that were expropriated—Freeport Sulphur's Moa Bay property and the United States Government's mine at Nicaro—were rehabilitated by Iron Curtain technicians. Nickel and cobalt are now being produced by Cuban mining engineers. Moa Bay, the Cubans claim, is running at full capacity. There is talk of building a refinery in Cuba. If it were not for the effective opposition of the United States, a European consortium would now be at work exploiting these resources. Exports of nickel are increasing steadily without outside help.

Washington's efforts to prevent Britain, France, Spain, Japan and a few other non-Communist nations from trading with Cuba and granting credits have been a partial success. By the same token, they are a partial failure.

Britain's Leyland buses are a case in point. British engineers in Cuba are supervising the building of a $100-million fertilizer plant to be completed in 1971. An export credit for five years on $45-million worth of British equipment brought an American protest, but to no avail. Cuba is Britain's third largest market in Latin America.

Franco's Spain has been the chief provider of the fishing vessels which have brought a new industry to Cuba—deep-sea fishing. Cuban fisherman can now be seen off the coasts of Labrador and Brazil, catching cod, hake, herring and tuna, mainly for export. Japan has also sold Cuba several large fishing boats. France has sent bulldozers and railway engines. Most of the breeding bulls that are Fidel's pride and joy come from Canada, which at all times has rebuffed American pressures to break relations with Cuba.

There has been only one—a vital one, to be sure—impediment: the small amount of hard currency available to buy the capital goods that Cuba needs. In a year like 1968, when drought reduced the sugar crop, Castro probably would have had no more than $150 million to spend. However, Cuba's credit rating is good.

One must be chary of trade statistics in dealing with Cuba. However, an estimation of the foreign trade situation that would be valid enough for 1968 was made by a United States House of Representatives subcommittee on Latin America covering the year 1966.

According to this study, 23 percent of Cuba's trade is still with non-Communist countries. In descending order of importance, the chief countries are Spain, Canada, Britain, Japan, France and the United Arab Republic.

Soviet aid was put at the familiar figure (really just a guess which the Cubans claim is grossly exaggerated) of $1,000,000 a day. Aid from other Soviet-bloc states was said to be about $300,000 daily. In 1966, the subcommittee wrote, Cuba had $950 million in imports and $630 million in exports. The deficits are manageable because of long-term, low-interest credits from the Soviet bloc.

Carlos Rafael Rodríguez, the Minister in charge of economic planning, headed the Cuban delegation to the twelfth session of the United Nations Economic Commission for Latin America (ECLA) in Punta del Este, Uruguay, in April 1967. The report he made to the conference was, like all the others, favorable to his own country, but as a technician reporting to experts he took care to avoid exaggerated claims. On the subject of rationing, he was able to deliver a shrewd thrust:

> The detractors of the Cuban Revolution have attempted to misrepresent its effects on the living standards of the population by

pointing to the existence of rationing in Cuba. Of course, rationing, as is known, indicates one thing: that consumption levels in Cuba are not determined by social or wealth differences, but that the establishment of equality in the distribution of the essential elements of life ensures that every Cuban has the right to receive an equal share of the products or articles available to society.

On the other hand, what the detractors of the Revolution would never publish is a table of rationed consumption in our country, side by side with the estimated consumption of workers and peasants in the rest of Latin America. This comparison would permit the peoples of America to know the great progress that the Revolution has made in Cuba.

It is still a fact in 1968 that shortage of some basic foods, such as rice and milk, and defective distribution cause unending popular discontent. As Goldenberg points out in his book *The Cuban Revolution* (page 256), the *per capita* consumption of food in 1958 was higher than the *per capita* figures when general rationing was introduced on March 19, 1962. This is most probably true, but the use of such figures is misleading for the simple reason that in prerevolutionary years *"per capita"* was an average. Some people ate very well while a great many more ate very poorly. In 1962 and afterwards, the *per capita* calculation has a different meaning: Every Cuban gets the same amount of food, which means that people in the lowest income brackets—the most numerous—have been eating more than they did before the revolution.

The program that Fidel Castro has found more difficult to fulfill than any other is housing. In the first year or two of the revolution, as with so much else, he had wildly exaggerated hopes and embarked on impossible projects. Every developing country, with its expanding population, has special problems in this field, and Cuba is no exception. However, Fidel raised hopes and has had to disappoint them. As Juan de Onis, the *New York Times* correspondent, wrote in a dispatch from Havana, published on February 11, 1968:

> Housing remains a sore problem. Most rural families still live in a wooden *bohío,* a type of rural hut, common here. The huts have a thatched roof, a dirt floor and no running water or electricity. And

in Havana itself many multistory dwellings look more like over-crowded, rundown tenements.

The Rodríguez report to the ECLA meeting, which was later published in Havana, was most impressive—and justly so—in the fields of public health and education. Castro's revolution has every reason to take pride in its accomplishments in these sectors.

> In our country [Rodríguez said], there is no involuntary un-employment, nor does anyone go to sleep without eating because he has no money. More than 140,000 families in the cities no longer pay rent for their dwellings since the end of 1965, and rent will be completely abolished in 1970. Medical services have been extended to the most remote parts of our island. Before the Revolution, thousands of persons, mostly children, died because they could not be transported to a far-off and costly medical center. . . .
>
> The number of hospitals has increased in the past two years from 144 to 162, with the largest rise found in the rural hospitals which increased from 34 to 46. It would be well to remember that before 1959 there was not a single rural hospital in Cuba. . . .

The Cubans claim—I believe correctly—that tuberculosis and poliomyelitis have been eliminated insofar as this is possible in any modern country. The former children's scourge of gastroenteritis is now close to being completely eradicated.

Fidel Castro is most proud of the revolution's record in education. The *New York Times* correspondent, Juan de Onis in the dispatch from Havana mentioned above, gives the following figures:

> The most basic reform has been the crash program in education. There are 1.3 million children in grade school here now, 180,000 secondary school students on scholarships, and 40,000 university students. These figures are nearly double prerevolutionary levels.
>
> This education is geared essentially to technical and vocational training. Thousands of young men and women are now in jobs after completing courses in technical schools that were just getting under way three or four years ago.

Critics of the Cuban Revolution, both American and Cuban, while granting the great quantitative advances in education, deprecate the results on two counts—quality and Marxist indoctrination.

So far as quality is concerned, it was inevitable that with so many teachers fleeing to the United States, and with so great an increase in pupils and schools, standards had to fall. At first, in many schoolrooms, it was a case of "the blind leading the blind"; then graduates moved in and kept one step ahead of their pupils. Finally, after five years or so, qualified teachers were numerous enough to raise standards to a fair average—and that is about where matters stand now.

There was one year—1961—when Fidel Castro instituted a campaign to wipe out adult illiteracy completely. There has been no parallel to that extraordinary—and surprisingly successful— effort in any country in modern times. Illiterate adults were brought up to primary-grade literacy in 1961 and the campaign was continued with the aim of bringing all Cubans up to the sixth grade.

The question of Marxist indoctrination is one of establishing values and attitudes. The American and Cuban-exile idea that Marxism-Leninism is being taught to all pupils in Cuba is, of course, wrong. "Scientific" Marxism would mean nothing to pupils except in the universities, and in a few "Schools for Revolutionary Instruction." Fidel Castro himself could not pass an examination in the subject. I doubt that anyone high in his government could, except Carlos Rafael Rodríguez. However, it may be different in the future as boys and girls can join the Communist youth movement at high-school age.

The real "indoctrination" comes in less definite terms. There is no religious teaching—although no atheistic teaching either.

All boys and girls are now educated within a Cuban totalitarian system that glorifies the "socialist world" and vilifies "Yankee imperialism." They and their professors are deprived of knowledge of the world outside Cuba and are given distorted or strictly limited pictures of life and events in other countries. Foreign books and magazines are scarce.

This is partly a reflection of Fidel Castro's intense desire to "free" Cuba from United States domination in cultural and social, as well as political and economic, fields. He wants education, like everything else, to be *Cuban*.

However, unlike that imposed by the leaders in the Soviet bloc,

Cuba's cultural life—in the fields of painting, sculpture, dancing, music (even the Beatles), theater and writing—has a remarkably free rein. The noted painter, Wilfredo Lam, while he lives most of the time in Paris, shows his work and is greatly honored in Havana. René Portocarrero, whose pictures are usually abstract, lives in Havana and cannot begin to fulfill the commissions he gets. He told me all artists can work exactly as they please.

Alicia Alonso has trained a splendid ballet company. Alejo Carpentier, Lisandro Otero, Ledesma Lima and the young Edmundo Desnoes are doing distinguished work in novel-writing. Nicolás Guillén, one of Latin America's most famous contemporary poets, is an enthusiastic Fidelista. So is César López, who heads the Writers' Union. For the first time, Desnoes told me in 1967, Cubans are reading books in large numbers—Kafka, for instance.

I mentioned "values and attitudes" because I have met many Americans and Cuban exiles who feel that it is better for children not to be educated at all, or get very little education, than to be "indoctrinated by Marxism." My own feeling on seeing hundreds and even thousands of children from poor rural and urban families now being fed, clothed and getting medical care, where before they were ragged, unhealthy and ignorant, is that things are better now.

The new generation is growing up educated, trained and healthy. A great deal of attention is paid to sports in the schools and universities. This is mainly due to Fidel Castro's own passion for and proficiency in a number of sports, but also to the fact that his former Mayor of Havana and present Minister of Education, José (Pepe) Llanusa, was an Olympic basketball player and is a fiend when it comes to physical education. A school to train teachers for that purpose is flourishing in Havana. Llanusa, incidentally, is one of the early Fidelistas and not only is very close to Castro but has been gaining influence in recent years.

In any event, Marxism-Leninism is not a disease; if there is a change of regimes later, it can be shed easily. As an ideology, it is a superficial feature of Cuban life.

Meanwhile, no one can take the credit for a remarkable advance in education away from Fidel Castro, and the revolution he has made. One reason the economy has lagged is that Cuba puts an extremely high proportion of her national budget—much the highest in Latin America—into education. The figures run about three times what they were in prerevolutionary years—and the money is now honestly spent. The Ministry of Education used to be notoriously graft-ridden.

"We believe," Fidel said in a speech on August 30, 1966, "without false boasting, without false pride and without vanity, that such is the effort made by our country in education that it is the country where the greatest educational effort has been made in modern times. This is recognized by UNESCO."*

One of the greatest problems at the beginning of the revolution was the "brain drain" when thousands of teachers, technicians, educators and specialists went into exile. Castro's problem, now that he has trained a new generation for these professions and is getting larger numbers every year, is to keep them happy. The phenomenon of "rising expectations" is at work.

Trained men and women expect a higher economic and social status than the average. But Cuba's is a social revolution where "all men are equal."

It is true that some are more equal than others, but Fidel is using all his charisma to instill a willingness for sacrifices on behalf of the revolution. This is part of his constant effort to minimize the importance of materialistic rewards and emphasize revolutionary ideals. Defeat or success in a battle of that kind is relative.

Engineers, doctors, nurses, teachers, military officers—technicians and professionals of all kinds—are pouring out of schools and universities now. Fidel could boast in his January 2, 1968, speech commemorating the ninth anniversary of the revolution,

* The reference is to a 1963 report of the United Nations Economic, Social and Cultural Organization, which said that the increased budgetary expenditures for education in Cuba far exceeded any other educational budget in Latin America.

that more Cuban engineers would be getting their diplomas in the course of the following three years than in all the years of this century up to 1959. "We already have more doctors, and better ones, than before the revolution," he said.

Quantitatively, there is no reason to doubt figures of this sort. Qualitatively, doctors and engineers are not made so quickly. The important facts are that Cuba is compensating for the early brain drain and that thus far the young graduates are supporting the revolution. A high proportion of them, after all, would not have had the opportunity to learn their professions before 1959, for economic or racial reasons.

In a speech on July 26, 1966, Castro dealt with the gibes of his foreign critics who threw statistics at him.

"What family today is evicted from its home?" he asked rhetorically. "What worker today is not entitled to retirement? What worker does not have his work assured? What sick person is denied a room in a hospital and does not have all he needs without its costing him a cent? What child goes without schooling? What youth cannot attend a technological institute with an opportunity to go to a university?

"These stale leftists—for lack of a better name—appear not to have taken these facts into account when thinking about the economy. They think in terms of the bourgeois seeking tons of this and tons of that. What is more, in addition to tons of this and tons of that, we will also speak and give them impressive figures, because this is the reason we have been preparing conditions during these years."

When I talked with Castro about the economic situation in 1966, he assured me that the Cubans are not going to make the mistake that the Russians made of trying to increase agricultural production by increasing acreage and using virgin land.

The way to do it, he said, is the way it is done in Europe, which is to concentrate on increasing production in already developed farms with better methods, more fertilizers, irrigation, more mechanization, better strains of cattle, better types of grain, fruits and vegetables.

This was a different Fidel Castro from the one I spoke to on the same subject in 1959 and 1960. I would guess that the economy hit bottom in the year 1962, when rationing had to be introduced, when food was scarce and discontent was widespread.

One of the most important things to be said about the Cuban economy after ten years of revolution is that, in every respect and every field, it is better organized. The first five years were the worst; the second five years have been, paradoxically, the hardest period. It will remain hard for several years, but the base is stronger now. Each industry, such as sugar, cattle, coffee, nickel, hydraulic resources, foreign trade, is fairly well organized and well run.

One of the many errors made by the Castro regime was to ask for and expect too much from the Soviet bloc. The Russians and Czechs were experts, not amateurs like the Cubans. They could see what was wrong with the optimistic and unrealistic plans that Fidel Castro, Che Guevara and others were making. They saw that much of the help they were giving was being wasted; their advice was not being followed. In February 1964, Che Guevara complained in a speech that Soviet exports to Cuba had fallen 30 percent short of the trade agreement with Cuba.

Fidel should have expected nothing better in the light of the Cuban performance and considering that it is an old Russian custom to promise the maximum and let fulfillment depend on availability and political considerations. Moscow's one great hold over Fidel Castro is the economic dependence of Cuba on the Soviet bloc. To expect the Russians not to employ that weapon, however carefully, would be naïve. They are not "utopian Marxists."

The Chinese Communists were less cautious; they struck hard and suddenly at the end of 1965 by cutting down on their rice exports to Cuba and on their sugar imports from Cuba. The reasons seemed clear. China was in the midst of Mao's cultural revolution and their internal economy was upset. Moreover, Peking could not be continually happy over the fact that Cuba was dependent on the Soviet Union.

Fidel Castro has at all times avoided taking sides in the Sino-Soviet quarrel. His thesis is that he is making a Cuban revolution, even if it be within the "socialist world." But China is in no position to give him extensive economic and military help. Only

Russia can do so. There has been no break with either side, but there have been quarrels with both. When Peking cut the rice supplies, Fidel was furious—and when he is furious, he explodes.

"We are not to blame and no one can blame us for this problem which has arisen," he said in a speech at Havana University on March 14, 1966. "Because the only alternative . . . is for us to have remained silent in the face of what constituted a veritable felony, a veritable blackmail, a veritable treachery against proletarian internationalism, such as depriving us in a difficult year of almost half of the rice they had sent to us the year before, and to do so on the last month of the year and in one of the years when our nation is undergoing the worst difficulties."

The speech went on in a similar vein, including an accusation by Fidel that the reduction in rice exports "was carried out clearly for political reasons." The blow came, as he said, when stocks of Chinese-import cotton, thread, needles, and "a tremendous number of articles" were "practically exhausted."

It was indeed a hard blow for Cuba, but it should not have been so unexpected. The romantic, utopian streak in Fidel's character keeps getting him into trouble. One of his grievances against Moscow with regard to the missile crisis was that Khrushchev had ignored "proletarian internationalism." So far as the present rulers of the Soviet Union and Communist China are concerned, there is no such thing.

It is possible that Fidel's idealism—if it can be called such—has an appeal to younger Communists and radicals all over the world. There have been signs of this over the last few years. In that case, his personal variant of Trotskyism may pay off politically. Meanwhile, the bread, butter and guns come from blasé, hardheaded, nationalistic rulers in the Kremlin.

Castro's blast against Peking, however, did not mean that he had opted for the Muscovite side. His continuing quarrel over how to bring about revolution in Latin America is one piece of evidence. That there has been no break with Peking is another. Communist China continued to send Cuba the reduced exports of rice and went on buying sugar at the same high "political" price as Russia paid—about six cents a pound.

Political necessity led Fidel Castro to make Cuba economically dependent on the Communist bloc, and it led Washington into a trade embargo. In an economic sense, this is sheer idiocy for both sides. Cuba's natural market will always be the United States, but it is useless quarreling with history. Politics is the guiding factor, not economics.

Castro showed his own streak of Machiavellianism and realism when, in August 1968, he supported the brutal and imperialistic Russian invasion of Czechoslovakia, although cautiously and with reservations. Whatever disapproval he may have felt was overcome by his economic dependence on the Soviet Union; his fear of a Russian-American *détente* in which Cuba could be sacrificed; his unwillingness to take sides with the Western democracies; and his dissatisfaction with Cuban-Czech trade relations.

# 9 THE WORLD OUTSIDE

WHEN FIDEL Castro entered Havana in triumph on January 8, 1959, he looked around for new worlds to conquer. Cuba was now "territorio libre"—free territory—but there was all the rest of Latin America, groaning under the yoke of "Yankee imperialism." His reach went across the oceans to Africa and Asia. And he has gone on reaching out.

Cuba is the primary task, but he wants to bring the blessings of revolution, as he conceives them, to all oppressed peoples and to all underdeveloped nations on the globe. He does not see himself simply as a Cuban making a Cuban revolution. He stands as a towering figure in the history of Latin America, but this is not enough. The David who took on the American Goliath is not afraid to tackle the Soviet and Chinese giants. His world is full of romance and Holy Grails and deeds of derring-do.

Meanwhile, he cultivates his little Cuban garden. The foreign adventures are real and mean much to him, but they are marginal. When Che Guevara was killed in October 1967, and all Fidel's hopes of guerrilla victories in Latin America were set back, this was not a decisive blow to his own revolution, or even to his determination to resume the guerrilla struggle. It was a severe jolt and he suffered a grievous personal loss, but the Cuban Revolution went on as before. Put in perspective, Fidel's foreign adventurism represents perhaps 5 percent of his time, energy and resources. The other 95 percent is devoted to his revolution.

However, Cuba is not "an island" in the game of power politics which Fidel Castro is trying to play. It is a part of what he calls the "socialist world," and it is a Latin-American country whose fate is tied to nineteen other Latin nations and to the "Colossus of the North" 90 miles from his shore.

Castro's idealism has its element of realpolitik. In his book *Trujillo* (page 424), Robert D. Cressweller asserts that there was "the practical but entirely cynical 'understanding' between Trujillo and Castro, which Johnny Abbes [Trujillo's "Himmler"] had promoted. The two Caribbean outcasts agreed to stop fighting each other and to concentrate on their other problems." Trujillo was a monster and Johnny Abbes a gangster-killer of the worst type.

I do not know if there was such an "understanding," but Fidel Castro has his Machiavellian side. He has done his best to help the former Ghanaian President, Kwame Nkrumah, now in exile in Guinea. Nkrumah was one of the most shamelessly corrupt of African leaders. As has been mentioned, Fidel had no scruples about seeking help from ex-President Prío Socarrás of Cuba, although Prío represented what the Castroites were revolting against.

On the reverse side, some of the outstanding figures of the hemisphere—Muñoz Marín of Puerto Rico, Betancourt of Venezuela, Figueres of Costa Rica, Frei of Chile—have been targets for vicious campaigns of Cuban propaganda and, in the case of Venezuela, active subversion. "Independence" for Puerto Rico was on the agenda of the student conference that Fidel went to join in Colombia in 1948 at the time of the *Bogotazo,* and he still agitates for it. These men—moderate, democratic, friendly to the United States without being subservient—sought reforms, not revolutions. They all became enemies of the Castro regime when it turned radical, dictatorial and then communistic.

Fidel's antagonism is understandable, but it is couched in outrageous terms. He is playing in a rough game with the odds against him, so he hits out hard and mercilessly. No quarter is asked and none given. When he fights, no holds are barred.

It is in the nature of a revolutionary to be *against*, not *for*. Fidel Castro is against the United States and against every Government in Latin America except the Mexican, which has refused to ostracize Cuba, although it is careful not to be pro-Fidelista.

The Latin-American problem, from Fidel's viewpoint, is that all these governments are naturally antirevolutionary. They are all, by Castroite standards, conservative. In nearly all of them the army is master and is linked to the traditional ruling classes. Some of the Governments are democratic, but they are as far from revolution, for different reasons, as the military dictatorships.

Fidel Castro sees only one way out—to encourage and back revolutions in every possible country of Latin America, using the same tactics of guerrilla warfare, urban resistance and mass support that were so successful in Cuba.

He would find little agreement with his belief that the conditions which were obtained in Cuba could be reproduced elsewhere in Latin America. Che Guevara publicly recognized that this was improbable, but went to his death seeking to make it a reality. However, many students of Latin-American affairs would agree that only revolution, or its equivalent, could break up the traditional concentration of wealth and income in the hands of a small minority of landowners, businessmen, bankers, military officers and politicians.

The Cuban Revolution is a Latin-American phenomenon and Latin America is part of the underdeveloped southern half of the world. The United States's problem with the Cuban Revolution is not the simple one of Communism, but the profound, complex question of a whole mass of people on the move from the backwardness of poverty, ignorance, disease and despair toward what they hope will be a better life. If the United States had succeeded in its efforts to overthrow the Castro regime in Cuba, it would have solved nothing definitive—in Cuba or elsewhere.

One cannot kill ideas, or blockade them, or declare them incompatible and expect them to melt away. Cuba can be isolated in a material sense, but the Cuban Revolution cannot be isolated; Fidel Castro cannot be declared a non-person. We live in an age when all people—the poor, the underprivileged, the black people under white rule—are demanding social justice. It is Fidel's thesis —and not his alone, of course—that the only way to get it is by violent revolution. The American thesis, in its idealistic form, was best expressed by President Kennedy: "Our unfulfilled task," he said, "is to demonstrate that our democratic, capitalistic, free-enterprise system is better for underdeveloped countries than the totalitarian systems, that it will provide the social justice which the masses demand."

The emphasis should be on *"unfulfilled* task." The United States has not proved its case, nor has the Alliance for Progress, nor has Castro's Marxism-Leninism. This is Fidel's "unfulfilled task." He feels sure that he will fulfill it in time, and he wants the other Latin-American countries to follow the "Cuban Path." This policy, paradoxically, has brought him into conflict with the Soviet Union as well as with the United States.

The Latin-American country which has been the most shot-at target of the Cuban revolutionists is Venezuela. Geographically, it is easily reached; it had a strong Communist party and radical student movements which could—until Fidel's quarrel with Moscow—be supported with arms and money. Two guerrilla nuclei, one in the western mountains and one in the eastern range, were able to operate, while terrorist groups worked in the capital of Caracas.

The guerrillas and Communists have, to date, been only a nuisance in Venezuela. Under Presidents Betancourt and Leoni, the country has made reforms. It has great resources in its oil and iron, and it is one of the countries where the United States would intervene at all costs against a threat of revolution. American investments in the oil industry exceed $2 billion. Venezuela, because of its oil and its location, is strategically vital to the United States.

But in spite of everything, Fidel keeps on trying. He knows there is not going to be a revolution in Venezuela but he gains something by causing trouble.

It was not always so. President Betancourt helped Fidel when he was fighting in the Sierra Maestra, and wanted to keep on helping him as long as he thought that the Castro revolution would be a liberal, democratic one. Fidel told me once that when he sent the two groups of guerrillas to the Dominican Republic in June 1959 to fight against Trujillo, "Romulo Betancourt was in the operation with us."

I wrote in my notes in 1963 that Fidel said to me, "I don't know why Betancourt turned on us; I think it must have been United States pressure." I told Castro that the Venezuelan President and we Americans thought that he had turned against Betancourt and not vice versa, which he emphatically denied.

In Professor Robert F. Smith's book *Background to Revolution,* there is a chapter by Professor C. A. M. Hennessy of Warwick University on Cuban nationalism which, he acutely points out (page 20), "has often lost touch with political reality." He continues:

> This was shown when the nationalists of the 1890's were prepared to devastate the island and so create the conditions for United States intervention rather than accept Spanish reforms. It has been shown, too, in Castro's own brand of nationalism when, on occasions, he has seemed prepared to invite the apotheosis of national martyrdom in the holocaust of a new war. There is also the fact that Cuban nationalism, whether in Martían or Castroist form, has always been couched in Latin American and universalist terms, not those of a narrow Cubanism. That is why the Castro revolution has seen itself as having the messianic mission of "turning the Cordillera of the Andes into the Sierra Maestra of Latin America."

Fidel Castro used the phrase about the Andes in a speech he made on July 26, 1960. The complete sentence was less threatening, for he said, "We promise to continue making the nation the example that can convert the Cordillera of the Andes into the Sierra Maestra of the hemisphere." However, he added, "If they want to accuse us of desiring a revolution in all America, let them accuse us."

This is just what he did want, and what he has been working for in vain ever since he took power in 1959. He does not seem to have calculated that his actions in this field would bring about counteractions by every Latin-American Government and by the United States, as happened in Bolivia. I remember arguing with him early in the revolution that his destruction of the entire officer corps of Bastista's armed forces—by dismissal or arrest, or by driving them into flight—frightened every military officer in Latin America. He would not accept the argument.

The "example" that Cuba set was the most vivid kind of warning. Instead of making revolution easier and more likely in Latin America, it has made it harder and costlier.

Che Guevara was shrewd enough to realize this early in the game. In the previously cited article he wrote for *Verde Olivo* of April 9, 1961, he noted that

> certain conditions existed which, though not peculiar to Cuba, will be difficult to exploit again by other peoples, because imperialism . . . learns from its mistakes. . . .
>
> This means that imperialism has learned, fundamentally, the lesson of Cuba, and that it will not again be taken by surprise in any part of our twenty republics, in any of the colonies that still exist, in any part of America. This means that great popular battles against powerful invasion armies await those who now try to violate the peace of the sepulchers, the *Pax Romana*. This is important because if the Cuban War of Liberation with its two years of continual combat, anguish and instability was difficult, the new battles that await the people of other parts of Latin America will be infinitely more difficult.

Che Guevara showed remarkable prescience in this passage, which was written four years before President Johnson intervened in the Dominican Republic because he feared "another Cuba." However, Fidel was not interested in the Dominican Republic, where he knew he could do nothing and had no contacts. The questions he asked in 1966 when I saw him were more logical: "What would the United States do if there were uprisings in four or five countries at the same time? What would they do if there is a revolution in Brazil? or Peru?" He and Che Guevara were working to achieve exactly that result in and from Bolivia.

The greatest harm that Fidel Castro can do to the United States is to make an economic success of the Cuban Revolution. The strongest propaganda point that Washington has had in Latin America for years is that "Communism has failed in Cuba; it cannot succeed in the Western Hemisphere." Should Fidel's present plans and hopes work out and Cuba become economically prosperous, this would be infinitely more effective in encouraging revolution in Latin America than any number of guerrillas.

It is not, however, an immediate danger. Meanwhile, Fidel will go on encouraging guerrillas for their nuisance value and the United States will do everything it can to make the Cuban economy a permanent failure. Washington was able, after several vain efforts, to enlist all the other Latin American countries except Mexico in lining up against Cuba, economically and politically.

Castroite Cuba has been a pariah so far as the Organization of American States is concerned since a hemispheric conference in Uruguay in January 1962. At Punta del Este the United States managed to persuade thirteen of the twenty states and to bribe Duvalier's Haiti for the necessary fourteenth vote to get a two-thirds majority for a resolution excluding Cuba from the inter-American system. Paradoxically, Cuba is still a member of the OAS, since there is no provision in the Bogotá Charter for expulsion of any country.

"You may expel us but you cannot extract us from America," said President Dorticós who was at the conference. "You may put us out of the Organization of American States, but the United States will have a revolutionary Cuba ninety miles from its shore."

All the Latin members, plus the United States, voted for a resolution recognizing that Cuba's alignment with the Soviet Union was "incompatible" with the inter-American system. Later in the year, all the countries supported the United States quarantine against Soviet ships in the missile crisis.

As no Latin country has traded with Cuba since 1964, and none except Mexico has diplomatic relations and a transportation connection with Cuba, the island is isolated in the hemisphere. Canada maintains diplomatic and trade relations, but no commercial passenger planes or ships are permitted.

Except for the Central American countries and Venezuela, which had good reasons to fear Cuban subversion, there was little or no enthusiasm among the Latin American states to respond to American pressures and to ostracize Cuba. When Brazil and Argentina became military dictatorships, their governments naturally were happy to follow an anti-Fidelista line.

In general, however, the Latin countries resent "Yankee" pressures and feel very strongly about North American intervention in their affairs. When President Johnson sent 30,000 marines into the Dominican Republic on April 28, 1965, because of almost certainly false information that "another Cuba" was threatening, it was a profound shock to all the Latin countries.

The United States feared another revolution. The Dominican Communists were few and of no importance, but there was a liberal, radical, anticonservative drive behind the uprising against a military government which was sustaining the *status quo*. The Dominican Reds got into the struggle, of course, as Communists will against any anti-government revolt in Latin America.

Moreover, the United States was determined to show Fidel Castro and all of Latin America that it would go to great lengths to prevent "another Cuba" especially against uprisings that could be labelled Communist. It did not matter how far imagination or fears had to be stretched to apply the black name of Communism to a movement.

President Kennedy, incidentally, formulated this general policy in a speech he made to the Inter-American Press Association in Miami on November 18, 1963, a few days before he was assassinated.

"The American States," he said, "must be ready to come to the aid of any Government requesting aid to prevent a takeover linked to the policies of foreign Communism rather than to an internal desire for change. My own country is prepared to do so. We, in this hemisphere, must also use every resource at our command to prevent the establishment of another Cuba in this hemisphere."

President Johnson's phraseology was much the same. "The American nations," he said on May 2, 1965, "cannot, must not and will not permit the establishment of another Communist government in the Western Hemisphere."

As it happened, Fidel Castro had nothing to do with the Dominican uprising. He was caught by surprise and in no position to help the rebellious forces if he had wanted to. Americans can argue that if they had not intervened, Castro would have—which cannot be proved or disproved. The Johnson Government was satisfied at having demonstrated to all Latin-American leftist movements that the United States will not stand for "another Cuba." This was considered a salutary lesson for Latin-American Governments—a demonstration of American power.

Whether the United States could or would put on such an expensive display of force, while Vietnam is tying up all the spare armed forces, is doubtful—especially if an uprising occurred in less accessible parts of the hemisphere than the Caribbean. (In Bolivia in 1967, it was simply necessary to provide some arms and counterinsurgency help.) The United States is in somewhat the same position as the Soviet Union. One can be sure that Moscow, today, would be appalled at the idea of having to support "another Cuba" in Latin America. There was not the remotest chance that the Russians would help the Dominican rebels. They do not have the resources, nor do they want to get into a conflict with the United States over any other Latin-American country.

This is Fidel Castro's quarrel with Russia. He wants to stir up revolutions, by violence, in Latin America. The Russians want to trade with the Latin-American countries. Their orders to the Muscovite Communist parties are to seek political power gradually through the equivalent of popular fronts. The freakish result is a United States and a Soviet Union working together to keep the peace in Latin America while a furious Fidel Castro raves against both of them. (The pro-Moscow Bolivian Communists sabotaged Che Guevara's guerrilla operation.)

The now famous Fidelista phrase that "the duty of every revolutionary is to make a revolution" is best known as coming from the Second Declaration of Havana, published on February 4, 1962, five days after the OAS resolution mentioned above. Examined too closely, the phrase seems like a truism or an exercise in tautology, but the significance is by no means banal. The idea has run through the years like the theme of a fugue in many speeches and pronouncements by Fidel Castro.

Castro has made a number of addresses in the last six years emphasizing his determination to back revolutionary violence in Latin America against Moscow's wishes. This has been called by Communists a "deviationist position" and "doctrinal heresy," which it no doubt is. To use a positive word, it is one aspect of *Fidelismo*. Marxism-Leninism Cuban style is what Fidel Castro says it is.

Here is a typical passage from an important speech he made on March 13, 1967:

"We conceive of Marxism as revolutionary thought and action. Those who do not have a truly revolutionary spirit cannot be called Communists. Anybody can call himself an eagle without having a single feather on his back. . . . If in any nation those who call themselves Communists do not know how to fulfill their duty, we will support those—even though they do not call themselves Communists—who behave like real Communists in the struggle. Revolutionaries who have revolutionary spirit will end up Marxists. . . .

"This [Cuban] Revolution will maintain its absolutely independent position to which peoples who know how to fight have a right. We proclaim to the whole world that this Revolution will continue on its way; that this Revolution will pursue its own line; that this Revolution will never be anyone's satellite or be subjected to anyone's conditions, and that it will never ask anyone's permission to maintain its posture, be it in ideology or in domestic and foreign affairs."

Five months later, Fidel was still fuming. He made a speech at the closing ceremony of the Latin American Solidarity Organization (LASO) in Havana on August 11, 1967 in the midst of Che's Bolivian adventure:

"Anyone who wants to wait for ideas to triumph first among the masses, in a majority fashion before revolutionary action is initiated, will never become a revolutionary," he said. . . . "What distinguishes a real revolutionary from a false one is precisely this:

one will act to carry the masses; the other waits for the masses to acquire the spirit before beginning to act. . . .

"Let no one dream that he will achieve power peacefully in any nation on this continent. . . . This does not mean that one should take a gun tomorrow in any place and begin to fight. This is not what I mean. What we are talking about is the ideological conflict between those who want to wage a revolution and those who do not."

This speech, like the one he made on March 13, 1967, was a long cry of defiance against Moscow and its policy of seeking change in Latin America by peaceful, political methods and meanwhile doing as much trade as possible with Governments that had embargoes against Cuba and were doing everything they could to make life difficult for the Cubans and their revolution. Fidel's outrage was naïve—or "utopian" or too idealistic. He takes "socialist solidarity" seriously. At the same time he realizes that what he called "the evident Marxist truths" in the LASO speech "constitute a series of old clichés that should be abolished."

"The very Marxist literature," he went on, "the very revolutionary political literature, should be rejuvenated, because by dint of repeated clichés, catchphrases, and catchwords that have been repeated for thirty-five years, nothing is conquered, nothing is won."

It may be that this is the voice of the new generation of revolutionaries speaking. It would be too easy to shrug it off because Fidel Castro's guerrilla campaign in Latin America has had a setback, or because Cuba is still a weak, dependent country. There is something about the "Old Guard" Communists in the underdeveloped countries which seems tired, blasé and too cynical for the younger men and women to whom Fidel Castro could mean more than Leonid Brezhnev or—to pick the most famous old Communist of Latin America—Luis Carlos Prestes of Brazil.

"Today we are the only nation which has built, or is building, socialism in Latin America," Castro boasted in an address on August 30, 1966, "the only nation which has freed itself completely from imperialism. But we are sure that all the rest of the nations will follow that road. We are that banner and that banner will never be lowered; that flag will never surrender."

This was before the death of Che Guevara and the collapse of
the guerrilla movement in Bolivia, but it is typical even now of the
way Fidel Castro feels. In July 1968 Castro wrote in his introduction to the diary of Che Guevara in Bolivia (Spanish edition published in Havana, pages xxii–xxiii):

> Those who fight to the end . . . symbolize the type of revolu-
> tionaries and of men whom history in this hour calls upon for a
> truly hard and difficult task: the revolutionary transformation of
> Latin America.

Fidel (page xxvi) saw Che's last gesture as one that would

> illumine the consciences and direct the struggle of the peoples of
> Latin America, because the heroic battle-cry of Che will reach the
> receptive ears of the poor and exploited for whom he gave his life,
> and many hands will stretch out to take up arms and win their final
> liberation.

"We do not belong to any faction," he said in the August 30,
1966, speech which was made to the Confederation of Cuban
Workers [CTC]. "We do not belong to any international Ma-
sonry. We do not belong to any Church. We are heretics. So, let
them call us heretics. . . . Regardless of who wages the revolution, it will be magnificent. The important thing is that there
should be a revolution. We believe there will be a revolution [in
Latin America]. We say this because we believe it, because we are
certain of it."

Fidel, as usual, was overoptimistic about the imminence of
revolution in Guatemala, Venezuela, Peru, Bolivia. I remember his
questioning me closely more than once about Brazil—where instead of a revolution he was to see a military counterrevolution
which brought joy to Washington. In any event, the Brazilian Communist party, still headed by the veteran Luis Carlos Prestes, is
pro-Moscow and is seeking change through political means and
not through violence.

Fidel said on January 16, 1963, "We do not deny the possibility
of peaceful transition, but we are still awaiting the first case."

Castro is not far out of line in this respect with the thinking of
liberals like Senator J. W. Fulbright, one of the United States's

wisest and most sophisticated minds. "A true revolution is almost always violent and usually it is extremely violent," Fulbright said in a lecture at Johns Hopkins University in May 1966. "Its essence is the destruction of the social fabric and institutions of a society, and an attempt, not necessarily successful, to create a new society with a new social fabric and new institutions."

Americans, he went on to say, have such "a lack of understanding or empathy for the great revolutions of our time" because of the success and unusually good fortune of the American experiment in popular government. As a result, "our sympathy dissolves into hostility when reform becomes revolution; and when Communism is involved as it often is, our hostility takes the form of unseemly panic. At the same time, our abhorrence for violence from the left has been matched by no such sensibilities when the violence comes from the right."

He used President Johnson's intervention in the Dominican Republic as an example of supporting "a corrupt and reactionary military oligarchy" against "democratic forces."

Incidentally, the Arkansas Senator thought that the Castro revolution "may be emerging from extremism" into a period of moderation—which was a wrong, or premature, guess.

Fidel's defiant proclamation "Let them call us heretics" was picked up and expatiated upon by Régis Debray in *Revolution in the Revolution?* which was first published in Havana on January 16, 1967. The little book is not important in itself because it is not original. The ideas came from Fidel Castro, and by derivation from Che Guevara, who used them in his book *Guerrilla Warfare.*

The USIA may well have been right in saying that Debray was attempting to formulate "a philosophical rationale for his [Castro's] ideas, a doctrinal base with which to justify his open intervention into the international affairs of every Communist party in Latin America." Debray had been in Havana, where he was seeing Fidel in the autumn of 1966 when his pamphlet was written.

The "heresy" is against Moscow-style Marxism, which the Cuban "Old Guard" Communists kept trying to persuade Castro to accept until he hit them again in the second "Escalante Affair" at the beginning of 1968.

Debray (i.e., Fidel Castro) argues that guerrilla warfare, not political organization, is the most important requirement in Latin America. The Cuban Revolution is the example to be followed, for it has made a "decisive contribution to revolutionary experience and to Marxism-Leninism."

The basic idea is that "it is necessary for the guerrilla force to take all the functions of command, both political and military." In Cuban terms, the army in the *sierra* gives the orders and the party or movement in the *llano*—the plain or the cities—carries them out. Che Guevara gave his life for these ideas.

Cuba's—which is to say Castro's—bid for leadership in Latin America was put in official form in the Final Proclamation of the Latin American Solidarity Organization (LASO) conference in Havana, August 11, 1967. The following are numbered paragraphs chosen from the twenty in the document:

1. That it is the right and duty of the peoples of Latin America to make revolution.

5. That the armed revolutionary struggle is the primary path of the revolution in Latin America.

10. That the guerrillas, as the embryo of the armies of liberation, are the most effective means for initiating and developing revolutionary struggle in the majority of our countries.

11. That the leadership of the revolution demands, as an organizational principle, the existence of a unified political and military command as a guarantee for its success.

13. That solidarity with Cuba and collaboration and cooperation with the revolutionary movement in arms are unavoidable duties of an international type for all anti-imperialist organizations of the continent.

14. That the Cuban Revolution, as a symbol of the victory of the armed revolutionary movement, is the vanguard of the Latin American anti-imperialist movement.

18. That the struggle in Latin America strengthens its bonds of solidarity with the peoples of Asia and Africa, the socialist countries, and with the workers of the capitalist countries, particularly with the Negro population of the United States who simultaneously suffer class exploitation, poverty, unemployment, racial discrimina-

tion, and denial of the most elementary human rights and who are an important force to be considered in the context of the revolutionary struggle.

20. That we have approved the statutes and created the permanent committee with headquarters in Havana of the Latin American Solidarity Organization which is the genuine representation of the peoples of America.

The proclamation ends with the slogan (which incidentally was displayed in large letters behind the speakers' stand, along with a photograph of Che Guevara): THE DUTY OF EVERY REVOLUTIONARY IS TO MAKE REVOLUTION.

All this is pure *Fidelismo*. Every country of Latin America was represented in Havana but generally not by its official Communist party. Other Communist and non-Communist nations sent delegations.

The most sensational figure there was the man introduced as the "delegate of honor representing the people of the United States, Comrade Stokely Carmichael." Carmichael, ex-chairman of the Student Non-Violent Coordinating Committee, is, with H. Rap Brown, one of the two most militant exponents of Black Power. Judging from what I was told in October 1967 when I was there, Carmichael made a deep impression in Havana.

It was perhaps a mistake for Americans to dismiss so lightly his fanatical specter in Havana, and to ignore the paragraph (No. 18 above) in which the racial conflict in the United States is placed "in the context of the revolutionary struggle." This is where it belongs. The assassination of Martin Luther King on April 4, 1968, drove that lesson home. Fidel Castro—from his own point of view—was clever in grasping this fact and exploiting it. He has two effective propaganda instruments to use against the United States—Vietnam and segregation—and he tries to make the most of them.

When I was in Cuba in 1966 I was shown some film documentaries (the Cubans have turned out some remarkable ones) including the famous *Now,* with Lena Horne singing the title song. It is a horrendous series of pictures of American Negroes being beaten and tortured and having dogs turned on them in the Deep South. It was unrelieved horror with no intimation that such behavior was not the normal thing in all of the United States, or that nearly all Americans deplore such excesses more than Cubans ever can, and are deeply ashamed to boot. It was a true "hate" film which was shown in many places in the world, as well as in Cuba.

Cubans understand Stokely Carmichael's appeal to violence and they are in accord with him. "What else did we do at Moncada?" Haydée Santamaría, who was President of the LASO conference, asked me. I gathered that Castro was genuinely impressed by Carmichael, aside from the fact that Black Power activities in the United States are indirectly helpful to him.

There is also Castro's sense of a universal revolutionary mission which he holds in all sincerity.

"We feel more sympathy for a poor, exploited Negro in the South of the United States," he told Lockwood (page 251), "than for a rich Cuban. Our country is really the whole world, and all the revolutionaries of the world are our brothers."

Another paragraph of the LASO proclamation—No. 13 on "solidarity with Cuba"—must have aroused some feelings in the Communist world. Just as one can talk of Fidel's "Trotskyism" in his desire to stir up revolution in this hemisphere, so one can talk of his Stalinist-type "socialism in one country"—Cuba. Just as he used the Cuban Communist party as an instrument to carry out his revolution inside the country, so he used the example of the Cuban Revolution and his own charisma to further his policy of the "armed revolutionary struggle" in Latin America. He would paraphrase Lenin's saying to read that "the road to hemispheric Communism lies through Havana."

It is a policy which is getting nowhere, if it is not going backwards as a result of Che Guevara's death, but it is too soon for Washington to write off Cuba, in Schlesinger's phrase, as an unimportant "mendicant Communist regime in the Caribbean." Ten years is not a long time for a social revolution. Besides, much of Latin America is in what the Brazilian economist, Celso Furtado, calls a prerevolutionary state.

And Fidel Castro is still young. He can count on something that President Kennedy once said: "Those who make peaceful revolution impossible will make violent revolution inevitable."

The similarity between Fidel Castro's ideas of violent revolution and Mao Tse-tung's policies and writings has often been noted. Yet there are important differences, too.

Fidel could agree with Mao's famous dictum: "Political power comes out of the barrel of a gun." But he would not agree with the sentence from *Problems of War and Strategy* that followed: "Our principle is that the Party commands the gun, and the gun will never be allowed to command the Party." In Cuba, the Communist party, as such, commands nothing.

Castro would be more in agreement with other Maoist ideas. Stuart R. Schram's introduction to Mao's *Basic Tactics* gives (page 25) "the three essential principles of the central role of the army, the importance of the rural base areas, and the protracted character of the struggle." Also (page 35): "In Mao's view, the supreme manifestation of conscious activity is provided by man at war." Schram writes (page 40) of "Mao's passionate desire to believe in the relevance of his own experience," which is pure pre-Fidelism. And (page 41) Mao, like Castro and Che Guevara after him, believes in the "revolutionary 'countryside' against the imperialist 'cities.' "

> The *campesino* [peasant] class in America will provide the great liberating army of the future, as it has already done in Cuba [Che Guevara wrote in the *Verde Olivo* article already cited]. . . . The possibility of triumph by the popular masses in Latin America clearly appears in the form of guerrilla warfare, carried out by an army of *campesinos* that defeats the oppressor army in a frontal assault, takes cities by attacks from the countryside, and dissolves the oppressor army as the first stage in destroying completely the superstructure of the previous colonial world.

This is Fidelism. The likeness to Maoism is coincidental. The policy did not work for Che Guevara, but Castro still believes that he has the right ideas. On a much bigger scale, the Cubans believe the ideas worked for General Nguyen Giap in Vietnam. Giap wrote (in *People's War, People's Army*):

Expanding guerrilla war, combined with the total political mobilization of the masses, can defeat the imperialists and their puppets, obsessed by a mechanistic approach to war in which weapons are all-important.

It is Vietnam that Fidel Castro has had his eyes on in recent years, not Communist China. He is emotionally identified with Hanoi. At the same time, he realizes that so long as the United States is involved in Vietnam it will not attack Cuba.

Theodore Draper calls violence "the chief issue binding Castro's Cuba and Mao's China." I would say that there is no direct link; it is a case of parallel courses, as Draper also notes.

Fidel won his revolution by guerrilla warfare without reading Mao Tse-tung's writings, and he believes that this is the way Latin Americans should win revolutions. In recent years he has preferred to notice that General Giap started using the tactics of "national liberation" warfare in Vietnam before Mao in China.

In this, as in so many other ways, it must be said that Fidel Castro is self-taught. One of the keys to his character and to his actions is that he does things in his own fashion. This is why there is no "line," no "thread," no pattern that can explain him or what he has done unless it derives from his own person and his own character. Theodore Draper often recognizes this, but without accepting it as a satisfactory explanation for Fidel's acts.

In the article "Castro and Communism" for *The Reporter* of January 17, 1963, he wrote:

> [Castro] has, in fact, institutionalized his personal instability by refusing to stabilize his revolution, on the ground that a revolution that stops going forward ceases to be revolutionary. He has never operated from a firm political center but has always associated himself with ideas and movements that seemed most able or willing at different times to serve him. In a sense, he has subordinated himself to them on condition that they subordinate themselves to him. . . .
>
> He did not come to Communism by the path of any other Communist leader, and his circumstances do not permit him to develop like any other Communist leader. In a sense, Castro does not belong in or out of any movement "naturally." As a personality, he could easily fit into the most contradictory movements from the extreme

Left to the extreme Right, as long as it was *his* movement and the future seemed mortgaged to it.

In my judgment, Fidel Castro picks up these "movements" as he would a coat, putting them on, taking them off, throwing them away or keeping them—but it is the same Fidel Castro in all cases. This Fidel Castro would not embrace a movement of the "extreme Right" because he could not be himself, and he could not carry out the sort of social revolution he always had in mind, however vaguely at first.

This is not the same as following a "line," for he had none to follow. The Marxism-Leninism which he proclaimed in 1961 is *Fidelismo* with a Marxist-Leninist camouflage. It is the coat that he is wearing now and may wear to the end, but it will not inhibit his determination to go his own way insofar as circumstances permit.

There is much talk of "The Path" in Cuba today, but Fidel Castro has not found it yet. As Haydée Santamaría said to me, *"Fidel está buscando"*—Fidel is searching.

He has a goal: to make Cuba, for all Cubans, a prosperous, healthy, progressive and independent country. This has always been his aspiration. It was so when he was a university student, when he led the attack on the Moncada Barracks, when he fought his two-year guerrilla war in the Sierra Maestra—and it is still his goal today. He has gone by different paths and used different methods, but the direction has never changed.

Professor Hugh Thomas of Reading University wrote in the *New Statesman* of August 26, 1966:

> Castro is both a man of action and an intellectual guide. But the fact is many Cubans believe that this particular ruler is only too likely to be assassinated sooner or later. A policy of assassination appears indeed to be the only positive one which the Johnson administration has up its sleeve where Cuba is concerned.

If not "a silver bullet" sent by the U.S. Central Intelligence Agency, it could be done by a fanatical or deranged Cuban prepared to commit suicide. Of course, Fidel could have a heart attack or a genuine accident.

An international conflict that could develop from the Middle

East might lead the Government in Washington to decide that the Castro regime must be liquidated. The price would be very high in American and especially Cuban lives and Cuban property, but it could be done. Castro's enemies have always speculated hopefully on the possibility that the Soviet Union might cut off its trade and aid to Cuba, either through exasperation with Castro or by a deal with Washington. This is possible but unlikely.

With each passing year the revolution has been gaining strength. Its institutions and the way of life it has introduced have become ingrained. Other Cubans than Fidel Castro have gained experience, although none has his charisma. If Castro were removed, the army, the police and the whole mechanism of maintaining order would continue to function; the Communist Party of Cuba would still provide a political framework and instrument of government; the chances are that the revolution would continue.

The most delicate period, Fidel once said to me when we were discussing the danger of assassination, would be immediately after he was killed. There would be a period of great uncertainty internally and a temptation for the United States to use this as an excuse to intervene. Fidel is certain that the revolution will carry on, and so are his associates. In present circumstances, Raúl Castro would be the one to take over the premiership.

Ernesto Che Guevara was never in line for the top position in Cuba, whatever happened. Although he had been granted all the rights of a native-born Cuban citizen, he was always thought of as an Argentine and, in any event, he was a man who remained alone. When he left the Cuban government forever around April 1, 1965, it was to lead a new crusade of guerrillas—somewhere, anywhere. The end came two and a half years later in a remote corner of southeastern Bolivia. Juan de Onis, the *New York Times* correspondent, went to Pucará, Bolivia, some weeks later and obtained what proved to be the true story of what happened. Che's diary and Fidel's introduction to it provided corroboration.

Che, who was leading a guerrilla band of mixed nationality, had been slightly wounded and captured in a gorge a mile from a village called La Higuera.

"He was held overnight in the schoolhouse," de Onis wrote in a dispatch printed on December 3, "questioned by Bolivian officers and executed the morning of October 9 on orders received by radio from armed forces headquarters in La Paz, the Bolivian capital."

In another article, published on March 7, 1968, de Onis added a few details. An American CIA agent questioned Che for a few hours in the schoolhouse.

> At about 11 A.M. the conversation was interrupted by a burst of gunfire in the adjoining room in the two-room schoolhouse. A wounded Bolivian guerrilla had been slain.
> Mr. Guevara was silent for a moment, then spoke again.
> "They are going to kill me, but that will not stop the revolution," he said. "The revolution will triumph."

A Bolivian NCO came in and the CIA agent left. De Onis continued:

> Despite his wound Mr. Guevara got to his feet and said: "You are going to see how a man dies." [Castro's version of Che's last words was "Fire! Do not fear!"]
> Four shots killed him instantly.

Afterwards, the highest Bolivian authorities lied about how he died, lied about the disposition of his body, and lied about what Che is supposed to have said. They even burned down the schoolhouse in La Higuera. That way, there would be no shrine, because there was no body, no place of death, no known burial place—only a name for history.

Guevara had left a letter with Fidel on April 1, 1965, when he departed. To protect Che, Castro kept it secret until October 3, at which time he read it to the Central Committee of the Cuban Communist party. In it Guevara said that he felt that he had fulfilled his duty to the Cuban Revolution:

> I have lived magnificent days. . . . Other lands of the world demand the aid of my modest efforts. I am able to do what is denied

to you by your reponsibility as head of Cuba, and the hour has come for us to separate. Let it be known that I go with a mixture of joy and sorrow. Here I leave the purest of my hopes as a creator, and the dearest of my dear ones—and I leave the people who took me in as a son.

Soon after disappearing Che wrote a letter to his parents (his mother died before he was killed) which was published in Cuba in the spring of 1967:

MY DEAR OLD ONES,

Once again I feel pressing against my heels the sides of Rosinante; I am back on the road with my shield on my arm. . . .

It may be that this letter will be the last. I do not seek it, but it is within the logical calculations of probabilities. If it be so, I send you a last embrace.

I have loved you very much, only I did not know how to express my affection. I am extremely rigid in my actions and I believe that sometimes you did not understand me. It was not easy to understand me, but believe me—just today.

The relations between Che and Fidel, while intimate, admiring and friendly at all times, could hardly have been smooth. Che was drifting away from the Cuban Revolution while Fidel remained heart and soul bound up in it. The revolution had ceased to provide Guevara with the action, excitement and satisfactions that he needed. By 1964, he had become more dogmatic than he had been before, or than Fidel, for all his protestations of Marxism-Leninism, could ever be.

Che Guevara was a permanent revolutionary. He was at his best and happiest making the Cuban Revolution, but once it was made, it was hard for him to sit behind a desk and sustain an interest. His economic ideas had gone badly. The future that stretched before him was more desk work, more drudgery. He was discontented. He and Fidel were no longer comrades-in-arms.

He felt a sense of mission as fierce and deep as that of any priest going to savage lands to convert the heathen. What Che Guevara wanted to do was to go to the lands where the people were oppressed and help them to make a revolution. He believed in Fidel's theories of guerrilla warfare and violent revolution, and he wanted to lead that kind of crusade in person, whatever the hardships and dangers.

His decision was natural, and from what Carlos Rafael Rodríguez said to me at the time of his death, which others confirmed, Che Guevara told Castro in the autumn of 1964 that he wanted to go away. Fidel apparently tried to dissuade him at first, but then worked with him on the elaborate Bolivian plan. Only a few other intimates knew, because Guevara had to be protected as long as possible from the CIA and the sort of mobilization with the help of United States counterinsurgency forces that caught him and killed him in Bolivia.

Some of Che's associates in the Cuban Government expressed wonder to me that he had stayed in Cuba as long as he did. Faustino Pérez, who first knew Che in Mexico when the *Granma* expedition was being prepared, told me that Guevara's idea from the beginning was to help Fidel make the revolution in Cuba, and that his task would then be over.

Although Che was given the rights of a native-born Cuban citizen, he always seemed a little out of place, which I ascribed to his unusual character, but in the long run it amounted to the fact that he could not feel about Cuba in the way that Fidel Castro and the other Cuban leaders felt.

This does not mean that Fidel and Che did not remain close friends until the end. There is ample proof of that now. Fidel's loyalty went to the extent of his indignantly denying to me in 1966 that Che had made any serious mistakes in the industrialization program—"just minor ones of little importance about a factory here or there." Che had no such modesty about his early mistakes.

Fidel at all times knew where Che was during the mysterious period when he was out of sight and helped him with arms and money. The doubts that were cast on the authenticity of the April 1, 1965, letter were on a par with the reports that the two men had quarreled bitterly and even that Castro had had Guevara killed. Fidel Castro lives in a suspicious and hostile world, the lonely world of all "Chief Leaders" in small or big, democratic or totalitarian nations.

Che Guevara was the only leader of any stature in the guerrilla movements of Latin America. This is why his death was such a blow to Cuban hopes of sustaining a series of pressures that would, in time, cause the disintegration of certain governments. In the Sierra Maestra, the guerrillas fighting Batista had some extremely bad moments, especially at the beginning, but they had Fidel Castro and he, in turn, had some outstanding leaders in his brother Raúl, Che Guevara, Camilo Cienfuegos and the fanatically brave Negro commander, Juan Almeida, who is now the Cuban army commander.

In the countries where Fidel had been supporting the guerrillas—Guatemala, Venezuela, Colombia, Peru and Bolivia—there had already been setbacks to the national groups and some deaths among their leaders. Only Che Guevara, with his magical name, his experience, his unlimited courage and determination, provided a ray of hope.

His death, therefore, was not only a great personal sorrow to Fidel and to Che's companions from the Sierra Maestra days; it was a stunning blow to the guerrillas of Latin America and to Castro's policies. Those policies are not going to change—Fidel believes in them—but it will be a long time before he can count on effective results.

Che Guevara knew that he was making no progress in Bolivia. One of the mysteries about his death is why he should ever have believed he could win over the Bolivian Indians. As he wrote in his diary, they are "as impenetrable as stones." His "call to battle," his efforts to persuade them that they had nothing to lose but their misery, his vision of revolution—all these were obviously meaningless; "you could see that they did not believe you." Che and many of the others were foreigners in Bolivia. They would not have been believed even where they were understood. They would certainly be betrayed by the peasants, who would be bribed by Bolivian army officers.

The United States acted quickly, sending down counterinsurgency specialists to advise and probably lead the Bolivians, some of whose officers had been trained in the United States.

The only possible support for a revolution in Bolivia would have come from the tin miners of the plateau, who were organized and armed, and who had fought and won in the revolution of 1952. But their leaders were corrupt; the Communist party was in tune with Moscow, not Havana, and it was not seeking revolution.

A part of Fidel Castro and his career died with Che Guevara. By an extraordinary coincidence for me, I happened to be in Havana as the news about Che gradually trickled through and doubt became certainty. I shared the Cubans' sorrow, for I liked and admired Che Guevara despite the fact that we disagreed so completely in our ideas and hopes. He was in the Sierra Maestra when I went up on February 17, 1957. I was in the Cabañas Fortress in Havana when he walked in to take command, his broken arm in a sling, at the beginning of 1959. There were long talks—arguments, really—in the small hours of different nights when he was so incongruously the president of the National Bank of Cuba. And there I was in Havana in October 1967, in at the death, so to speak—a quixotic and natural death for Ernesto Che Guevara.

Carlos Rafael Rodríguez told me that Che had said to him before he left Cuba, "You know, it is my fate to die as a guerrilla and I will die as a guerrilla—somewhere."

The picture of Che Guevara sitting at the president's desk in the National Bank was always completely out of focus. He knew he didn't belong. It was not affectation on his part to sign the Cuban banknotes simply "Che." It was his way of expressing contempt for money as such. Like Fidel, Che Guevara was an anarchist at heart and did not approve of a money economy.

Rodríguez said he remembered a long conversation with Fidel Castro in the Sierra Maestra as victory was approaching, in which Fidel said, "Once we have won our victory here, I want to go to Santo Domingo and help make a revolution there, and then to Guatemala, and then Peru." Rodríguez told me that he argued with Fidel—as he did later with Che—that it was a duty and a necessity to stay and make a success of the Cuban Revolution—

which Fidel decided to do after his initial hesitation about the role
he would play.

Castro's heart was with Che Guevara as he went out from Cuba
like a knight of old to conquer the giants and monsters of imperialism who peopled his nightmarish world. He left a wife and four
young children—one a baby a year old. Someone close to the
family said to me that he loved them all very much, was a most
affectionate father, and left them with sorrow—but something
stronger beckoned and called to him, and he went.

For me, Che Guevara, unlike Fidel Castro, was not a man of
our times or a man of the future. No doubt his ghost will brood for
a time over the Cordillera of the Andes which he had hoped, in
Fidel's phrase, to turn into another Sierra Maestra, or where, in his
own phrase, he hoped to make a second or third Vietnam. But Che
was too strange a man. His character was different from Castro's;
he was withdrawn, the opposite of flamboyant or demagogic, never
seeking publicity, austere in his habits. He seemed to use the
minimum necessary to keep alive, even to smoking his inevitable
cigars down to the shortest stub.

However much one disapproves of his Marxist philosophy, his
destructive appeal to violence and hatred, his naïve and faulty
economic ideas, Che Guevara shaped up as a man whose flame
burned with an extraordinary purity. He dedicated himself to
others and gave his life for others. The passion he felt and the
suffering he forced himself to endure had a profound religious
quality.

The instinct that drove Che Guevara from Cuba was a true one.
He had not been fulfilling the mission that he saw for himself.
Cuba no longer needed him; others he felt did, and he gave himself
to a cause that encompassed the poor and oppressed and that he
was sure would end for him in some such death as he met in
Bolivia.

He did not seek to be a martyr so as to live in history, as a
missionary would aspire to live in heaven—but he will live, and
it is arguable that he is worth more to the revolutionary cause as a
dead martyr than he was as a living guerrilla.

Guerrilla warfare has a certain degree of continuity and perhaps
permanence in Latin America, as in the world at large. It will not

end with the death of Che Guevara and the breakup of his band in Bolivia. Within the hemispheric movement for national liberation, or whatever it is called, Che Guevara will be a legendary figure and an inspiration. Even in life he was a figure out of legend—not quite real, not down-to-earth, not quite human.

This, perhaps, is why it was uncomfortable for one to be with him. His ideas, by normal, pragmatic standards, were false, impractical, even antiquated. For existing society, they were destructive. His name will live because of his ideals, his dedication, his courage and a certain romantic aura that surrounds a man who lives to sacrifice himself for a universal cause.

There really was something quixotic about it, but only the obtuse would claim that the world defeated Don Quixote. As Fidel said to me in the time of mourning, "There was only one Che." He truly was, in Castro's elegiaic tribute, "the most extraordinary of the companions in the revolution."

The last article that Che Guevara wrote—and in retrospect, the most important—was sent to Havana from Bolivia and published as a special supplement by the new magazine, *Tricontinental,* on April 16, 1967, six months before he was killed. It contained his most passionate expression of the need, as he put it, "to create the Second or Third Vietnam or the Second and Third Vietnam" in Latin America. It is an eloquent expression of *Fidelismo:*

> America constitutes a more or less homogeneous ensemble, and over almost all its territory, North American capitalistic monopolists maintain absolute primacy. The governments which are puppets, or at best weak and timid, cannot oppose the orders of the Yankee masters. The North Americans have reached the height of their political and economic domination. They cannot go much further. Any change in the situation could turn into a retreat from its primacy. Its policy is to hold what it has conquered. Its line of action at present is reduced to the brutal use of force to prevent liberation movements, whatever form they may take.

As an example, Che Guevara gave the American intervention in the Dominican Republic in 1965. But guerrillas in isolated places and the masses in the cities must go on fighting.

Many will die [he wrote prophetically] victims of their errors; others will fall in the hard conflict that approaches; new fighters and new leaders will arise in the heat of the revolutionary struggle.

He saw the United States having to send more and more troops, as in Vietnam, for the Americans must be beaten "in a great global confrontation" in places far from their familiar surroundings:

It will be a long, cruel struggle whose front will be in guerrilla hideouts, in the cities, in the houses of combatants, where the oppressors will seek easy victims among families, in the massacre of peasants, in the villages or cities destroyed by enemy bombs. . . .

Hatred as a factor of the struggle, implacable hatred of the enemy, [will provide] an impulse beyond the natural limitations of the human being and will convert him into an effective, violent, selective and cold machine for killing. Our soldiers have to be like that; a people without hatred cannot triumph against a brutal enemy.

For Che Guevara, over whom death was hovering—and he knew it—the *Tricontinental* article was a testament, a valedictory, whose words will live in this revolutionary era—terrible words, but not without their idealism to make a better world out of hatred and blood and struggle.

"Our mission, in the early hours, is to survive," he wrote. This was what he could not do. The closing passage of the article was so widely quoted at the time of his death that it has already become famous:

For we are proud of having learned from the Cuban Revolution and its Maximum Leader the great lesson that is to be drawn from his actions in this part of the world: "What matter the dangers and sacrifices of a man and a people, when the fate of humanity is at stake?"

All that we do is a battle cry against imperialism and a cry for the unity of peoples against the great enemy of humankind: the United States of America. In whatever place death surprises us, let it be welcome, if only this, our call to war, reach a receptive ear and another hand stretches out to pick up our weapons, and other men prepare to intone the mournful dirge to the staccato singing of machine guns and to new battle cries of war and victory.

The ceremony of mourning in the Plaza de la Revolución in Havana on the night of October 18 was surely the most fervent that the Cubans had held in the course of the revolution. The profound silence of the immense crowd who listened to Fidel Castro's moving oration—one of the best he has ever made—was a most poignant tribute of respect.

It had always been hard to grasp what place Che Guevara held in Cuba during his years there. But his death left such a sense of tragedy and loss that his hold on the Cuban people must have been much greater than it had seemed.

Che Guevara also left an "unfulfilled task." Fidel Castro will not abandon it.

When my wife and I were in Cuba in November 1963, we asked Fidel, "What about the attempted subversion of other Latin-American countries that Washington complains of all the time?"

"Of course," he said, "and why not? The CIA is doing everything to Cuba that you accuse us of. It is training saboteurs and guerrillas; it is supplying counterrevolutionaries with arms and matériel; it is supporting raids by sea and air, and landing parties on Cuba; it is flooding Latin America with anti-Cuban propaganda; it is using its great influence on every country in Latin America against us.

"If the United States can do all these things, why can't we try to do the same things?"

What he said was true, and its logic was inescapable—unless one accepted the American premise: that the United States was on the side of right, justice and goodness, and the Cubans on the side of wrong, injustice and evil. Using this argument, it is all right for the United States to employ every method, however underhanded and illegal, to destroy Castroism, and it is wrong for the Cubans to fight back with the same weapons.

The CIA is forcing Castro to keep an extensive and expensive guard against raids, sabotage and plots to assassinate him. However, Fidel has been able to use these operations as internal propaganda to rally the Cuban people around him, and to depict the United States as a deadly menace to Cuba—which it is.

The two-way operation is fairly sophisticated on the Cuban as well as on the American side. The Russians have provided the technical means and advice. Latin American guerrillas are trained in Cuba and sent back to their native countries. The Cuban embassies in Paris, Prague, Madrid and Mexico seem to be the main diplomatic channels—with the American embassies watching them.

During the Latin American Solidarity Organization conference in Havana in the summer of 1967, two Cubans who confessed to being agents of the CIA were put on display for the foreign newspapermen. One of the prisoners said that the CIA had given him radiotelegraph training for six months and that it had later trained him in demolition, the use of weapons and the carrying out of infiltration missions. The CIA also furnishes the agents with false credentials, he said.

Cuba's role in insurgency, according to a report of the House of Representatives Subcommittee on Inter-American Affairs dated July 3, 1967, is

> predominantly that of coach, prompter and tireless propagandist. . . .
>
> Several thousand Latin Americans have been trained and indoctrinated in Cuba. Insurgent groups have also received financial assistance and military supplies from Cuba. . . . In addition to conducting insurgency training, Cuba also engages freely in psychological warfare.

The United States Information Agency and its Voice of America likewise engage freely in psychological warfare. "Who is subverting whom?" Fidel Castro asks. The answer depends on the angle of vision. Both sides have a sense of righteousness; each considers the other to be evil. There is a mini-Cold War going on between the United States and Cuba, and it will continue so long as Castro and a Communist government exist in Cuba.

So far as can be seen, the CIA has failed in Cuba, even without counting the Bay of Pigs fiasco. The best that can be said, from the CIA's point of view, is that it forces Castro to maintain larger military, police and militia operations than he would otherwise need.

This adds to the cost of governing and interferes with the economy. The effect on the stability of the Castro regime is, if anything, what Cubans would call *contraproducente* (counterproductive).

"What good are the agents and counterrevolutionaries and their pinpricks doing to the United States?" President Dorticós asked me irritably. "What misinformation is the CIA getting that can make them think that this sort of operation is effective?"

Fidel Castro and Che Guevara asked me much the same question on occasions. The answer is that revolutionary Cuba is an enemy, and that it is the business of the CIA to do just what it is doing. What is less excusable is that the CIA does seem to get more misinformation than truth from Cuba. It works from an emotionally biased basis, using United States agents and Cuban informers who see Communism and the Castro regime as evil, sinful and heretical. The overwhelming majority of Cubans do not feel the same way.

"The capture of CIA agents," Fidel told the LASO conference in August 1967, "has become so routine here that it is something that takes place every week. Many times publicity is not given to it because it is absolutely no news to anybody."

Castro's problems with the United States—and vice versa—are compounded by the falsities, distortion and ignorance in the mass media on both sides of the Florida Straits. The United States has a free press within any practical meaning of the phrase, but this cannot overcome lack of knowledge and understanding, or the emotional hostility that Communism in general and Fidel Castro in particular meet on the mainland. Cuba does not have a free press. Its distortions and falsehoods are deliberate, but there, too, emotions prevent understanding.

Fidel was frank with Lee Lockwood (page 128), in replying to the question why "the Cuban press writes so one-sidedly about the United States":

> I am not going to tell you that we don't do that. It's true, everything that we say about the United States refers essentially to the worst aspects, and it is very rare that things in any way favorable

to the United States will be published here. We simply have a
similar attitude to the attitude of your country. I mean that we always try to create the worst opinion of everything there is in the
United States, as a response to what they have always done with us.

And so the game of "tit for tat" goes on.

At the time of Hurricane Flora—in October 1963—there was
great devastation, homelessness and a shortage of food and medicine. The American Red Cross offered to help. Fidel Castro immediately rejected the offer. It was hard for Americans to understand the *pundonor* of a Spanish nation like Cuba in a case of this
sort. Help from a government which was doing everything it could,
short of war, to destroy them would have been demeaning to
Cubans, although they wanted and would have accepted help from
Americans acting as Americans and not officially. The Cuban reaction was undoubtedly understood by other Ibero-Americans and
by Spaniards.

Cubans, like all other members of the "socialist world," continually refer to the United States and "Yankee imperialism" as
"the common enemy." For Cubans this phrase has a special meaning. No other nation in the Communist bloc is geographically close
to the United States. None has had the long history of economic,
social and strategic relations which Cuba has had with her "formidable neighbor"—to use José Martí's apt phrase.

Consequently, when Fidel Castro raves against "the common
enemy" of mankind, he has a much more intense feeling than the
attitude of the other Communist states—with the obvious exception of North Vietnam. When Premier Fidel Castro thinks about
the United States, he thinks of it primarily as the enemy of Cuba.
Logically, if the United States felt that it had to fight a war against
Communism, it should be fighting in Cuba, not in Vietnam.
History is neither logical nor inevitable, but the Cubans will never
cease worrying about the intentions of the United States toward
them. Nor will they ever cease to remain as militarily strong as
possible.

"Unquestionably, the United States today represents the most
reactionary ideas in the world," Fidel Castro told Lee Lockwood
(page 188). "And I think that they cause grave danger both to the
world and to the people of the United States themselves."

When Lockwood asked him what he meant by "reactionary ideas" Fidel replied, "I mean especially its role of world gendarme, its desire to impose outside its frontiers the kind of government system it thinks other states and other peoples should have."

Castro is not alone in making this criticism. He was thinking of Vietnam as well as of Latin America. The Cuban Revolution identified itself wholeheartedly with the North Vietnamese from the moment that President Johnson began to escalate the war in Vietnam in the spring of 1965. The Cubans cannot help materially, but the propaganda value to Hanoi is worth something in the Western Hemisphere. Cuba has a powerful radio station (built by the Russians) on which North Vietnam's case is presented daily. For Cubans, 1967 was the "Year of Solidarity with Vietnam."

One of the most important results of the Cuban Revolution in the Western Hemisphere is the Alliance for Progress. It is chiefly associated with President Kennedy, who gave it a name, a coherent philosophy and an organization. As has been mentioned before, the challenge of the Cuban Revolution, with its emphasis on social and economic reforms, had to be met throughout Latin America. The Alliance for Progress, which was put into treaty form in August 1961, was the answer.

Unfortunately for Latin America, the sense of alarm and urgency over the Cuban Revolution did not last. The concept of the Alliance was splendid—that all the Governments of Latin America should produce working plans and money to bring to pass reforms in the fields of agriculture, education and public health. The United States furnished $1 billion a year in aid until 1968–69.

Previously, the aid went solely to industries and infrastructural projects which benefited the ruling minorities far more than the masses. Since the program asks that landowners, bankers and businessmen give up some of their wealth and privileges for the general good, the Alliance calls for the equivalent of a voluntary social revolution. This goes against centuries of tradition in Latin America.

The Alliance for Progress is not working well, but it cannot be written off. Foreign aid has been reduced steadily by the United States Congress. Latin Americans do not yet feel threatened sufficiently by revolutionary pressures to make the suggested sacrifices in taxation, agrarian reform and the like. The United States proved in the case of the Dominican Republic that it will protect them against leftist revolutions.

Fidel Castro has, for years, been pointing out that he is doing what the Alliance for Progress is trying to do. Thus far, he has been right in asserting that the ruling classes elsewhere in Latin America will not voluntarily make the sacrifices which are required. The Alliance, he once said to me, using a favorite word of his, is "utopian." Thus, the only answer from his point of view is violent revolution.

> Until 1959 [Dudley Seers wrote in the *Political Quarterly,* April–June 1963], Latin America had seemed within the sphere of American influence. It provided a chain of military alliances covering the southern flank; its votes in the United Nations were usually available on critical issues; its materials and foodstuffs could be purchased by the exports of American manufacture; it was a secure field for American investors. This state of affairs had lasted so long that it seemed part of the natural order; it was institutionalized in the Organization of American States.

And along came Fidel Castro! The shock effect of the Cuban Revolution on the United States and on Latin America was profound. The effort to brush it off now for a variety of reasons—the isolation of Cuba, the failure of guerrilla tactics everywhere they have been tried, the weakness and divisions in all Latin-American Communist movements, Fidel Castro's loss of prestige and influence—is premature.

Among the irreversible factors brought into focus by Cuba is that United States relations with Latin America will never again be as Professor Seers described them above. Fidel Castro came along at a moment in hemispheric history when many Latin-American countries were faced with the necessity of making drastic structural changes in social and economic spheres. Some of the countries were—and are—ripe for revolution, even though the revolutionary forces may be held in check for many years to come.

History is on the side of Castroites, although probably not in the form of Marxism-Leninism. There are other ways of making social revolutions, although in the present state of Latin-American affairs change is more likely to come from the extreme left than from the extreme right. The socioeconomic structure of Latin America, with its militarism and small, conservative, traditional ruling class, is close to Fascism. The Peronist regime in Argentina, for instance, was a Fascist variation.

On the other hand, one of the striking features of Latin-American history is the absence of ideologies. This has been a reason why Cuba's Marxism-Leninism has no appeal in its doctrinal form.

Some Cubans see Castro's foreign policy as a bid for leadership of the "Third World." There is a tendency among Cuban intellectuals to regard the Soviet Union as a second-rate power and the United States as the only first-rate one. The Russians, it is argued, lost their predominance as a result of the missile crisis. The Communist world is divided. Moreover, in Cuban terms, the Soviet Union is becoming more of a capitalistic power than a communistic one.

At the same time, Fidel argues that the United States has not "resolved the problems of a single underdeveloped country in the world." And as Castro told Lockwood (page 191):

> The only thing that can resolve the problems of hunger and misery in the underdeveloped countries is revolution—revolutions that really change social structures, that wipe out social bonds, that put an end to unnecessary costs and expenditures, the squandering of resources; revolutions which allow the people to devote themselves to planned and peaceful work.

By rejecting a role either for the Soviet Union or for the United States in the underdeveloped nations, Fidel Castro opens the field for himself and his revolutionary ideas. He is seeking the support of the young and adventurous everywhere in the world, and rather especially in the Communist bloc outside the Western Hemisphere.

Fidel Castro does have an appeal which extends far beyond the island of Cuba. He has global ambitions and a messianic temperament. His voice is the voice of the restless young people of our

times—the younger generation coming into power in many nations. When it does, Cuba may not be so isolated.

The isolation, it should be noted, is from the Soviet Union as
well as from the United States and Latin America. The missile
crisis was a turning point in that respect. Cubans learned what they
should have known—that the Soviet bloc was no real protection
for them and that their country was expendable. From that time
onward, Fidel Castro concentrated on working out Cuba's problems in as independent a fashion as possible. His eccentric foreign-
policy line became more pronounced.

The immense popularity that the Soviet Union once enjoyed in
Cuba has waned. At the same time the Chinese Communists are
regarded with suspicion. Fidel is, therefore, finding it easy to continue to emphasize to the Cuban people the Cuban aspects of his
revolution. At the same time, he wants to keep Cuba within what
he calls the "socialist world."

An example of Castro's truculent policy of independence was
his refusal to send a delegation to the preliminary "world conference" of Communist nations in Budapest in February 1968, although the Soviet Union had invited him to send one. An editorial
in *The Times* of London on February 26, discussing the absentees,
said: "In Latin America Castro flies his lonely, independent standard like some transatlantic Tito."

Tito, however, received help from the United States in 1948 and
afterwards, and he could play his independent role without being
economically dependent on the Soviet Union. Castro is gambling,
thus far rather shrewdly, that Cuba's value to Moscow is important
enough to allow him—unlike Czechoslovakia—to take great
liberties and get away with them. Cuba is not alone in defying the
Soviet Union; it may be that a "Communist Third World" is shaping up.

However, the Russians, like the Americans, are going through
with the process of isolating Cuba. Castro seemed to have won a
great triumph when eighty-two countries sent delegations to Havana for the Afro-Asian-Latin-American Peoples Solidarity Organization (AALAPSO) conference, January 3–15, 1966. The Soviet Union and Communist China were represented. However,
little of value came out of the meeting from Castro's point of view

except a decision to hold a "Latin American Solidarity Organization" (LASO) meeting in Havana in midsummer, 1967. There, Fidel and Cuba were dominant and imposed their militant revolutionary policies, but the Soviet bloc continues its peaceful political policy in Latin America. Communist China is far away and otherwise engrossed.

When I was talking to Fidel about the American press in 1967, and trying to persuade him to allow a permanent *New York Times* correspondent to return to Havana, I made the point that the ignorance about Cuba in the United States was complete.

"It is in Russia, too," Celia Sánchez chimed in. I had the impression that Fidel also had a poor opinion of the Russian journalists in Havana. I ascribed it to the general disillusionment with the Soviet Union in Cuba, and to the differences between them.


As Fidel has stated with pride, Cuba has never broken diplomatic relations with any country. He provoked President Eisenhower into breaking relations between the United States and Cuba. He insisted on establishing diplomatic relations with East Germany although he knew it would lead to Bonn's breaking off relations. When Albania became a pro-Chinese maverick and other Communist countries broke relations with her, Cuba refused to follow suit.

Although the Castro Government favored the Arabs against Israel in the June 1967 war and afterwards, relations with Israel were not interrupted. Nor have they ever been with the Vatican.

This is one of Fidel's ways of showing his "independence," but there is also a strong feeling that Cuba—due to what Castro calls "Yankee imperialism"—has been dangerously isolated in the Western Hemisphere. The more diplomatic and trade links that can be maintained, the better for Havana. It is a field where Fidel's streak of pragmatism operates.

He knows that there is no chance in the foreseeable future to reach a mutually agreeable understanding with the United States. When I asked him in October 1967 about a reconciliation with

Washington, he answered with one word: "Impossible!" The election of Richard Nixon as President of the United States would have strengthened this belief.

On the American side I am reminded of something Winston Churchill said in a debate in the House of Commons in June 1946: "There are no people in the world who are so slow to develop hostile feelings against a foreign country as the Americans, and there are no people who, once estranged, are more difficult to bring back." (One can add, "especially where Communism is involved.")

At various times—particularly in 1963 and 1964—Castro talked vaguely of the possibility of negotiations with the United States. In an interview with Richard Eder of *The New York Times,* published on July 6, 1964, Fidel spoke of his willingness to withhold support of Latin American revolutionaries if the United States would agree to cease supporting "subversive activity against Cuba." He expressed a willingness to discuss compensation for expropriated American properties and also a willingness to release political prisoners.

The year before—in a television interview on June 5—Fidel had likewise said that he would talk about "indemnifications and all those things." He came back to the subject several times in speeches.

The United States was not interested. The policy has remained firm—that Cuba's military, economic and political dependence on the Soviet Union and her subversive activities in Latin America were not negotiable. Fidel Castro could say the same thing—the American demands were not negotiable. They would mean unconditional surrender and giving up his revolution. Nothing could be more "impossible" from Fidel's point of view.

Senator Fulbright, sensible and moderate as always, was one of the few voices in American public life urging acceptance of the Cuban Revolution and living with it "as a disagreeable reality." He said this in a Senate speech on March 25, 1964. He urged Americans to give up the "myth" that the Castro regime was going "to collapse and disappear in the immediate future." He was derided for his pains and ignored.

This is not a rational period of world history—if there ever was one. Not that Fidel Castro is any more rational than the next man.

"So," he said in a speech closing the international Cultural Congress in Havana on January 12, 1968, "there exists an enemy who can be called universal, and if there ever was in the history of humanity an enemy who was truly universal, an enemy whose acts and moves trouble the entire world, threaten the entire world, attack the entire world in one way or another, that real and really universal enemy is precisely Yankee imperialism. And to the degree that humanity takes note of this problem, it will mobilize; to the degree that it understands this problem, it will begin in one way or another to act."

To act, in Castroite terms, is to rebel: "The duty of every revolutionary is to make revolution." The year 1968 was designated as "The Year of the Heroic Guerrilla" as "a mark of veneration, affection and profound remembrance for our heroic Major Ernesto Guevara."

# 10 CASTRO'S COMMUNISM

FIDEL CASTRO was more than willing to turn Marxist-Leninist and to make his regime a Communist one, but it had to remain *his* revolution and the Communism had to be personal, special, revolutionary—and Cuban. There is nothing in the "socialist world" like Cuban Communism. Moscow, echoing Washington, thanks its lucky stars that there is only one Fidel Castro.

Those who want to trace the permutations and combinations whereby the old Communist Partido Socialista Popular (PSP), the 26th of July Movement, the Directorio Revolucionario and the remnants of past political parties were first combined into the Integrated Revolutionary Organizations (ORI) in 1961, which became the United Party of the Socialist Revolution (PURS) in 1963, and the Communist Party of Cuba (PCC) in 1965, can do so. The Cubanologists have faithfully recorded each step.

In the Communist countries, the party is the mechanism of legitimacy and continuity. When Lenin died, the party provided a leader in Stalin. When Stalin died, the leadership again came out of the party. When Mao Tse-tung dies, the same will happen. The mechanism is there, because power resides in the Communist party.

This is not the case in Cuba. The resounding proof that it was not and will not be came in the two cataclysmic "Escalante Affairs" of 1962 and 1968. The reason is simple. The Cuban Revolution is, and always was, Fidel Castro's revolution.

Aníbal Escalante, who had been secretary general of the PSP during the Batista regime and was an "Old Guard" Communist of thirty years' standing, made his first mistake (as I have said previously), in trying to get control of ORI for the PSP. Of course, as a faithful Communist he was doubtless acting under Moscow's orders. The Slavic Russians have been no more able to understand the Cuban *Gallego,* Fidel Castro, than the Anglo-Saxon North Americans have.

Escalante put his own PSP men in every position that he could; he was issuing directives on his own and, in general, acting independently of the Cuban Government. Fidel's closest and most trusted supporters—the men and women who had been with him from Moncada and the Sierra Maestra—were being bypassed.

It was obvious that Escalante was riding for a fall. It came in a television speech by Castro on March 26, 1962. The broad target was sectarianism but the direct attack was against Aníbal Escalante and the Partido Socialista Popular.

"Was it real power?" Fidel asked in his address. "No, it was not real power. It was a formal power. It was a fictitious power. There was no real power in the hands of that comrade."

Castro made it clear that this was not a break with Communism or the PSP. He paid his respects to the "old Communists" and in return asked modesty of them.

"From this moment on," he insisted, "every difference between old and new, between the *sierra* and the *llano,* between him who threw bombs and him who did not, him who studied Marxism and him who did not previously study Marxism, must cease once and for all. From this moment on, we must be one and united."

Aníbal Escalante was banished gently to Prague where he stayed for a few years. The entire Administration—political and economic—was overhauled by Fidel, Raúl Castro and Che

Guevara, who put in their own provincial, municipal, factory and state-farm representatives.

Moscow had no choice but to accept and even applaud. The PSP yielded meekly. It had seemed as if the Cuban Communists were taking over, and it remains a mystery why Castro permitted them to go so far before cracking down. Had he let Escalante operate for many more months, the subsequent cleanup would have shaken the whole revolutionary structure from top to bottom. At that, it took Fidel about six months to reestablish complete control for himself and the small clique of companions under him who are the effective rulers of Cuba.

Incidentally, the purge of the "Old Guard" came at a time when the economy of Cuba was in an especially bad state. Fidel was in a position to let it be believed that the PSP leaders deserved much of the blame—which was unfair. However, the crackdown was essentially a reassertion of Castro's power and of his determination to keep control of the Cuban Revolution through the instrumentality of *his* men, not the PSP's and not Moscow's. Moreover, the "Marxism-Leninism" that he had proclaimed less than four months before was to be what he said it was, not what the Cuban Communists or the Kremlin thought it was.

There was no essential change in the Cuban Revolution as a result of the first "Escalante Affair." At no time in the revolution have the Cuban Communists or Moscow had more power than Fidel Castro. (The missile crisis concerned nuclear missiles, not Cuban politics.) The belief that Fidel was a puppet in the early years of the revolution was one of the basic errors of the United States State Department and of some American scholars.

Castro, and everyone else, thought that the "Old Guard" Communists had been taken care of once and for all. The political situation calmed down. The PSP passed into history. Aníbal Escalante came back to Cuba, ostensibly to live and work in quiet. The loyalty of the famous trio of "old" Communists—Carlos Rafael Rodríguez, Blas Roca and Lázaro Peña—was never in question.

In October 1965, PURS (the United Party of the Socialist Revolution) was turned into the Communist Party of Cuba (PCC), and one of Fidel's closest and most loyal colleagues—

Armando Hart, who had been Minister of Education—was made party organizer. Once again, it looked as if the Cuban Revolution was at last being institutionalized. Blas Roca was put at the head of a considerable group of scholars, lawyers and revolutionary followers, to draw up a new constitution.

When I was in Cuba in May 1966, Hart, Roca and other leaders thought that the PCC would be ready for its first national congress in mid-1967. But when I was back in Cuba in October 1967, nobody talked of a national congress, and I had the impression that Fidel Castro was losing interest in the Partido Communista de Cuba.

The reason became clear early in 1968. Aníbal Escalante and some of the "Old Guard" Communists were at it again. Since they were orthodox, pro-Soviet Communists they surely were following orders from the Kremlin. Escalante had been working in an obscure post as administrator of a state farm.

At the end of January 1968, the rarely convoked Central Committee of the PCC was brought together to hear a scathing, 15,000-word denunciation by Raúl Castro, as Minister of the Armed Forces.

Escalante and about forty members of what was called a "microfaction" of the Communist party were tried and convicted for "anti-party" activities. This time Escalante was sentenced to fifteen years' imprisonment, and eight other members of the clique were given twelve-year sentences. All were expelled from the party.

Ostensibly, the "microfaction" had merely been trying to rehabilitate Escalante and give him the opportunity to help his pro-Soviet friends to rise in the bureaucracy and Community party. However, the activity must have been more serious than that for the Castro regime.

A second secretary of the Soviet Embassy was involved and had been sent home in 1967. Raúl Castro also disclosed that a Russian, who headed a group of police advisers, maintained regular contacts with Escalante, who was accused of passing "false information" to the Russians. Raúl's complete report was published over a period of three days by the Cuban press, and the state radio gave hours of time to it.

The sentences [wrote Juan de Onis in *The New York Times* on February 3, 1968], while not severe by Cuban standards, left no doubt that the Castro regime was setting an example through Mr. Escalante of what happens to members of the revolutionary structure who seek support in the Soviet-led Communist world to oppose Mr. Castro.

The affair . . . also served as a warning to the Soviet Union not to meddle in Cuba's internal politics despite Cuba's economic dependence on the Soviet Union.

The serious feature of the second "Escalante Affair" was that Moscow was trying to undermine and weaken Fidel Castro. This is what the American Government is also trying to do. In striking out so hard and so openly against Escalante and the men he enlisted, Castro was hitting at the Russians.

He could do so with impunity because the Soviet Union is in no position to let him down. Aside from the value to it of a Communist regime in the Western Hemisphere—even a recalcitrant one—Moscow would suffer a serious reverse in the Communist world and vis-à-vis Peking if it allowed the Cuban Revolution to fail for lack of its help. This should be even more true now after the reactions to the invasion of Czechoslovakia.

For those interested in the meaningful developments of the Cuban Revolution, it is time wasted to read the dreary and bewildering pages speculating on the minutiae of Communist influence. The Cuban Revolution is a complicated phenomenon. There is no need to make it a guessing game in unimportant details of momentary interest.

Another exercise in futility in the books and articles by Cubanologists who are authorities on Communism and Marxism has been their efforts to interpret the revolutionary process in Cuba in terms of Marx, Lenin, Stalin, Trotsky, Mao Tse-tung—or whatever orthodoxy, philosophy or practice operated in past decades.

The dynamism of the Cuban Revolution and the individualism and nationalism of Fidel Castro may lead to surprising changes. The man who took the Cuban Revolution into Communism could conceivably take it out one of these days. He has the power to do it, should the practical possibility arise. There is no such possibility today and no desire to abandon "socialism"—but this is today. In some tomorrow the situation could be different.

In Cuba power resides in Fidel Castro, Premier, Secretary-General of the Communist party, Commander-in-Chief of the Armed Forces and, in both practical and popular terms, *Jefe Máximo*—the Chief Leader.

Since one man cannot run a country of 8,400,000 people all by himself, many powers have to be delegated. The leader is always temporarily at the mercy of the efficiency and loyalty—or the lack of them—of a great many officials. Fidel is a phenomenal worker. An eighteen-hour day, seven days a week, is normal. Nevertheless, the administration of even a small country has to be carried out by many thousands of officials. This was one of Castro's most painful problems in the first five years or so of the revolution. He was completely inexperienced himself in every respect—administrative, political, economic, financial, diplomatic. For months he did not have supreme power. The only men and women he could trust—those who had been close to him in the struggle against the Batista regime—were even a little younger and just as inexperienced as he was. Some, like Camilo Cienfuegos, Efigenio Almeijeiras and Juan Almeida, were almost illiterate.

He had military commanders who knew no more about the sophisticated techniques of modern warfare than firing rifles and machine guns in the jungles as guerrillas could have taught them. There was Che Guevara, who knew nothing about banking and who instinctively despised money, heading the National Bank of Cuba and directing the industrialization of the economy.

The radical revolutionary process alienated and then drove away the great majority of those who could have helped Castro to run the economy and make his drastic reforms in every field. The old political parties—with one exception, the Communist PSP—were discredited and divided, with no outstanding leaders. The old military commanders were—with good reason—swept away. The old diplomats, with very few exceptions, could not be trusted. The old generation—all but a few of them—belonged to the past.

There were only the young men and women—idealistic, eager,

hardworking, honest, loyal. Yet all were not loyal. There were the traitors—traitors to Fidel Castro, at least: Díaz Lanz, Hubert Matos, the Bay of Pigs invaders.

An administration, an army, a government had to be constructed out of just about nothing, in the midst of chaos and hostility, while the great power that for sixty years had dominated Cuba directed all its hostile efforts to destroy the Castro regime once it saw where the revolution was going.

Considering these things—and they are a summary of the true situation—one can grasp the extraordinary accomplishment of Fidel Castro. It was he who held the chaotic structure together, who defended his revolution against its enemies, who inspired a generation with enough faith and loyalty to support him and to bear hardships in the hope of better times to come. It was he who used the Communists, Cuban and Russian, to help him make his revolution—as he is using them today.

Fidel Castro went down the road that he calls Marxism-Leninism. Along the way, he had to construct an "apparatus." It was a chore; he was bored with the process; he had little faith in it, and no intention at any time to allow the *apparatchiki* to have or to seize any power.

So he took his time—an endless time, for the process is still going on in the eleventh year of the revolution. He let others do the organizing at first, until he saw what Aníbal Escalante could do with ORI, the Integrated Revolutionary Organizations which was the first and preliminary form that the inevitable party took. Now he has a passionately loyal admirer and a capable administrator, Armando Hart, organizing the Communist Party (PCC). I suspect that Fidel Castro, privately, considers the party to be a necessary evil in its ideological guise.

The formula for the Cuban Revolution is what it has always been—Fidel Castro plus the masses. However, Castro has to reach the masses in more ways than by making speeches at meetings or on the radio and television. There is an infinite number of tasks to be carried out in a modern nation. In an authoritarian regime, the men who perform these tasks must be controlled, through a chain of command, from above. The machinery to do this is provided by the Communist party of Cuba. It is nothing more or less than a machine, run by Fidel Castro and his powerful group of *compañeros*.

The fact that the party has no power, in or by itself, makes it fundamentally different from Communist parties in the Soviet and Chinese blocs, and it is different in construction also. Cubans, in fact, believe that they are breaking new ground in the Communist world and, in the process, creating something especially Cuban.

"We do not deny the importance of the party in the organization, the movement, or whatever it is called," Fidel conceded grudgingly in a speech on August 30, 1966. "However, a party is not a party just because it is called a party. A party is not Marxist-Leninist just because it is listed as Marxist-Leninist. . . . To wage revolutionary warfare a party or a Marxist-Leninist organization is necessary."

However, having said that, he did not give the Communist party of Cuba the right "to wage revolutionary warfare" except as his instrument of policy or government. There is no evidence that the Central Committee of the PCC, or the National Directorate or Secretariat of the PURS which preceded the present party, made any decisions on their own.

When ORI, which was always conceived as a preliminary organization, was formed in 1961, Castro had the idea of choosing its members by a unique system. The first conflict over Escalante interfered with his plans, but he began to put them into effect when the United Party of the Socialist Revolution was suddenly created in 1962. The same system is now being used in the PCC.

Emilio Aragonés, who has been on a secondary level of leadership since the 26th of July Movement days, explained the process this way:

> We convene general meetings of workers who freely and democratically elect the best, exemplary comrades, those who are best in production, those who best cope with the tasks set by the Revolution, those whose past is without blemish and who are at present rendering outstanding services to the cause of socialist construction.

These "exemplary comrades" pick the party members who form a cell, or primary organization. Then, by a similar process, a district committee, a regional committee, a provincial committee and the Central Committee for all of Cuba are formed.

By the time the Central Committee is reached, Fidel Castro has stepped in. Each member is satisfactory from his point of view. The "democracy"—if it can be called such—has ended. The real power lies in the six-man Secretariat and, at the top, an eight-man Politburo. Fidel and Raúl Castro and President Dorticós are in both bodies, which Fidel heads as Secretary General. Thus, the whole construction is a pyramid leading up to him.

For all the lip service that he pays it, the PCC seems curiously detached from Fidel Castro. He has not shown any real interest in it, nor does he yet show signs of giving it any power. He rarely attends a meeting. The party, in all its branches, had not been completely formed at the end of 1968. The Constitution, which Blas Roca (who is a member of the party Secretariat) is putting together, will be years in the making.

Unlike the economy, on which he is working with frantic speed, Fidel is remarkably deliberate when it comes to the politics of Marxism-Leninism. It is not a priority in his mind. The party structure is being completed; the Constitution is being drawn up—but there is no hurry.

His chief anxiety in the political field is to avoid "sectarianism" —the crime that Aníbal Escalante committed twice. This is a part of Castro's instinct for, and insistence upon, "unity." His critics interpret it as a demand for loyalty and obedience by all to him. His followers see it as a desire to make a homogeneous structure in which all Cubans will work harmoniously and voluntarily for the good of the country and the triumph of the revolution.

Perhaps there is not much difference in the two points of view. Those who believe in the Cuban Revolution look to Fidel Castro as their leader. He, in turn, identifies his ideas, hopes, ideals and desires with what is best for the Cuban people. He believes he is interpreting the will of the people—Rousseau fashion—and therefore that Cuba now has "democracy." If enough Cubans agree with him, then he has a form of democracy, although not the kind that came down from Magna Carta.

The PCC is like other Communist parties in forming an elite. Its membership—again like the other countries—will be kept relatively small. It will be an amalgam, a channel, an instrument, an example, an apparatus, a framework, a foundation—anything and everything but a governing body.

Fidel Castro—most emphatically in his onslaught against Escalante and the "microfaction"—has given notice to Moscow to keep hands off. The situation does not resemble Czechoslovakia's. The Chinese have not tried to "muscle in" and have no reason to do so.

Kalman H. Silvert, one of the most knowledgeable students of Latin-American affairs in the American academic world, discusses Cuban Communism and the revolution in his book *The Conflict Society,* of which a revised edition was published in 1966. He says on page 30:

> The Cuban example is all the more dangerous because it is not identified only with Communist parties; the Marxist-Leninist ideological tag was adopted by the present Cuban regime to indicate something native, something special to the Latin American experience and somewhat independent of the slavish devotion to Moscow which so long has characterized the policies of the Communist parties themselves. . . .
>
> A distinction must then be drawn between Russian-oriented Communists and Cuban-type Marxist-Leninists to appreciate fully the new strength of this part of this part of the Left in Latin America and thus the new task of the anti-Marxist opposition.

The Partido Communista de Cuba is Fidel Castro's party. But it is, in its fashion, a Communist party—or, as he prefers to say, a Marxist-Leninist party. Even if Fidel were assassinated, or to die of heart failure, the PCC would still not have the power to take over and govern. What will happen when the men and women of the *sierra* are gone will be for another historian to relate.

The Government of Cuba is in the hands of a small group not held together by party discipline, but by loyalty to Fidel Castro, by a remarkable *esprit de corps,* and by a fervent belief in the ideals and the future of the Cuban Revolution. Not one of them, except for the two old Communists, Rodríguez and Roca, has any deep or genuine ideological feeling about Communism. That includes Fidel Castro, despite his constant professions of Marxist-Leninist faith in every speech he makes. "The best lack all conviction, while the worst/ Are full of passionate intensity," as Yeats wrote in "The Second Coming."

Fidel, as I have said, uses Communism; he finds it valuable, but that is different from believing in the Communist ideology. His reliance in government, in carrying out his program, in the multitude of institutions that he has created, is on a person or persons he trusts and believes can make a success of carrying out a policy.

Someone who was present at one of the earliest meetings on planification told me that Fidel, as usual, let people talk, and even make decisions. At this conference he suddenly asked, "Planification—isn't it like a straitjacket?" "Yes," someone said, "in a sense it is." Whereupon Castro exploded: "Nobody is going to put *me* in a straitjacket!"

This was, and is, characteristic. He has learned to be more patient and to see the necessity of making plans, even though some of those he makes are overoptimistic. He still has the habit of setting a goal (10,000,000 tons of sugar by 1970, for instance) and feeling that he has made a "plan." His technicians then set frantically to work to do the real planning, knowing that if he has asked the impossible he will recognize the fact in time and find explanations.

The difficulty is a basic one with Fidel Castro—he cannot stand being restricted or under any orders or discipline. This is undoubtedly the main reason why he would not join any Communist party until he could make one of his own, which he runs and which is fashioned to suit his needs. Orthodoxy, in politics as in religion, is unnatural to him.

As time passes, his Communism becomes more and more heterodox. It could have been predicted that Cuba, like Yugoslavia, Czechoslovakia or Romania, would not conform to a Stalinist pattern. Those who believed that Cuba's economic dependence on the Soviet Union would force the country to follow a satellite role were reckoning without Fidel Castro. Carlos Rafael Rodríguez, who is an orthodox Communist, told me in 1967 that the Russians and Eastern Europeans do not consider Castro or his Cuban system to be Communist.

All the same, they are Communist. An aberrant or a maverick belongs to the species, despite eccentricities. Mexico has a one-party political system in which Presidents are chosen by their predecessors, but Mexico can legitimately be called a democracy because it has so many democratic institutions. Cuba is Communist because no other name suits its political system. Besides, Castro never stops calling it that, and he is the one who decides.

It has to be kept in mind that social revolution, whether Communist or not, has no deep roots in any Latin American country. The Mexican Revolution began in 1910 and it had no repercussions in the hemisphere. It antedated the Bolshevik Revolution and consequently had no Communist links.

As Professor Richard Morse of Yale University has written, Marxism made virtually no impact on Latin America in the nineteenth century. The structure of society was feudal, paternal, hierarchical, static. It was nationalism, not Marxism, that introduced some dynamism after World War I. The appeal of Fascism and Nazism in Argentina, Brazil, Chile and a few other South American countries was a combination of militarism and a belief that the Axis powers were going to win World War II.

Political systems of a doctrinaire nature, such as Fascism, Socialism and Communism, have never had a strong appeal to Latin Americans. They are not interested. When the Cold War began and the United States tried to make the Latin Americans see Communism as evil, heretical, sinful and dangerous, the Latins could not go along. Washington was able to force the Latin countries to sign treaties and resolutions condemning Communism (as at the Inter-American Conference of 1954) but they meant nothing. The worst dictatorships in Latin America blithely signed solemn professions of liberal-democratic faith.

This situation has changed only superficially. The missile crisis shocked Latin Americans into a realization that the Cold War could endanger them, but this was a nationalistic reaction against the intervention of the Soviet Union. It was not anti-Communism in the North American sense. It was power politics.

In a similar way, the hostile Latin-American reaction to Cuba is not due to the fact that the Castro regime turned Marxist-Leninist. The hostility and fear are against the revolutionary ideas and practices of Castroite Cuba. Every Government is afraid of revolution in its own country. There is no strong Communist party in any Latin-American nation. The Indian peasants and workers are slower to rebel than the much more sophisticated Europeans. The students and intellectuals are nationalistic; they do not look to Moscow or Peking.

Fidel Castro did not do so when he made his insurrection. The Cuban Communists opposed and sabotaged him until near the end, when they saw that he was going to win. The whole background of Latin-American indifference to, and ignorance of, Marxism in the Communist form helps to explain why Castro's "Marxism-Leninism" came so late and fits so badly, even today. This is without counting Fidel's personal unsuitability for Communist discipline and orthodoxy.

What applies to him in that respect applies to Cubans in general. They are as temperamentally unsuited to a Communist system as any people on earth. This does not mean that they are unsuited to a dictatorial system or a highly centralized government. It is in the Latin-American tradition to have personalized, paternal governments. Cuba never has known a democracy as pervasive as the systems existing in Mexico, Costa Rica, Uruguay or Chile. General Batista, in or out of the presidency, had run Cuba for the better part of twenty-five years. The freedom that existed was license for a small number of citizens at the top. The "free press" was subsidized by succeeding governments; the "free labor unions" had corrupt, government-appointed leaders; "free education" did not extend to rural areas, and so forth.

The great majority of Cubans, therefore, have not found it difficult to accept a *Jefe Máximo* who says he has a Marxist-Leninist government, and who does have totalitarian dictatorship whatever it is called. Those who rebelled against the Communist trend and fled abroad, or plotted and tried to return, are a middle- and upper-class minority for the most part.

So far as I have been able to tell, Cubans accept Communism as Italians did Fascism or Spaniards do Falangism. It is convenient to belong to such parties, and often necessary. Jobs, promotion, power, social position often come through party zeal or at least membership. With a change of regime, the membership can be shed. When the Allies invaded Italy in 1943 and moved up the peninsula, it was hard to find an acknowledged ex-Fascist; they were all anti-Fascists. I suspect that something of the sort will happen one day in Cuba, or else Fidel's Marxism-Leninism will be so watered down and aberrant that not even the American Government will care.

Some Cubans and foreign students of the revolution believe that the turning point came with the missile crisis of 1962. This is an arguable thesis. It does seem as if the shock it gave to Castro made him realize that Cuba had to go it alone as much as possible, and that Cubans had to work out their own problems one by one in a practical, trial-and-error way, forgetting about scientific Marxism. This was the beginning of the extraordinary study phase of Castro's career when he applied himself to reading every book on agricultural techniques and practice that he could get hold of. The "science" he went in for was agrarian, not ideological.

In the interview I had with Fidel Castro for *War/Peace Report* of December 1967, he spoke enthusiastically of plans and hopes that sounded much like the way Spanish anarcho-syndicalists talked to me in the vivid dawn of the Spanish Civil War.

"We are planting coffee and citrus trees everywhere, as you can see," he said.

"In the 1970s we are going to have so much coffee and fruit that we will give it freely to people—and sugar, too. Just because they get it free will not mean that they will consume much more than they need. We give the peasants houses, and build them free. We give them fertilizers, implements, everything they need. All we ask is that they plant what we tell them to plant and work their farms diligently and well. These are all small proprietors owning their own land in the surroundings of Havana.

"Our system is gradually working, through experimentation, and now with much success, to create a society in which money will become unnecessary except for certain things that cannot be acquired in other ways. It will take a long time, but we do not believe in the materialistic concepts of capitalism or of other types of Communism in which money is the incentive.

"Men live for other things than money. The incentives must be to guarantee them a decent life in which they and their children are educated, cared for, housed, fed and acquire culture. They must be given dignity and in return must learn that their work is a contribution to the good of all the people and the state. This is true Marxism-Leninism as we see it, but it is not Communism as it is practiced in Russia, Eastern Europe or China. We are working out our own Cuban system, to meet our problems and satisfy our people."

Despite what Fidel claimed, this is not "true Marxism-Leninism." It is true *Fidelismo*. It must be taken seriously because Fidel Castro is trying to turn it into reality. However, if it should prove as utopian as it seems, and if it does not work, Fidel Castro is not going to stick with these ideas and go down with them. He will change, as he has changed in the past. His enemies cannot count on his regime's collapsing because he makes mistakes. Errors can be corrected. It is not his idealism which has saved him through these years; it is his pragmatism.

In a conversation with Foreign Minister Raúl Roa on October 19, 1967, I suggested that Fidel was getting too utopian. He said he was discussing the same question with President Dorticós and they decided that for one or two percent Castro is obsessed by ideologies, plans and ideas, but for the rest he has his practical side—working in the rural areas or with government people, doing things. If the ideas do not work out in practice, Roa argued, Fidel changes them as he did with the policy of industrialization. He and Dorticós agreed that one must not take Castro's enthusiasms too literally. They are hopes and ideals in which he believes passionately at the time—and then sometimes learns are impractical or impossible.

Carlos Lechuga, the former ambassador who has been working in cultural affairs, said much the same things to me.

"Fidel makes his dreams come true," he argued. "When he talks of a society without money, he has already made rents free for many Cubans and rent will soon be free for all. Schools are free, with free meals, and in many cases clothes and lodging. Most of all, his dream of making a radical social revolution has come true. When we are with him, we are carried away by his faith and enthusiasm—and so is Fidel. While he talks he walks on air, but in the countryside, for instance, he always has a keen eye for how the fields are planted, which breeds of cattle should be crossed, whether to grow coffee or citrus trees or both on a particular field, and so forth."

On the same trip, when talking to Haydée Santamaría, who directs the Casa de las Américas in Havana, she made the point which so many of Castro's associates emphasize.

"The Marxism-Leninism of December 1961 was a phase," Haydée said. "Fidel is not following any ideology. He is seeking his own way—he alone." And she added sadly and cryptically, "He has everybody against him."

Raúl Castro, too, brushed aside my fears about his brother's "utopianism." While Fidel's nature is excessively enthusiastic and optimistic, Raúl asserted that Fidel knew when he had made a mistake and had no hesitation in correcting it.

When I made the point that ever since the famous Marxism-Leninism speech of December 1, 1961, Fidel is stuck with the label, and that everything he does must be called Marxism-Leninism, Raúl answered philosophically, "Well, Marxism is a flexible concept; it allows for development and change."

One of the government leaders, who had better be nameless, referred to Communism in Cuba as *una mística*—a mystique. For most of them there is a Cuban Revolution that has taken a Communist form while always remaining Cuban. These revolutionary leaders, whom I have known and watched for years, feel very strongly that they are Cubans, not Communists in an ideological sense but simply in a practical, working, Fidelista sense. Yet they do consider themselves Communists now. It is as if the international Marxist world of Communism were turned into a Cuban nationalistic movement. The distinctions are subtle, but they could have vital meaning in an emergency, or at some future date.

Certainly, Fidel has not allowed his Marxism-Leninism to grow into a dogmatic system. He keeps it flexible, adjusting it to the

Cuban temperament and character and to the special needs of the revolution. Otherwise it would cease to change and grow; it would lose dynamism and in the process force the Cuban Revolution into a rigid framework. Fidel is at all times wary of what he calls, disparagingly, "theoretical Marxism."

"What do we accomplish," he asked in a speech on September 28, 1964, "if a peasant is able to recite the materialistic concept of history or the dialectic concept of nature or the problems of the class struggle from memory, if he does not know how far one cane stalk should be planted from another, if he does not know the amount of fertilizer that must be put into the ground and if he does not know how material goods are produced? . . . The revolution is in the first place a matter of creating a new means of production."

He kept harping on such ideas. In an important address he made on October 3, 1965, at the time the creation of the PCC was proclaimed, he said:

"It is impossible to expect that in a contemporary world so heterogeneous, under such diverse circumstances—a world made up of countries at the most dissimilar levels of material, technical and cultural development—that we conceive of Marxism as something like a church, a religious doctrine with its Rome, its Pope and its Ecumenical Council.

"It is a revolutionary and dialectical doctrine, not a philosophical doctrine; it is a guide for revolutionary action, not a dogma. To try to press Marxism into a type of catechism is anti-Marxist."

One of the aberrant features of Cuban Communism is its attitude toward religion and the Church. It has always been nonsense, of course, to believe that because Fidel Castro proclaimed himself to be a Marxist-Leninist, he and his associates are atheists who believe that religion is the opium of the people.

I have never seen or heard Fidel do or say anything against religion. He expelled about a hundred and forty Spanish priests from Cuba in 1960–1961 for purely political reasons. He gladly saw some four hundred Cuban priests go for the same reasons. He protested earnestly to me afterwards that he had done everything he could to keep on good terms with the clergy and to favor them as much as he could. But he would not permit anyone, frocked or not, to try to destroy the revolution. A great many priests have come in since 1961 to replace those who left.

"I don't care whether a person is religious or not, or what religion he believes in," Castro said to me once, and this was confirmed to me in Church quarters as well as by his associates.

It would not have been at all surprising if Fidel had been anticlerical because he had good historic reasons to be so and it is in the Cuban tradition. The Catholic Church in Cuba was part of the landowning-military-aristocratic establishment under the Spaniards. The hierarchy supported Spain against the rebels in the wars of independence. Freemasonry, as a reaction, was strong, and in this century the influence of the Americans brought many converts to the Protestant sects.

During the Republic, the clergy were a part of the small ruling class. From a half to two-thirds of the priests, even when the revolution began in 1959, were Spanish-born. They neglected the rural areas. In all of Cuba there were only 700 to 750 priests for a population of 7,000,000.

The hierarchy of the Cuban Church was in the weakest possible position when Fidel Castro took over. There were glowing exceptions, like the Archbishop of Santiago de Cuba, Enrique Pérez Serantes, who will be recalled for his courageous stand at the time of the Moncada Barracks attack. (Incidentally, toward the end of 1963 he told my wife and me that freedom of worship in Cuba at the time was "total.")

Pope John XXIII was elected a few months before the triumph of Castro's insurrection. Pope John's great encyclical of April 1963—"Mater et Magistra"—had its effect on regimes like Fidel Castro's.

"One must never confuse error and the person who errs," the Pontiff said of the Communists, "not even when there is a question of error or inadequate knowledge of truth in the moral or religious field. The person who errs is always and above all a human being. . . ."

Of course, Pope John added, citing his predecessor, "Salvation and justice are not to be found in revolution, but in evolution through concord. Violence has always achieved only destruction. . . . And it has reduced men and parties to the difficult task of rebuilding, after sad experience, on the ruins of discord."

It is this wise balance of regret with tolerance, understanding and patience that the Vatican has kept throughout the course of the Cuban Revolution. There was never any thought of breaking diplomatic relations on either side. The Cuban Ambassador to the Holy See, Luis Amado-Blanco, was the only Communist diplomat present throughout the Ecumenical Council sessions. The Vatican knows it is going to outlast the Castro regime.

The Papal Internuncio, or Chargé d'Affaires, in Havana through most of the revolutionary decade, Mgr. (now Bishop) Cesare Zacchi, has been very popular with Castro and the other leaders. He is on friendly personal terms with them and admires the humanistic aspects of the revolution while he necessarily deplores its Communism.

When the Partido Communista de Cuba was formed in 1965 and a sudden excess of Marxist zeal became evident, Mgr. Zacchi was worried. The problem that arose was not Marxist atheism but whether a man or woman could be a devout, practicing Catholic and a good revolutionary. Logically, there was a conflict of interest. The idea in the back of some leaders' heads was that no man could serve two masters.

Llanusa became Minister of Education about the time the PCC was created. Someone told me that he had had a "traumatic experience" as a youth which made him very anticlerical and even antireligious. He made it easier for students to engage in sports than to go to church on Sunday mornings. Minister of the Interior Ramiro Valdés is also rated as strongly anticlerical.

The Catholic private schools and the University at Santa Clara were taken over early in the revolution. There are, however, two flourishing seminaries for priests in Cuba today.

Believers were not persecuted and not prevented from going to church and taking their families with them. They did find it difficult for a while to get good posts in the government or state industries and farms. One reason was a persistent belief that the United States Central Intelligence Agency worked through priests and the faithful on the theory that they were anti-Communist and hence anti-Fidelista.

When I returned to Cuba in October 1967, the situation had improved for the Church and for the faithful. The government no longer interfered in any way with religious practices, although I had the feeling that a deeply religious person would arouse some misgivings among the leaders—not because of his religion but for political reasons.

Most Cuban men are typically Spanish in being nonreligious or anticlerical, but not antireligious. This is true of the revolutionary leaders who, so far as I could tell, do not think of their Marxism-Leninism in connection with religion. They are not atheists.

Haydée Santamaría told me that her brother Abel, who was killed so brutally in the Moncada Barracks attack, was an atheist. She felt that the "Movement" would worry if a member went to confession, since a priest could not be trusted not to divulge what he heard. Other leaders I spoke to did not feel this way.

Faustino Pérez, who combines religion with Communism in a typically Latin way, told me of an incident when a group of Argentine Marxists went to see Fidel and one of them asked whether Marxism was not contrary to Christianity. Fidel, he said, replied, "Marxism is for the poor, and whatever is for the poor is Christian."

I found in my papers a page printed in Havana for the revolutionary "faithful," headed PALABRAS DE FIDEL (Sayings of Fidel):

> The true Christian is one who loves his neighbor, who sacrifices himself for others, who fulfills the doctrines of Christ and gives what he possesses to the poor and if it be necessary abandons everything that he has to go and serve others. Leave the temples and go into the fields to succor the ill, to plant trees, to build houses, to help the Agrarian Reform, to weave and embroider gowns for children who have no clothes! This truly is Christian. But to go to the doors of the temple to conspire against one's fatherland is to be a Pharisee, and never to be Christian.

Cubans continue to take the sacraments, have their children baptized, get married in church and seek priests to administer the last rites—all with government knowledge and consent. Certainly Fidel Castro does not disapprove.

The fact that there is no religious teaching in the schools and that the whole educational system is geared to a communistic way of life, even if only formally, means that the generation coming along will have only what religion is inculcated at home. Already church attendance is almost entirely confined to older people and to young children taken along, perforce, by their mothers.

Since religion in Cuba is historically and traditionally weak, there is little resistance to Communism from that direction. In Latin-American countries like Colombia and Peru it would be different. Cuba, in this respect, was easier to take into the "Marxist-Leninist" camp than any of the other Latin-American countries would have been.

The Cuban Revolution, it should be noted, was not at all like the Mexican, in which the revolutionaries were antireligious as well as anticlerical. The Mexicans were in conflict with the Catholic Church; Fidel Castro and the Cuban revolutionaries were at no time against the Church—they were against certain priests, and for political reasons, as I have stated.

While I find myself frequently in disagreement with Andrés Suárez because he makes so many mistakes owing to his not having been in Cuba since 1960, I would agree with his conclusion on Cuban Communism (page 240), as well as with much else in his awesome array of documentation:

> We do not know of any Communist state so far that is not under the control of a party organized according to Lenin's rules. But in Cuba, as we know, the original Leninists have been reduced to insignificance. Only in October 1965 was the party of a "new type" created, but under the direction of Castroites, not Leninists. . . .
>
> It is highly doubtful to me that the Cuban regime can legitimately be called Communist in the sense in which I interpret the word, that is, a state ruled by the leading nucleus of a party organized according to Leninist norms. We cannot rule out, however, the possibility that history may have a new experience in store for us.

This will be true of Cuban history so long as Fidel Castro is alive and running his revolution. His Marxist-Leninist government today is a charmed circle, a club, a closed corporation into which it is almost impossible to break. In recent years, when one talks to

Fidel about his own "microfaction," he positively glows. "It has never been better," he says, praising the high quality, the fine performance, the smoothness of daily work, the splendid organization of the government and the party leadership. The amateurishness, he feels, is gone. I suppose it would be hard to find anywhere in the world a group of young men and women who have had such a fiery, even agonizing trial. Those who survived are good; they learned the hard way.

"Nothing," Fidel says emphatically, "can now break the strength or unity of this government."

And when he says "nothing," he means Moscow and Peking as well as Washington. He believes in "socialist solidarity," but on his own violent, revolutionary and Cuban terms.

# 11    FIDEL CASTRO'S REVOLUTION

**⧉⧉** THAT DYNAMO named Fidel Castro—twenty-seven years old when he led the attack on the Moncada Barracks, thirty-two when he entered Havana in triumph, an incredible forty-two on August 13, 1968—is driving ahead with undiminished speed. Where is he going? What will happen to Cuba?

Fidel's life, like the revolution that he has made, is a continuing process. He has not changed; he has developed, matured and—he claims—is becoming more and more radical as the years pass. Life is just as exciting, adventurous and challenging as it ever was. The flame that burned so brightly in younger days has not consumed him, nor can one even see it diminish or flicker.

On my many visits to Cuba, when I would wait seemingly endless hours and days to see him, I would always think that this was like waiting for Godot. There was something unreal or mythical about Fidel—but then, unlike Godot, he would show up, and no one could seem more solid, real, touchable, understandable. But afterwards the figure would recede again; the image would lose its clarity. Men like him are clear and simple only to those who stand far off.

Yet there is the testimony of those who work with him in running the Cuban Revolution—the men and women who lived and fought, suffered and triumphed with him. They worship Fidel. They have their blind spots, yet they know Fidel Castro better than any others of his contemporaries do. The greatest tribute that has been paid over the years by what is now known as the "Generation of '53," is their loyalty, trust, admiration and—by no means least—their affection.

These still-young men and women—now in their late thirties—are a remarkable lot. Every revolution has its galaxy: individuals whom later historians write books about, as books have been written about Che Guevara. None of the social revolutions of this century was so entirely the work of youths. At thirty-two years of age in January 1959, Fidel was just about the oldest of the revolutionary leaders in the 26th of July Movement who were to get control and remain the masters of Cuba. The few older men who came in a little later—Osvaldo Dorticós, Raúl Roa, Carlos Rafael Rodríguez, Blas Roca—were middle-aged.

I remember sitting with a group of eight or ten of the leaders at table one evening in 1960 in a barracks near Pinar del Río when Fidel asked me how old I was. When I said "sixty," a sudden awed silence descended on the room, as if it could not be that anyone they knew was so old. On later trips I felt more and more like a *revenant* coming back from a past age, for a post-Batista generation had come into the picture, and now men like Armando Hart—thirty-seven or thirty-eight years old in 1966 when I spent an afternoon with him—was talking of the youth: the new young people taking office, running factories and farms, becoming army officers.

"This revolution, fortunately," Fidel said in a speech on March 14, 1966, "is a revolution of young men, and we hope that it will always be a revolution of young men."

Below the top leadership, the great majority of revolutionary workers and leaders are between twenty and thirty years old. Only the young can stand the strain, can disdain luxuries, can blossom with hope and enthusiasm, can respond to idealism and feed on it in place of money and the things that money could buy. Only the young can see a light in a distant future and know that they will live to reach it and that it will materialize because of their loyalty and zeal.

By no means every youth in Cuba feels that way, but it has been one of Fidel Castro's accomplishments that he has inspired a new generation of Cubans and a majority of them—insofar as it is possible to tell—support him. They are not rebellious against him, as he was against General Batista. Fidel provides an outlet for the revolutionary spirit which is agitating the youth of every nation on both sides of the Iron Curtain.

"Young Russians," Laura Bergquist of *Look* magazine wrote in an article that was published on April 9, 1963, "like recent visitor Evgenii Evtushenko, are fascinated by youthful, vocal, zealous revolutionary Cuba, so different from middle-aged, not very revolutionary Russia. Back in Moscow, Fidel Castro has the glamorous attraction of a movie idol, far more so than old Nikita."

And Draper wrote in *Castroism* (page 127):

> Castro cut across all classes; he established a mass relationship primarily with his person, not with his ideas, and so could change his ideas without changing the relationship. This was especially true of his appeal to the youth, always the vital force behind him. We are accustomed to "class analyses," but we have yet to devote enough thought to a "generational" struggle that cuts across classes and even wins converts from the younger generation of the class marked out for destruction.

Castro is one of a handful of outstanding figures in Latin-American history and the only one—as I said before—to have achieved worldwide fame and influence during his lifetime.

> Quetzalcoatl, Columbus, Bolívar, and Castro are the supreme myth figures of Latin America's major historical ventures [Professor Silvert writes at the opening of a chapter on Cuba in *The Conflict Society* (page 228)]. They represent not only glory but

also the sadness of failure in their inability to reach the ideals of their grand aspirations. . . . Bolívar lived the frustration of the revolutionary who in a traditional world could impart only form but not substance. And Fidel Castro is the first to lead an Iberian country into quasi-modern social organization, choosing the black path of charismatic totalitarianism for his tempestuous passage. Whether even Cuba's way of storming the gates of contemporary life is preferable to a continuance of the indignities and uncertainties of the present political life of the Latin American republics is the question that most disturbs modernizers who also are of democratic commitment.

I would say that whether Castro's way is preferable is for Cubans, and not democratic modernizers, to decide. I believe that a great many Cubans are willingly following Fidel as he "storms the gates of contemporary life."

Dr. Silvert's judgment on the role of Cuba in this process (page 243) is acute:

For those whose perception is not blurred by their distance from understanding the modern world, Cuba has demonstrated the clear difference between neutralism and overt commitment to the Soviet bloc, between pragmatic statism and totalitarian *dirigisme,* between the ghetto of self-willed inferiority in which Latin America has for long wallowed and the real possibilities for emergence into the modern community of nations. Never again will we be able to say that Catholic Latin America is immune to Communism; but never again shall we be able to say, either, that Catholic Latin America is immune to modernism.

The implication in Silvert's use of the term "modernism" is that there is a hardheaded, practical, pragmatic side to Fidel Castro along with his idealism. The two sides of his character work with and for each other. He has survived—and with him the Cuban Revolution—because for all his utopianism, he never neglects the bread and butter for the will-o'-the-wisps.

"In my revolutionary experience," he said in a speech on August 30, 1966, "I have never been better informed than when I talk to the people, when I meet with workers, with students, with peasants. In my lifetime I have known two universities, one in

which I learned nothing and another in which I learned everything."

There is no head of government that I have known, or read
about in newspapers or history books, who carries out the tasks of
his office the way Fidel Castro does. He is the itinerant Premier,
rarely in an office, hardly ever in the same place for more than a
few days, sometimes in the capital of Havana, but more often
elsewhere.

There are few Cubans who have not seen him in the flesh, few
technicians, workers and peasants who have not seen him in their
factories and sugar mills or on their farms. Watching Fidel meeting, mingling with and talking to these people—as I have often
done—I have been impressed to see how natural they are with
him, how lacking in any servility, and how simply he talks to them,
without any sense of superiority, condescension, or the slightest
arrogance. He is at home with the so-called "common people,"
joshing them, pepping them up, joking, but always with the serious
purpose of getting them to work harder. The sense and the use of
authority are there, but disguised.

By every instinct of his nature he is a countryman, of peasant
stock, born and brought up on a farm. It has been interesting in
these latter years to see him revert to type. The atavistic pull of the
land is a factor behind his concentration of Cuba's economy on
agriculture. This is the heart of the Cuban Revolution and, to twist
the image, Fidel's heart is in the land. I was out in the countryside
with him on my trip to Cuba in October 1967, and wrote for
*World/Peace Report:* "At one point, as we drove through a lovely
stretch of pasture, with cattle on our left and trees ringing the field,
Castro said: 'Ah, Matthews, this is where I would like to retire. I
could be happy here.' "

He was dreaming; he would wither away without the thrills and
the heady wine of power which he has now imbibed for a
decade. He fools himself at times with the belief that he can step
aside and even retire young. What he cannot imagine, as he told
Lee Lockwood (page 181), is growing old and not being able "to
climb mountains, to swim, to go spear-fishing, and to do all those
things that please me."

Fidel feels certain that power has not corrupted him in Lord

Acton's meaning of a spiritual corruption. Yet he has the "absolute power" that Acton wrote "corrupts absolutely."

He spoke his heart when he told Lockwood (page 180):

> We love the Revolution as a labor. We love it just as a painter, a sculptor, or a writer may love his work. And, like him, we want our work to have a perennial value. . . . Revolution is an art. And politics is also an art. The most important one, I think.
> The revolution is not made for the sake of revolution itself; it is made in order to create the best conditions for the development of the material and spiritual activities of the human being.

The mixture of idealism and pragmatism is in those words. There lies Fidel Castro's life. Whatever he says—and, like Mirabeau's remark about the young Robespierre, Castro believes everything he says—he will not give it up in the foreseeable future. He can be killed or he can die suddenly, but today Fidel Castro lives only for his revolution.

For him, revolution is good in a moral as well as a material sense. It is this deeply felt conviction that leads him into his appeal for what is known as the "permanent revolution," the idea that a revolutionary spirit must be maintained, and by other than simply materialistic incentives.

"The reactionaries mistrust mankind," he said in a typical asseveration. "They think that a human being is still something of a beast—that he only moves under the lash of a whip. They think that man can perform noble things motivated merely by an egotistical interest. . . . The revolutionary believes in man; he believes in the human race. If one does not believe in a human being, then one is not a revolutionary."

These words were spoken on January 29, 1967, at San Andrés de Caiguanabo in Pinar del Río Province, where Fidel went to inaugurate some buildings on a big new development. He was combining the practical with the idealistic.

"These ideas are in conflict throughout the world," he said, "these ideas which we can call revolutionary and reactionary. They have to do with ways of building socialism, of constructing Communism. In many places, reactionary ideas are gaining strength and are making inroads. Faith in man is lost. In our land, revolutionary ideas gain strength. Faith in the human being grows."

In an address on September 30, 1966, he said, "What I am most grateful to the Revolution for, and what I am most willing to die for, is that I have felt myself a human being because of the Revolution. I have felt like a man with dignity. I have felt that I am something among my people, that I am something in my fatherland. . . . We must stimulate these factors of conscience among the people. We must stimulate these moral factors among the people, besides the effort to satisfy their material needs."

It will be noted that in the end he puts in the pragmatic touch about satisfying the "material needs" of the people. It is this balance for which he is groping, in the knowledge that his utopia has to have solid foundations.

Cubanologists in the United States have wasted their time in doctrinal arguments about Cuban socialism, and/or Cuban Communism. Andrés Suárez, in his *Cuba,* solemnly writes of Castro's heresy in proclaiming "the parallel construction of socialism and communism" (page 237).

Without taking much trouble, I can cite three occasions when Fidel took the orthodox line.

"We face nothing less than  the task of constructing socialism," he said in a speech on August 30, 1966. "We face nothing less than the task of marching toward Communism."

In speaking to Lee Lockwood (page 137), Castro stated: "When will the revolutionary process end? When we arrive at Communism."

"Let us make our Marxist-Leninist, socialist-Communist revolution," he declared in his September 30, 1966, address. "We do not say that we will reach socialism. We do not say that we will go through socialism to reach Communism. And we will reach Communism by the road of Marxism-Leninism."

Fidel Castro is at his most confusing in playing with doctrinal ideas, which he neither understands clearly nor believes in, except when he can give them his own definition. He does know, of course, that the third and fourth stages of Marxism are Socialism and Communism. In Cuba he is trying, in a general sense, to apply the guiding principle of Marxist socialism: "From each according to his ability, to each according to his work." And he has in mind the gradual transition to Communism which will be: "From each according to his ability, to each according to his needs."

However, he is going about it in his own peculiar way. Back on July 13, 1960, Premier Khrushchev ruefully remarked in a press conference, "The Cuban people are following a course of their own choosing. It is said that it is the Communists who are running all the affairs there. If that were true, the Cuban Revolution would have proceeded in a different way."

In his speech of August 30, 1966, when he was arguing against his "orthodox" critics, Castro warned, "Let each build his Socialism or Communism as he sees fit, but please let him also respect our right to build our Socialism and Communism as we wish."

Later in the same address he showed how far his socialistic ideas had gone. "The policy being followed," he said, "is this: If a thing is indispensable, and if it is necessary, it is given free or sold at cost."

Sir Henry Marchant, who was British Ambassador in Cuba from 1960 to 1963 (and was incidentally one of the most skillful and understanding envoys that the revolution has had), revisited Cuba and wrote an article for *The Times* of London which was published on February 6, 1968:

> Together with these more practical problems, Castro has declared himself preoccupied with visions of a Cuban utopia, where neither private property nor money would exist. Free housing, transport, telephones, theatres, cinemas and free burial are already in prospect; but according to *Granma,* the official party organ, overtime and extra pay, for "over-fulfillment of norms" are on their way out. The "new Cuban man" will work not for "material inducements" which have a negative effect on the workers' consciousness but for reasons of honour; he will regard his work not as "another piece of merchandise" but as a contribution to the communal effort of building the new communist society.

More dreams! Here is a piece of reality which showed up in Fidel's August 30, 1966, address to the Confederation of Cuban Workers (CTC):

"Almost no Cuban towns have a sewage plant, nor do they have sewage pipes," Fidel said. "All the towns want their sewage plants. All the towns, of course, want their sewage pipes laid. All the towns want their schools. All the towns want a medical dispensary or a hospital. They all want their roads, sports fields, stadiums, and in addition they all want the economic development of the area. In addition, they all want housing. But in addition to housing they want fresh milk in the morning for breakfast. In order to have milk there must be dairies, and to have dairies with hygienic milk there must be cement. . . .

"We believe that the revolution and its work have much to be proud of. It has attained great successes. However, the task before us is so overwhelming, so enormous, that what we have done is nothing, nothing in comparison with the tasks ahead. As the revolution develops, needs grow and the recognition of what we can and must do also grows. Our obligation becomes greater."

Yet Fidel could rightly add, "There is not a single city, town or village in this country where a school, a dispensary or hospital, or an industrial installation has not been built."

This is the picture as a whole as the tenth year of the revolution ends—much done and more yet to do. North Americans who speak so disparagingly of the Cuban economy forget the dreadful ghettos of their own cities and the widespread areas of poverty against which "war" is being so feebly waged. Scholars who proffer statistics to show that things were better before the revolution forget that most Cubans could not live on those statistics. They ignore the graft and corruption, the gambling and prostitution that have now gone.

On a recent trip to Cuba I had a telephone call from an anonymous, obviously middle-aged man who spoke in excellent Cuban-accented English.

"Mr. Matthews," he said, "I hope you will go back to the United States and tell the truth about what our poor country is suffering."

Other Cubans would ask what he meant by "our country." It

once was his and other privileged persons' country, and it was a fine country for them—and that country has been ruined. But "our country"—for the parents of poor children, for most peasants, for the overwhelming mass of the youth—was not *his* country. It is a better country in a great many respects now, and this is a "truth" along with other, unpleasant truths that can be said.

No one can deny that Fidel Castro and his revolution have brought tragedy to thousands of Cuban families. Revolutions can no more be made without bringing suffering to many people than wars can be fought without sacrificing lives. But at least, revolution is a mechanism by which tyranny, corruption and injustice are overthrown—almost the only mechanism known to modern man in the underdeveloped two-thirds of the world. Fidel Castro says the revolution must be violent, but it need not be.

The unhappiness varies. There was the young woman my wife encountered at a Havana hairdresser's who was very unhappy indeed. Her distress was caused by—in a descending order of importance—the scarcity of cosmetics, the shortage of food, and the lack of freedom—although "freedom" seemed to mean freedom to buy what one wanted. "The revolution does not let you be a woman," she said.

We lunched that day with some Cuban friends of many years' standing. The revolution had been a great tragedy to them. They were ill and old; their son had been arrested and sentenced to twenty years' imprisonment on the Isle of Pines, where he had already been for twenty-eight months. They had been unable to see him for eight months. Another son and the wife's relatives were in the United States, but they could not join them. They could see nothing good in the revolution. Their world had gone, never to return.

This sad story can be countered—and many times over from my experience—by happy stories of happy families. If Fidel Castro brought some tragedy to some families, I believe that it is demonstrable that he brought a better life to a majority of Cubans—if not always today and for the older generations, then for tomorrow and for the youth.

My wife and I spent a day with a group of Havana University students a few years ago. They said that they were Marxist-

Leninist but were not sure what that meant or even when they crossed into that camp. They simply followed Fidel Castro.

When asked how they so cheerfully accepted a regime without liberty, they laughed. I, who was American, and my wife, who was English, had thought we were asking a simple and obvious question. But those Cuban boys and girls had no consciousness of being deprived of liberty, and they could not seem to grasp what the term meant to us.

In prerevolutionary years, freedom of the press meant a venal, subsidized press responding to government and industry; elections were frauds won by corrupt politicians and military officers; capitalism and free enterprise were a system that enriched a few Cubans and American investors, while most Cubans remained poor. Those youths never knew what real democracy, capitalism and freedom were, so they could not feel the lack of something that they did not have.

What was true of them was true of Fidel Castro and all the young men and women who came along with him. To this day, Fidel does not understand what liberal democracy, in the Anglo-Saxon sense of the term, means. But neither do other Cubans, or other Latin Americans—or Asians, for that matter.

There is no good reason why they should. Democracy, Anglo-Saxon style, is not a God-given religion or a categorical imperative. It is not even the only type of democracy. The objections to Castro's form of government should not be based on its Marxism-Leninism, which is simply another political and economic system that Cubans should be left alone to enjoy—if they do enjoy it. What is wrong is that Fidel Castro has deprived Cubans of basic rights that they should have under any system—and that the Czechs, the Romanians, the Poles, the Yugoslavs and other Communist nations, even the Russians, are now fighting to obtain.

The Cubans' lack of true freedom before the revolution does not mean that there is no such thing as freedom—or democracy. Of course, Fidel Castro says, and believes with all his heart, that his system is democratic because it is a true expression of the will of the masses. But Fidel summons up this "general will" like the conductor of an orchestra bringing out the strains of a symphony from the musicians at his feet. He is a superb conductor, and the music is good, but there is no freedom, except to get up and walk away. Or, like Robespierre, Castro would say, "No freedom for the enemies of freedom."

Of course, freedom—like truth—is not an absolute and it depends on a point of view. I am reminded of the concluding paragraph of a series of articles about Communist China which Felix Greene wrote for the *Observer* of London in October 1961, and later published in book form:

> A Chinese uses the word "freedom" in a very personal, down-to-earth, non-theoretical sense. He is not talking about abstractions, but experience. He means that he is at last free to eat and not to starve; he is free of the landlord and the money-lender; he is free to learn to read and to write; he is free to develop skills which would otherwise remain hidden; he is free to send his children to school, and when they are ill there is a doctor to help make them well; he is free to look at the future with hope, not despair. For him these are all new freedoms. And it's not such a bad list.

For millions of Cubans these are all "new freedoms" which have been brought to them by the revolution. They would agree that it is "not such a bad list," and they know that they have Fidel Castro to thank for such "freedoms."

Besides, as Fidel asked me, "Can one tell a Negro in Cuba that he has no liberty, and tell a Negro in Alabama that he has liberty?"

Among the developments that turned Cuba's middle class against Castro was his embrace of the Negroes, his insistence on giving them equality in schools, jobs, apartments, clubs. They saw this as a class warfare and it was, to a certain extent, given that form; but there was a genuine humanism behind the policy and a true revolutionary sense. Besides, Fidel, as I have said, has no feelings about race or color, which means that he is not prejudiced in favor of Negroes, either.

One of the most distinguished scholars in Latin America—the Mexican, Daniel Cossío Villegas, in a lecture he gave at the University of Nebraska in 1962, offered two main reasons for what he called "Latin American sympathy for Cuba":

"The principal element of popular sympathy," he said, "is that the Cuban Revolution has sought to benefit the poor, the defenseless, those who are in the majority in any society. A second principal element—still held—is that the only aim of the Cuban revolutionaries is the welfare of the people, and that they pursue this so sincerely and honestly that they place it before all else."

That lecture was given before the missile crisis turned the sympathy of many Latin Americans into fear, and before Castro's policy of supporting guerrillas and violent revolution reached its peak. Yet the reasons which Dr. Cossío Villegas gave for Latin-American sympathy still exist because they are based on a correct understanding. They are like money in the bank that Fidel Castro may someday be able to draw upon.

As the first decade of his revolution ended, Fidel Castro could say like the Abbé Sieyès after the French Revolution: "I survived." He has led a charmed life.

He is better guarded now than he used to be, as I discovered on my latest trip to Cuba, but it is still—and always will be—his custom to mingle with people and expose himself to crowds. Major Rolando Cubelas, who plotted in 1966 to kill Fidel with the help of a Miami-based, CIA-supported organization headed by Manuel Artime, had in his possession a rifle with a telescopic sight when he was picked up. Fidel's luck holds out.

That the Cuban Revolution not only held out but is stronger than ever at the end of 1968 when this book is ending is equally remarkable.

"The most significant thing that can be said of our revolution," President Dorticós remarked to me five years ago (and Che Guevara had said the same thing a few days before) "is that despite our errors, despite the counterrevolutionaries, despite everything that the United States has been able to do against us, the revolution has survived and is stronger than ever."

That I should be able to write the same words five years later is even more striking. Yet it is in the nature of a radical social revolution, such as Cuba is experiencing, to last a long time. The French Revolution (and I would consider that Napoleon carried it on) lasted from 1789 to 1815—if it has yet ended. The Mexican Revolution, which began in 1910, did not level off until Lázaro Cárdenas ended his presidential term in 1940. The Bolshevik Revolution, starting in 1917, is only in these years petering out into a form of conservatism. The Chinese Revolution, which triumphed in 1949, is far from over.

By these historic standards, the Cuban Revolution is still young. So is Fidel Castro, and so are the men and women of the Sierra Maestra who surround him and help him to run his revolution. They are all, as I have said, making plans stretching to 1975 and 1980. If his luck and health hold out, Fidel will be only fifty-four years old in 1980.

I am not, of course, predicting this or any other duration for the revolution or for Fidel Castro. If there is such a thing as a foreseeable future, one can only say that the still perfectly healthy, physically powerful and young Fidel Castro should go on living and working for a great many years to come. On the same basis, the situation today leads to one conclusion—that the Cuban Revolution is also going to last many more years.

These are the bases on which all those dealing with Cuba—writers, exiles and Governments—must, or should, operate.

For the Cuban exiles, there are harsh and bitter prospects which are being recognized by many refugees only in recent years. What is even harder for them to accept—although it is demonstrable beyond any question of doubt—is that the Cuba they left has gone into history. It no longer exists. It has been transformed so profoundly that there is no more possibility of reversing the revolution than there is of putting an egg back into its shell after it has been broken.

I find it extraordinary that so acute an observer of the Cuban Revolution as Theodore Draper should reject such an inescapable conclusion. However, he does so (in an article for *The New Leader* of April 13, 1964) by putting up a straw man: the claim others make that *Communist* revolutions are irreversible. This is not the point so far as Cuba is concerned. The point is that *social* revolutions of a profound nature, which transform the political, economic and social structures of a nation, are irreversible. Communism has nothing to do with it.

One can legitimately reduce the argument to the absurd. All rural children in Cuba are now going to school and being clothed and fed. Will a government of Cuban exiles, installed by Washington, send them back to hovels and take the shoes off their feet? Cuban Negroes now, for the first time in the history of the island, have equality. Will a counterrevolutionary government force a return to the previous inferior status? Are graft, corruption, gambling and prostitution going to be restored to their previous disgracefully high levels?

I am not for a second imputing any such desires to Theodore Draper or to the responsible and patriotic Cubans in the exile colonies. But if the Cuban Revolution is "reversed," what else could happen to a greater or lesser degree?

> Yet [Draper writes in the article I mentioned (which is essentially an attack on Senator Fulbright's ideas)] if there is one place in the world where Communism can be "reversible" it is Cuba. Those who are willing at this stage to give up all hope and effort to bring down the Castro regime must take into account the total magnitude, the full enormity, of this decision. It is not right or just for them to wash their hands of all responsibility by pretending that the decision has been made for them.

This is emotional nonsense. Senator Fulbright had sensibly suggested that Castro's Cuba should be regarded as a "nuisance" and that the United States should learn to live with it. Willy-nilly, this is exactly what the United States has been doing since the Bay of Pigs fiasco in 1961, although it does everything it can in its halfhearted way to make life difficult and costly for Fidel Castro and the Cuban Revolution.

One can regret that the Cuban Government is Communist, but there is no "enormity" in letting Cubans work out their destiny in whatever form they choose. There is not going to be another nuclear crisis.

United States relations with Cuba can become normal, if not friendly, only as part of a global settlement in which the Communist bloc is allowed to go on disintegrating while each Communist nation settles its own problems. The Soviet Union is not ready for this as Czechoslovakia learned.

Fidel Castro's anti-Yankeeism—his diatribes against "Yankee

imperialism"—are not the result of his Marxism-Leninism. They come from Cuban nationalism with its complex historic, economic and political background. He is defending his revolution against the threat that he sees coming from the United States. So long as Washington demands nothing less than unconditional surrender— and this is still the case—Fidel Castro and a majority of the Cubans will go on fighting and will, if necessary, go down fighting.

"We are located ninety miles from Yankee imperialism," Fidel said on January 2, 1965. "It is a situation in which no other country of the socialist camp finds itself. We are thousands of miles away from the socialist camp, the only socialist country in this hemisphere. That is why we need to be armed; that is why we need those weapons and those cannons."

This was a theme he has repeated since 1965—and it was an old theme then. He sees Cuba as a beleaguered country, and in depicting it as such, he wins support from the Cuban people. As I have written before, he believes that the United States is going to lose its preeminent power.

"Nearly all the world nowadays is revolutionary, but not the United States," he said to me in 1963. Since then there has been the Vietnam War with its devastating impact on the United States economy. Castro hopes while we Americans dread. The first of his problems is to continue to survive; and second is to make a success of his revolution.

Thus far Fidel Castro has done the first and is in process of doing the second. He needs time, and, judging from the way things look at the end of 1968, he is going to get a certain amount of it. The great assets of technical knowledge and expertise that flowed out of Cuba in the early years of the revolution are gradually being replaced. Writing of the fiftieth anniversary of the Bolshevik Revolution, *The Times* of London said in an editorial:

> And, though for years the revolution suffered from the disastrous loss of talent with the destruction of the old educated classes, the great spread of higher education has untapped the stores of new talent in all ranks; it is one of the greatest gains in the revolution.

One could use virtually the same words of the Cuban Revolution except that ten years are not fifty years, and in Cuba the process is just now bringing results. The tragic conclusion for the Cuban refugees—even in the professional classes—is that with each passing year they are needed less and less.

Few of the young men and women in Cuba today even know the names of the refugee leaders from prerevolutionary days, and no one wants them back except the few older folk who live in, and long for, the past. The young exiles who fought at the Bay of Pigs are equally unwanted. For the younger generation of Cubans they all make up a mass of faceless men who have no place in the new Cuba. Even when changes in revolutionary governments come, as with Italy and Germany, it is the ones who stuck it out who come to the top, not the ones who fled.

This is part of the tragedy that accompanies all revolutions. "What is even more cruel, all [the exile's] ties are loosened and he ends up a stranger in his own land," wrote Madame de Staël, who was exiled by Napoleon for twelve years. He is a stranger because his land has been transformed, because a new generation has grown up, because the jobs are taken by others, because even the meaning of life has changed.

> In Cuba [Rufo López-Fresquet, Castro's first Minister of the Treasury, courageously told a conference at the Inter-American University in Puerto Rico in March 1967] people are living with a scale of social, political and economic values distinct from that which existed before Castro. Especially the young, the women, the Negroes, the poor, the farmers, the students, and the military. . . .
>
> It is logical to think that a very different social being is in process of formation. . . . In thinking of the future it is necessary to consider that the Cuban who remains in Cuba until the present situation ends will differ from the one who has migrated and the one who existed before Castro took power. If the change takes place this year, we will find 8,000,000 Cubans of this new type.

One might say that this was Fidel Castro's most spectacular accomplishment. It was on a trip to Cuba in November 1963, nearly five years after the revolution began, that I sensed the change in the Cuban people. I wrote in my notes:

A revolution is a fiery experience for everybody involved in it, and fire hardens when it does not consume. The leaders are working well together, and for the first time I had a feeling that the revolution was functioning as a popular movement in many respects. The people have, naturally, learned too. They were euphoric and bewildered in the early stages. The dynamism of the revolution, the shifts, the bitter internal struggle over Communism, the defection of the right—all these things kept the nation in confusion and turmoil.

Cubans are an intelligent people, and it stands to reason that they have at least grasped what a social revolution means, what is required of them, what they may or may not hope for. Naturally, a great many of them may hate it, but at least they have come to understand. There is a purposefulness which is rare in Latin America today, and new in Cuba.

Even Fidel's Marxism-Leninism has a freshness about it that cannot be found behind the Iron Curtain where one or two generations have been brought up with Communism from childhood. In Cuba, Communism came as something new; it was approached— by all but the minority who fled—with open, inquiring minds, disposed to accept, wanting to be convinced, but at first still diffident. In 1963 I felt that some of the novelty had worn off. Marxism-Leninism had become a Cuban phenomenon.

Life has now assumed a familiar rhythm, a beat which is familiar not because the tune is old but because it is new, like the Beatle-style songs so popular in Cuba today. Fidel Castro—hated or worshiped—has always provided excitement. Each day a new life begins and the Lord only knows what the next day will bring. Very often, not even Fidel Castro knows.

Living, in many ways, is drab in Cuba today. The cities are clean but they are dingy because paint cannot be spared. Clothes are strictly rationed. The food is adequate but monotonous and, in the restaurants, expensive and awful. Cabarets, with their gay night shows, are now closed. The people are ignorant of world affairs because their newspapers and radio stations feed them only blatant Communist, anti-Yankee propaganda. As each year passes, Cuba becomes less and less Latin-American, less a part of the Western Hemisphere. Drab, yes; but dull, no!

The list of weaknesses could be lengthened—rationed products are sometimes hard to get; there are not enough doctors, not enough medicines, not enough housing. These and other failings breed discontent, discouragement, cynicism, complaints. Yet no one feels that the discontent even remotely threatens rebellion. The good features of the revolution are there to counterbalance the bad—and so is the powerful military and police structure. The Administration has a basic solidarity now which Cubans feel, but which is not visible from outside the country.

Yet the fundamental fact is unchanged: Fidel Castro runs the revolution. He made it, and it will go where he tells it to go. I did not think in 1959, 1960 and 1961 that Fidel had any deep feeling for the people, the masses, the peasants. Now one must say that he has shown such feeling.

Those associates who know him best—and much of the Cuban public—credit him with a humanity, a love of the people, a desire to live for them and to make their lives better; but was he really like that in 1959? Did I exaggerate his thirst for power? Or did he have it then and has he mellowed today? Is he, as his principal in the Belén preparatory school sensed so many years ago, a consummate actor? a man of many parts? And if he is, what else could he be doing but playing himself in a drama that he wrote? He is always Fidel Castro, but Fidel is a baffling character who disguises himself so well and so often that he makes the real man elusive, mysterious, aloof, unreachable.

I still say: "By their works ye shall know them." The safest judgment is to look at what Fidel Castro has done—those things which I have written about in this book—and then decide what manner of man he is. It will be a personal opinion. For all Cubans, all North Americans, all of us who know him, it will be a biased opinion. No one can be objective about Fidel Castro except those divorced from Cuban affairs and open-minded about Communism. This is the case with most Europeans, but not with any American—North or Latin—and not with citizens of Communist nations or the underdeveloped countries of the world.

I have my personal opinion. In a paper I gave in October 1959, at a conference at Stanford University, I said of Fidel, "He is an emotional, inexperienced, confused, amateurish, willful, arrogant young man." I also added that "it is equally true to say of him that he is a decent, honest, brave, sincere, idealistic young man, who thinks he is being democratic and wants to be, and who passionately desires to do what is best for his people and his country."

I would say today that he is no longer inexperienced and that he is in many respects professional and not amateurish. Otherwise, I would not, today, change a word.

Arthur Schlesinger, Jr., after his experience in the White House during the disastrous Bay of Pigs invasion, said that as a historian he had often used newspaper accounts but would no longer trust them. I had earlier come to an opposite conclusion; as a journalist I had often used history books, but I now realized how "history" was written, and I no longer trusted the historians.

There are few historians wise enough to say, with G. M. Trevelyan in one of his last lectures (to the National Book League of London on May 30, 1945): "It is still too early to form a final judgment on the French Revolution, and opinion about it (my opinion certainly) is constantly oscillating."

There are details concerning Fidel Castro and the Cuban Revolution on which one is entitled to pass "final judgments," but only details. Fidel and his revolution must wait a long time for anything more than tentative judgments.

Opinions made without understanding are worthless. There was no keener observer in England of what happened in France during the French Revolution than Edmund Burke—and there was no one who was more blind to what it meant.

I have always felt that the French Revolution was the most significant political event of the modern age—allowing for what it borrowed from the American Revolution. The Cuban Revolution is a direct descendant of the French Revolution, and its importance to Cuba and to Latin America derives from the fact that it is in the line of the social revolutions begun by France.

André Malraux reported in his *Antimémoires* (page 194) a long discussion with Jawaharlal Nehru in New Delhi in 1958:

I had already encountered [Malraux wrote of India], and I was later to encounter many times, this presence of [revolutionary] France. . . . And in all cases where the revolution was not made by the proletariat but by the people, the teachings of the French Revolution, the exaltation of the fight for justice proclaimed from Saint-Just to Jaurès, passing through Michelet and above all Victor Hugo, retain a prestige at least the equal of Marxism.

Fidel Castro has studied the French Revolution and he knows the debt that he owes to it but, of course, he could not create a contemporary political system out of Jacobinism.

He does not live in the past. Nothing could be further from the truth than to say, as Draper does in *Castroism* (page 230), that Fidel "found the past far more inspiring and sustaining than the present."

Ten minutes spent with Castro would show the folly of such a belief. He lives, passionately and exuberantly, in the present and future. The zest, the eagerness and the optimism of the man are almost overwhelming when one is in his presence. Ahead of him he sees a New Jerusalem, and he rushes toward it with the same boundless faith that led him into his earliest adventures, and will lead him into new ones.

Che Guevara, in *Guerrilla Warfare,* wrote that Danton's slogan was best for a revolution: *"De l'audace, et encore de l'audace, et toujours de l'audace!"* Consciously or not, that is Fidel Castro's motto for the Cuban Revolution. If he and the revolution come a cropper—as they almost did in the nuclear missile crisis—it may well be from an excess of audacity.

A prominent Cuban exile—anti-Fidelista, of course—remarked at a dinner I attended in Washington, where the conversation was on the whole full of criticism of Castro, that the President of the United States, the Prime Minister of Britain and the Premier of the Soviet Union can easily make a great mark in the world. For the Premier of a little Latin American country like Cuba to do so is a truly remarkable feat. This sense of Cuba's having been put on the world map, and having provided a figure of global stature who is Cuban and Latin-American, is strong except among the most embittered exiles.

It is not by considering only the negative aspects of such a man—his failures, his mistakes, his sometimes immoral methods, his deceptions, his weaknesses and foibles—that one arrives at a valid judgment. One does not explain Julius Caesar by his amorality, his epilepsy, or the colossal mistakes from which he spent so much time extricating himself. Historians do not rely on Cicero's correspondence.

Christopher Brooke, of the University of Liverpool, in his *From Alfred to Henry III,* speculates on why Thomas Becket changed toward Henry II (page 179–80):

> It is unlikely that these questions will ever be answered satisfactorily, because their answer must depend on reconstructing the logic of a world which is irrecoverable, and on fathoming the mysteries of a deep and complex character, one who puzzled his contemporaries as much as he puzzles us. . . . No set of events in the twelfth century is better recorded than the dispute of Henry II and Thomas Becket; we have twelve or so *Lives* and some 800 letters from which to reconstruct the story. But the central character remains an enigma.

Honestly written history is like that. Most of the hostile books and articles by Cubanologists and the United States State Department and White House use an invalid progression. They go from what Fidel Castro said to what he did—or did not—do. When the time comes for future historians to strike a fair balance (there will never be a final one), the task will be to study what Castro has done, and, insofar as his multitudinous words are concerned, to see whether there is not a basic, fundamental consistency.

I believe there is. I believe that Fidel Castro always wanted to rebel against, and overturn, the existing structure in Cuba and to create a new structure that would bring honesty to government and a decent life to all Cubans. By every instinct of his nature and character, consciously and unconsciously, he believed himself to be the instrument to achieve such a transformation in Cuba. Having assumed power, he believed that what was good for Cuba would be good for all of Latin America, and the underdeveloped "Third World."

The flood of diatribes about his "betrayal" of the revolution derive from selective, hostile, subjective emotions and reasoning. It is easy to find any amount of inconsistency in some details of what Fidel said he would do and in some of the methods he said he would use. These inconsistencies are the commonplaces of history, and similar criticisms are applicable to innumerable historic figures.

They were applied for instance, to President Lyndon B. Johnson who promised again and again during the presidential campaign of 1964 that he would not send "American boys" to Vietnam to fight a war that Asiatics should fight. History will not judge Johnson by what he said he would or would not do; it will judge him by what he did. There was no "betrayal" either in his case or in Castro's. They both later faced situations in which they felt they had to act differently than they had thought. They can be criticized for having done the wrong things, or praised for having done the right things, according to the point of view. President Johnson, in fact, changed his Vietnam policy once again, this time toward de-escalation, at the end of March, 1968.

Carlos Rafael Rodríguez once said to me that he could not conceive of Fidel Castro "as a horse pulling a carriage in a certain direction." I preferred to say that a leader of Castro's type is like the pilot of a ship in a storm—one wonders if the buffeting is driving the ship where the pilot does not want it to go, or is driving it faster than he wants it to go.

On my last trip to Cuba before writing this book—in October 1967—I had more than ever the sense of a continuing process, a development, of the way Fidel is searching for new ideas, new ways of doing things. He was not going to stand still; no book was going to write *finis* to his career. When I asked him about the famous autobiography that everyone has talked about for years, for which poor Carlos Franqui has collected enough material to fill eleven volumes to date, Fidel shook his head.

"I don't want to write history," he said. "I want to make it. Anyway, the most important 'history' is what the revolution has done and is doing, and this cannot be finished yet because it is still in process."

Starting in November 1963, I believed and wrote—as the

Cuban revolutionaries did—that the revolution was beginning to be institutionalized. After all, a communistic type of structure was being formed. Now that five years have passed and the Cuban formula is still Fidel-Castro-plus-the-masses, with the Communist party of Cuba simply providing a channel and a framework, I would say that institutionalization, if it comes at all, is only a future prospect. The requisite—that Castro be willing to relinquish power to a totalitarian party—is not in sight.

As early as November 1959, well before the "Marxist-Leninist" period, I wrote in my notes: "The pattern is Fidel and the masses." In October 1967, on my latest visit to Cuba, I was writing the same sentiment. In its simple way, this fact about the Cuban Revolution provides an apt example of the French saying *"Plus ça change, plus ça reste la même chose."*

The Cuban Revolution has a mass character because Fidel Castro gave it that form. It did not exist in the beginning. His systematic destruction of the men, the parties, the movements and institutions which stood between him and absolute power was what permitted him to make a mass revolution.

Now everybody, willingly or unwillingly, is a participant in the revolution. There is still the element (figures vary from 100,000 to 400,000) who want to emigrate and are waiting their turn to do so. These, for the most part, are older men and women with children, who have relatives in the United States. They are almost all from the middle class. (Castro is not trying to hold them back, for they are a liability to him, but the rate of departure has been regulated by the United States's willingness to provide transportation.)

For the rest, Fidel said to me, "Cubans have a real sense of revolution now, a true understanding." This did not prevent him from branding a great many thousands of shopkeepers, vendors and self-employed as "counterrevolutionaries" in his startling speech of March 13, 1968, putting an end to what little private enterprise remained in Cuba.

This is a typical case of *l'audace*. Often Castro seems to be driving the Cuban people to limits that are dangerous for his revolution. He asks so much of them that one wonders, Is he not asking too much? He could miscalculate, if only because his own

faith and self-confidence are so great that he blinds himself to the
fact that men and women normally respond to simple and tangible
motives.

> Ordinary men are not often moved to action by a direct appeal to
> abstract ideas [Professor Fagen wrote in the article on "Mass Mo-
> bilization in Cuba"]. Not "building socialism," but rather com-
> radeship, ambition, social pressure, or fear probably motivate the
> Cuban office worker who volunteers to cut sugar cane on the
> weekend. Similarly, visions of a brave new world may be instru-
> mental in keeping a few agricultural reformers working after hours,
> but the average Cuban peasant is probably kept in harness by some
> combination of necessity, habit, ignorance and hope of material
> gain. The Cuban leaders are well aware that widespread popular
> participation cannot be achieved by appeals to nineteenth or even
> twentieth century abstractions. On the other hand, both for political
> and ideological reasons, they are committed to a mobilization
> strategy that included the use of ideas as well as the use of the
> carrot and the stick.

It is because Fidel Castro has offered the Cuban people a great
many "carrots" and is sparing with the "stick" that he is still in
power with a functioning and progressing revolution in 1969. He
agreed, in a conversation I had with him at the beginning of 1959,
that his revolution would succeed only if he could make it an
economic success. But it has been a major problem for him that to
reach economic viability he must ask the Cuban people to accept
many hardships along the way. He asks for their faith as well as
their support.

In general, it seems true, as Fidel and his associates claim, that
the most significant change which has taken place in the Cuban
people in recent years is their understanding and support of the
revolution. By tradition, Cubans have a revolutionary spirit which
has had no scope in the  generations since the wars of independence. To say that this spirit now exists arouses the skepticism or
disbelief of outsiders, yet there is much evidence that it is real and
widespread.

There is a drive, an *élan,* that now comes from the masses. Without this, the revolution could not continue. A police state would
not hold the Cuban people down.

I would agree with a personal opinion that Lee Lockwood, who has followed the Cuban Revolution since it began, gives near the end of his book on Castro (page 281):

> An outsider who devotes all his attention to constructing theories about [the revolution] runs the risk of failing to understand its essential values, which are human and organic, and, being in flux, tend to resist intellectualizing. It is almost necessary to go to Cuba to see for oneself to truly understand this. There is in Cuba today much of the same spirit of excitement, of a sense of purpose, of a moral momentum, of a people making their own destiny, that charged the air when Castro's Revolution swept into power seven years ago.

My only disagreement with Lockwood is that he wrote that it is "almost" necessary to go to Cuba to see for oneself. It *is* necessary, and this is why, for me, so much that has been written abroad, and especially in the United States, about Fidel Castro and the Cuban Revolution is mistaken and misleading.

The upheaval in France, which reached a startling climax in May and June 1968, came out of the same explosive brew as the Cuban Revolution. All over the world university students, for different reasons and with differing goals, struck the first blows, as Fidel Castro and his young followers did in 1953.

Orthodox, Moscow-directed Communist parties were forced reluctantly to tag along, as in Cuba, behind youths who were to their left—more radical, more rebellious, more revolutionary. Trade union leaders, like those in Cuba, sided at first with governments and employers against the students whom they considered as extremists, putschists, Trotskyists and, above all, anarchists. Youth, which raised the banner of revolt, was leading toward a too-uncertain future.

The anarchical element—so typical of the Cuban Revolution—has been a characteristic of the "student power" uprisings everywhere. The common features are an idealistic revulsion against established order and always—as was the case in Cuba in the preliminary phase—demands for liberty, democracy, participation in government and economy. The Vietnam War was, understandably, a hated symbol for the youth movements in every country.

Just as the Cubans named their rebellion after a symbolic date—the 26th of July—so the French students formed a 22nd of March Movement and a 5th of May Movement. Charismatic leaders like Rudi Dutschke in West Germany and Daniel Cohn-Bendit in France rose out of the ferment. It followed naturally that among the photographs displayed by students everywhere were those of the martyred Che Guevara and (to a lesser extent, for he is almost an elder statesman now) Fidel Castro.

Violent and direct action brought results which peaceful agitation could not have achieved. During the dramatic explosion that paralyzed France, everyone recognized the link to the Revolution of 1789. And everyone said and wrote, "France will never be the same again." The world will never be the same again, and the year 1968 proved that Fidel Castro and the Cuban Revolution were not aberrations. They are symptoms and symbols of our times. The inevitable reaction from the right could not restore the lost world, as the monetary crisis of November 1968 proved.

Jung pointed out somewhere in his writings that Columbus, "by using subjective assumptions, a false hypothesis, and a route abandoned by modern navigation, nevertheless discovered America."

Fidel Castro, by breaking with the United States, on which modern Cuba has depended for its very existence, and by destroying or driving out the industrial, banking, landowning, professional and entrepreneurial classes which ran the country, has made a successful social revolution in Cuba.

This would still be true if the government were overthrown tomorrow, along with Castro and his faithful group of associates. The revolution would continue; it cannot be overthrown; it cannot be reversed; it is an ineradicable fact of Cuban history.

This, I repeat, is Fidel Castro's greatest accomplishment: the achievement that gives him—whether one approves or disapproves —a stature that no other Cuban has remotely attained. In fact, as a revolutionary, there is no comparable leader in Latin-American history.

Simón Bolívar, one of the noblest figures in the history of the Western Hemisphere and one who accomplished marvels, nevertheless had to say bitterly at the end of his great career, "To serve the revolution is to plow the sea." He had lived to see his efforts at revolution and social reform fail. Fidel Castro could be killed tomorrow, but his revolution would endure.

As the English historian, H. A. L. Fisher wrote: "But there is a nemesis which attends the policy of political assassination. The victim may fall, but the cause survives, strengthened by the martyr's blood."

"Life and death can be noble and beautiful," Haydée Santamaría said to Carlos Franqui, speaking of the attack on the Moncada Barracks in 1953 (page 56 of Franqui's book), "and they are both the same: one defends one's life or one sacrifices it without haggling."

"The cosmic bellyache" of our times, to use H. L. Mencken's wonderful phrase, is caused by the twin manifestations of revolution and wars of national liberation. Fidel Castro invented neither of these contemporary torments, but he is the outstanding figure of his generation in bringing them to Latin America.

He wears his revolution with a difference. He is no Madero or Lenin or Mao Tse-tung. He speaks for today's generation, in and out of the Communist world. Cuba is not his confine; it is the homeland from which he looks across boundaries and seas to where his ambitions and ideals lure him.

And yet listening to Fidel Castro make the funeral oration at the ceremony for Che Guevara in Havana on October 18, 1967, as I did, I could feel some of the revolutionary spirit of the Sierra Maestra come back.

It was a comrade's speech, which evoked the great days now long gone and sought to stir the embers of the fire that Che's death threatened to smother in the guerrilla campaigns of Latin America. One had to know what those Sierra days meant to Fidel Castro and the small group of men and women who survived the epic struggle to sense the nostalgia and the sadness behind the words that Fidel spoke.

"Every time I see Fidel," Haydée Santamaría said to Franqui (page 54), "every time I speak to him, or see him on the television, I think of the others, of all those who are dead, of those who live and think of Fidel—of the Fidel whom we have known and who is always the same. And I think of the revolution, which is always the same as the one that we led at Moncada. . . ."

I, too, think of the young Fidel Castro I first saw in the jungle shrubs of the Sierra Maestra on February 17, 1957, and of the revolution he started to make in January 1959, and I, too, say these are the same man and same revolution—Fidel Castro's revolution.

# Bibliography

Attwood, William, *The Reds and the Blacks*. New York, Harper & Row, 1967.

Batista y Zaldivar, Fulgencio, *Cuba Betrayed*. Vantage Press, Inc., 1962.

Casuso, Teresa (translated by Elmer Grossberg), *Cuba and Castro*. New York, Random House, Inc., 1961.

Conte Agüero, Luis, *Cartas del Presidio*. Havana, Editorial Lex, 1959.

———— *Fidel Castro, Vida y Obra*. Havana, Editorial Lex, 1959.

Cressweller, Robert D., *Trujillo: The Life and Times of a Caribbean Dictator*. New York, The Macmillan Company, 1966.

Debray, Régis, *Révolution dans la révolution?*, Paris, Librairie François Maspero, 1967. Also *¿Revolución en la revolución?*, Havana, Casa de las Américas, 1967. Also (translated by Bobbye Ortiz) *Revolution in the Revolution?*, New York, Monthly Review Press, 1967.

Desnoes, Edmundo, *Punto de Vista*. Havana, Instituto del Libro, 1967.

Drachkovitch, Milorad M. (editor), *Marxism in the Modern World*. Stanford, Stanford University Press, 1965.

Draper, Theodore, *Castroism: Theory and Practice*. New York, Frederick A. Praeger, Inc., 1965.

———— *Castro's Revolution: Myths and Realities*. New York, Frederick A. Praeger, Inc., 1962.

Dubois, Jules, *Fidel Castro*. New York, Bobbs–Merrill Company, Inc., 1959.

Franqui, Carlos, *Le Livre des Douze*. Paris, Gallimard, 1965.

Goldenberg, Boris, *The Cuban Revolution and Latin America*. New York, Frederick A. Praeger, Inc., 1965.

Guevara, Ernesto Che, *El Diario del Che en Bolivia*, Havana, Book Institute, 1968.

—————— *La Guerra de Geurrillas*. Havana, Departamento de Instrucción, 1960. Also (translated by J. P. Morray) *Guerrilla Warfare*. New York, Monthly Review Press, 1961.

—————— *Man and Socialism in Cuba*. Havana, Book Institute, 1967.

—————— *Pasajes de la Guerra Revolucionaria*. Havana, Ediciones Unión, 1963. Also (translated by Victoria Ortiz) *Reminiscences of the Cuban Revolutionary War*. New York, Monthly Review Press, 1968.

Hilsman, Roger, *To Move a Nation: The Politics of Foreign Policy in the Administration of John F. Kennedy*. New York, Doubleday & Company, Inc., 1967.

Johnson, Haynes, and others, *The Bay of Pigs: The Leaders' Story of Brigade 2506*. New York, W. W. Norton & Company, Inc., 1964.

Lipset, Seymour Martin, and Solari, Aldo (editors), *Elites in Latin America*. New York, Oxford University Press, 1967.

Lockwood, Lee, *Castros' Cuba, Cuba's Fidel*. New York, The Macmillan Company, 1967.

López-Fresquet, Rufo, *My 14 Months with Castro*. New York, The World Publishing Company, 1966.

MacGaffey, Wyatt, and others, *Cuba: Its People, Its Society, Its Culture*. New Haven, Human Relations Area Files Press, 1962.

Mao Tse-tung (translated by Stuart R. Schram), *Basic Tactics*. New York, Frederick A. Praeger, Inc., 1966.

Matthews, Herbert L., *Cuba*. New York, The Macmillan Company, 1964.

—————— *The Cuban Story*, New York, George Braziller, 1961.

Merle, Robert, *Moncada, Premier Combat de Fidel Castro*. Paris, Robert Laffont, 1965.

Meyer, Karl E., and Szulc, Tad, *The Cuban Invasion: The Chronicle of a Disaster*. New York, Frederick A. Praeger, Inc., 1962.

Nelson, Lowry, *Rural Cuba*. Minneapolis, University of Minnesota Press, 1950.

Rojas, Marta, *La Generación del Centenario en el Moncada*. Havana, Ediciones R., 1964.

Schlesinger, Arthur M., Jr., *A Thousand Days*. New York, Houghton Mifflin Company, 1965.

Seers, Dudley (editor), *Cuba: The Economic and Social Revolution*. Chapel Hill, The University of North Carolina Press, 1964.

Selser, Gregorio, *La Revolución Cubana*. Buenos Aires, Editorial Palestra, 1966.

Silvert, Kalman H., *The Conflict Society*. New York, American Universities Field Staff, Inc., 1966.

Smith, Robert Freeman, *The United States and Cuba: Business and Diplomacy, 1917–1960*. New York, Bookman Associates, 1960.

———— *What Happened in Cuba?: A Documentary History*. New York, Twayne Publishers, Inc., 1963.

———— (editor), *Background to Revolution: The Development of Modern Cuba*. New York, Alfred A. Knopf, 1966.

Sorensen, Theodore C., *Kennedy*. New York, Harper & Row, 1965.

Suárez; Andrés, *Cuba: Castroism and Communism, 1959–1966*. Cambridge, Mass., The M.I.T. Press, 1967.

Taber, Robert, *M–26: Biography of a Revolution*. New York, Lyle Stuart, 1961.

Toynbee, Arnold J., *Acquaintances*. New York, Oxford University Press, 1967.

Urrutia Lleo, Manuel, *Fidel Castro & Company, Inc*. New York, Frederick A. Praeger, Inc., 1964.

Zeitlin, Maurice, *Revolutionary Politics and the Cuban Working Class*. Princeton, Princeton University Press, 1967.

# Index

Abbes, Johnny, 276
Acton, Lord, 52–53, 341
Adams, John Quincy, 46, 48
Agramonte, Roberto, 135
Agrarian reform (1959), 240–41, 261
Agrarian reform (1963), 262
Agriculture
  cooperatives in, 239, 261–62
  diversification of, 245, 263
  food shortage in, 238–39, 266
  irrigation programs for, 248
  nationalization of, 262
  plans to develop, 271
  tobacco in, 263–64
Agüero, Luis Conte, 20, 28, 64, 65, 155
  Castro's letters to, 80–81
  on "La Historia me absolverá," 74
Alliance for Progress
  Johnson and, 167
  launching of (1961), 56
  partial success of, 308

Alliance for Progress (cont.)
  as result of Cuban Revolution, 307
Almeida, Juan, 95, 100, 117, 126, 298, 319
Almeijeiras, Major Efigenio, 95, 108, 154, 253–54, 319
Almeÿeiras, Gustavo, 73
Almeÿeiras, Machaco, 73
Alonso, Alicia, 269
Amado-Blanco, Luis, 36, 332
Aquinas, Thomas, 80
Aragonés, Emilio, 321
Arbenz, Jácobo
  Guevara's help to, 87–88, 119
  overthrow of (1954), 56, 206
Arendt, Hannah, 134
Army, see Rebel Army
Artime, Manuel, 214, 348
Attwood, William, 236

Baldwin, Hanson, 210, 212
Barguín, Colonel Ramón, 140

Batista, General Fulgencio, 25, 34, 326
  attempt to kill, 110–11
  brutality under, 51, 67, 125, 145
  on Castro's 1957 interview, 107
  counter-terrorist forces of, 125
  coup of (March 1952), 50, 57, 62
  end of term of (1944), 61
  flees (Jan. 1959), 129, 139
  interviewed (1957), 113
  last offensive of (May 1958), 126–27
  presidential election held by (Nov. 1958), 128
  U.S. support for, 56–57
  view of July 26th Movement, 81
Bay of Pigs invasion (Apr. 17, 1961), 199–215
  bombing preceding, 207
  CIA's role in, 202, 206–7, 213–14
  Cuban exiles involved in, 203
  development of invasion, 207–8
  impact of, 199
  leadership during, 200
  prisoners taken during, 221–22
  strategy in, 204, 208–9
  U.S. forces in, 210–11
  victory in (Apr. 19), 213–14, 223
Bayamesa, La (Cuban national anthem), 64
Bayo, Colonel Alberto, 86, 89, 90, 163
Ben Bella, Ahmed, 160
Bender, Ray, 214
Bendix, Reinhard, 141
Bergquist, Laura, 338
Betancourt, Romulo, 276, 278–79
Bloch, Marc, 30
Bogotazo (Colombian uprising of Apr. 1948), 24–25
Bolívar, Simón, 363
Bonsal, Philip, 53, 152, 158, 160, 163
Bosch, José M., 135
Brezhnev, Leonid, 285
Brooke, Christopher, 357
Brown, H. Rap, 289
Brown, John, 16
Buchanan, James, 48
Burke, Edmund, 355
Butler, General Smedley D., 49

Cabell, General C. P., 169
Cantillo, General Eulogio, 129, 139
Cárdenas Lázaro, 86, 349
Carlyle, Thomas, 9
Carmichael, Stokely, 289, 290
Carpentier, Alejo, 269
Cartas del Presidio (Castro), 20, 78–81
Castillo Armas, Colonel Carlos, 206
Castro, Agustina (sister), 17
Castro, Angela (sister), 17
Castro, Ernma (sister), 17
Castro, Fidel, 15–38
  arms purchased by, 200–1
  attachment to his son, 29
  attitudes of
    to dogmatism, 83
    to manual work, 251–52
    to money, 34–35, 319
    to the people, 354
    to racism, 36, 347
    to religion, 35–36, 330–31, 333–34
    to totalitarianism, 161
  birth of, 17
  "black legend" around, 24–26
  breaks with Ortodoxo Party (1956), 82
  characteristics of
    anti-Americanism, 46, 56–57, 121, 158, 197–98, 350–51
    attention to detail, 118
    attraction to the land, 340
    capacity for self-deception, 136, 184, 230
    charisma, 31, 141–42, 209, 309–10, 362
    concern for publicity, 105–6, 109
    courage and determination, 25, 31–32
    fighting spirit, 95–96
    humaneness, 125
    independence, 292–93, 310
    integrity, 24
    as loner, 32–33
    lust for life, 356
    personal appearance, 36–37
    physical fitness, 21, 27
    puritanical quality, 253–54
    rhetorical brilliance, 30, 148

Castro, Fidel (*cont.*)
  characteristics of (*cont.*)
    toughness, 104–5
  Communists and
    Castro opposed, 177, 326
    Castro's position on (1959),
      176
    Communists brought into
      power, 156
    Communists in secondary posi-
      tions, 205
    Communists used, 144, 320,
      324
    first contacts, 121–22
    forced collaboration, 195
    national unity as basis for
      alliance, 176
    as natural allies, 178
    old-guard and, 182, 287–88,
      315–18
  counterrevolutionaries fought by,
    151–53
  democratic ideals of, 108
  devotion to, 76–78, 124, 337
  *dolce vita* disease fought by, 154
  education of, 21–23
  execution of war criminals and
    (Jan. 1959), 47
  factors influencing policies of,
    37–38
  family relationships of, 17–20
  faith in guerrilla warfare of, 99–
    100
  five-point program of, 233
  grows beard, 103–4
  Guevara and, 296–97, 300
    Castro on Guevara's death, 286
    Guevara's influence, 175
    Guevara's loyalty, 88–89
  hopes to come to terms with
    U.S., 311–12
  ignorance of U.S. by, 195–96
  imprisonment of
    Boniato Prison, 78
    Isle of Pines, 78–81
  increasing radicalism of, 235,
    236
  interview of (Feb. 1957), 106–7
  invasion of Czechoslovakia sup-
    ported by, 274
  Jacobin tradition followed by, 140

Castro, Fidel (*cont.*)
  Latin America and, 276–77, 281,
    321
    attempt to overthrow Trujillo
      (1947), 26–27
    Betancourt and, 278–79
    Castro's prestige in, 275
    efforts to revolutionize, 236,
      277, 279–80, 283–84, 286
    *See also* Latin America
  as lawyer, 23–24
  leads battle of Santo Domingo
    (June 1958), 126–27
  as leader of Third World, 309
  leads offensive on Santiago de
    Cuba (Nov. 1958), 129, 139
  Lenin compared with, 96–97, 141
  Mao Tse-tung and, 291–92
  march to Havana (Jan. 1959),
    139
  marriage and divorce of, 28–29
  Martí's influence on, 45–46
  Marxism-Leninism of, 165–66
    adherence (Dec. 1961), 184,
      188–89
    Castro on Marxism, 284
    development toward, 172–74,
      185–87
    as *Fidelismo*, 293
    lack of dogma in, 329–30
    national unity as basis for, 181
    study of Marx (1954–55), 187
    unorthodoxy of, 327
  meaning of rebellion to, 57–58
  middle-class origin of, 61
  military service re-introduced by
    (Nov. 1963), 255
  Ministry of Interior established by
    (1961), 201
  nonviolent agitation by (1955),
    83
  potential successor to, 294
  peasantry and, 157, 261
  plot to assassinate, 202, 348
  policy lines of (1956), 123–24
  propaganda used by, 289–90,
    303–4
  quoted
    on accomplishments of Revo-
      lution, 271

Castro, Fidel (*cont.*)
  quoted (*cont.*)
    on agrarian reform and co-
        operatives, 261
    on anti-U.S. propaganda, 305–
        306
    on atomic war, 227–28
    on beginnings in Sierra Maestra,
        97–98
    on bureaucratization of econ-
        omy, 248–49
    on Cuban Revolution, 93, 271,
        341–44
    on Cuban sovereignty, 233
    on deceitfulness of Kennedy,
        207
    on economic problems of Latin
        America, 166–67
    on educational achievements,
        267, 270
    on exiles, 242–43
    on Guevara's death, 286
    on imperialism, 313
    on Marxism, 284
    on missile crisis, 233–34
    on national unity, 81
    on nature of a revolutionary,
        284–85
    on necessity of Communist
        Party, 321
    on the people, 339–40
    on propaganda, 73
    on prostitution, 252–53
    on revolutionary government,
        335
    on social justice, 278
    on socialism, 285
    on solidarity with U.S. Negroes,
        290
    on sugar, 255
    on unfulfilled promises, 138
    on U.S. intervention (1898), 40
    on U.S. role as world police-
        man, 306–7
  Rebel Army created by, 151
  runs for Congress (1952), 62
  Schlesinger on, 211
  Sino-Soviet quarrel and, 272–73
  spoils system destroyed by, 50
  as symbol of the future, 221

Castro, Fidel (*cont.*)
  takes power
    becomes Prime Minister (Feb.
        1959), 137
    beneficiaries of, 148
    compared with Lenin, 141
    composition of first govern-
        ment, 135–36
    fights corruption, 143
    problems, 132–33, 144
    program, 138
    reluctance to assume premier-
        ship, 80–81
    struggle for power, 124–25
    supreme power of, 243, 319
    victims, 134, 148
  trip to U.S. (Apr. 1959), 160–61
  at U.N. (1960), 169–70
  utopian ideals of, 327–29
  Vietnam war and, 292
  working class and, 258–60
  writing of "La Historia me
      absolverá" by, 72–74; *see
      also* "La Historia me absol-
      verá"
  *See also* Bay of Pigs; Missile
      crisis; Moncada Barracks
      attack; Sierra Maestra
Castro, Fidelito (son), 28–29
Castro, Juana (sister), 17, 19
Castro, Lidia (sister), 17, 37, 72, 73
Castro, Lína Ruz de (née González;
    mother), 17–19
Castro, Pedro Emilio (brother), 17
Castro, Ramón (brother), 17–19
Castro, Raúl (brother), 17, 23, 80,
    108, 175, 230, 248, 298, 322,
    329
  on armament of Rebel Army, 200
  on Castro's determination, 31
  on Castro's optimism, 95
  communism of, 173–74, 178, 187
  Escalante affairs and, 315, 317
  faith in guerrilla warfare, 100
  in *Granma* expedition, 83, 95
  in Moncada Barracks attack, 66
  myths about, 17
  named Minister of Armed Forces,
    153

Castro, Raúl (*cont.*)
  in offensive on Santiago de Cuba (Nov. 1959), 129
  as potential successor to Fidel, 294
  raids led by (June 1958), 120
  religion and, 35
  role in missile crisis of, 227
  in Sierra Maestra, 117
Castro y Argiz, Ángel (father), 17, 18, 34
Casuso, Teresa, 20, 29, 90
Central Intelligence Agency (CIA), 119
  assumptions of, 151
  criticized, 203
  counterrevolutionaries helped by, 152, 202
  explosion of *La Coubre* and, 180
  Guevara discredited by, 88
  Guevara's death and, 295
  overthrow of Arbenz (1954), 56, 206
  role of, in Bay of Pigs, 202, 206–7, 213–14
  sabotage by, inside Cuba, 227, 304–5
  subversion efforts in Latin America by, 206–7, 303
Central Planning Board (JUCEPLAN), 243
Céspedes, Carlos Manuel de, 97
Charter of Bogotá, 215
Chiang Kai-shek, 219
Chibás, Eduardo, 62, 82
Chibás, Raúl, 124
Chomón, Fauré, 111, 118, 124
Churchill, Winston, 170
CIA, *see* Central Intelligence Agency
Cienfuegos, Camilo, 95, 114, 129, 298
  in charge of Havana (Jan. 1959), 140
  death of, 154
  faith in guerrilla warfare, 100
  illiteracy of, 319
  march to Sierra de Escambray and, 126, 127–28
  raids led by (1958), 117
Cienfuegos, Osmani, 154

Cienfuegos revolt (Sept. 1957), 111
Clay, Henry, 48
Cohn-Bendit, Daniel, 362
Committees for the Defense of Revolution, 201–2
Communism
  brought about by pressure, 166
  of R. Castro, 173–74, 178, 187
  by choice, 165
  Cuban brand of, 187, 314–15, 324–27
  freshness of Cuban, 353
  as goal, 342–43
  Hart on Cuban, 191–92
  in Latin America, 326
  on need to fight, 282
  in U.S., 191, 194, 209–10, 305
  *See also* Castro, Fidel—Marxism-Leninism of
Communist Party of Cuba (PCC), 181
  building of, 320
  Castro as Secretary-General of, 319
  function of, 321
  as framework, 359
  lack of leadership by, 334
  membership of, 323
  organization of, 322
  *See also* Castro, Fidel—Marxism-Leninism of
Constitution of 1940, 74–75
  Castro's promise to restore, 74
Consumer goods, 245
Cossío Villegas, Daniel, 347–48
Crespo, Luis, 95, 104
Cressweller, Robert D., 276
Cromwell, Oliver, 16
Cuba
  anti-Americanism in, 46, 55, 350–51
  economic situation of (Jan. 1959), 135; *see also* Economy
  effects of Platt Amendment on, 41–43
  gangster politics in (1940s–50s), 63–64
  land ownership in (after 1898), 51–53

Cuba (*cont.*)
  Latin American relations with, 276–77, 281, 326
  natural wealth of, 93, 264
  in 1920s, 45
  political isolation of, 310–11
  post-revolutionary population growth in, 242
  pre-revolutionary political system in, 50–51
  pre-revolutionary social situation in, 58–61
  religion in, 333–34
  richness of soil in, 263
  sabotage work in, 227, 304
  strategic position of, 47–48
  struggle for independence of, 39–41
  U.S. control of economy of, 52–54; *see also* Economy
  U.S. intervention in, 49–50
Cuban Revolution, 336–64
  achievements of, 344
  anarchist element in, 361–62
  basis for judging, 355–57
  betrayal of, 74, 113, 121, 137, 358
  Castro on, 93, 341–44
  Communism as goal of, 342–43
  Dorticós on, 348
  failings of, 353–54
  faith in man and, 341–42
  institutionalization of, 191, 294, 359
  irreversibility of, 349–50, 362–63
  made by youth, 337–38
  mass character of, 359
  nature of, 147–48
  new values brought by, 352–53
  socialist nature of, proclaimed (Apr. 1961), 182–83
  suppression of freedom in, 183, 346–47
  tragedies brought by, 345
Cubelas, Major Rolando, 202
Cushing, Richard, 127

Dalton, Hugh, 246
Danton, Georges, 134

Debray, Régis, 89, 99, 287
  on Castro's attention to details, 118
  on importance of guerrilla warfare, 288
  on learning through experience, 98
  on Sierra Maestra, 113
de Gaulle, Charles, 160
del Pino, Rafael, 26, 45, 91
del Río Chaviano, Colonel, 67, 69, 70
Democracy, 108, 346
Desnoes, Edmundo, 15, 269
Díaz, Julio, 95
Díaz-Balart, Mirta (wife of Castro), 28–29
Díaz-Balart, Rafael, 28–29
Díaz Lanz, Major Pedro, 152, 320
Diplomatic relations, 311
  with Communist countries (1960–61), 170–71
  with Vatican, 332
  U.S. breaks (Aug. 1960), 163
Dominican Republic
  effects of intervention in, 282
  intervention in (1965), 215, 223
Dorticós Torrado, Osvaldo, 175, 193, 230, 281, 305, 322
  age of, 337
  becomes Marxist, 173
  on Cuban Revolution, 348
  named president, 156
Dostoevski, Feodor, 161
Drachovitch, Milorad M., 168
Draper, Theodore, 23, 60, 100, 121, 137, 149, 189, 204
  on Batista, 57
  on Castro's entry in Havana, 147
  on Castro's illusions, 230
  on Castro's independence, 292–93
  on Castro's opposition to military service, 255
  disputed, 10–11, 100–1, 174, 349–50
  on food shortage, 238
  on *Granma* expedition, 99
  on Moncada Barracks attack, 67
  on nature of Castroism, 123

Draper, Theodore (*cont.*)
  on personality cult, 338
  on relations between Guevara and
    F. Castro, 175
  on sugar economy, 52, 244
Dubois, Jules, 22, 24, 26
Dulles, Allen, 206
Dulles, John Foster, 56, 206
Dumont, René, 163
Dutschke, Rudi, 362

Eccles, Admiral H. E., 212
Echevarría, José Antonio, 111
Economy (Cuban)
  development of fishing industry,
    264–65
  early errors in, 149–51
  exodus of professionals and, 242
  exploitation of natural resources,
    264
  foreign trade and, 265
  hampered by bureaucracy, 248–49
  hurricane Flora as blow to (Oct.
    1963), 246–47
  new role for women in, 260
  sabotage in, 304–5
  scarcity of consumer goods in,
    245
  Soviet bloc aid to, 241, 272–73
  state of (Jan. 1959), 135
  state controlled, 243, 256
  U.N. report on, 250
  U.S. control of prerevolutionary,
    52–54
  U.S. embargo on, 162, 238
  *See also* Agriculture
Education, 267–71
  budget for, 270
  indoctrination through, 268
  nature of, 267
  physical, 269
  training of professionals and, 270–
    71
  for workers, 258
Eisenhower, Dwight D., 56, 160,
    162, 163, 194, 196, 205, 311
El Patopo, 114, 115
El Uvero, attack on (May 1957),
    110, 130

Ellender, Allen J., 128
Employment, full, 246, 250
Escalante, Aníbal, 182, 315–18, 320
Escalante affairs, 190
  first (1962), 315–16
  second (1965), 317–18
Espín, Vilma, 100, 108

Fagen, Richard F., 191, 360
Fajardo, Manuel, 103–4, 108, 120
Felix, Christopher, 202
Figueredo, Pedro, 64
Figueres, José, 276
Fisher, H. A. L., 363
Fishing industry, 264–65
Food shortage, 238–39, 266
Franco Generalísimo Francisco, 17,
    33
Frankel, Max, 171
Franqui, Carlos, 20, 63, 94, 97, 101
Frei, Eduardo, 276
Freidel, Frank, 41
Fulbright, J. William, 286–87
  call to recognize Castro's govern-
    ment by, 312–13, 350

García, Calixto, 95, 100
García, General Calixto, 40
García, Guillermo, 95, 108, 118
Gardner, Arthur, 113, 127
Giap, General Nguyen, 291–92
Goldenberg, Boris, 41, 60, 125, 149
  disputed, 10, 101
  on totalitarianism, 257
Gómez, General Maxímo, 40, 45,
    128
*Granma* expedition, 83–95
  attempts to organize general strike
    and, 89–90
  Draper on, 99
  Guevara wounded in, 95
  invasion plans of, 83–85
  landing of (Dec. 1956), 91–94
  preparations for, 87, 89–91
  rumors following landing, 106,
    188
  trial following, 113–14
Grant, Ulysses S., 48

Grau San Martín, Ramón, 27, 34, 51, 61, 156
Greene, Felix, 347
Guerra, Eutimio, 45, 102–3
Guerrilla warfare
  Debray on, 288
  faith in, 99–100
  Guevara on, 114–15
  in Latin America, 278, 301
  qualities demanded of guerrillas, 116
Guevara, Major Ernesto "Che," 31, 35, 38, 126, 230, 272, 356
  Arbenz and, 87–88, 119
  attitude toward money, 319
  background of, 87
  becomes Marxist, 173–74
  Castro and, 296–97, 300
    Castro on death of, 286
    influence on Castro, 175
    loyalty to Castro, 88–89
  in charge of Havana (Jan. 1959), 140
  death of, 275, 286, 295, 298–99
  economic mistakes of, 149
  Escalante affair and, 315–16
  fall of Santa Clara and, 129
  faith in guerrilla warfare, 100
  family relationships of, 300
  as legendary figure, 300–1
  limited Marxist knowledge of, 191
  march to Sierra de Escambray and, 127–28
  mourning ceremony for, 303
  non-Communism of, 88
  as president of National Bank, 299
  quoted
    on accidental nature of Cuban Marxism, 193
    on death, 286
    on development of the Revolution, 190–91
    on early economic errors, 150–51
    on Guerra's betrayal, 102–3
    on guerrilla warfare, 114–15
    on his leaving Cuba (Apr. 1965), 295–97

Guevara, Ernesto "Che" (cont.)
  quoted (cont.)
    on implications of Platt Amendment, 41–42
    on peasantry, 257–58, 291
    on qualities demanded of guerrillas, 116
    on revolutions in Latin America, 280
    on sugar, 53, 162
    on U.S. domination, 301–2
    on U.S. fear of Cuba's independence, 179–80
  raids led by (1958), 117
  stature of, 298, 337, 362
  wounded, 95
Guijano, Carlos, 115
Guillén, Nicolás, 269
Gunther, John, 49
Gutiérrez Menoyo, Elroy, 118

Halperin, Ernst, 159
Hart, Armando, 124, 317, 320, 337
  Cuban Communism explained by, 191–92
Hart Phillips, Mrs. Ruby, 106
Hay, John, 40
Hemingway, Ernest, 180n–81n
Hennessy, C. A. M., 279
Hernández, Melba, 65, 70, 72, 73
  devoted to Castro, 77–78, 124
  Granma expedition and, 90
  letter received by, 86
  naming of July 26th Movement and, 81–82
Hilsman, Roger, 204, 211, 229–30
Hitler, Adolf, 123
Housing, 266–67
Howard, Lisa, 190

INRA (National Land Reform Institute), 144, 243
Instituto del Libro (Havana), 15

Jefferson, Thomas, 48
John XXIII, Pope, 331–32

Johnson, Haynes, 204
Johnson, Lyndon B., 33, 48, 214, 215
  Alliance for Progress and, 167
  basis for judging, 358
  Dominican Republic intervention and, 280, 282–83, 287
Jolly, Richard, 59
July 26th Movement, see 26th of July Movement
JUCEPLAN (Central Planning Board), 243
Jung, Carl, 362

Keating, Kenneth B., 229
Kennedy, Jacqueline, 222
Kennedy, John F., 48, 51, 194, 204, 222
  Alliance for Progress and, 56, 167, 307
  Bay of Pigs and, 208–10, 214–15
  Castro on, 207
  Cuban policy of, 206, 213, 236
  interviewed, 217–20
  meets Khrushchev, 169
  in missile crisis, 213, 226
    call up of reserve troops, 228
    Kennedy's brilliance, 235
    Kennedy's reactions, 231
    warns Soviet Union, 229
  on nature of revolutions, 290
  on need to fight Communism, 282
  press criticized by, 216
  on superiority of capitalism, 278
Khrushchev, Nikita S., 170, 182
  on defense of Cuba, 228
  fails to understand Castro, 226
  meets Kennedy (1961), 169
  missile crisis and, see Missile crisis
King, Martin Luther, 289
Knox, John, 80
Kotman, François, 80

"La Historia me absolverá" (History will absolve me; Oct. 16, 1953), 24, 70–76
  background history of, 72–73

"La Historia me absolverá" (cont.)
  importance of, 73–74
  prophetic quality of, 74–76
  reissue of (1958), 76
  writing of, 70
La Coubre (ship), 180, 200
Labor force, 254–55; see also Peasantry; Working class
Lam, Wilfredo, 269
Landsberger, Henry A., 156
LASO (Latin American Solidarity Organization), 288–89
Latin America
  absence of ideologies in, 309
  Castro's prestige in, 275
  CIA subversion in, 206–7, 303
  communism in, 326
  Dominican Republic intervention and, 282
  economic problems of, 166–67
  effect of Cuban Revolution on, 308
  effect of missile crisis on, 231, 325
  guerrillas in, 278, 301
  postwar U.S. policies for, 56
  relations with Cuba of, 276–77, 281, 326, 347–48
  roots of social revolution in, 325
  U.S. support in, 281–82
  USSR and, 195, 283
  violent revolutions supported in, 236, 277–80, 283–84, 286
Latin American Solidarity Organization (LASO), 288–89
Lechuga, Carlos, 328–29
Lenin, Vladimir I., 80, 96–97, 123, 140–41, 314
Leoni, Raúl, 278
Letters from Prison (Castro), 20, 78–81
Lima, Ledesma, 269
Lincoln, Abraham, 132
Lipset, Seymour Martin, 156
Llanusa, José "Pepe," 124, 269, 332
Locke, John, 80
Lockwood, Lee, 11, 18
  on Castro's fighting spirit, 96
  on Cuban Revolution, 361
  at El Uvero, 130

López, César, 269
López-Fresqet, Rufo, 135, 137, 145,
    163, 253
  on blowing up of *La Coubre*, 180
  on C. Cienfuegos, 154
  on new values, 352
Lowenthal, Richard, 140
Luther, Martin, 80


McCarthy, Francis L., 92
MacGaffey, Wyatt, 61
Machado, Gerardo, 139
  brutality under, 51
  ousted (1933), 45, 50
  U.S. support for, 49
McKinley, William, 43
Malraux, André, 355
Manifesto of 26th of July Move-
    ment, 99
Mao Tse-tung, 89, 123, 147, 291–92,
    314
Marat, Jean-Paul, 134
Marchant, Sir Henry, 343
Marinello, Juan, 176
Martí, José, 27, 34–35, 55, 306
  Castro influenced by, 45–46
  on death, 64
  national unity and, 81
  renewed popularity of (1920s), 45
  revolt led by (1895), 40
  warning of, 44
Marx, Karl, 80, 187
Marxism, *see* Communism
Masferrer, Rolando, 125
Mathews, Thomas, 251
Matos, Major Hubert, 104, 152–54,
    320
Matthews, Nancie, 106
Mencken, H. L., 363
Merle, Robert, 35, 72, 173
  on Moncada attack, 67, 69
Mesa, Liliam, 107
Mexican expedition, *see*: *Granma*
    expedition
Meyer, Karl E., 204, 205
Mikoyan, Anastas, 170, 200, 234
Miller, Edward G., 216
Milton, John, 80

Mintz, Sidney W., 53
Mirabeau, Conte de, 341
Miret, Pedro, 91
Miró Cardona, José, 124, 135, 137
Missile crisis, 223–34
  Bay of Pigs invasion compared
    with, 199
  Castro on, 233–34
  decision to install missiles, 223–25
  effect on Latin America of, 231,
    325
  as humiliating experience, 200,
    224, 232
  motives behind, 216, 226–27, 230
  photographic evidence in, 229
  settlement of, 232
  Soviet buildup in, 228
  types of missiles installed, 230–31
Moncada Barracks attack (July
    1953), 45, 63–72
  Castro's capture of, 69–70
  Castro's trial after, 70–72
  as failure, 66–67
  leadership at, 64–65
  as symbol of rebellion, 57, 63
Monroe, James, 48
Monroe Doctrine (1823), 216, 235
Montané, Jesús, 64, 65, 73
Morgan, William, 118
Morse, Richard, 325
Mujal, Eusebio, 128, 258
Muñoz Marín, Luis, 276
Mussolini, Benito, 123


National Land Reform Institute
    (INRA), 144, 243
Nehru, Jawaharlal, 355
Nelson, Hugh, 46
Nelson, Lowry, 39
Nixon, Richard, 33, 205, 311
Nkrumah, Kwame, 276


Onis, Juan de, 266, 267, 294–95, 318
Organization of American States
    (OAS), 281
Ortiz, Fernando, 52
Otero, Lisandro, 77, 82, 269

Paine, Thomas, 80
País, Frank, 101, 110, 114
  death of, 90
  organization of general strike and,
    89
Palma, Tomás Estrada, 45
Pazos, Felipe, 33, 106, 124, 135,
    158
Pazos, Javier, 106, 107, 167
PCC, see Communist Party of Cuba
Peasantry
  Guevara on, 257–58, 291
  importance of, 157
  improved life of, 257
  pre-revolutionary conditions of,
    261
Peña, Lázaro, 316
Pérez, Crescencio, 95, 126
Pérez, Faustino, 63, 87, 107, 172,
    248, 297
  Castro's optimism and, 94–96
  faith in guerrilla warfare of, 100
  in Granma expedition, 92–94
  loyalty of, 124
  religion and, 333
  Resistencia Cívica organized by,
    106
Pérez Jiménez, General Marcos, 139
Pérez Serantes, Archbishop Enrique,
    67–69, 331
Platt Amendment (1901), 41–43
Portell Vilá, Herminio, 43, 44
Portocarrero, René, 269
Prestes, Luis Carlos, 285, 286
Prío Socarrás, Carlos, 34, 124, 156,
    276
  lends money to Castro, 90–91
  liberal regime of, 51
  political affiliation of, 61
  resigns, 62
Public health, 267


Quevedo, Miguel Ángel, 90, 135


Ray, Manuel, 135, 154, 214
Rebel Army
  creation of, 151
  militia as part of, 201

Rebel Army (cont.)
  Russian arms and training for,
    200–1
Redondo, Ciro, 95
Resistencia Cívica (Urban Resist-
    ance), 101, 106
Revolution
  Carlyle on, 9
  Castro on, 133
  defined, 132
  economic development and, 54–55
  Fulbright on, 286–87
  J. F. Kennedy on, 290
  nature of, 131
  necessity of, 38
  Saint-Just on, 146
  See also Cuban Revolution
Rivero Agüero, Andrés, 128
Roa, Raúl, 172, 204, 253, 328, 337
Roa, Raulito, 253–54
Robespierre, Maximilien de, 134,
    341
Roca, Blas, 177, 178, 316–17, 328
Rodríguez, Carlos Rafael, 17, 20,
    121, 171, 190, 268, 297, 299,
    316, 358
  on achievements in public health,
    267
  age of, 337
  as head of INRA, 243
  on living standards, 265–66
  profile of, 177–78
Rodríguez, René, 100, 106
Roig de Leuchsenring, Emilio, 41
Rojas Rodríguez, Marta, 71
Roosevelt, Franklin D., 160
Root, Elihu, 48
Rousseau, Jean-Jacques, 80
Rubottom, Roy R., Jr., 216
Rusk, Dean, 194, 231
Russia, see Soviet Union


Saint-Just, Louis de, 134, 146
Salisbury, John of, 80
Salvador, David, 157
Sánchez, Celia, 20, 108, 230, 311
  becomes Marxist, 172
  Castro's relations with, 32–33, 37

Sánchez, Celia (*cont.*)
  on Castro's 1957 interview, 109
  on El Uvero attack, 117
  faith in guerrilla warfare, 100
  on Moncada Barracks attack, 63
  on movement's strength (1957), 112
  profile of, 116–17
  in Sierra Maestra, 101, 130
Sánchez, Guerrito, 107
Sánchez, Universo, 94–96, 100
Sánchez Mósquera, Lieutenant Colonel Ángel, 127
Santamaría, Abel, 64, 66, 77–78, 333
Santamaría, Haydée, 63, 65, 70–72, 77–78, 124, 290
  faith in guerrilla warfare, 100
  on life and death, 363
  naming July 26th Movement and, 81–82
  religion and, 333
  in Sierra Maestra, 101
Santiago de Cuba, offensive on (Nov. 1958), 129, 139
Santo Domingo, battle of (June 1958), 126–27
Sarría, Lieutenant Pedro, 69
Sartre, Jean-Paul, 55, 134
Schlesinger, Arthur, Jr., 51, 169, 209, 216, 290, 355
  on Bay of Pigs, 204–5, 207, 211
  on Castro's isolation by U.S., 223
  opinion on missile crisis, 224–25, 230, 232
  on Washington's ignorance, 212
Schram, Stuart R., 291
Seers, Dudley, 59, 60, 308
Selser, Gregorio, 24, 82
Sierra Maestra, 93–130
  battle of Santo Domingo (June 1958), 126–27
  beginnings in, 97–98
  Castro's interview in (1957), 106–10
  Cienfuegos revolt and (Sept. 1957), 111
  documents and speeches from, 123
  El Uvero attack from (May 1957), 110

Sierra Maestra (*cont.*)
  forces in (1957), 105
  as groundwork, 113, 115–16
  Guerra's betrayal in, 102–3
  hardships in, 103–4
  leadership in, 129–30
  march to, 93–97
  march to Sierra de Escambray from, 127–28
  military strategy in, 124
  morale in, 99–101
  radio messages from, 118
  raids from (1958), 117–18
  C. Sánchez on, 130
  urban resistance inspired by, 128–29
Silvert, Kalman H., 323, 338–39
Smith, Earl E. T., 49, 127, 129
Smith, Sir Norman, 26
Smith, Robert F., 11, 43, 46, 159
Social classes, *see* Peasantry; Working class
Solari, Aldo, 156
Somoza, Luis, 207
Sorensen, Theodore, 204, 230
Soviet Union
  aid provided by, 193, 200–1
  disillusionment with, 310–11
  Latin America and, 195, 283
  second Escalante affair and, 318
  seen as friend, 197
  sugar bought by, 256
  *See also* Missile crisis
Spanish-American War, (1898), 40
Stevenson, Adlai, 207
Stalin, Josef, 314
Strachey, John, 191
Suárez, Andrés, 25, 60, 149, 174, 191
  on Castro's opposition to dogmatism, 83
  on Communist participation in government, 205
  disputed, 10, 101
  on lack of party leadership in Cuba, 334
  on Matos' resignation, 153
  on national unity, 176
Sugar industry
  Draper on, 52, 244

Sugar industry (*cont.*)
  emphasis on production in, 262–63
  Guevara on, 53, 162
  labor force for harvests in, 254–55
  production goals (1970s), 237
  return to economy based on, 244
  state ownership of, 256
Sugar Act (1934), 53
Szulc, Tad, 204, 205

Taber, Robert, 111
Tabernilla, General Francisco, 110
Talmon, J. L., 134
Tannenbaum, Frank, 141
Ten Years War (1868–78), 40
Thomas, Hugh, 293
Tito, Marshal, 310
Topping, John, 127
Trevelyan, G. M., 355
Tró, Emilio, 25
Trujillo, Generalísimo Rafael Leónidas, 26–27, 129, 276
26th of July Movement
  formation of Resistencia Cívica, 101
  fund-raising activities of, 86
  link to Ortodoxo Party of, 82
  Manifesto of, 99
  organization of Resistencia Cívica and, 106
  meeting of (Feb. 1957), 106–10
  naming of, 81–82
  strength of (1957), 100, 112

U Thant, 234
Unemployment, eradicated, 246, 250
United States
  anti-revolutionary position of, 43
  basis for policy of, 205–6
  Batista supported by, 56–57
  Castro and
    attempts to get rid of Castro, 197
    break in diplomatic relations, 163
    Castro's visit to, 86
    isolation of Castro by, 223

United States (*cont.*)
  Castro and (*cont.*)
    relations with Castro (1958), 119–21
  Communism in, 191, 194, 209–10, 305
  Cuba in strategy of, 47–48
  Cuban economy owned by, 52–54
  double standard of, 303
  executions and reactions in, 145–46
  Latin American support for, 281–82
  post-war Latin American policies of, 56
  pre-revolutionary Cuba supported by, 49–51
  possibility of reconciliation with, 312
  pressures by, 162, 170, 238
  in Wars of Independence, 40–42
  *See also* Bay of Pigs; Central Intelligence Agency; Missile crisis
Urban resistance (Resistencia Cívica), 101, 106
Urrutia, Manuel, 31, 114, 136–39
  at *Granma* trial, 75
  resignation of, 155–56
USSR, *see* Soviet Union

Valdés, Ramiro, 100, 126, 151, 201, 202
Vallejo, Major René, 236
Varona, Antonio de, 124
Verdeja, Santiago, 107–8
Vietnam war
  Cuba's attitude to, 307
  deescalation of, 358
  impact on U.S. economy of, 351
  as nationalist war, 212–13, 215
  youth's reactions to, 362

Waldo, Thayer, 203
War of Independence (1895–98), 44
Warfare, *see* Guerrilla warfare
Weber, Max, 31
Webster, Daniel, 48

Wedgwood, C. V., 33
Werth, Alexander, 160
Wood, General Leonard, 48
Working class
    complaints of, 258
    full employment for, 246, 250
    support for revolution of, 259–60

Yanés Pelletier, Lieutenant Jesús, 78

Ydígoras Fuentes, Miguel, 206
Yeats, William Butler, 324
Youth
    anarchism and, 361–62
    radicalism of, 361
    reverence for, 337
    revolutionary spirit of, 338

Zacchi, Bishop Cesare, 36, 332
Zeitlin, Maurice, 54, 157, 259–60

## ABOUT THE AUTHOR

Before his retirement in 1967, Herbert L. Matthews worked as a reporter, war correspondent and editorial writer of *The New York Times* for 45 years. He was the chief *New York Times* correspondent covering the Spanish Civil War, and was the foreign reporter who first interviewed Fidel Castro in the Sierra Maestra Mountains in 1957 when the Cuban government and the world press believed him and his movement both to be dead. Ernest Hemingway wrote of him: "Herbert Matthews is the straightest, the ablest and the bravest correspondent writing today . . . he stands like a gaunt lighthouse of honesty." This is his eighth book.